FIVE THOUSAND AMERICAN FAMILIES—

PATTERNS OF ECONOMIC PROGRESS

VOLUME I

An Analysis of the First Five Years of the Panel Study of Income Dynamics

James N. Morgan
Katherine Dickinson
Jonathan Dickinson
Jacob Benus
Greg Duncan

Conducted Under Contracts with the Office of Economic Opportunity
(Responsibility for this project has been transferred to the Office of the Assistant Secretary
for Planning and Evaluation, Department of Health Education, and Welfare)

SURVEY RESEARCH CENTER
INSTITUTE FOR SOCIAL RESEARCH
THE UNIVERSITY OF MICHIGAN

ISR Code No. 3568

Five Thousand American Families—Patterns of Economic Progress, Volumes I and II
Library of Congress Catalog Card No. 74-62002
ISBN 0-87944-153-4 paperbound
ISBN 0-87944-154-2 clothbound

Published by the Survey Research Center of the Institute for Social Research
The University of Michigan, Ann Arbor, Michigan 48106

First Published 1974
Second Printing 1974
Manufactured in the United States of America

We dedicate this analysis with affection and gratitude to the families who make up our panel. Their inexhaustible good temper is reflected in the high response rates which make these data valuable. As a representative sample they speak very well for the kindness of the United States population.

CONTENTS

Foreword   ix

Preface   xi

INTRODUCTION   1

Chapter 1   CHANGE IN GLOBAL MEASURES   11
James N. Morgan

Chapter 2   FAMILY COMPOSITION   99
James N. Morgan

Chapter 3   WAGE RATES OF HEADS AND WIVES   123
Katherine Dickinson

Chapter 4   LABOR SUPPLY OF FAMILY MEMBERS   177
Jonathan Dickinson

Chapter 5   TRANSFER INCOME   251
Katherine Dickinson

Chapter 6   INCOME INSTABILITY   277
Jacob Benus

Chapter 7   EDUCATIONAL ATTAINMENT   305
Greg Duncan

Chapter 8   SUMMARY OF FINDINGS   333

Appendix A   SAMPLE WEIGHTS AND INDEPENDENT SUBSAMPLES   341

Appendix B   SAMPLING ERRORS   345

Appendix C   TECHNIQUES OF STATISTICAL DATA ANALYSIS   357

Appendix D   CATEGORICAL INTERACTIONS IN LINEAR REGRESSION MODELS   365

Appendix E   DICHOTOMOUS DEPENDENT VARIABLES   375

Appendix F   MEASURES OF ACHIEVEMENT MOTIVATION AND COGNITIVE ABILITY   381

Appendix G   THE COMPOSITION OF INCOME AND OTHER POLICY-RELEVANT CHARACTERISTICS OF FAMILIES AT DIFFERENT LEVELS OF WELL-BEING   387

Glossary   415

Index   425

FOREWORD

Nearly a decade has elapsed since passage of the Economic Opportunity Act of 1964 which declared that United States policy was "to eliminate the paradox of poverty in the midst of plenty" by opening to all the opportunity for education and training, for work and for living "in decency and dignity." Since passage of the Act there have been many proposals for reducing or eliminating poverty, some of which have been acted on. Nonetheless, few people would now claim that progress in realization of the goal has been rapid.

At times, it is hard to escape the conviction that part of the failure must be ascribed to either a lack of will or a lack of concern on the part of the public and their elected representatives. But surely this does not fully explain why elimination of poverty is taking so long. Clearly a lack of understanding of the dynamics of family income generation and maintenance has contributed greatly to the failure to formulate effective programs for dealing with poverty and to the very limited success of the programs which have been carried out. Elimination of poverty requires not only the will to do so, but also knowledge of what to do. Humans and their institutions and social systems are not simple and are far from being understood well enough to make the intent to eliminate poverty equivalent to the reduction of poverty.

One of the primary barriers to achievement of needed knowledge and understanding has been the inadequacy of data available for testing and estimation of hypotheses bearing on family income dynamics. The Office of Economic Opportunity deserves much credit for recognizing the critical need for improved behavioral understanding. It also deserves credit for perceiving that bold new steps would be necessary to secure a data base capable of providing the essential understanding of income dynamics.

One of the truly path-breaking steps taken by OEO was to finance the important and now famous negative income tax experiments carried out by the Institute for Research on Poverty at the University of Wisconsin with the help of Mathematica Incorporated. The second truly innovative step aimed at securing a more adequate data base was to finance and help plan the panel study of family income dynamics conducted by the University of Michigan's Survey Research Center.

The panel study represents a unique effort to reach the very limits of what is achievable by sample survey techniques in collection of needed evidence on family income dynamics. Not only has the study succeeded in collecting information on a rich assortment of background and current attributes relating to families and associated individuals, but it has succeeded in following a panel of families and individuals, including movers and split families, over more than five years. In addition, it has collected important information on the local labor market environments specific to the panel members. The body of data collected by this study will clearly be a landmark collection of data which will be used by social scientists for research on family income dynamics for years to come.

These two volumes report on what has been learned so far from the ongoing panel study and provide an appropriate testimonial to the wisdom of the substantial support provided by OEO. James Morgan and the rest of the staff involved in preparing this book, are to be congratulated both for providing social scientists with the single most important addition yet made to the stock of data on family income dynamics and for so ably presenting their initial results in analyzing these data. Their work has significantly improved our basic understanding of poverty and its causes and has enhanced the opportunity to create meaningful policies for elimination of poverty.

Guy H. Orcutt
October 1973
New Haven, Connecticut

PREFACE

Many people in The Research and Plans Division of the Office of Economic Opportunity and elsewhere were involved in the planning of this project. It was undertaken in the belief that a longitudinal study would provide OEO with a better source of information on the dynamics of family economic status than was available in our annual census survey of the poor.

It would not have been possible to carry out these plans without the cooperation of thousands of respondents, hundreds of interviewers, scores of editors and coders, and a variety of specialists, advisors, and analysts. It is impossible to thank them all individually. James Smith first saw the value of designing this as a panel study. We are particularly grateful for his help and also for the close collaboration we have received from many other staff members at OEO, among them Tom Glennan, Ned Gramlich, Lester Klein, Robert Levine, Jonathan Lane, James Lyday, Tom Tomlinson, and John Wilson. The Urban Institute has been generous with advice and money and we have also profited greatly from the help of our own Economic Behavior Program's Advisory Committee whose members include Robert Ferber, Lawrence Klein, F. Scott Maynes, Guy Orcutt, James Tobin, Peter de Janosi, Arnold Zellner, and Arthur Goldberger

In the Institute for Social Research this project benefited from the work of specialists in sampling, interviewing, coding and data processing, and the helpful advice of numerous colleagues. The late John B. Lansing was in charge of the project for ten months during 1969-70 and contributed both to its organization and to the analysis of the data. Nancy Baerwaldt worked on the administration, documentation, and analysis of the study from the beginning until 1972, and is the joint author of a study of intrafamily transfers. Barbara Thomas, Paula Pelletier, and Karen Liss developed the complex computer file management procedures.

The development of measures of cognitive ability and of achievement motivation that could be taken in a very few minutes in a voluntary household interview situation was the responsibility of Joseph Veroff, Kent Marquis, Lou McClelland, and Robert Hubbard, with the helpful advice of John Atkinson.

The complex problems of merging two samples, designing the weights, and estimating sampling errors had the benefit of the expert work of Irene Hess, head of the SRC Sampling Section, and Thomas Tharaken (now of the University of Trivandrum, India), and the advice of Leslie Kish. The final design of questionnaires and administration of the field work involved Charles Cannell, John Scott, head of the Field Section, Jane Peppard, Arlene Lewis-Beck, Tracy Berckmans, and others. Joan Scheffler, head of the Coding Section, contributed to the development and supervision of the coding procedures. The final editing of this volume was done by Doug Truax and Linda Stafford.

Conducting such a large scale study over five years would have been impossible without the staff of talented and dedicated people within the Economic Behavior Program of the Survey Research Center.

Joan Brinser, who was also involved in the editing of this volume, has overseen the field work and it is mainly because of her patience and persuasiveness that this panel is still representative of the population. Beverly Harris and Tecla Loup have assisted in virtually every aspect of this research. They have supervised the coding and editing of the interviews for many years, and the consistency of the data is to a large extent due to their efforts. Priscilla Hildebrandt has been of great assistance by preparing many early manuscripts, and more recently by facilitating the computer analysis for this volume. Bonnie Lawrence's programming skills were invaluable in preparing the complex data files for this project. Charles Stallman has also provided assistance both in processing the data and in the computer work.

Susan Finlayson has prepared many of the questionnaires and manuscripts of this study. These volumes have benefited enormously from her skills, organization, and good-natured persistence. She was ably assisted by Priscilla Hildebrandt and Wanda Lemon.

Finally, the design, execution and documentation of the study has been the responsibility of the authors of this first volume. Research Associate Katherine Dickinson, in particular, coordinated and directed the whole process with its many deadlines and complex arrangements. Assistant Study Directors Jonathan Dickinson, Jacob Benus, and Greg Duncan also undertook operational responsibilities. Jonathan improved the statistical sophistication of all our analyses. Jacob worked with the Sampling Section in the development of sampling error estimates. And Greg has made extensive contributions to several chapters in both of these volumes.

James Morgan
Ann Arbor

INTRODUCTION

History

This study was initiated by the Research and Plans Division of the Office of Economic Opportunity in order to supplement and complement the regular assessments of poverty being conducted by the Bureau of the Census. It was felt that interpretation of national trends and added insights into factors affecting changes in family well-being would require both following the same people over an extended period of time and collecting from them a much richer mixture of economic, behavioral, and attitudinal information.

Since many policy issues focus on the bottom of the income distribution and on minority groups, the initial sample included a subset of about 2000 families from the Census' Survey of Economic Opportunity, which had already over-sampled the groups of interest. The Census study families were selected from those with incomes less than twice the official poverty line who had also been willing to sign a release form. This sample was combined with a fresh probability sample from the Survey Research Center's national sampling frame to provide about another 3000 families.

The family is not an unchanging unit; hence, the study followed the heads of the 1968 original panel families and also all members of those families who left home. If a female sample member married a nonsample member, we interviewed him in order to secure the full family financial information. The earnings information of a nonsample member in a sample family became part of the data base, since that income affected the sample family. We arrived at a set of weights to account for initial variations in sampling rates, variations in nonresponse rates and complexities affecting probabilities, such as potential overlap of the two samples and marriage to nonsample members.

After some initial losses, the response rate of the panel has been very high, and because of the cooperation of respondents the field costs have not risen much in spite of inflation and the scattering of the original clustered samples. No longer clustered locally in small groups, they now live in twice as

2

many counties as in 1968. The fact that we paid respondents, from the second interviews forward and again for sending in an annual address correction post card, clearly helped us to keep in touch with them.

The study was originally planned to last for five years, but it was decided in 1972 that it would be important to measure the outcome variables -- employment, earnings, income, housing and family change -- over a longer period. Costs were to be kept down by using telephone reinterviews wherever possible, and by restricting the questionnaire to a third of its original size. The only additions to the basic outcome variables were background information on new family heads and a short new series of questions on day care for children of working parents.

A study of change requires repeated measurement of the same variables. Each year we have measured the money and nonmoney components of family income, people's behavior patterns in crucial areas like planning ahead, risk avoidance, and striving to improve things, and some of their relevant attitudes. Most family background questions were asked in the first two interviews, but they were repeated whenever a new family head appeared. Improvements and additions to the questionnaire are spelled out in Volume I of the documentation.[1] These include improvements in the questions on food consumption and family planning and the addition of questions on commuting costs, from the second year onward, and on "intelligence" and achievement motivation in the fifth year only.

Purposes

The major purpose of this study is to see what causes changes in the economic sell-being of families. In particular, we seek variables which are subject to change by public policy and which help to change a family's well-being. We rely on two things: the diversity of attitudes and behavior of individuals, and the "natural experiments" provided by changing environment, opportunities, public policies, and unemployment levels. The potential impact of certain proposed new policies can be assessed by looking at the situations of those eligible for or likely to be affected by them.

It may be difficult to use these data to study the effects of policies which have not been tried. But we can extrapolate from findings about the short-term adjustment that families make to income changes, to possible effects of changes in income maintenance programs. Or we can see whether personal efforts by the poor to improve their situation do in fact help them climb out of poverty.

----

[1]See A Panel Study of Family Income Dynamics, 2 Volumes, Survey Research Center, Institute for Social Research, University of Michigan, Ann Arbor, Michigan, 1972.

People's backgrounds -- where they grew up, their formal education -- are not subject to change in the short-run, but must be taken into account to derive unbiased estimates of other effects. Characteristics like age, race, and sex are unchanging also, but their effects on earnings, employment, and consumption can be altered by public policy. Environmental factors such as the level of unemployment or public school expenditures are clearly changeable.

Beyond the well-studied demographic, environmental, and institutional variables are attitudes and behavior patterns which may affect economic well-being. A major attempt was made in this study to measure such attitudes and behavior patterns.

For economy in analysis, we grouped individual attitudes or behavioral reports into composite indexes, examined the effects of these indexes, and investigated the components of any index that seemed to matter to find which ones were important. The reader should approach the descriptive titles of these groups cautiously: risk avoidance, planning ahead, connectedness to potential sources of information and help, economizing, and so on. Their components are defined in the Glossary, in Appendix E, and more specifically in Volume II of the basic documentation.

If we find some potentially changeable factors that affect changes in economic status, it may be possible to increase economic well-being while reducing dependency on public welfare programs. But we need to recognize the implications of finding, on the other hand, that few changeable factors make any difference in economic status. It may be that substantial numbers of families must remain dependent on a system of transfers to keep them out of poverty. We do not intend to propose policy solutions to poverty-related problems. Our purpose is to explain the static and dynamic determinants of economic well-being and its changes.

Advantages of a Panel

Reinterviewing the same families over an extended period has a number of advantages which seem to make it worth the costs. Measurement of change is, of course, more accurate than one could get by relying on memory or by comparing two independent samples a year apart. The sampling error of a mean difference is substantially smaller than the sampling error of the difference in two means. There is also growing evidence that the quality of information improves in the reinterviews. Differential improvements can distort the analysis of changes and in some analysis we concern ourselves with this problem, but certainly from the second interview onward even the changes are much better measured.

We can estimate short run adjustments, examine the accuracy of people's own expectations and plans, and sort out long run trends from short run fluctuations. Year-to-year changes in income are partly reversible fluctuations and partly long term trends. Particularly for increases in income it is difficult to distinguish the two without several years of data, yet the implications of recovery from a bad year versus an increase in permanent income are quite different.

In measuring attitudes and behavior patterns, reinterviews are also useful in improving the quality of measures by averaging out "noise." It is clear from the data that there is substantial random fluctuation in most such measures, so that the main advantage in repeated measures of attitudes is less in assessing their trends, which are often small or non-existent, than in improving precision.

Data Base

The data base for the present analysis is five waves of full interviews, the last one taken in 1972. There were 5060 families as of that time. Only 42% of them have remained unchanged in composition since the first interview in 1968. Some are drastically different because they contain members of the original families who have split off to form new families. The most dramatic example is the one we mentioned earlier of a sample woman marrying a nonsample husband. He becomes head of the family and is interviewed, but the earlier records would be for her parental family.

There are 24% of the families in early 1972 who have changed heads since 1968. These changes are handled in two ways. First, we can analyze separately families with different change patterns, or concentrate analysis on families with the same head for all five years. Second, we also have a second data file consisting of 18,000 individuals. We have, for each individual, a record which includes his or her own situation (work hours, income, relationship to head of family) and all the information about the family in which the individual lived for each year.

The information for a family collected in 1967 may appear in several records of the final family sample, since it is relevant for all families which sprang from that original family. It will appear in the records of each individual as of 1972. This is perfectly correct, if one thinks of a sample of families in 1972 and a sample of individuals as of 1968 who have been followed for five years.

The weights keep the results representative of the non-institutional population of the continental United States, but do not indicate the number of interviews, and it is the latter which determines the sampling stability of a finding about any subgroup. For example, families in the lowest quintile of family money income/needs in any one of the five years make up some 35% of all families, but they account for more than half the total interviews in 1972.

The data have not been adjusted for inflation except in one or two instances and are in "current dollars", even though the Consumer Price Index rose about 5% per year and the food component of the Index rose slightly more than that. The USDA's estimates of weekly food costs at different adequacy levels for persons of each sex and age group are repriced regularly in the Family Economic Review, and they show similar but not identical increases. The disagreement about which index should be used to adjust official Federal poverty levels is sure to be exacerbated by recent dramatic price increases in food. We have used a constant measure of food needs and of annual family income needs, unadjusted for inflation. It can be thought of as an adjustment for differences in, or changes in, family composition, and will go up slightly over time for unchanged families with children growing older and increasing food needs.

This leaves the reader free to make whatever translation for inflation and/or for increases in average real incomes he chooses. One might argue that in order to leave the family no worse off, current dollar income relative to a needs standard, which changes only for changes in family composition, should rise at a rate somewhere between the rise in the cost of living and the rise in average money incomes.

Special Variables

An essential ingredient of behavioral research is the translation of what can be measured in an interview, or about the environment of each family, into variables with theoretical meaning. Procedures vary from mechanical combinations, as in factor analysis or least-space analysis, to purely deductive-theoretical combinations. In any case there is always some danger of wrong construction or misinterpretation. Our strategy has been to use theory wherever possible and in addition to rely in some areas on a two-stage approach. Sets of attitudes or of behavioral reports are combined into simple additive indexes with neutralization of items irrelevant for a particular family. Then we see whether that index has any effect on the criterion variables such as the trend in the family's economic status. If it has no effect, then presumably none of its components do either and we can dismiss them all. If there is a linear effect, we can check the components, but there is reason to believe that they will all matter. If there are non-linear effects we can check the components for complementarity, substitutability, or the presence of components that do not matter. For example, if there is no effect until an index reaches its highest levels, one might conclude that the components were complementary, that all of them must be favorable before anything happens.

Other special variables are more structured by theory or definition; these are described in the Glossary in alphabetical order. There is a substantial literature behind some of them, particularly the measures of achievement motivation and of "intelligence," as well as separate documentation on our development of those two measures. The food and income needs of the family were derived from USDA and HEW procedures. Environmental information about the county was derived from public records and from annual mail questionnaires to the state directors of unemployment compensation.

One way of avoiding arguments about the adequacy of minimum poverty standards is to use the ratio of family income to a needs standard, allowing the reader to use any cut-off point he likes. Such a ratio is easy to adjust for inflation or the cost of living. Much of the analysis focuses on the ratio of family money income to the official needs standard. But we move in two directions -- analyzing changes in the components of that ratio (changes in family composition, in work hours of head and wife, in wage rates) and comparing more elaborate and sophisticated composite measures of well-being which include non-money components of income, deduct some costs of earning income, and even include the amount of time left to enjoy that income.

Statistical Procedures

With a rich body of data, many competing theories, and uncertainty as to how the measured variables relate to the theoretical constructs, we are not testing one well-specified theoretical model. Rather, we are attempting to determine which of a large collection of possible factors actually influence change in family economic status, and in what combinations. The statistical procedure starts with systematic search and selection, using multivariate procedures which impose few restrictive assumptions (see Appendix C for descriptions of those procedures).

Modern computers are so powerful, and our data so rich, however, that we are in danger of "capitalizing on chance," of finding some intriguing result which fits some neat theory and of inferring that the expected relationship exists in the real world. To avoid such a trap, at the suggestion of the National Advisory Committee of the Economic Behavior Program, Survey Research Center, we divided the sample into four independent part-samples, and did most of our searching on part of the sample. We used the independent fresh data to test whether the findings would hold up. Sometimes we did this by fitting the final model, usually by multiple regression, to the full sample, examining whether the effects held and doubling any differences. We also tested the stability of our results by trying alternative measures and transformations of the data.

In both searching and assessing-testing we used multivariate methods in order to avoid assigning to one variable what is really the effect of something correlated with it. Since many of our variables have no clear scale, we used methods that can deal with categorical variables. For explanatory variables it was simply a matter of converting categories into sets of dichotomous or "dummy" variables with values of 0 or 1. For categorical dependent variables we resorted to a new searching program (THAID), but at present we have no way of testing a final model in this situation.

Our purpose is to build a credible picture of the world by trying a variety of approaches to see which factors persist after we have explored many variations in measuring variables, applied several statistical procedures, and examined all of the subpopulations.

We want to see whether anything subject to change through public policy or personal effort matters in the changing economic fortunes of families. Unchangeable background factors must be included in the analysis, and the effects of some of these, like race and sex, are subject to change. What is new about this study is the combination of such standard background variables with measures of the attitudes and behavior patterns which might be expected to affect people's economic progress.

In the case of such attitudinal or behavioral concepts as confidence, risk avoidance, or planning ahead, we apply an analysis strategy which says that if a simple additive combination of elements that are not negatively correlated has *no* effect on the family's economic progress, then it is unlikely that any of the components do either. Hence, we can test a set of additive indexes, and only when the combination does something do we need to ask whether it is only some of the components or all of them that matter, and whether they operate additively or cumulatively. For convenience we shall refer to these combinations by picturesque descriptive terms, such as sense of personal efficacy, connectedness to sources of information and help, and the like, hoping that the reader will keep in mind that this is a shorthand way of referring to a combination of elements no better than the questions that created them.[1]

---

[1] See Glossary for details of each index, the documentation for still more detail, and for an evaluation see Katherine Dickinson, "Investigation of the Attitudinal and Behavioral Indexes," working paper, July 1972.

One note of warning. Interviewing was done in the spring of 1968 and each following spring, but the reports on flows in income, consumption, and work hours refer to the previous calendar year, 1967 and subsequently. This would cause no problem in referring to years except that the status reports on family composition, whether currently employed or in the labor force, and even short run rates of flow such as food consumption and food needs are measured as of the time of the interview. We shall mostly be referring to the year of the income flow, 1967-71, but when we discuss change in family composition, for instance, we discuss changes from 1968 to 1972. While we are analyzing five waves of interviews and have five years of income and work measurements, we have only a four-year span. Hence, if prices went up 5% per year, the prices in 1971 were only 20%, not 25%, higher than in 1967.

One of the great problems of quantitative social research is that it is never so exciting or simple or clean as the hypotheses it sets out to test. Frequently there are several conflicting hypotheses, each one fascinating and having clear policy implications, but the real world has a way of agreeing with none of them. The truth often falls between the competing hypotheses and cannot be summarized with any passion, certainly not without unconscionable sacrifice of precision. First searches of the data produce new hypotheses, almost all of which must be rejected or qualified when a systematic analysis is done.

The capacity of the human mind to find regularities, focus on the unusual, and combine things is such that there is great danger of pouncing on findings that "fit." The reader should be warned that in spite of everything, negative conclusions are more trustworthy than positive ones. If we are unable to find any evidence that a certain variable matters, even for some subgroups of the population, then in the absence of serious measurement problems it is likely that it does not matter. But if we find an intriguing relationship for which we can elaborate a neat theory, the possibility remains that it is a chance finding. Even with all our attempts to search half samples and check with the fresh data, the final runs often produce new and interesting speculations which can only be regarded as new hypotheses.

Presentation of Findings

The first volume focuses systematically on the main question: What has determined the paths of individual family well-being over this period in time? After an overview which stresses the crucial importance of changes in family composition and our inability to explain the remaining changes in overall family well-being, we turn to the components: changes in wage rates earned and hours worked. Throughout, we search not for the obvious and well-known influence of unchangeable background factors, but for the important marginal effects of environmental, behavioral, or attitudinal variables which may be subject to change by persuasion or public policy.

We also examine in the first volume transfer incomes, the instability of income (as distinguished from its level or trend), and educational attainment of the new generation. A final chapter summarizes the findings.

The second volume contains a series of related but somewhat special studies of housing, mobility, food consumption, family planning, nonmoney rewards from work and their correlation with money rewards, the incidence of selected taxes and subsidies, and the investment of time in children. All these are thought to have policy implications, but we have attempted to limit our conclusions to what we have found, not extrapolating or combining them with other information and/or values in an attempt to make public policy.

Chapter 1

CHANGE IN GLOBAL MEASURES

INTRODUCTION

Our sample of 5060 families covers a wide range of possible economic histories -- from stable, middle-aged families with few changes in size, labor force
participation, or composition to families where individuals have retired, divorced, or split off from a parental home during the years 1968 to 1972. We will
analyze many of the details of what happened during this period, but it is useful
to start with an overall picture and to provide some feeling for the relative importance of the components of economic well-being.

The definition and measurement of well-being are important problems that
must be faced at the outset. Our data allow us to go far beyond the simple income measures that have traditionally been available. Adjustments can be made
for family size and composition, labor, capital and transfer income of all family
members, costs of earning income such as commuting and child care expenses,
imputed rent from owning a home, money earned through home production activity,
and even for leisure time. In the first section of this chapter, various measures of economic status are developed and their intercorrelations are presented.

The availability of these measures of economic status over a five-year
period enables us to analyze some of the dynamics of family well-being. On a
very simple level we are able to contrast a family's situation in the first and
last years to see the extent to which families change their relative ranking in
the distribution of well-being. The well-being measure used for this is total
family money income relative to a family's needs. Results of this analysis are
presented in Section II.

Observations of family well-being over time also permit a more satisfactory
definition of a low income or poverty population. If all families with a low
income in a single year could be observed over several years, it would be found
that some are only transitory members of a poverty population while the remainder
are its permanent members. We again use total family income relative to needs as a

well-being yardstick and define two important subpopulations. The first we call the "target population." It consists of all families who were in the bottom quintile when ranked by family money income/needs for *any one* of the five years of the study. This group of families is the focus of much subsequent analysis. In order to avoid one-sided conclusions, analysis is not restricted to this group but is expanded to include those who are not poor. A description of this target population is given in the third section of this chapter. The second subpopulation of interest is made up of families falling in the lowest income/needs quintile for *every one* of the five years. These we call the "persistently poor." They will be described in Section IV.

Changes in the economic status of families are complicated by, and are also the result of, changes in the compositions of the families themselves. Before analysis of the changing economic status of changing families can proceed, an attempt must be made to relate the two phenomena. This topic, which is analyzed in a necessarily cursory way in the fifth section of this chapter, is the subject of the entire chapter which follows this one.

The richness of the data allows us to search for the determinants of changes in some global measures of family well-being. The five years of information can be thought of as a set of natural experiments, providing a sample of families in different situations, and with different behavior patterns and attitudes. We are able to see if there are things people believe or do that get them into or out of poverty or that affect, in a more general way, changes that occur in their economic status. We also attempt to assess the extent to which external environmental conditions which may be subject to change by public policy affect the economic fate of families. These issues are so important that several alternative measures of economic well-being are investigated with several different definitions of change in these measures over time. The analysis of them is presented in the sixth and seventh sections of this chapter. Variations in concept and definition of change did not alter the basic conclusions of this analysis: people's economic experiences are largely either the result of their backgrounds or of unmeasured and perhaps random events. But we also discover that major changes in family composition and labor force participation so dominate the overall picture that these large changes may well mask the smaller marginal results of other factors. For this reason, later chapters look more closely at the *components* of the changes in well-being and at subpopulations where individuals have some freedom of choice. To place this subsequent analysis into perspective, the final section of this chapter considers how the changes in some global measures of well-being relate to changes in their components.

ANALYSIS

I. Intercorrelations Among Measures of Economic Status

A family's well-being is dependent upon many complex factors. In measuring the average level, the time trend, and the instability of family economic status, it is clearly not enough to look only at such common measures as family money income or the earnings of the family head. Vast differences in family well-being can be created by income from capital, other earners, nonmoney income such as the free rent of an owned home, and by differences in the number of people to be supported. Some attention should also be paid to the amount of leisure time left to enjoy the income after it is earned. To account for these elements of family well-being we have developed a series of measures, each more sophisticated than the previous one. Our analysis of trends and levels of economic status will focus on one or two measures, but it is useful at the start to see how they are related to one another and to learn which components are dominant.

Correlations among the various measures of economic status are relatively high, but not so high that we can be indifferent about which one we use. There is a substantial difference in economic well-being when we account for different family compositions by dividing by a standard of needs. Allowing for the leisure time a family has also makes a difference, but the weight (exponent) we give leisure in the measure is so arbitrary that we cannot insist on its importance. The details are given in Table 1.1 for a single year, 1971, only. The table arranges eleven measures of economic status in order of complexity and comprehensiveness, starting with the head's hourly earnings and progressing to some rather complex "utility" measures that include leisure. Food consumption relative to an estimate of the food needs is also included in order to show its correlation with measures of economic status. This relies on the tradition that, particularly at the lower income levels, the adequacy of food consumption is an indicator of the family's income adequacy.

The first measure of status is the head's hourly earnings and the second is the head's annual earnings, a figure equal to his wage rate multiplied by his annual hours of work.[1] To these earnings we add the wife's earnings and capital income such as rent, interest, dividends, royalties, and business and farm income not previously allocated to labor. This yields our third measure of economic status, taxable income of head and wife. Finally, by including transfer income

---

[1] We actually obtain these measures by asking the family head about his annual hours and annual earnings and dividing the two to obtain hourly earnings.

TABLE 1.1

Correlations among Various Indicators of Well-Being
(1971 Income)

	Head's Hourly Earnings	Head's Annual Earnings	Head and Wife Taxable Income	Total Family Money Income	Money Income/ Needs	Well-Offness: (Money Income/ Needs)$^{1/2}$ (Leisure)$^{1/2}$	Net Real Income	Net Real Income/ Needs	Well-Offness*: Using Net Real Income	Deducting Commuting Time and Costs	(Net Real Income- Housing Costs/ Food Needs)$^{1/2}$ (Leisure)$^{1/2}$	Food Costs/ Food Needs
Head's Hourly Earnings		.82	.77	.73	.63	.58	.70	.60	.51	.49	.44	.23
Head's Annual Earnings			.92	.85	.71	.60	.82	.67	.52	.49	.44	.25
Head and Wife Taxable Income				.94	.83	.71	.90	.79	.62	.59	.54	.27
Total Family Money Income					.86	.76	.98	.83	.70	.67	.61	.26
Money Income/Needs						.91	.82	.98	.85	.83	.82	.44
"Well-Offness" Use of Money Income							.74	.92	.98	.96	.93	.42
Net Real Income								.82	.70	.68	.60	.25
Net Real Income/Needs									.90	.87	.85	.46
"Well-Offness" Use of Net Real Income										.99	.94	.43
"Well-Offness" Using Net Real Income and Deducting Commuting Time and Costs											.92	.40
(Net Real Income-Housing Costs/Food Needs)$^{1/2}$(Leisure)$^{1/2}$												.47
Average Value	$3.57	$7089	$9060	$10,894	3.36	102.6	$10,550	3.24	102.4	99.4	173.3	2.10
Standard Deviation	$3.54	$7012	$8540	$ 8,397	2.53	36.5	$ 7,162	2.10	32.5	31.8	63.6	1.00

*Well-Offness = (Income/Needs)$^{1/2}$(Leisure/Person)$^{1/2}$

MTR 1073

for the family and taxable income of other earners, we obtain total family income, the most commonly used measure of a family's resources.

These concepts are somewhat unsatisfactory indicators of economic well-being since they make no adjustment for the number of people who must share this income. Families are ranked better when we divide money income by a standard of needs which is based on family composition.[1] The structure of our measure of needs follows the same logic as those that are the basis for the U.S. official poverty standards. It starts with a measure of what an adequate diet would cost for the family, allows for economies of scale in consumption, expands that to take care of all the other needs, and introduces another adjustment for the economies of scale in housing and otherwise caring for larger families.

The focus of these measures of economic well-being is on ranking people rather than selecting arbitrary cutoff points. Accordingly, a major subpopulation which we shall often study separately is the group of families which, according to money income/needs, are ranked in the lowest fifth of all families during at least one of the five years of the survey. A detailed description of this group is presented later in this chapter. We refer to them as the target population since many government programs are "aimed" at them. Such families account for about half of our particular sample, but are only slightly more than a third of the nation's families.[2]

Our next measure takes into account the leisure that the family has to enjoy its income. Leisure time and income/needs are in different units so we cannot add them, but we can multiply them together. If we assume that the combined measure should have the characteristic that a 10% increase in both income/needs and in leisure makes the family 10% better off, then the two exponents should add to 1.0. We have made them each equal to ½, arbitrarily.[3]

---

[1] See the Glossary for a detailed description of this measure.

[2] We weight our data, of course, to preserve the representative nature of the findings, but the added numbers of families with low incomes increase the reliability of conclusions about them.

[3] There are also some problems with defining leisure. We have deducted 8 hours a day for sleep, and no more, in order to avoid negative leisure for a few hard working souls. We have deducted from the remaining 5840 hours a year what we call "nonleisure hours" which include home production time, work hours, commuting time, housework hours, unemployment (8 hours per day unemployed), and illness (16 hours a day for the first 8 weeks and 12 hours a day after that). This assumes that the remaining time is enjoyable leisure, which may be an exaggeration, particularly for retired people. Finally, some decision about whose leisure to count had to be made; we decided to count leisure time only for the head and wife, averaging the two so the number would be comparable with single-headed families.

The first six measures consider the total gross income the family receives but we can improve our measure of the family's control over resources by including estimates of income in kind a family receives and by subtracting the costs of earning income.[1] We then divide this "net real income" by needs and account for leisure time.

Two final adjustments are made using the leisure-adjusted measures. The first deducts commuting cost from income and commuting time from leisure. The second attempts to remove the distortions from subsidized housing costs and the disproportionate housing costs of older people still living in a family home now too large for their needs. The housing costs are deducted from net real income and the result is related to the food needs measure.

In Table 1.1 we can see that the correlations among various measures of well-being drop as soon as we introduce the adjustment for family composition (divided by needs), and they drop further when we account for differences in leisure. They also drop when we improve the measure of income by going to net real income, and again when we deduct commuting time and costs.

Each of these measures correlates well with the family's food consumption relative to an estimate of food needs. One must remember that at the lower levels food consumption differences may mean the difference between an adequate diet and an inadequate one, while at the top levels they may mean only differences in luxury. Those who can afford to eat out in restaurants add to their expenditures but not necessarily to their nutrition. The adjustment for family composition (going to income/needs) increases the correlation of economic status with food consumption, while the correction for leisure (going to well-offness) reduces it slightly. Interestingly, the status measure which takes account of housing costs has the highest correlation with food consumption. One might think this was the spurious result of having the same denominator on both sides, but the measurement error in food needs is small and the theoretical logic is strong. People in subsidized housing *can* afford to spend more of their remaining income on food, and those paying a large fraction of their income for housing might well be constrained to eat less.

It might seem that the correlations in Table 1.1 are high, but the extent to which one concept accounts for the variation in the other is given by the *square* of these correlations, and the introduction of family composition (needs)

---

[1] Specifically, we add imputations for the value of home production, the net rent implicitly earned on equity in a house, and the value of free goods and services and subtract the cost of child care for working mothers, union dues, and estimates of federal income tax.

produces relatively low correlations. Any analyst who wants to array families according to their ability to pay taxes or their need for help or who wants to measure inequality may well consider making at least some of these adjustments.

We focus much attention on family money income/needs, partly because the additional possible improvements in the income measure are relatively small, and partly because the adjustments for leisure are so speculative. Even then we have a complex problem of analysis since family money income/needs is itself made up of components which may be of different levels of importance and which may be affected by different things.

Of the 5060 families in the sample, 25% have acquired a different head during the course of the study and among those with the same head, some 13% (10% of all families) were not in the labor force in 1967 or in 1972, 1% entered the labor force between 1967 and 1972, and 13% were in the labor force in 1967 and not in 1972, most of the last group having retired during the period. Hence, analysis must either take account of these changes or be restricted to families with the same head and a head who was in the labor force all along. When we do restrict the sample we analyze, the reader must keep in mind that many dramatic changes in well-being are occurring to those who have been excluded from that analysis.

II.   Patterns of Transition

Changes in economic status lower the inter-temporal correlations, that is, how well the first year predicts the fifth. For families with the same head for all five years, the correlation between almost any income or well-being measure in the first year with that same measure in the fifth year is relatively high, for instance around .64 for income/needs. For families with different heads, the correlation drops to .29 for income/needs. The pattern of transitions can be shown if we cross-tabulate a measure for 1967 against the same measure for 1971. In most of our analysis we do not adjust for inflation, partly because there are too many possible ways to do it and the estimates of changes in prices and in real income are still subject to revision, and partly because it is arguable whether one should adjust only for changes in prices or also for changes in real standards of living. For transitions in income/needs, however, it appeared essential to make such an adjustment.[1] Tables 1.2 and 1.3 show the "before" (1967) and "after" (1971) distributions of family income/needs and the combinations or

---

[1] A series of unadjusted tables of transitions in various income measures appears in the Appendix to this chapter as Tables A1.1 through A1.7.

TABLE 1.2

Income/Needs in 1971 According to Income/Needs in 1967[a]
(for all families)

Family Income/Needs in 1971 (adjusted for inflation)	Family Income/Needs in 1967						
	Less than .60	.60-.99	1.00-1.49	1.50-2.99	3.00-4.49	4.50-	All
Less than .60	38	13	6	2	1	0	5
.60-.99	26	33	13	5	3	2	10
1.00-1.49	17	26	34	12	4	2	14
1.50-2.99	15	23	38	54	29	15	37
3.00-4.49	3	5	7	22	40	26	21
4.50-	1	1	2	5	23	55	13
	100%	101%	100%	100%	100%	100%	100%
Number of Cases	670	896	898	1600	657	337	5060
Percent of Sample	6	10	14	39	20	11	100

Cramer's V = .37

[a]The data have been adjusted for inflation.

MTR 1058

TABLE 1.3

Income/Needs in 1971 According to Income/Needs in 1967[a]
(for families with the same head all five years)

Family Income/Needs in 1971 (adjusted for inflation)	Family Income/Needs in 1967						
	Less than .60	.60- .99	1.00- 1.49	1.50- 2.99	3.00- 4.49	4.50-	All
Less than .60	<u>44</u>	9	4	1	0	0	4
.60-.99	29	<u>39</u>	15	4	1	0	9
1.00-1.49	15	28	<u>38</u>	10	3	1	13
1.50-2.99	9	18	37	<u>57</u>	24	9	36
3.00-4.49	3	5	5	23	<u>45</u>	26	23
4.50-	0	1	1	5	27	<u>64</u>	15
	100%	100%	100%	100%	100%	100%	100%
Number of Cases	419	594	645	1147	498	265	3568
Percent of Sample	5	10	14	39	20	12	100

Cramer's V = .44

[a]The data have been adjusted for inflation.

MTR 1058

transitions for all families and for those with the same head.[1] The tables show
that there is a good deal of change in status, even among families with the same
head, and also a good deal of improvement, even in real terms. There are more
people with increasing income/needs ratios than with decreasing ones. More important, there are substantial numbers with changed status, even if, as in Table
1.3, we consider only families with the same head for all five years, where about
half are in a different group after four years.

Two working papers by former members of the Office of Planning, Research
and Evaluation Staff of the Office of Economic Opportunity have looked at transitions of families over the first four waves of the study. Jonathan P. Lane
(1972) compared families below the poverty level in one year with those with a
four-year average below the poverty level.[2] He also compared the data with the
Census (CPS data) and looked at transitions out of poverty. Lester Klein (1972)
used a threshold of some width that a group had to cross in order to be called
upwardly mobile, thus avoiding the inclusion of people right at the borderline
whose improvement was very small.[3]

III. Who Is In the Target Population?

The availability of five years of information on a large number of families
enables us to get a better look at transitory and permanent members of the poverty population. It is customary to define poverty by some absolute income or
income/needs level. Those below that level are "poor," those above it are "non-
poor." But in any one year, many families below the line will be there only
temporarily. Only over several years can those persistently poor be sorted from
those temporarily poor.

The single year poverty line used here is the level of total family income/
needs which separates the lowest fifth of the population from the rest, so in any
given year exactly 20% of the families will fall into this bottom fifth. As the

---

[1] The 1971 needs standard is adjusted to allow for the 24% increase in food costs
during the period between 1967 and 1971. Table 1.2 is for all families and
Table 1.3 is for all the families with the same head all five years, eliminating
the splitoffs and the widowed or divorced women. It would be possible to
adjust using the 21% increase in the Consumer Price Index for all items, but
particularly for low income families national indexes place too little importance on food and it is food costs that determine the poverty standards.

[2] J. P. Lane, Who's Poor, One Year vs. Four Year Perspectives in Counting Low
Income Families, May 1972.

[3] Lester Klein, A Partitioning Algorithm for Studying Income Dynamics, 1972.

time period is expanded from one year to five, considerably more than 20% of the families will have been in the bottom income/needs quintile. In our sample, 35% of the families were in the bottom quintile in at least one of the five years. This definition of a poverty population adjusts both for inflation and for increasing real standards of living in the nation and at least crudely takes care of differences in family resources, composition, and needs. In much of the analysis which follows in this and other chapters, we take a separate look at these families.

We need to answer two questions. The first is "Who among the entire population are in the target population?" One way of thinking about the fact that 35% of the sample is in the target population is to consider that a family's chances of falling into it are about one in three. Many things can be expected to influence this chance. Families with older, retired heads will have a greater than 35% chance; those with highly educated heads will have a much smaller chance. We systematically consider how various demographic, background, and related policy relevant variables affect the chance of a sample member falling into the target population. Fewer than one quarter of the families (24%) in the target population (9% of all families), were in the bottom fifth of the income/ needs distribution *every one* of the five years. We shall call those that were the persistently poor, because they were persistently at the lower end of the distribution. The second question concerns these families: "Who among the target population are persistently poor?" Given that a family is in the target population, its chances of being persistently poor are about one in four. The way in which this chance relates to demographic, background, and related policy relevant variables is the subject of the next section.

Many factors could be expected to relate to a family's chance of falling into the lower fifth of the income/needs distribution in any one of five years. Old age, low education, and rural residence are a few examples. This section will relate a family's chance of being in the target population to a standard set of demographic and environmental variables: age, education, test score, motivation, race, city size, distance to a large city, the sex-marital-child status of the head of the household, and the unemployment rate in the county of residence in 1971. The simple association (eta-squared) between each of these variables and the chance that a family is in the target population is given in Table 1.4.[1]

The simple relationship between age and the chance of being in the target population is shown in Figure 1.1. As would be expected, both the very young and

---

[1]See the Glossary for an explanation of the variables and of eta-squared.

22

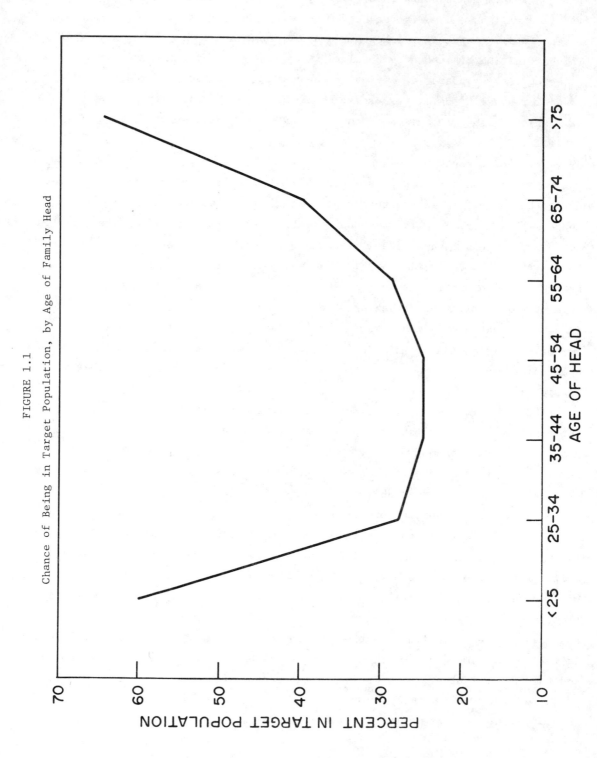

FIGURE 1.1

Chance of Being in Target Population, by Age of Family Head

TABLE 1.4

Association (eta-squared) between Several Demographic,
Background and Policy Variables and a Family's Chances
of Being in the Target Population

Variable	Eta^2
Age	.081
Education	.118
Test score	.089
Race	.067
City size	.024
Distance to a large city	.025
Sex-marital-child status	.086
Motivation	.043
Unemployment rate	.006
Change in family composition	.040

very old have a much higher than average chance of falling into the target population than those between the ages of 25 and 64. In the multivariate analysis which follows, only heads in the 25-64 year age group will be included.

Another variable which is related to target population membership is change in family composition. But we will exclude it from multivariate analysis due to its circularity.[1] Different probabilities of being in the target population by types of family composition change are presented in Table 1.5. Families which undergo the least change have the smallest probability of being in the target population. The probability seems to rise with the complexity of the particular

TABLE 1.5

Chance of Being in Target Population
by Change in Family Composition

Family Composition Change	% in Target Population	Number of Observations
No change in family members	28.7	1767
Same head and wife only	29.4	1572
Same head, changed wife	37.9	229
Wife became head	50.0	247
Female head got married	40.2	168
Family member other than head or wife became head	53.4	743
Female family member other than head or wife married	51.0	283

[1]By circularity we mean that economic status can lead to changes in family composition as well as be altered by these changes.

change. Widowed, separated, and divorced women and splitoff children have a better than 50-50 chance of being in the target population. While these complex family changes are associated with being in the bottom fifth of the income/needs distribution at least one of the five years, it will be seen in the next section that their associated probabilities of being there *all* five years (i.e., being persistently poor) were much below average.

To see the gross and net effects of the various predictors on the chance of being in the target population, a dummy variable regression was run which included all variables as predictors.[1] Table 1.6 presents the relative importance of each of the independent variables (as indicated by their β^2) in their prediction of the probability of being in the target population. Of all the variables, three dominate: education of head, sex-marital-child status, and race.

TABLE 1.6

Relative Importance (β^2) of Predictors of the Probability of
Being in the Target Population
(for all families with heads age 25-64)

Predictor	β^2
Age	.004
Education	.051
Test score	.008
Race	.029
City size	.009
Distance to a large city	.012
Sex-marital-child status	.061
1971 Unemployment rate in county	.002
Motivation	.004

$$R^2 \text{ (adjusted)} = .261$$

The way in which the probability of being in the target population relates to the years of education of the head of the household is presented in Figure 1.2. It shows that there is a monotonic and nearly linear relationship between increased education and the reduced chance of being in the lowest quintile of income/needs for any of the five years. Those with less than a sixth grade education have a slightly greater than 50% chance; those with more than high school have a less than 25% chance.

---

[1]This regression was actually the second analysis stage; the first used the more flexible AID program to check for interactions among predictors. The sex-marital-child status interacted variable was specified *a priori* and the AID showed no substantial interactions. See Appendix C on statistical procedures.

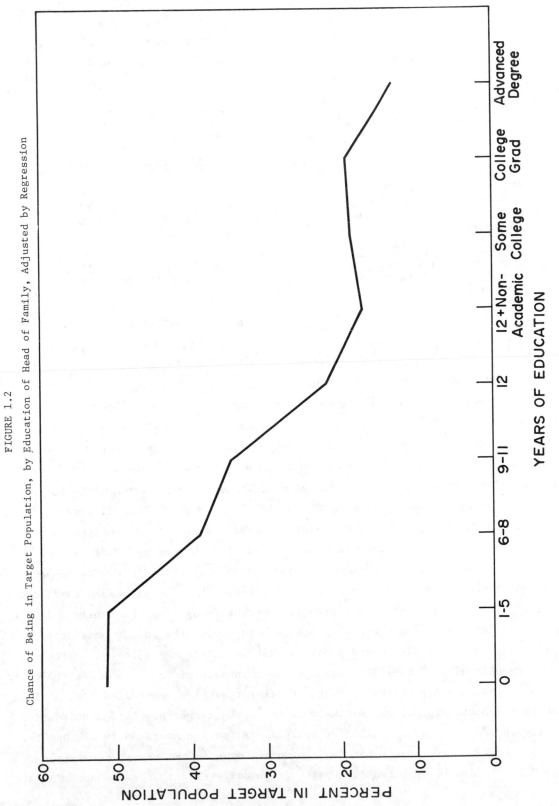

FIGURE 1.2

Chance of Being in Target Population, by Education of Head of Family, Adjusted by Regression

The sex, marital, and child status of the head of the household were combined into a single variable. The unadjusted and adjusted chances of being in the target population by categories of this variable are presented in Table 1.7.

TABLE 1.7

Unadjusted and Adjusted Chance of Being in the Target Population,
by Sex, Marital and Child Status of Head of Household,
All Families with Head Age 25-65

	Unadjusted %	Adjusted %	% of Cases
Male Head			
married, no children	15	16	22.6
married, children at home	21	23	48.7
unmarried	40	38	8.7
Female Head			
no children at home	37	36	11.4
children at home	63	54	8.5

Female headed households have a considerably higher chance of being in the target population than those with male heads. The adjusted chance of being in the target population for all families with male heads is 22.4%; for families with female heads the chance is about twice as much -- 43.6%.

The presence of children increases the family's chance of being in the target population. This is to be expected, in part because the definition of target population was made from a measure of income relative to family needs. These needs will increase with additional children and they will rarely be offset by increases in family income. The effect of children differs between the households headed by males and those headed by females. Much of this difference is undoubtedly due to the fact that children are more likely to affect the labor force participation of females than males. Families headed by a male in which there are children living at home have a 23% chance of being in the target population; those without children have a 16% chance. For female-headed families, children make a much greater difference. Over half (54%) of the families in which children are present and a female is head are in the target population, while only 36% of female headed families *without* children are in this category.

Race is also of considerable importance in determining a family's chance of being in the target population. With no other variables controlled for, a black family is about three times as likely to be in the target population as a white family (60.2% for blacks, 21.6% for whites). A Spanish American family has two and a half times the chance that whites do of being in the target population (53.9%). It can be expected that part of the difference in these chances is due to differences in factors that increase employability and earnings: education, age, sex, rural residence, test score, motivation, and so on. Yet when we control for these and all other variables, the black family's chance of being in the target population is still twice as great as the corresponding white family's chance (46.3% for blacks vs. 23.7% for whites). Spanish American families fare only a little better than the blacks: 42.6% of them are in the target population. All of the remaining variables included in the analysis had quite weak relationships with the family's chance of being in the bottom fifth of the income/needs distribution in any one of the five years. The full detail of the regression is given in Appendix Table A1.8. It is important to note that neither individual achievement motivation, as we measured it, nor unemployment in the county seemed to matter, even with the background variables taken into account.

IV. Who Among the Target Population are Persistently Poor?

As stated earlier, we define the persistently poor to be those families in the bottom fifth *every one* of the five years. These families comprise about 24% of the families in the target population and some 9% of the *total* population.

The chance of being persistently poor will be related to the same set of variables used in investigating a family's chance of being in the target population: age, education, test score, race, motivation, city size, distance to a large city, the sex-marital-child status of the head of the household, and the unemployment rate in the county of residence in 1971. The simple measure of association (eta^2) between each of these variables and the probability of being persistently poor is given in Table 1.8. None of the numbers in this table are very surprising; it is presented to help gain a perspective on the multivariate analysis which follows. Again, family composition is not included in the multivariate analysis because of the circularity it would introduce. Table 1.9 shows how the chance of being persistently poor is related to the various family composition changes.

Target population families with no change in either head or wife over the five years have the highest chance of being persistently poor. Those families with a splitoff -- of son or daughter as head or of daughter as wife -- have the lowest probability. This situation contrasts sharply with findings noted earlier which show that the probability of being in the target population is greatest for those families which have changed most (see Table 1.5).

Before turning to multivariate analysis, two restrictions on the sample need to be made. Figure 1.3 shows the relationship between the head of the household's age and that family's chance of being persistently poor. As would be

TABLE 1.8

Simple Association Between Several Demographic, Background,
and Policy Variables and a Family's Chances of Being Persistently Poor[1]

Variable	Eta^2
Age	.080
Education	.099
Test Score	.079
Race	.038
City Size	.020
Distance to a large city	.019
Sex-marital-child status	.023
1971 Unemployment rate in county	.013
Motivation	.018
Change in Family Composition	.044

MTR1082

----

[1]See Glossary for definitions of variables like test score and motivation.

TABLE 1.9

Probability of Being Persistently Poor
by Change in Family Composition

Family Composition Change	Percent of Target Population Persistently Poor	Number of Observations
No change in family members	33%	742
Same head and wife only	27	794
Same head, changed wife	12	111
Wife became head of household	20	159
Female head got married	11	98
Family member other than head or wife became head	14	493
Female family member other than head or wife married	7	179

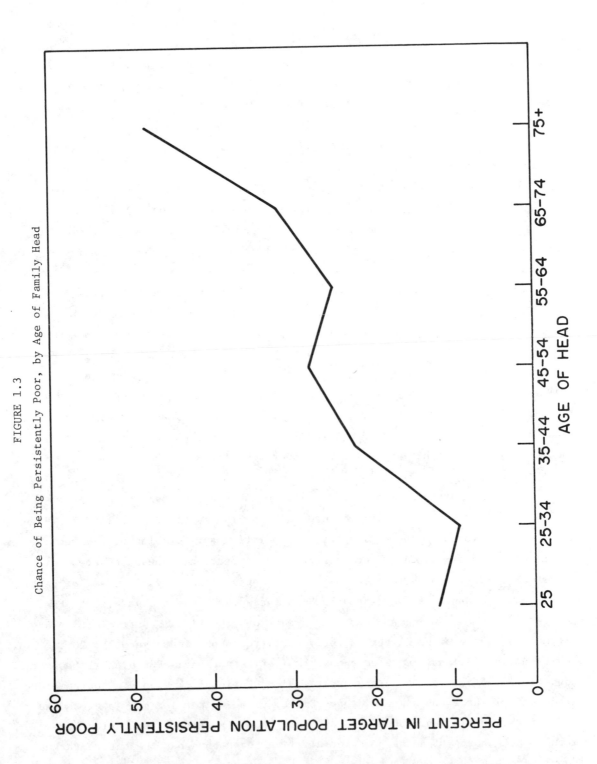

FIGURE 1.3

Chance of Being Persistently Poor, by Age of Family Head

expected, those older than 65 years have a considerably higher probability of being persistently poor than do younger persons heading households. Most of the persistently poor over 65 years are retired and would be unable or unwilling to rejoin the labor force under any circumstances. To make the target population reasonably homogeneous with respect to potential labor force participation, those older than 65 or younger than 25 years are excluded from the subsequent analysis. Because we find that many of the important variables depend critically on the race of the family we also present separate results for the entire population and for blacks only.

The importance of the various predictors on the chance of being persist-ently poor is presented in Table 1.10 for both the entire population and for blacks only. For both groups the sex of the head of the household and whether there are children at home matter most in determining that family's chance of being persistently poor. Table 1.11 shows how the chance of being persistently poor varies among families with male and female heads, with and without children.

As with the chance of being in the target population, a family's chance of being persistently poor is about twice as great if a female rather than a male heads the family (28% vs. 12%). Also consistent with the earlier findings for the entire target population is the fact that children in a household consider-ably increase the chance of being persistently poor. For the chance of being in the target population, however, children in the household made the most differ-ence in families where the head was female. Table 1.11 shows that children about double the chance of being persistently poor regardless of whether the head is male or female.

The effect of education on the chance of being persistently poor is as strong as it was with a family's chance of being in the target population. Fig-ure 1.4 shows for both the entire target population and for blacks only how the chance of being persistently poor depends upon education. These "chances" are adjusted for differences in age, test score, motivation, city size, sex of head, and all of the other independent variables included in the analysis. For the entire population, having at least six grades of education is sufficient to drop a family's chance of being persistently poor from approximately 40% to 20%. Additional educational increments make smaller reductions. For blacks, however, education's effect is not nearly as dramatic. While blacks who did not complete grade school share the same high probability of being persistently poor as the rest of the population, those who have more than six years of education have a much *higher* chance of being poor for all five years than has the entire target population. For the entire target population, six grades is sufficient to drop

TABLE 1.10

Relative Importance (β^2) of Predictors of the Probability
of Being Persistently Poor - for the Entire
Target Population and for Black Members Age 25-64 Only

Predictor	β^2	
	Entire Population	Blacks Only
Age	.011	.029
Education	.038	.027
Test score	.012	.008
Race	.034	-
City size	.006	.039
Distance to a large city	.012	.009
Sex-marital-child status	.045	.111
1971 Unemployment rate in county	.005	.006
Motivation	.004	.016

R^2(adjusted) = .182 R^2(adjusted) = .226

MTR1082

TABLE 1.11

Unadjusted and Adjusted Chance of Being Persistently Poor,
by Sex, Marital and Child Status of Head of Household,
for Target Population Families with Head Age 25-65

	Unadjusted %	Adjusted %	% of Cases
Male Head			
married, no children	10	8	12.6
married, children at home	18	19	38.7
unmarried	15	16	12.9
Female Head			
no children at home	20	18	15.9
children at home	35	36	20.0

MTR1082

32

Chance of Being Persistently Poor, by Education of Head, Adjusted by Regression

FIGURE 1.4

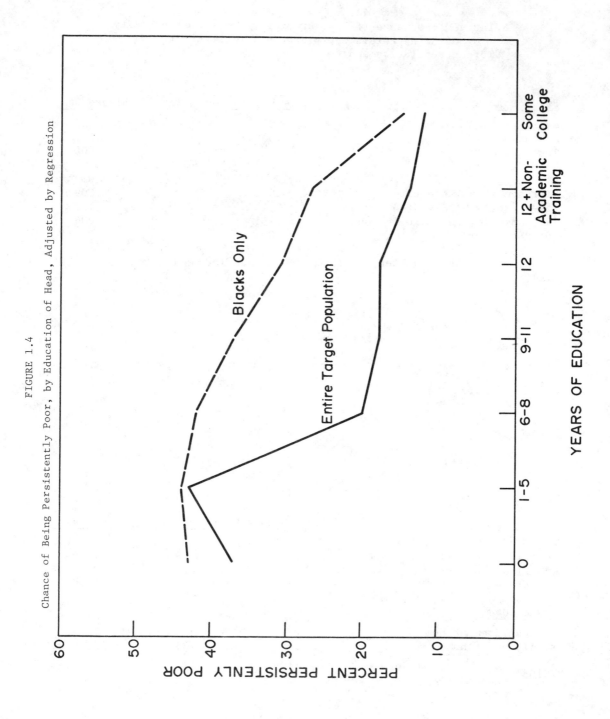

the chance of being persistently poor to about one in five. For blacks, it takes at least some college education to do this.

Attempts to explain why education pays off much more for whites than for blacks have pointed to differences in the *quality* of education for the two groups. While quality differences may produce some of this effect, it would be absurd to argue that they account for most of it. To do so one would have to equate the quality of white sixth grade education with that of black high school education. The alternative explanation of black-white differences is that a given amount of education pays off differently for blacks and whites in the labor market. Although these data do not directly prove that there is pervasive discrimination in the labor market against blacks in amount of and remuneration for employment, that explanation is entirely consistent with the findings.

The test score variable also affects the chances of a family being persistently poor -- an effect which also depends on the race of the family.[1] Figure 1.5 shows how the adjusted probability of being persistently poor depends upon the test score of the head of the household. Recall that the adjustment procedures hold constant the education, sex, age, and other important variables of the family's head. For the entire target population, there is a nearly monotonic decrease in the probability of being persistently poor with high test scores. For blacks, the relationship is weaker and erratic; only those in the highest test score category have less than a three in ten chance of being persistently poor.

Distance to a large city is an important predictor of whether a family is persistently poor or not. The adjusted chances of being persistently poor for the different distances are given in Figure 1.6. It shows that those living within 30 miles of a large city have a considerably smaller chance of being persistently poor than those in more rural areas. This effect is the same for blacks as it is for the entire population.

The effect of the size of the largest city in the area is considerably greater for blacks than for the entire target population. The adjusted chance of being persistently poor for these two groups by city size is given in Figure 1.7. For the entire population there is little relationship between the two variables. For blacks, however, larger cities clearly *decrease* the chance of being persistently poor, perhaps by widening job opportunities. Those in areas where no city is as large as 50,000 run about a 50% chance of being persistently

---

[1] The test was a sentence completion test of cognitive ability, designed for this study but still subject to the usual qualifications about such tests. See the Glossary.

34

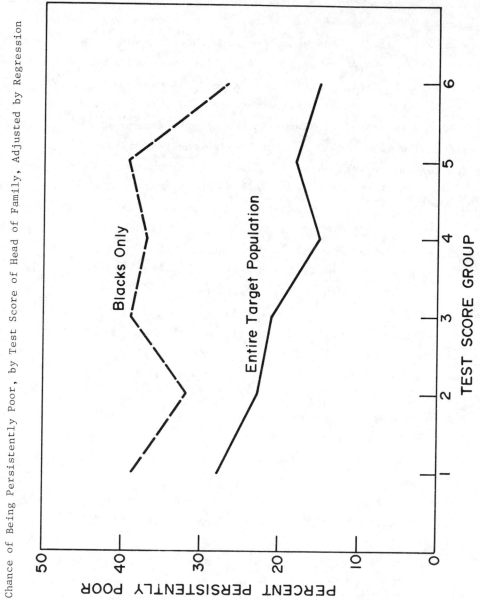

FIGURE 1.5

Chance of Being Persistently Poor, by Test Score of Head of Family, Adjusted by Regression

FIGURE 1.6

Chance of Being Persistently Poor, by Distance to a Large City,
Adjusted by Regression

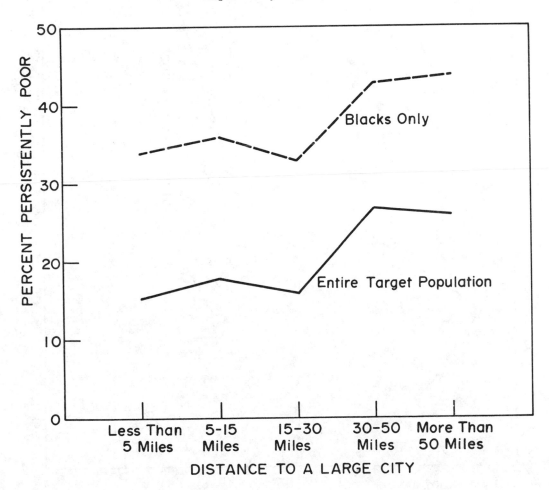

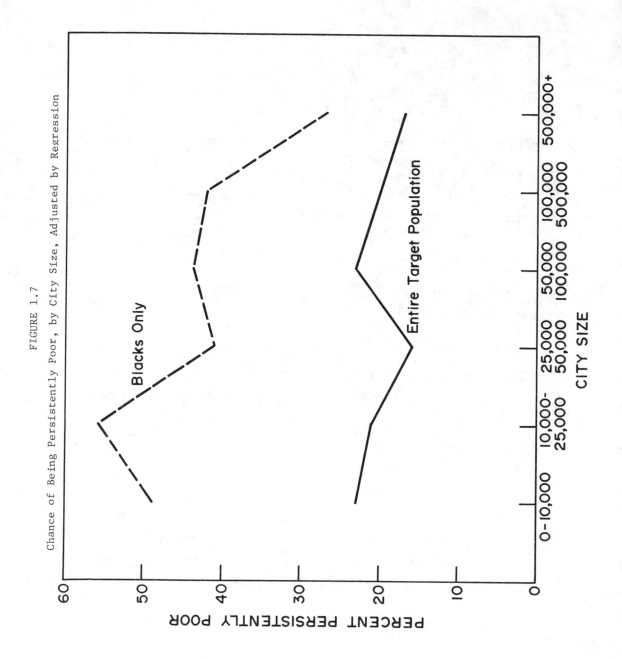

FIGURE 1.7

Chance of Being Persistently Poor, by City Size, Adjusted by Regression

poor, those in areas where the largest city is larger than half a million have less than one chance in three of staying poor.

The overall effect of race on the chance of being persistently poor is large, even after adjustments for the other variables. Table 1.12 shows the unadjusted and adjusted chance of being persistently poor by racial category. Its numbers are quite remarkable. The simple (unadjusted) proportion of white target population families who are persistently poor is less than one-half of the fraction of black target population families who are persistently poor. Conventional wisdom holds that much of this difference is due to the fact that blacks have less education, have a higher proportion of families headed by females, or live more often in rural areas. Yet when we control for these factors with regression and calculate what the difference in the chance of being persistently poor is for a black and a white with equal education, test score, motivation, sex, distance to a large city, county unemployment rate and so on, we still find that a black is more than twice as likely to be persistently poor as his white counterpart. We cannot pinpoint the cause of these racial differences. We can, however, report the negative finding that racial differences in the chances of being persistently poor are *not* due to the other variables included in our analysis.

TABLE 1.12

Unadjusted and Adjusted Probability of
Being Persistently Poor, by Race
(for target population families)

Race	Unadjusted %	Adjusted %	Number of Observations
White	.14	.16	593
Black	.37	.33	1067
Spanish American	.27	.23	66
Other	.08	.12	18

The other variables affect the chance of being persistently poor in less systematic and interesting ways. The county unemployment rate, a policy related variable, has an insignificant effect, as does our measure of achievement motivation. The full detail of the unadjusted and adjusted proportions of persistently poor for all explanatory variables are given in Appendix Table A1.8.

V. Effects of Change in Family Composition

Having seen what affects the level of a family's well-being and leads to the persistence of poverty, it would be natural to turn next to a systematic study of changes in well-being. But it is already obvious that there are very

large changes in well-being associated with changes in family size (and needs)
and with the presence of other earners or working wives, that would swamp the
effects of wage increases of the head as well as changes in the amount of work he
found available. Hence, we turn directly to an examination of some of these very
large changes to see whether we can deal with them in some systematic way that
will avoid dividing the sample into subgroups for separate analysis. We first
use a set of categories focused on changes in family composition, ignoring
changes in labor force participation. We then present a table of initial levels
and changes between 1967 and 1971 for families with changes in composition during
the period (see Table 1.13).

We are looking at the 1972 sample of families. They are classified according to their history over the previous four years. Some will be newly formed
(from children leaving home or from divorces) while others will have lost members
who died or formed new families or have gained children.

The ten groups of family composition change account for very little of the
difference in initial *level* of income for the whole sample, but they do account
for a substantial amount of the variance in the *change* in income and in income/
needs. Income changes vary from an 81% increase where the head got married to a
50% decrease for single women who left their parental homes (splitoffs). The
changes in income/needs vary from a 60% increase in families where people other
than the head or wife left (mostly children moving out) to an 8% decrease for
those same single female splitoffs.

When we focus on the target population, the same pattern appears, but much
more intensely, so that the ten groups account for more of the variance. For
this low income group there are substantial differences in initial income and
therefore a substantial fraction of that variance is also accounted for. This is
partly an artifact, since splitoffs from well-off parental families can be in the
target population, because they are poor *after* they leave home and being poor any
one year qualified them for the target population. Similarly, the target population can include those who got out of poverty by marrying another earner or
leaving a poor family.

Some of the changes obviously affect the denominator of the income/needs
ratio; such changes included getting married, being a single splitoff from a family, having fewer family members other than head and wife (children left home),
or being divorced, widowed, or separated. Some changes are also likely to affect
the family income, such as being a divorced woman or a splitoff. Wherever there
is a different head, the income of the original head is usually lost and a different main income gained; but needs may also decrease in this situation so that

TABLE 1.13

Initial Income and Income/Needs and Percent Change 1967 to 1971
By Change in Family Composition

	All:					Target Population:				
	% of Families	1967 Income	% Increase 1971/1967	1967 Income/ Needs	% Increase 1971/1967	% of Families	1967 Income	% Increase 1971/1967	1967 Income/ Needs	% Increase 1971/1967
No Change in Family Members	42	8239	33	2.81	27	35	3080	36	1.12	29
Same Head - More or Different Family Members	15	8540	46	2.55	30	13	4602	45	1.27	29
Same Head and Wife - Fewer Family Members	14	10750	31	2.38	60	12	4991	34	1.01	58
Same Head - Remarried	2	7479	81	2.56	49	1	4285	120	1.44	92
Same Head - Widowed, Divorced, Separated	3	8650	19	2.54	57	3	5361	1	1.47	40
Different Head - Wife became Head	6	7994	-15	2.34	0	8	5607	-33	1.62	-17
Different Head - Single Male Splitoff	4	9667	-41	2.34	1	6	8448	-50	1.86	-6
Different Head - Female Became Head	4	9910	-50	2.41	-8	8	8532	-62	1.94	-33
Different Head - Married Male Splitoff	6	9478	14	2.38	39	7	6181	36	1.47	71
Different Head - Not Original Sample Member	4	9750	3	2.18	36	6	6774	10	1.42	62
ALL	100	8895	22	2.58	30	99	5001	13	1.33	24
Number of Cases	5060					2608				
Percent of Variance Accounted For*	.02	.13		.01	.05		.21	.20	.09	.09

*Square of correlation ratio (ETA^2): see Glossary

MTR 1043F

income/needs can go in either direction.

The proportion of 1972 families represented by these various groups given at the left of Table 1.13, indicates that there are substantial numbers of families involved in dramatic changes in composition that affect their economic status. The tables in the Appendix to this chapter provide more detailed information on levels and changes in work hours, food consumption, head and wife's taxable income, leisure hours, food needs, and family needs. They also provide information on the level and change of a number of these items tabulated for *individuals*, including the children, rather than families, which is equivalent to weighting each family according to its size. The same pattern of dramatic differences persists, particularly in the *changes* from 1967 to 1971 for families with changed composition, and need not be described in detail.

In fact, these differences in families based on changes in their composition have almost no relationship with the changes in income of the individuals within the families. If we take only individuals with some income in both 1967 and 1971 who were 18 or older in 1968, the ten groups account for 6% of the variance in individual incomes among the 5227 individuals, but they account for less than half of one percent of the variance in the *change* of individual income.

Changes in Family Composition and Labor Force Participation

Even where a family has the same head and wife over the entire period, there can be dramatic changes in economic status because of changes in the labor force participation of the head, the wife, or others. Again, these changes are much larger in magnitude than those which might result from the head working harder or getting a better job. Thus they deserve study on their own and must be taken into account if we are to see whether anything else matters.

Table 1.14 shows a new set of categories of change in family structure and in wage earners. They start with some small groups where the head of the family was never in the labor force, where the head was not in the labor force in 1967 but was in 1972, and where there was a working head in 1967 but not in 1972.

The next nine categories encompass all the combinations of change in number of family members and in the presence of other earners. We only count as an increase in other earners the situation where the earnings of wife *and* others went from less than $500 (in 1967) to more than $2000 (in 1971). Similarly, a decrease in other earners means that the family had earnings from wife and/or others of more than $2000 in 1967 and less than $500 in 1971.

The last five categories include most of the cases with a different head -- the first three of them being largely splitoffs, and the last two largely women

TABLE 1.14

Change in Income and in Income/Needs

By Status and Change in Family Composition and Labor Force Participation

(for all 5060 families)

Family and Labor Force Status and Change	1967 Family Money Income	% Change in Family Income 1967-1971	1967 Family Income/ Needs	% Change in Income/ Needs	Average Age of Head	% of Families
Not in labor force 1967-1972, under 65	4146	11	1.13	29	49	3.0
Not in labor force 1967-1972, 65 or older	3611	22	1.63	23	76	8.7
Entered labor force during period	5254	73	1.38	99	46	0.6
Left labor force during period	6558	3	2.59	1	64	9.5
No change in other earners, same number in family	10,004	36	3.17	32	46	26.0
No change in other earners, more family members	8417	55	2.57	33	35	9.2
No change in other earners, fewer in family	11,700	32	2.61	67	49	11.0
More other earners, same number in family	9845	82	2.43	76	43	3.4
More other earners, more family members	6504	118	2.23	69	39	1.2
More other earners, fewer in family	10,360	72	2.16	92	47	1.3
Fewer other earners, same number in family	10,603	-4	3.63	-9	48	0.8
Fewer other earners, more family members	11,843	-3	3.74	-8	32	1.4
Fewer other earners, fewer in family	12,388	-18	3.33	16	45	1.4
Single man, not head in 1968	9671	-40	2.32	2	26	3.6
Married man, not head in 1968	9612	8	2.32	38	27	9.9
Single woman, not head in 1968	10,317	-54	2.32	0	24	2.5
Widowed woman, not head in 1968	8825	-28	2.80	11	59	2.5
Divorced or separated woman, not head in 1968	9621	-21	2.46	0	34	4.0
Total Sample					46	100.0
Percent of variance explained by the 18 groups (eta squared--see glossary)	.14	.21*	.08	.11*	.65	

*Variance of absolute change.

MTR 1066

who became widowed or divorced. An examination of the last column of the table reveals that *only 26% of the families had the same head in the labor force the entire time and experienced no change in family size or in important other earners.* In the target population only 12% were in that stable group (Table 1.15). Change in well-being is obviously affected by many things other than the hours and wages of the head of the family.

The 18 groups account for a substantial fraction of both the level and change in family income and in family income/needs. This is true for the whole sample and even more so for the target population. The reader may want to subtract 20% from the percentage increases to adjust for the increase in prices during the period.

We need not describe the changes in detail, since they are all what one would expect. In brief, they reveal that: more earners increase income, more members increase needs and decrease the income/needs ratio, retirement decreases income, and splitoffs usually have less income than the original family. The average ages of the heads in these groups vary greatly, of course, and the groups account for 65% of the variance in age in the whole sample and 72% in the target population. Families with added members usually have younger heads (who were having children), lower initial incomes, and greater increases in incomes.

In later stages, where we restrict the analysis to units which have the same head in the labor force for all five years, we still can have substantial changes in family economic status because of changes in family size or in other earners, or both.

The implications of these findings are clear. Change in economic status is largely the result of major events such as entry into or exit from the labor force, change in numbers of other earners, or change in family size. These changes dwarf any results from the head's wage increases or marginal changes in his working hours. Indeed, it is possible that these major events are more easily under the control of individuals than their hours or earnings. They can marry, encourage other family members to go to work or to leave home, use birth control, or even double up with relatives more easily than they can secure a wage increase. On the other hand, many of the changes are the expected and almost inevitable life cycle changes: entry into the labor force by the head, appearance of other major earners, increase in family size, decrease in family size, and retirement. How much their timing is subject to personal decision we do not know, although we show in the next chapter that children are more likely to leave home when the initial dwelling has a shortage of rooms relative to a standard of adequacy. It is useful, then, to attempt an overall analysis of the

TABLE 1.15

Change in Income and in Income/Needs

by Status and Change in Family Composition and Labor Force Participation

(for 2608 families in the target population)

Family and Labor Force Status and Change	1967 Family Money Income	% Change in Family Income 1967-1971	1967 Family Income/ Needs	% Change in Income/ Needs	Average Age of Head	% of Target Population Families
Not in labor force 1967-1972, under 65	3470	16	.95	25	48	7.1
Not in labor force 1967-1972, 65 or older	2134	33	.94	37	77	15.7
Entered labor force during period	4199	90	.79	149	43	1.3
Left labor force during period	3576	-2	1.33	-5	62	12.8
No change in other earners, same number in family	4200	45	1.18	42	43	11.7
No change in other earners, more family members	4783	51	1.35	27	37	6.4
No change in other earners, fewer in family	5733	34	1.15	72	48	7.0
More other earners, same number in family	4878	132	1.01	149	44	2.1
More other earners, more family members	3732	192	.99	197	33	1.1
More other earners, fewer in family	5138	156	.92	162	46	0.9
Fewer other earners, same number in family	5849	-11	2.05	-24	53	0.5
Fewer other earners, more family members	9341	-45	2.75	-55	31	0.5
Fewer other earners, fewer in family	7546	-44	1.88	-17	46	1.0
Single man, not head in 1968	8453	50	1.86	-6	25	6.3
Married man, not head in 1968	6463	26	1.45	69	26	12.6
Single woman, not head in 1968	8828	-66	1.94	-32	24	4.7
Widowed woman, not head in 1968	6776	-55	2.08	-36	60	2.7
Divorced or separated woman, not head in 1968	7520	-39	1.79	-21	34	5.6
Total Sample					47	100.0
Percent of variance explained by the 18 groups (eta squared--see glossary)	.27	.24*	.13	.15*	.72	

*Variance of absolute change.

MTR 1066

entire sample that accounts for these differences and changes in family structure while asking simultaneously whether there are also other things which affect the overall changes in family well-being.

VI. Analysis of Trends

Even though in later chapters we examine the trends of components of well-being measures such as hours of work, wage rates, and changes in family composition, it is useful to conduct an analysis of trends in some of the more global measures of well-being. It is possible that different people choose different routes to solve economic problems -- some may double up to increase incomes more than needs, others may marry another earner, take a second job, or encourage a wife to go to work or the children to leave home. Rather than explain which of these alternatives was chosen, it may be easier to see the forces that affect the overall result. The simplest measure of well-being that seem appropriate and closest to traditional data is total family money income relative to a needs standard. It ignores nonmoney income, the differential costs of earning income, and the somewhat erratic nature of housing costs, but it does make some adjustment for changes in family composition.

Our interest is in explaining the trend in income/needs over the five years but it is surprisingly difficult to develop a measure of *trend* that does not have substantial correlation with average *level*. Since level turns out to be much more predictable than trend[1], analysis of any measure which uses only trend or combinations of level and trend will give misleading results. The measure used here comes from fitting a trend line to the income/needs for each of the five years and then dividing the average annual trend in income/needs by the five-year average *level* of income/needs. The resultant measure is the average annual percentage change in income/needs. For our entire sample of families, the average

---

[1] In an endeavor to see whether the same things affected both level and change of income/needs and whether the relationship between the two differed within the population, all possible combinations of three categories of level and three categories of trend were made into a single nine category variable. We then applied a computer programmed search technique (THAID) that sequentially divided the sample into groups that differed maximally in their *distribution over those nine categories* of level and trend. The results are complicated to present and need only be summarized here. The groups that were separated differed mostly as to *level* rather than *change* in income/needs, and the characteristics on which they were distinguished -- education, marital status, economizing, risk avoidance, and age -- were also things we know to be associated with economic status level.

of this measure was 5.9%[1] per year.

The search program AID was employed to determine which among the large collection of possible factors affect the trend in family money income/needs. Background, demographic, environmental, attitudinal, and behavioral variables were
used as predictors of the trend in money income/needs on half of the sample.
Those variables which were searched for explanatory power and their simple association with the dependent variable are given in Table 1.16 both for families
with the same head all five years and for those with different heads.

The attitudes and behavior patterns presumably can change so only the average of the measures for the first two years was used. It is questionable whether
the personality disposition "achievement motivation" is changeable -- according
to the original theory it is not, except where the next generation changes its
child-rearing practices. Among the remaining variables, some are of interest
because of their potential policy implications. Local unemployment, mobility and
family composition may well be influenced by public policy, as may the effects of
race and sex on economic status. Attitudes and behavior patterns may also be
altered by persuasion or education.

The simple associations between the predictors and the trend in well-being
given in Table 1.16 show that the usual background measures such as age, education, family structure, and family composition change have the strongest relationship with trend in family money income/needs. The attitude and behavior indexes have very low association with it. Before inferences about variables
affecting the trend in well-being can be made, three factors need to be taken
into account. First, although certain predictors may have a very small effect on
trend in well-being for the population as a whole, it could still be true that
they matter a great deal for certain important subgroups of the population. The
AID search program is designed to uncover such interactions and the results of it
will be presented first. Perhaps as important as finding these interactions is
finding that there are *no* important subgroups of the population for which policy
related variables matter. Negative findings are in many cases as important as
positive results and AID is well suited to provide evidence that certain variables are unimportant for the entire population and its major subgroups.

A second problem concerning inferences about factors affecting the trend in
family well-being is that any simple association between predictor and dependent

---

[1]Neither the needs standard nor the income levels are adjusted for cost of living
differences over time, so that this rate of change exaggerates the increase in
well-being. Such adjustments aren't crucial for this analysis which attempts
to differentiate among families.

TABLE 1.16

Simple Association (eta-squared) between Trend in Family Money Income/Needs
Relative to Five-Year Average Income and Various Explanatory Variables

Variable	Same Head All Five Years eta^2	Different Head eta^2
Age of head in 1972	.056	.010
Age of youngest child in 1968	.054	.039
Marital status of head in 1972	.003	.068
Sex of head	.003	.058
Race	.009	.025
Education of head	.013	.024
Change in family composition and membership 1968 to 1972	.029	*
City size in 1972	.004	.021
Unemployment rate in county (1968–71 average)	.001	.002
Change in residence	.006	.005
Test score	.011	.014
Achievement motivation	.009	.028
1968–69 average score on:		
Attitudes		
Sense of personal efficacy	.013	*
Trust in others	.004	*
Ambition and aspiration level	.006	*
Behavior		
Real earnings activity	.009	*
Economizing activity	.004	
Connectedness to sources of information and help	.005	*
Horizon	.020	*
Risk avoidance	.008	*

*Not available

MTR 1046

variable may be **the spurious result** of some third **variable.** To control for
this possibility, the variables are entered into a regression which will make adjustments for such spurious correlations. The results of these regressions will
be presented after the AID results.

A third factor important to the analysis of changes in global measures of
well-being is that the particular *measure* of trend in well-being may not be the
best one. Although the intercorrelation among most measures was seen in Section
I to be quite high, it is still possible that a different well-being measure may
produce different results. The family income/needs can be faulted because it
includes transfer income (the level of which may not be entirely within the control of the family) and income of family members other than the head and wife
(which also may be quite independent of decisions by the head and wife). AIDs
and regressions were, therefore, also run on the trend in total taxable income[1]
of head and wife. To see the effects of predictors of this taxable income measure, the sample was restricted to families where head and wife were the same for
all five years of the study and where the head was in the labor force both the
first and fifth years. The results of these analyses are in general quite similar
to those where money income/needs was analyzed; summary **tables and figures of**
the AIDs and regressions are presented in the Appendix to this chapter.

While trend in taxable income of head and wife seems a reasonable alternative measure to family income/needs, it is by no means the only one. Searches
were made on several other measures of well-being -- trend in taxable income of
the *family*, family income/needs trend defined as the percent **change** in the fourth
and fifth year average relative to the average of the first two years, taxable
income of head and wife trend defined by fitting a line through the average of
the first three years and the average of the second two years, and others. Analyses of these alternative measures were almost identical to those reported here.

The results of the AIDs on trend in family money income/needs for families
with different heads and the same heads for all five years are given in Figures
1.8 and 1.9, respectively. They need not be discussed in great detail because
they largely reaffirm the importance of changes in family composition or proxies
for these changes such as age, age of youngest child, and sex of head. What is
more important is that nothing **else much** mattered. Among families with a different head (who are composed mostly of sons and daughters who have split off and
formed their own households), those new heads who remained single are, in general, worse off than those who married. This is especially true of whites. For

---

[1]This includes business and farm income, rent, interest, dividends and earnings.

48

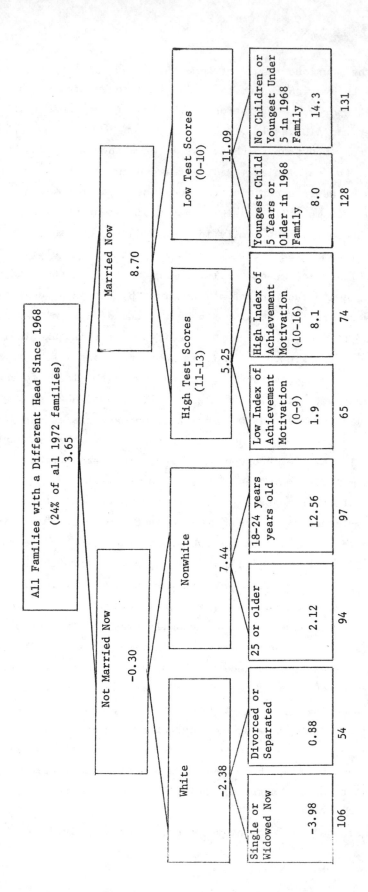

FIGURE 1.8

Average Annual Change in Income/Needs as Percent of Five-Year Average
(for all families with a different head in 1972 from 1968)*

All Families with a Different Head Since 1968
(24% of all 1972 families)
3.65

Not Married Now
−0.30

Married Now
8.70

White
−2.38

Nonwhite
7.44

High Test Scores
(11-13)
5.25

Low Test Scores
(0-10)
11.09

Single or Widowed Now
−3.98
106

Divorced or Separated
0.88
54

25 or older
2.12
94

18-24 years years old
12.56
97

Low Index of Achievement Motivation (0-9)
1.9
65

High Index of Achievement Motivation (10-16)
8.1
74

Youngest Child 5 Years or Older in 1968 Family
8.0
128

No Children or Youngest Under 5 in 1968 Family
14.3
131

Standard Deviation = 18.33

*Half Sample

MTR 1046

FIGURE 1.9

Average Annual Change in Income/Needs as Percent of Five-Year Average
(for families with same head all five years)*

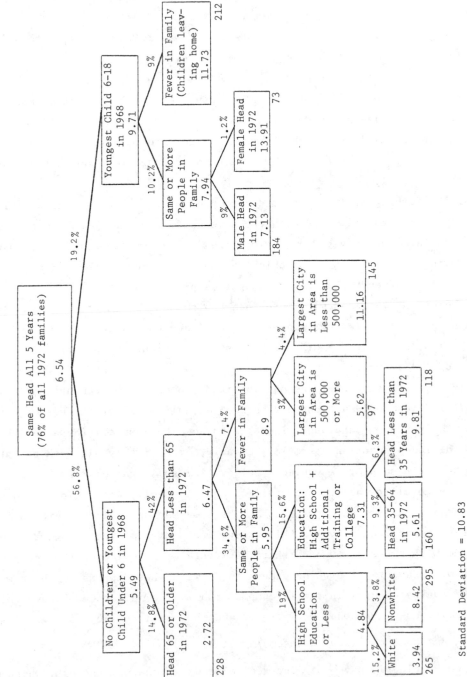

Standard Deviation = 10.83

% = percent of all 1972 families in group.

*Half Sample

MTR 1046

blacks, leaving home and remaining single results in an improvement in income/needs -- especially if he or she is younger than 25.

Among the married new-headed families (shown on the right side of Figure 1.8), those with *high* test scores seem to experience *less* improvement. This is perhaps due to the fact that they left a high-income family. This effect is offset by high achievement motivation for some, however.

For families with the same head for all five years, Figure 1.9 shows again the importance of the explanatory variables representing basic demographic forces that change family size and number of earners: age of youngest child, age of head or change in family size. Within some of the groups, however, education and race are important. Nonwhites have a greater percentage increase but are at a lower absolute level.

Only by forcing splits on second-best predictors could we find anything else of importance for families with the same head. In the group under 65 with either no children or only very young children, those who reported 11 or more behavioral evidences of planning or thinking ahead in 1968 or 1969 had a greater increase in income/needs than those doing less planning (8.68 vs. 5.67). And for a smaller group of 76 cases with more than a high school education and a stable or increasing family size, changing residences more than once during the interviewing period seemed to pay off or be associated with greater improvement in income/needs (11.12 vs. 6.13).

Aside from these borderline possibilities, none of the ten attitudinal or behavioral indexes could account for as much as half of 1% of the variance by splitting the group or subgroup. There is no need to test all these variables again on the independent half sample. Clearly, even if they did seem to matter on the other half sample, we wouldn't believe it, so we can dismiss them.

We can **conclude** then that overall changes in family well-being are dominated by changes in family composition and by some unchangeable background factors like education and race. Even within groups where most of these factors are constrained within narrow bounds, there is little or no evidence that people's attitudes or behavior patterns have much to do with what happens to their well-being. Of course changes in family composition may be influenced by environmental conditions or personal motives, or even by public policy.

Regression Analysis of Trend in Income/Needs

Since we clearly have some intercorrelated explanatory factors, which may be giving spurious exaggerations of the effects of each, and since there is very little evidence of systematic interaction effects, we turn to regression analysis.

Unlike our sequential searching procedure, it uses all the predictors simultaneously.[1] We will look separately at those in the low income or target population both because of their policy importance and because the patterns of causation may be different for them.

We keep as explanatory factors in the analysis any of the attitudinal or behavioral indexes which seemed to be important in any of the previous half-sample search analyses, for any subgroups. Table 1.17 shows the relative importance of the various predictors in two regressions, one for families with the same head for all five years and the other for the subset of those families who were in the target population. The difference between the gross and net effects reflects adjustments for intercorrelations among predictors, which usually reduce the estimated effects. In some cases, however, the pattern of correlations is such that one-way relations *hide* effects which show up in the adjusted coefficients of regression analyses. Notice that for the target population a number of factors have more powerful effects in the regression context than singly.

The test of the explanatory power of any of the predictors depends not only on the beta-squared measure of net effect, but also on whether the effect was monotonic and in the expected direction, which can be determined easily in a regression using categories of the predictors. Our combination of risk-avoiding activities in the first two years proved to be negatively associated with the rate of improvement in income/needs, implying that the disasters avoided did not affect enough people to show up in samples. Our index of planning activities the first two years had an irregular effect, and even what positive effect it did have may have been circular since it contains items about having a better job in mind and knowing something about that job. But those in the target population averaging five or more planning activities in the first two years did better. Our index of achievement motivation (measured in year five) had a serpentine relationship with the rate of increase in income/needs, high at both ends and in the middle.

The one variable -- education -- that helped to explain the *absolute* annual trend in income/needs, but not the trend relative to the five-year individual average, was probably really explaining *level* of income/needs and, hence, "explained" trend through the correlation of trend with level. The very highly

---

[1] Multiple regression with sets of dichotomies representing the subclasses of explanatory characteristics allows non-linear effects but assumes that the effects of the various characteristics like age and education are additive. It produces simultaneous estimates, adjusting the effect of each characteristic for the fact that it is correlated with other characteristics, that is, that people in one age group are not average on education and other things (see Appendix C).

TABLE 1.17

Factors Affecting the Five-Year Trend in Income/Needs
Relative to the Five-Year Average Level*
(for all families and for the target population)

	All		Target Population	
	Gross Effect[a]	Net Effect[b]	Gross Effect[a]	Net Effect[b]
Age of head in 1972	.045	.027	.044	.040
Age of youngest child in 1968	.034	.015	.031	.035
Change in family size or marital status	.031	.019	.019	.011
Education of head	.006	.002	.013	.009
Test score of head (1972)	.009	.008	.015	.011
Achievement motivation (1972)	.003	.002	.012	.016[c]
Horizon index (1968-1969)	.019	.006	.020	.014[c]
Risk avoidance index (1968-1969)	.005	.004[d]	.009	.011[d]
Residential mobility	.008	.002	.008	.003
Connectedness index (1968-1969)	.006	.006	.013	.015
Marital status, 1972	.003	.002	.004	.010
Sex	.000	.003	.000	.004
Race	.005	.005	.006	.006
Unemployment in county (1968-1971)	.003	.003	.003	.005

R^2 (adjusted)	.09	.12
Average annual rate of increase	.071	.069
Number of cases	3568	1647
Mean	7.06	6.86
Standard deviation	11.10	14.60

---

[a] Eta squared (square of correlation ratio): see Glossary

[b] Beta squared: see Glossary

[c] Effect not monotonic

[d] Effect opposite to expected

*For families with the same head all five years.

educated members of the target population, however, did very well (see Figure 1.10).

What, then, *does* affect the rate of improvement? Age does, of course, with the young moving up rapidly and those close to retirement age showing the effects of retirement. Figure 1.11 shows that age affected the target population less than the rest of the sample, particularly around retirement ages, presumably because fewer retired and/or their income dropped less because it was not high anyway. The middle-aged target population, however, shows a peak that may reflect the children leaving home.

The age of the youngest child identifies two types of family situations: families where the children are all in school so that the wife is able to work, or families where the children themselves are old enough to improve the family economic status by their own earnings or by leaving home. Figure 1.12 shows that families with children at these stages of growth experienced much more rapid improvement than families with very young children or with no children at all, and that the differentials were much larger for the target population.

The one behavioral index that did not seem to matter before, except for one analysis of those below 1.65 in 1969, but showed up here with the full sample and the simultaneous regression analysis, was one entitled "connectedness to sources of information and help." It is made up of such diverse connections as PTA, church, television, newspapers, bars or taverns, organizations, and labor unions. It is summed over the first two years only, to avoid the possibility that it was a result rather than a cause of an improving trend. Even more interesting is the fact that connections seemed more important in the target population than for the full sample. Not only was the net effect larger for them, but it was more monotonic and regular (see Figure 1.13). Perhaps it pays for the poor to have friends.

The predictor labeled "change in family membership" is a combination of change in family size for families with the same head and wife and, where the wife was not the same, the result of the head getting married or divorced. (All these data are for families with the same head for all five years.) Figure 1.14 shows that changing family size had more effect on needs than on income. An increase in the family size (mostly children being born) decreased the rate of improvement in income/needs, while a decrease *dramatically* improved it, since the older children leaving home reduced family needs more than a new baby increased them. The effects of marriage or divorce were startlingly absent in the target population, indicating that there the wives were more likely to be working,

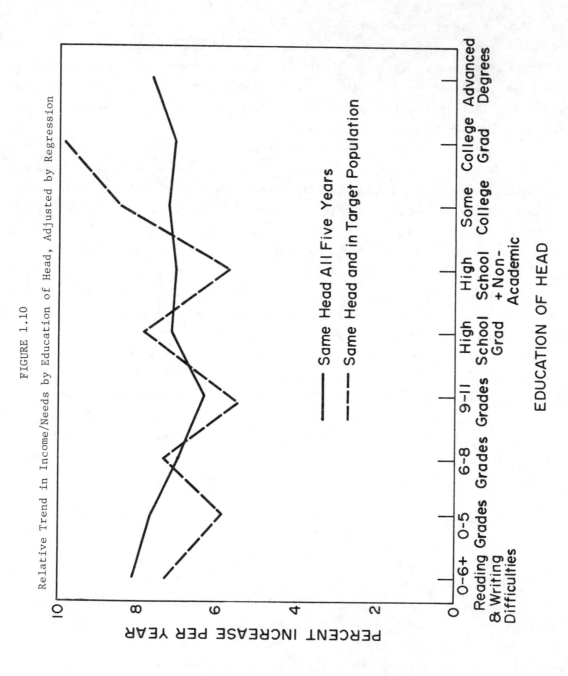

54

FIGURE 1.10

Relative Trend in Income/Needs by Education of Head, Adjusted by Regression

FIGURE 1.11

Relative Trend in Income/Needs by Age of Head, Adjusted by Regression

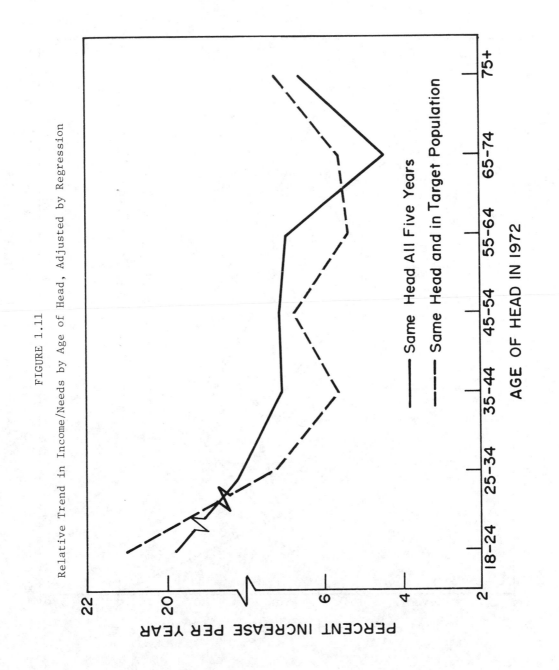

FIGURE 1.12

Relative Trend in Income/Needs, by Age of Youngest Child, Adjusted by Regression

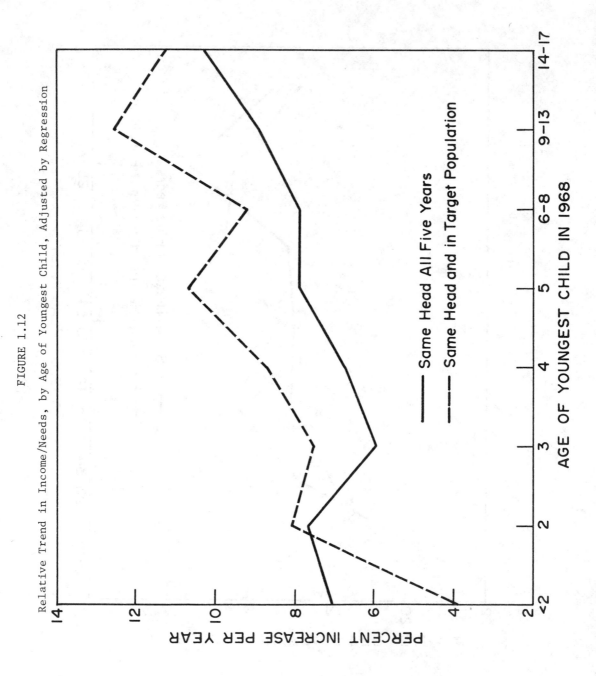

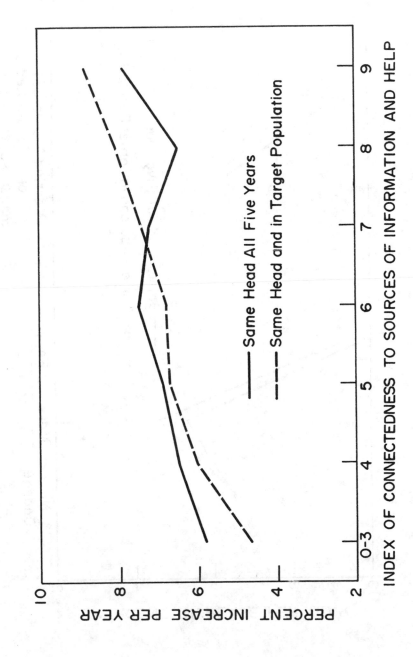

FIGURE 1.13

Relative Trend in Income/Needs, by Index of Connectedness, Adjusted by Regression

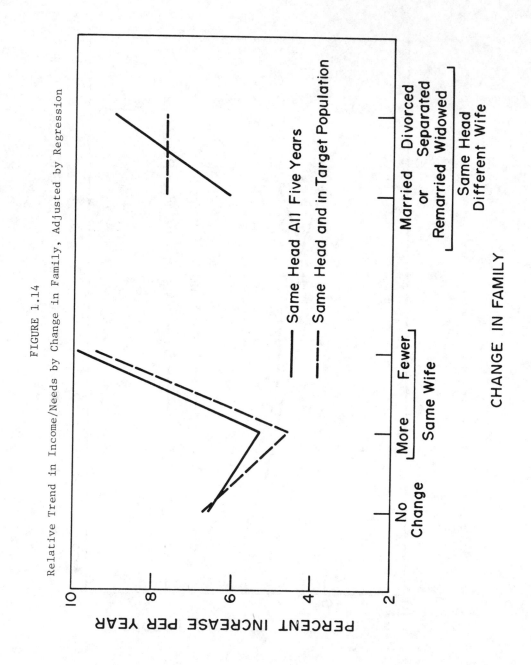

FIGURE 1.14

Relative Trend in Income/Needs by Change in Family, Adjusted by Regression

making incomes that were large relative to the husbands' incomes.[1]

There are a number of other meaningful differences, also borderline statistically but worth reporting because they are at least adjusted for the effects of changing family composition, age, and other factors.

Female headed units improved about 2% per year more rapidly than those headed by males in the target population, and 1½% per year more rapidly in the whole sample. Some of this was due to the improved standards of income maintenance which affected welfare mothers, as we shall see in Chapter 5; some perhaps is a real effect of the women's movement, as we shall see in Chapter 3.

Blacks improved nearly 2% more per year than whites in the target population and 1½% faster in the whole population. The oversampling of lower income and minority families provided enough cases so that the race and sex differences are both statistically significant.[2]

Those who changed residences two or more times during the period did marginally better in both groups, though it is difficult to decide whether this is a cause or an effect of improved economic status.

The one environmental measure we have, unemployment in the county, did appear to have an appreciable depressing effect on the rate of increase in income/ needs among the target population, provided that the average level over the four years 1968-71 was 6% or greater; differences below 6% unemployed did not seem to matter.

Where does this leave us? We eliminated some explanatory variables because a searching analysis of a half sample could not account for any appreciable amount of the variance over that half sample or over any of the major subgroups within it. Even those which seemed to have some effect proved to have little effect when tested in a simultaneous multivariate multiple regression model and an examination of the detailed patterns frequently showed relationships that were not in the direction predicted or that were curvilinear.

The factors that did have an effect were for the most part proxies for the usual changes over the family life cycle: age, age of youngest child, and change in family membership. These presumably affected the family composition and

---

[1] These findings are based on 110 and 118 cases in the full sample and 50 and 60 cases in the target population, with standard deviations about twice the means so they are of borderline statistical significance even considering that the differences between the target population and the full sample (including the target population) are smaller than the differences between the two separate populations.

[2] We assume that the sample design effects are reduced by the multivariate nature of these regression coefficients. See Appendix B.

therefore the needs estimate. They also affected the wife's work status. Factors which might affect the trend in earnings of the head -- education, test score, achievement motivation, planning -- all had small effects. The effects seemed larger for the low income or target population, but that may have been partly the result of the smaller sample size -- the adjusted multiple R-squared only rose from .09 to .12.

We should not expect to do well in explaining such a composite measure. It is for this reason that much of the subsequent analysis focuses on things which affect changes in the components: fertility, labor force participation of the wife, work and earnings of the head, and transfer incomes. We also focus on sub-populations where the head or the wife stayed the same.

We controlled for the effects of changing family composition by regression even though those changes may be subject to discretion and be affected by individual motivation or public policy. We did not control for the effects of changing labor force participation of the head or of others; these changes have large effects and may be so dominated by basic demographic forces such as age, the arrival or departure of children, marriage, and divorce, that they hide other forces more subject to change by public policy. Hence, we moved to an expanded regression analysis that included the more elaborate, 18-category classification of change in family composition and labor force participation which was used earlier in the descriptive tables showing the effects of those changes.

The results were dramatic; nothing much mattered in explaining the trend in family income/needs except the changes in family structure and in labor force participation, even when these were represented only crudely by a set of categorical predictors (see Table 1.18). Race remained powerful for the target population with the same head for all five years, and test score and our index of achievement motivation had some effect, but the index of connectedness had no effect at all. The unimportance of the other factors was also evident from the very small variations in the effects of the changes in family and labor force participation when they were adjusted by regression (see Table 1.19).

The basic results were not changed when we reran the regression for those with the same head for all five years reducing the number of classifications of family change, and reducing them still further for families with the same head and a head who was in the labor force in 1967 and in 1972.

VII. Who Climbs Out?

If most of the explanatory variables tend to explain levels of well-being better than they explain change, we must eschew attempts to explain level and

TABLE 1.18

Importance of Background, Environment, Attitudes and Behavior,
and Family Changes in Accounting for Trend in Family Money Income/Needs

	Full Half Sample		Target Population	
	Gross Effect[a]	Net Effect[b]	Gross Effect[a]	Net Effect[b]
Change in family composition or earners	.12	.13	.15	.14
Education	.00	.00	.02	.01
Age	.02	.00	.01	.02
Sex-Marital status	.01	.01	.04	.03
Test score	.00	.01	.01	.00
Achievement motivation	.01	.01	.02	.02
Real earning acts	.01	.01	.03	.02
Risk avoidance	.02	.01	.04	.01
Connectedness	.00	.00	.01	.00
Efficacy	.01	.01	.02	.01
Horizon index	.01	.01	.02	.01
Race	.01	.01	.03	.02
Unemployment in the county (average of 1968-1971)	.00	.00	.01	.00
R^2 (adjusted)	.17		.27	
Number of cases	2527		1357	
Mean	6.09		5.18	
Standard deviation	13.40		18.06	

[a]Percent of variance explained by that predictor alone = eta squared = correlation ratio squared (see Glossary)

[b]Beta squared, analogous to beta weight in numerical regression (see Glossary)

MTR 1068A

TABLE 1.19

Relative Trend in Income/Needs by Change in Family Composition
and in Labor Force Participation - Adjusted by Regression

	All		Target Population	
	Unadjusted Average	Adjusted Average*	Unadjusted Average	Adjusted Average*
Same head all five years:				
Head <65 and not in labor force	5.2	1.8	4.6	1.5
Head >65 and not in labor force	18.4	15.2	20.2	18.0
Head entered labor force	-0.4	-0.2	-1.6	-2.9
Head left labor force	5.2	4.6	6.9	3.8
Head in labor force and:				
No change in number of earners, no change in family members	6.7	7.3	7.2	8.6
No change in number of earners, more family members	6.4	7.1	6.1	8.7
No change in number of earners, fewer family members	11.8	12.3	12.5	12.5
Increase in number of earners, no change in family members	14.7	15.6	21.6	23.4
Increase in number of earners, more family members	12.5	12.2	19.7	18.9
Increase in number of earners, fewer family members	17.7	17.8	26.9	26.7
Decrease in number of earners, no change in family members	-3.5	-2.3	-8.7	-7.1
Decrease in number of earners, more family members	-4.5	-4.3	-16.7	-13.2
Decrease in number of earners, fewer family members	2.3	1.6	-4.5	-4.8
Different head:				
Single man	3.4	1.4	3.9	4.4
Married man	9.2	8.3	11.2	10.8
Single woman	-0.7	-1.2	-5.6	-2.7
Widow	-2.8	-1.5	-6.6	-1.6
Divorcee	-0.0	-0.5	-1.7	1.3
	$eta^2 = .12$	$beta^2 = .13$	$eta^2 = .15$	$beta^2 = .14$

*
Adjusted by multiple regression taking account of all the other variables
in Table 1.18.

change jointly and find some way to deal with change reasonably unpolluted by level. One traditional way is to examine who "crosses the line," however defined, between being poor and not being poor. Here we must deal with the inflation in costs of living. The "low cost weekly food needs" standards given in Family Economics Review rose by 20% between 1967 and 1971, or 5% per year, with only minor differences for various age-sex groups. If we want to look at change by comparing the average income/needs ratio for the first two years with the average for the last two years to reduce random fluctuations, then the span of time for adjusting for inflation is really three years rather than four, so the inflation was 15%. Hence, we can define three groups as follows:

Description of Group	Average income/needs in 1967 and 1968	Average income/needs in 1970 and 1971
Climbed out	Less than 2.00	2.30 or more
Fell into poverty (if only through inflation)	2.00 or more	Less than 2.30
Stayed poor or stayed non-poor	Less than 2.00 2.00 or more	Less than 2.30 2.30 or more

Table 1.20 shows the proportions of all 1972 families whose experience was in each of these three categories; they were 11%, 9%, and 80%, respectively. It also shows that changed family status matters. A major way to climb out of poverty is to get married, and a major way to fall into it is to get divorced, or to leave the parental home (split off).

It is useful to look at the fate of only those who were initially below 2.00. Thirty-four percent of the group eligible to climb out actually did so. Figure 1.15 shows that where the head remained the same, the main causes of financial improvement were education and ability. Being young also helped. Within each of the four final groups in Figure 1.15 the younger heads were more likely to rise above the poverty line.

Looking within income strata and studying the crossing of arbitrary lines is never completely satisfactory. Families whose status changed very little but enough to cross the line and those undergoing substantial change but not quite enough to cross it will be, in some sense, misclassified. We tried a few experiments which changed our criterion of "climbing out of poverty." We examined the trend in income/needs for those with an initial (1967) income/needs below 1.50 and those with a level in the middle year (1969) below 1.65. The analysis showed that the trend was explained by family composition change, education, test scores, planning acts or connectedness to sources of information. Many of these effects seemed to be working on *level* of income/needs through its correlation with trend.

TABLE 1.20

Proportion Who Crossed a Line (at twice the needs standard), by Change in Family Composition**
(all families as of 1972)[a]

Change in Family Composition	Climbed Out Income/Needs <2.00 in 1967-68 and >2.29 in 1970-71	Stayed (Above or Below) Rest	Fell In Income/Needs >1.99 in 1967-68 and <2.29 in 1970-71	Total	Number of Cases	Percentage of Families
Same Head and Wife						
No change	10	85	6	101	868	42
More or different family members	11	81	8	100	727	16
Fewer other family members	10	86	3	99	364	14
Same Head						
Head married (or remarried)	23	69	9	101	57	2
Widowed, divorced men	16	67	17	100	61	3
Different Head						
Previous wife is now head (widowed, divorced)	11	74	15	100	136	6
*Single man from sample	17	60	23	100	78	3
*Single woman from sample	5	72	23	100	131	4
*Married man from sample	20	71	8	99	243	6
Head from outside sample	16	66	18	100	162	4
All	11	80	9	100	2527	100%

*Mostly splitoffs.
**Using averages of 1967-1968 for start, and 1970-1971 for end and adjusting the standard up 5% per year for inflation.
[a]Half Sample
MTR1049B

FIGURE 1.15

Proportions of Initially Poor or Near-Poor Families Who Rose above the Poverty Line[*]
(for families with the same head all five years)[a]

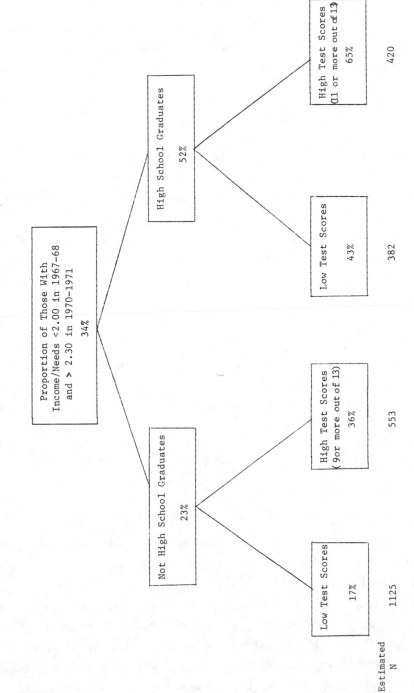

| Estimated N | 1125 | 553 | 382 | 420 |

*Using averages of 1967-1968 for start, and 1970-1971 for end and adjusting the standard up 5% per year for inflation

[a]Half Sample

MTR1049A

The method we used earlier was to divide the annual rate of increase in income/needs for each family by the family's average income/needs *level*. This assumes that there is a linear relationship between level and trend, with a line that goes through the origin. We examined the relation of trend to level for the families with the same head who was in the labor force in 1967 and still in it in 1972. The overall relationship was:

$$\begin{array}{l} \text{Annual increase in} \\ \quad \text{income/needs} \quad = .055 + .058 \text{ (five year average of income/needs)} \\ \quad (\text{Av.} = .254) \qquad\qquad\qquad (\text{Av.} = 3.42) \end{array}$$

$$R^2 = .09$$

An examination of subgroups according to the average level shows relatively similar regression coefficients between slope and level within each, and a relation between group average slope and group average level which is also similar, indicating no serious non-linearity.

The small positive intercept (constant term) indicates that the ratio of trend to level would be higher at the lowest levels, but there may indeed be a relatively greater improvement there. As we shall see later, there is a real tendency for the trend to be steeper at the very highest levels too, even relative to average level.

So dividing trend by average level seems justified, and since the variances are greater at the higher levels, this also reduces the heterogeneity of variances, and improves the statistical precision.

A similar analysis of the relationship for head's earnings gave a similar result, with the overall regression being:

$$\begin{array}{l} \text{Annual increase in} \\ \quad \text{head's earnings} \quad = \$107 + .056 \text{ (five year average of head's earnings)} \\ \quad (\text{Av.} = \$617) \qquad\qquad\qquad (\text{Av.} = \$9195) \end{array}$$

VIII. Components of the Variability of Well-Being

We have looked at the inter-family correlations among various measures of well-being, but it is also useful to look at the inter-family variability of the components of well-being and at the variability of changes over time in those components. Any measure which is made up of a sum, product, or ratio of other measures can be thought of as "determined" or "explained" by those components and their covariances. In the simple case of the additive components of money income (head's earnings, wife's earnings, capital income, others' earnings, transfer income), if the sizes of the components were independent of one another the components would fully "explain" the total. That is, if we used multiple correlation or regression, each of the regression coefficients would be 1.00, the

squared beta coefficients would add to 1.00 and the multiple correlation coefficient would be 1.00.[1]

There are, of course, some intercorrelations, particularly negative ones,
between other income sources and transfer incomes which would make them add to
more than 1.00. But the betas are still a useful measure, and they still depend
largely on the standard deviation of each component, which in turn can usefully
be thought of as a combination of its absolute size, and its relative variability
(relative to its mean). A component which is small in absolute size can account
for a lot of the variance if it has high variability relative to its size.
Hence, we give both the betas and the means and standard deviations of the components.

The extent to which inter-family differences in each of the five components
of family money income account for the differences among families in its total is
shown in Table 1.21 both for the whole sample and for the target population.
Head's labor income accounts for two-thirds of the differences between families,
for both populations. For the target population, head's earnings account for
more of the variability of income than of the level of income because of their
larger *relative* variability.

Perhaps the most surprising finding is that variations in earnings of family members other than the head or wife account for as much of the variation as
differences in the wives' incomes, and in the target population they account for
a great deal more of the variation than differences in wives' earnings. In the
target population, the average income of others is greater than that of wives
(many of these are female headed families with no wife), and *also* has a larger
relative variance. In the whole sample, wives account for more income on the
average than do other earners, but the relative variability of others' income is
so much greater that the standard deviations and the betas are about equal.

Of course, transfer incomes account for more of the differences among the
target population families, because they are a much larger fraction of their
total incomes.

When we turn to *change* in family money income from 1967 to 1971 we restrict
ourselves to families with the same head throughout all five years. Changes in

---

[1]Since the beta weights or normalized regression coefficients are merely the regression coefficients times the standard deviation of that predictor divided by
the standard deviation of the dependent variable, and since the regression coefficients are all 1.00, the betas vary only as the standard deviations of the
component "predictors" vary. With uncorrelated predictors, the squared betas
are also equal to the coefficient of partial determination, the relative importance of each component in "explaining" the total. See Glossary and Appendix C.

TABLE 1.21

Components of Total Family Money and Their Contribution
to Its Interfamily Variation

| Full Sample (N = 5060) | | |
Beta Squared*	Average (1971)	Standard Deviation
Head's labor income	.69	$7089	$7012
Wife's labor income	.08	1188	2391
Taxable income of others	.08	755	2380
Capital income	.09	783	2494
Transfer income	.05	1076	1902
	.99	$10,894	$8398

| Target Population (N = 2608) | | |
Beta Squared*	Average (1971)	Standard Deviation
Head's labor income	.62	$2814	$3418
Wife's labor income	.09	446	1323
Taxable income of others	.13	457	1579
Capital income	.07	278	1177
Transfer income	.12	1330	1543
	1.03	$5332	$4344

*
Beta is the "normalized" regression coefficient, i.e. $\dfrac{b_x \sigma_x}{\sigma_y}$

Positive and negative intercorrelations among the components presumably
have offset each other so that the betas squared add nearly to 1.00.

MTR 1071C

the head's earnings are the predominant explanation for changes in family income (see Table 1.22). In the target population, change in the head's income accounts for half the inter-family differences in family income change, even though the average change in head's income is only a fourth of the average change in family income. This is because, in this low-income population, there are great differences from family to family in the direction and amount the head's income changes.

Changes in the earnings of others account for more inter-family differences in income changes than changes in wife's earnings. Most wives tend to stay either in the labor force or out of it and to stay in the family. Other earners are commonly older children of the head, or extra adults, and are not apt to be permanent family members; many entered or left the labor force during the five years.

When we examine the components of head's earnings, namely, hourly earnings and hours of work per year, we must use logs to make them additive, but the beta-squareds will still show the relative importance of the two components. Table 1.23 shows that variations in hours are only *slightly* more important than variations in wage rates in accounting for variations in earnings for the full sample, but they are *far more* important in the target population. Unemployment is more common in the low income population and many people have extra jobs to make up for low hourly earnings.

Our most commonly used measure of well-being in this study is total family money income divided by an estimate of the family's needs. This can be thought of as the sum of two components: the log of income minus the log of needs. Table 1.24 shows that variations in *income* among families rather than variations in need (family size) account for most of the differences in income/needs.[1]

The overall implication of these analyses is that differences in the head's hours have the largest effect on differences in earnings, particularly among low income families, and that differences in the head's earnings in turn have the largest effect of any of the components in accounting for inter-family differences in family money income. Variations in family money income are, in turn, the dominant explanation of the differences among families in well-being (income/

---

[1] In this case not only do the beta-squareds add up to more than 1.00, but the one for income is itself more than 1.00. This means that if you increased income by one standard deviation, holding needs constant, the income/needs ratio would increase by more than one of its standard deviations. This is the classical "suppressor" effect that occurs when two correlated predictors have effects of the opposite sign (as in this case) or when two negatively correlated predictors have effects of the same sign.

TABLE 1.22

Components of Change in Total Family Money Income (1968 to 1971)
and Their Contribution to Interfamily Variation in Income-Change

| | All Families with Same Head All Five Years (N=3568) | | |
	Beta Squared	Average Change	Standard Deviation of Changes
Change in head's labor income	.64	$1656	$4557
Change in wife's labor income	.11	316	1933
Change in others' taxable income	.14	346	2153
Change in capital income	.17	301	2381
Change in transfer income	.08	479	1584
Totals	1.14	$3101	$5705

| | All Families with Same Head All Five Years and in Target Population (N=1647) | | |
	Beta Squared	Average Change	Standard Deviation of Changes
Change in head's labor income	.52	$ 366	$2727
Change in wife's labor income	.10	125	1180
Change in others' taxable income	.21	299	1722
Change in capital income	.10	134	1238
Change in transfer income	.11	528	1294
Totals	1.04	$1462	$3785

TABLE 1.23

Components of Head's Earnings and Their Contributions
to Variation among Heads

All Working Heads of Households	Beta Squared	Average of Logs	Standard Deviation (of Logs)
Hours	.45	3.22	0.32
Wage Rate	.41	0.54	0.30

Working Heads in Target Population	Beta Squared	Average of Logs	Standard Deviation (of Logs)
Hours	.67	3.10	0.44
Wage Rate	.29	0.31	0.29

MTR 1071D, 1071E

TABLE 1.24

Components of Income/Needs and Their Contribution
to Variation among Families, 1971

All Families (N = 5060)	Beta Squared	Average of Logs	Standard Deviation (of Logs)
Income	1.22	3.9098	.3700
Needs	.24	3.4929	.1649
Income/needs		.42	.3186

Target Population Only (N=2608)	Beta Squared	Average of Logs	Standard Deviation (of Logs)
Income	1.22	3.5988	.3720
Needs	.37	3.4775	.1897
Income/needs		.1319	.2895

MTR 1071C

needs).

By leaving out of our calculations the families with changed heads, we have underestimated the important role that changes in needs and in other earners play in families' well-being.

Some compromise will always be necessary between a global measure which incorporates many dimensions of well-being with a variety of components of income, and one with more limited focus that is easier to explain and understand. Total family money income/needs seems to be a good compromise, but we need to look at its components in a broader way.

There is another way to look at the overall pattern of changes during this period. We can decompose the trend in family income/needs relative to the five-year average level to see how much of the change is the result of each of the following factors: changes in needs, a remaining correlation with level (high levels allow larger relative changes), a change in the head of the unit (mostly splitoffs), and a change in the number of adults (and hence the number of potential earners).

Changes in the family account for substantial fractions of the variance, and little else besides age adds much (see Table 1.25). Indeed, the net effects are substantially *larger* than the gross effects.

Since we include families with changed heads, we measured at the *end* of the period not only achievement motivation and test scores, but also the indexes of risk avoidance, planning acts, and connectedness. Only risk avoidance seems to matter, and this time in the positive direction. This means, perhaps, that the successful can afford to do things to avoid risk, since our other analysis indicated a negative relation between initial risk avoidance and the improvement in economic status.

We can use this same decomposition with *individuals* rather than families, selecting those who are 18 or older in 1972 and in the target population. In place of the simple change in number of adults, and change in head, we created a nine-category explanatory characteristic:

Change in Family:

Same head 1968 to 1972, and this individual is:
    Head
    Wife
    Someone else (mostly a son or daughter)

Different head, and this individual is:

    A child of the original head, now:

        A married head of a unit
        A single head of a unit
        A wife
        Someone else

TABLE 1.25

Trend in Income/Needs Relative to Five Year Average –
Decomposition by Regression
(for all families)

	Gross Effect[a]	Net Effect[b]
Change in needs	.008	.090
Change in head	.011	.023
Change in adults	.025	.063
Level of income/needs	.001	.004
Age	.016	.019
Race	.009	.008
Education	.003	.002
All following were measures in 1972:		
Test score	.003	.003
Achievement-motivation[c]	.004	.003
Connectedness	.004	.004
Planning acts	.010	.003
Risk avoidance	.004	.011

$N = 5060$

$R^2 = .11$

$\bar{y} = 6.28$

---

[a] Eta squared or correlation ratio squared (see Glossary).

[b] Beta squared (see Glossary).

[c] Removing two "future-orientation" items from the index.

MTR 1076 A,B

Not a child of the original head (wife, grandchild, brother, cousin) and now:

> Head of a unit
> Not head of a unit

Table 1.26 shows that for the 4346 individuals involved, the change in the individual's own income accounts for nearly a fourth of the differences in trend of income/needs, but the "change in family" accounts for a great deal too. The actual pattern of annual change in income/needs is shown in Table 1.27 unadjusted and adjusted by regression.

Clearly, there are substantial minorities of individuals with dramatically different changes in economic well-being associated with changes in their family and living arrangements.

SUMMARY

As an introduction to the more detailed analysis of components of change in economic well-being and of subpopulations sufficiently homogeneous to study effectively, we have first examined the major components of economic well-being and the major subpopulations of family composition and its changes (and labor force participation). We find great heterogeneity and a great deal of change that has little to do with the gradual increase in earnings that is so often the focus of theoretical analysis.

As an introduction to our search for possible individual attitudes or behavior patterns or environmental influences that may affect changes in family economic status, we looked for overall effects after adjusting for some of the greatest differences in family composition or labor force participation. The result is clear: nothing individuals believe or do has an effect that persists consistently through the different statistical procedures and measures. While policy might produce changes in attitudes or behaviors that would affect people's economic fate, there are apparently not enough natural examples of such effects for us to support such programs. The full analysis must also ask whether any of these attitudes, behavior patterns, or environmental factors matter for subgroups and for components of economic change, such as changes in wage rates, hours of work or labor force participation.

The following summarizes our findings:

1. A number of measures of economic well-being were compared with one another, and although the intercorrelations are relatively high, they are not so

TABLE 1.26

Decomposition of Trend in Income/Needs by Regression
(for individuals 18 or over and in target population)

	Gross Effect	Net Effect
Change in individual income	.193	.233
Change in needs	.008	.032
Level	.026	.012
Change in family	.084	.152
Education	.014	.005
Motivation-achievement	.011	.008
Test score	.009	.006

N = 4346 (11 extreme cases omitted)

R^2 (adjusted) = .345

Standard deviation = 3.27

Mean = 1.03

MTR 1075

TABLE 1.27

Trend in Income/Needs by Change in Family
(for individuals 18 or older and in target population)

Change in Family	Annual Change in Income/Needs		% of Sub-Population
	unadjusted	adjusted	
Same Head, individual is:			
Head	.099	1.333	38.7
Wife	.099	1.489	18.9
Other	.151	1.568	13.1
Different Head, was child, now:			
Married head	.126	-1.101	4.3
Single head	-.114	-2.553	6.4
Wife	.255	1.547	6.0
Other	.250	2.469	1.4
Not a Former Child, now:			
Head	-.059	-.513	7.2
Not head	.331	3.646	4.1
			100.1

large as to make more sophisticated measures unnecessary. It seems essential to
relate income to some measure of need that takes account of family composition.
If we use the strength of the relationship to food consumption relative to needs
as a criterion, then the more complex measure of economic status is better than
income alone.

2. Transition tables showing the distribution of well-being in 1971 for
families at different levels in 1967 indicate that improvement dominates, although there is substantial change in both directions. Improvement continues to
dominate even when we restrict the analysis to units with the same head for all
five years and adjust the needs standard for inflation to eliminate fictitious
improvements.

3. Background and demographic factors like education, sex, and race are
most important in explaining a family's chances of falling into the lowest quintile of the income/needs distribution for any one of the five years of the study
(i.e., of being in the target population).

4. For those in that target population, the chance of being *persistently*
poor is greater for blacks and is affected somewhat differently by some explanatory factors. It takes much more education to improve a black's chance of
avoiding poverty than a white's. While county unemployment did not matter much,
the job market as reflected by size of the largest city and distance to its center matters more for blacks than for whites.

5. Changes in family composition and in the existence of secondary earners
not only have dramatic effects on changes in family well-being, but also affect a
substantial part of the population over a four year span. The changes affect
both aspects of our measure of well-being (income) and needs. Since families
with changes in membership are usually larger, there is a larger percentage of
individuals than of families affected by these changes.

6. Since level and change in status are difficult to disentangle, nine
combinations of level and change were developed and a programmed search was conducted for groups with different distributions over those nine categories. The
results are dominated by differences in *level*. It is much easier to find things
that distinguish groups by level than by change in status.

7. A searching multivariate analysis of the five-year trend in income/
needs relative to the five-year average finds that changes in family composition
dominate, even when the analysis is restricted to units with the same head for
all five years. Among units with different heads (mostly young people who left
home to set up their own households) high achievement motivation or *low* test

scores are associated with greater improvement in status, the latter presumably reflecting the low level of the family left behind. For families with the same head, other family changes (e.g., children born or leaving home) and education make a difference. There is some evidence that blacks are catching up, and that sample members moving during the period or planning ahead in the first two years experience greater improvement.

Even before checking these results by regression on the full sample, we tried different ways of measuring the trend in family money income/needs which were dominated less by the first and last years than the least-squares trend line. We also did similar overall search analyses of the trend in the taxable income of head and wife and in the taxable income of the whole family. And finally we took apart some of the attitudinal indexes into component subsets of individual questions. In general, the dominant importance of background and of changes in family composition and labor force participation remain. The few cases where some behavior or attitude of the respondents seemed to matter did not persist.

8. A simultaneous multiple regression analysis was then used in place of the sequential searching strategy on the full sample to test whether the previous results were really dependable. The analysis was done for the full sample and separately for the target population. Again the changes in family composition and labor force participation and the demographic background facts dominated the explanation of change in economic status. *If people's own attitudes or behavior or environment affect their economic situations, they must do it through changes in family composition or labor force participation.* We do not place too much faith in the target population findings that being connected to sources of information and help seem to affect the trend in income/needs, or that economizing seems to affect the trend of taxable income of head and wife, since the apparent effects did not generalize to the other dependent variables.

9. Among those who started at a low level of income/needs, some improve enough to more than make up for inflation. Changes in family composition are important here too, as is formal education and test score.

10. Finally, we decomposed the changes in income/needs into components using regression, once for families and again for all individuals 18 years or older and in the target population. The overall result of all this is that *we find that changes in family composition and in labor force participation so dominate changes in family well-being that nothing else seems to matter very much.* It is important to notice that we have devoted much energy to measuring attitudes, behavior patterns, a personality dimension (achievement motivation),

and environmental conditions like unemployment in the county. None of these measures account for much. It is time, then, to look at changes in family composition and labor force participation, and then examine earning rates, to see whether any policy-relevant variables affect them.

TABLE A1.1

Head's Labor Income in 1971 by Head's Labor Income in 1967

(for families with same head all five years)

1971	1967							All 1967 Income Group
	0	$1-1999	$2000-4999	$5000-7499	$7500-9999	$10,000-14,999	$15,000 or More	
0	83	25	7	6	4	3	2	18
$1-1999	12	41	10	3	2	1	1	9
$2000-4999	3	20	37	9	4	1	0	12
$5000-7499	1	7	28	21	9	4	1	13
$7500-9999	0	6	10	35	18	6	5	14
$10,000-14,999	1	2	7	23	55	38	4	21
$15,000 or more	0	0	2	3	8	47	88	13
	100%	101%	101%	100%	100%	100%	101%	100%
Number of Cases	561	546	877	717	406	352	108	3567
All 1971 Income Group	14%	11%	18%	22%	15%	15%	5%	100%

Rank Correlation (Kendall's TauB) = .70

Cramer's V = .49

MTR 1053

TABLE A1.2

Wife's Labor Income in 1971 by Wife's Labor Income in 1967
(for families with same head all five years)

	1967							All 1967 Income Group
1971	0	$ 1–1999	$2000–4999	$5000–7499	$7500–9999	$10,000–14,999	$15,000 or More	
0	84	36	27	21	17	0	100	66
$1–1999	9	32	11	9	0	0	0	13
$2000–4999	4	23	36	13	6	0	0	11
$5000–7499	2	7	20	24	4	40	0	6
$7500–9999	1	2	6	27	31	0	0	3
$10,000–14,999	0	0	1	7	42	61	0	1
$15,000 or more	0	0	0	0	0	0	0	0
	100%	100%	101%	101%	100%	101%	100%	100%
Number of Cases	2480	572	367	120	24	3	1	3567
All 1971 Income Groups	67%	14%	13%	5%	1%	0	0	100%

Rank Correlation (Kendall's TauB) = .54

Cramer's V = .35

MTR 1053

TABLE A1.3

Total Family Money Income in 1971 by Total Family Money Income in 1967
(for families with same head all five years)

1971	1967							All 1967 Income Group
	0–$1999	$2000–3999	$4000–4999	$5000–7499	$7500–9999	$10,000–14,999	$15,000 or More	
0–$1999	41	6	2	1	1	0	0	5
$2000–3999	42	40	19	7	2	1	0	12
$4000–4999	6	18	14	5	3	0	0	6
$5000–7499	5	19	31	21	11	3	2	12
$7500–9999	2	9	19	32	16	8	2	13
$10,000–14,999	3	6	10	26	50	33	14	24
$15,000 or More	1	3	5	8	18	56	81	28
	100%	101%	100%	100%	101%	101%	99%	100%
Number of Cases	440	732	303	754	495	558	285	3567
All 1971 Income Groups	8%	14%	6%	19%	17%	22%	13%	99%

Rank Correlation (Kendall's TauB) = .67

Cramer's V = .42

MTR 1053

TABLE A1.4

Head's Average Hourly Earnings in 1971
by Head's Average Hourly Earnings in 1967
(for families with the same head all five years)

| 1971 | 1967 | | | | | | All 1967 Income Groups |
	No Wage Income	$.01-1.99	$2.00-2.99	$3.00-3.99	$4.00-5.99	$6.00 or More	
No Wage Income	78	11	6	7	4	6	18
$ .01-1.99	12	39	7	3	1	2	13
$2.00-2.99	5	26	20	6	4	3	12
$3.00-3.99	1	13	35	16	6	2	14
$4.00-5.99	2	8	25	53	35	7	23
$6.00 or More	2	3	6	15	50	80	19
	100%	100%	99%	100%	100%	100%	99%
Number of Cases	647	1090	693	537	437	163	3567
All 1971 Income Group	16%	21%	19%	19%	18%	7%	100%

Rank Correlation (Kendall's TauB) = .64

Cramer's V = .48

MTR 1053

TABLE A1.5

Wife's Average Hourly Earnings in 1971
by Wife's Average Hourly Earnings in 1967

(for families with the same head all five years)

| 1971 | 1967 | | | | | | All 1967 Income Groups |
	No Wage Income	$.01- 1.99	$2.00- 2.99	$3.00- 3.99	$4.00- 5.99	$6.00 or More	
No Wage Income	84	31	26	20	21	47	66
$ .01-1.99	7	30	9	9	6	10	11
$2.00-2.99	4	26	24	7	9	0	10
$3.00-3.99	2	10	24	12	3	5	6
$4.00-5.99	2	2	14	42	37	18	5
$6.00 or More	1	1	3	9	24	20	2
	100%	100%	100%	99%	100%	100%	100%
Number of Cases	2536	623	259	72	54	23	3567
All 1971 Income Group	68%	16%	10%	3%	2%	1%	100%

Rank Correlation (Kendall's TauB) = .52

Cramer's V = .34

MTR 1053

TABLE A1.6

Money Income/Needs 1971 By 1967*

(for families with the same head all five years
and not retired or disabled)

1971	1967							All
	0-.59	.60-.99	1.00-1.49	1.50-1.99	2.00-2.99	3.00-4.49	4.50-	
0-.59	24	4	1	0	1	0	0	2
.60-.99	31	20	6	2	1	0	0	4
1.00-1.49	19	32	22	6	3	1	0	8
1.50-1.99	11	18	25	13	5	3	1	9
2.00-2.99	8	13	30	45	28	7	3	21
3.00-4.49	7	9	11	25	45	35	13	27
4.50-	1	4	5	8	18	54	83	29
	101%	100%	100%	99%	101%	100%	100%	100%
Number of Cases	317	445	541	461	531	434	219	2948
All 1971 Groups	4	8	13	15	25	23	13	101

Rank Correlation (Kendall's TauB) = .61

Cramer's V = .39

*Needs not adjusted for inflation; ratio should go up 21% just to offset
rising costs.

MTR 1055, 7.01

TABLE A1.7

Money Income/Needs 1971 By 1967*

(for all families)

1971	1967 0-.59	.60-.99	1.00-1.49	1.50-1.99	2.00-2.99	3.00-4.49	4.50-	All
0-.59	26	6	3	1	1	1	0	3
.60-.99	30	23	8	4	3	1	1	7
1.00-1.49	20	29	22	11	6	2	2	11
1.50-1.99	9	15	25	14	9	5	2	11
2.00-2.99	9	15	25	42	27	12	7	21
3.00-4.49	5	9	12	21	38	36	19	24
4.50-	2	3	5	8	16	43	69	23
	101%	100%	100%	101%	100%	100%	100%	100%
Number of Cases	670	897	899	754	846	657	337	5060
All 1971 Groups	6	10	14	15	23	20	11	100

Rank Correlation (Kendall's TauB) = .54

Cramer's V = .33

*Needs not adjusted for inflation; ratio should go up 21% just to offset rising costs.

TABLE A1.8

Unadjusted and Adjusted Percent of Entire Population in Target Population
And Percent of Target Population Persistently Poor
By Several Demographic, Background and Policy-Related Variables

Predictor	N	Unadjusted % in Target Population	Adjusted % in Target Population	Adjusted % in Target Population Blacks Only	N	Unadjusted % Persistently Poor	Adjusted % Persistently Poor	Adjusted % Persistently Poor Blacks Only
Age								
25-34	1101	.28	.31	.65	486	.09	.14	.27
35-44	957	.25	.26	.60	466	.22	.21	.35
45-54	928	.25	.24	.54	445	.28	.23	.39
55-64	707	.29	.24	.63	347	.25	.25	.51
Test Score								
<6	351	.61	.37	.64	284	.42	.29	.39
6-7	494	.51	.35	.60	354	.27	.23	.32
8-9	998	.32	.28	.62	522	.21	.21	.40
10	731	.24	.26	.62	288	.13	.15	.36
11	597	.18	.24	.56	178	.12	.19	.38
12	377	.13	.23	.47	95	.08	.15	.23
13	145	.10	.22	.51	23	.16	.29	.57
Unemployment Rate								
< 2%	34	.43	.41	.93	16	.00	.03	.11
2-3.9%	775	.26	.26	.55	346	.20	.22	.36
4-5.9%	1650	.28	.27	.63	857	.20	.20	.39
6-10%	1089	.25	.26	.59	453	.21	.21	.36
over 10%	145	.29	.32	.63	72	.23	.18	.22
City Size								
>500,000	1518	.24	.25	.59	783	.17	.17	.27
100,000-500,000	763	.20	.24	.58	306	.20	.20	.41
50,000-100,000	407	.29	.34	.71	183	.19	.24	.47
25,000-50,000	197	.25	.18	.47	74	.21	.18	.44
10,000-25,000	296	.33	.30	.67	130	.24	.21	.55
<10,000	506	.38	.29	.68	265	.24	.24	.48
Outside U.S.	6	.55	.71	--	3	.31	.48	--

TABLE A1.8
(continued)

Predictor		Unadjusted % in Target Population	Adjusted % in Target Population	Adjusted % in Target Population Blacks Only		Unadjusted % Persistently Poor	Adjusted % Persistently Poor	Adjusted % Persistently Poor Blacks Only
Distance to a Large City	N				N			
<5 miles	888	.30	.26	.60	481	.18	.15	.34
5-15 miles	1269	.20	.23	.58	578	.18	.18	.36
15-30 miles	485	.22	.25	.54	186	.16	.17	.31
30-50 miles	333	.26	.26	.60	136	.27	.27	.40
>50 miles	708	.37	.36	.72	359	.23	.25	.45
Outside U.S.	10	.37	.21	.62	4	.31	.20	.22
Education of Head	N							
0 grades	130	.69	.52	.85	108	.48	.38	.49
1-5 grades	184	.66	.51	.76	153	.53	.44	.44
6-8 grades	675	.44	.39	.73	433	.21	.20	.42
11 grades	810	.40	.35	.57	493	.19	.17	.37
12 grades	706	.21	.22	.47	271	.15	.16	.29
12+ non-academic	307	.15	.18	.50	84	.12	.16	.32
Some college	420	.14	.19	.57	102	.05	.13	.19
B.A.	266	.13	.20	.56	50	.09	.21	.23
Advanced degree	131	.05	.13	.37	12	.04	.20	.78
N.A.	64	.34	.29	.60	38	.12	.13	.20
Sex-Child Status	N							
Male: married, no children	662	.15	.16	.34	177	.10	.08	.02
children	1749	.21	.23	.48	683	.18	.19	.31
unmarried	293	.40	.38	.70	166	.15	.16	.25
Female: no children	402	.37	.36	.67	226	.20	.18	.31
children	587	.63	.55	.86	492	.35	.36	.57
Race	N							
White	2195	.22	.24	--	593	.14	.16	--
Black	1364	.60	.46	--	1067	.37	.33	--
Spanish-American	100	.54	.43	--	66	.27	.23	--
Other	34	.28	.32	--	18	.08	.12	--

TABLE A1.8
(continued)

Predictor	N	Unadjusted % in Target Population	Adjusted % in Target Population	Adjusted % in Target Population Blacks Only	N	Unadjusted % Persistently Poor	Adjusted % Persistently Poor	Adjusted % Persistently Poor Blacks Only
Motivation								
<2	114	.56	.38	.79	84	.33	.26	.50
<4	509	.41	.28	.67	317	.23	.18	.31
<6	984	.33	.29	.62	533	.22	.20	.39
<8	1012	.24	.26	.57	455	.20	.22	.41
<10	741	.19	.24	.62	273	.13	.17	.30
<12	308	.12	.23	.39	79	.11	.24	.51
12-14	25	.05	.22	.04	3	.00	.18	-.04

TABLE A1.9

Averages for First and Fifth Year of Two Measures of Economic Status, by Change in Family Composition
(for independent half sample of all families)

	Family Money Income			Head and Wife's Taxable Income			% of Families	# of Cases
	1967	1971	Mean Change 1971-1967	1967	1971	Mean Change 1971-1967		
Same Head and Wife								
No change in others, either	$ 8,322	$10,890	+2568	$ 7,415	$ 9,098	+1683	42	868
Some change in others, same number or more in family	8,646	12,785	+4139	8,101	11,155	+3055	16	427
Some change in others, fewer in family	10,936	14,413	+3477	8,846	11,833	+2987	14	364
Same Head--Not Same Wife (only for males)								
Head married now	6,763	12,958	+6195	6,320	12,057	+5737	2	57
Unmarried now (widowed, divorced or separated)	8,365	9,236	+ 871	7,693	7,912	- 81	3	61
Different Head								
Wife became head (widowed, divorced or separated previous wife)	7,661	6,400	-1261	6,177	2,622	-3555	6	136
*Some other sample person became head, and is single man	9,397	6,355	-3042	7,031	5,700	-1331	3	78
*Some other sample person became head, and is a woman	10,806	5,121	-5685	8,471	3,291	-5180	4	131
*Some other sample person became head and is a married man, or married a non-sample man	8,634	10,308	+1674	6,658	9,441	+2783	6	243
Head from outside family unit, or a previous female head whose husband returned	10,068	9,106	- 962	7,703	8,184	+ 481	4	162
All	8,864	10,884	+2020	7,633	9,041	+1408	100%	2527

*These persons are mostly "splitoffs"

MTR 1047

TABLE A1.10

Average for First and Fifth Year of Family Income and Hours, by Change in Family Composition
(for independent half sample of all families)

	Family Money Income Relating to Needs Standard**			Total Family Work Hours			Leisure Hours (of main adults)		
	1967	1971	Mean Change 1971-1967	1967	1971	Mean Change 1971-1967	1967	1971	Mean Change 1971-1967
Same Head and Wife									
No change in others, either	2.78	3.50	+ .72	4079	3724	- 355	3543	3868	+325
Some change in others, same number or more in family	2.59	3.31	+ .72	5215	5237	+ 22	3104	3360	+256
Some change in others, fewer in family	2.42	3.89	+1.47	5537	4833	- 704	3164	3526	+362
Same Head--Not Same Wife (only for males)									
Head married now	2.47	3.56	+1.09	3380	4843	+1463	3506	3515	+ 9
Unmarried now (widowed, divorced or separated)	2.52	3.68	+1.16	5061	2751	-2310	3331	3400	+ 69
Different Head									
Wife became head (widowed, divorced or separated previous wife)	2.37	2.35	- .02	4726	2650	-2076	3577	3850	+273
*Some other sample person became head, and is single man	2.34	2.62	+ .28	5561	2351	-3210	3120	3408	+288
*Some other sample person became head, and is a woman	2.51	2.36	- .15	5643	2159	-3484	3123	3819	+696
*Some other sample person became head and is a married man, or married a non-sample man	2.77	3.17	+ .90	5234	4670	- 564	3097	3490	+393
Head from outside family unit, or a previous female head whose husband returned	2.21	2.78	+ .57	5680	4531	-1149	3026	3521	+495
All	2.58	3.31	+ .77	4772	4022	- 75	3336	3666	+330

**Needs standard not adjusted for inflation and 1967 not adjusted for farmers.
*These persons are mostly "splitoffs"

MTR 1047

TABLE A1.11

Averages for First and Fifth Year of Food Consumption and Food Needs Standard for Families
(for independent half sample of all families)

	Annual Food Needs			Food Consumption**		
	1967	1971	Mean Change 1971-1967	1967	1971	Mean Change 1971-1967
Same Head and Wife						
No change in others, either	904	940	+ 36	1633	1941	+ 308
Some change in others, same number or more in family	1154	1387	+ 233	1828	2527	+ 699
Some change in others, fewer in family	1588	1174	- 414	2365	2281	- 84
Same Head--Not Same Wife (only for males)						
Head married now	774	1056	+ 282	1440	1918	+ 478
Unmarried now (widowed, divorced or separated)	1137	605	- 532	1850	1684	- 166
Different Head						
Wife became head (widowed, divorced or separated previous wife)	1073	748	- 325	1760	1328	- 432
*Some other sample person became head, and is single man	1537	489	-1048	1872	1440	- 432
*Some other sample person became head, and is a woman	1562	609	- 953	2324	1091	-1233
*Some other sample person became head and is a married man, or married a non-sample man	1327	1050	- 277	1948	1851	- 97
Head from outside family unit, or a previous female head whose husband returned	1674	994	- 680	2341	1719	- 622
All	1159	1004	- 155	1862	1968	+ 106

**Changed questions may affect comparability.
*These persons are mostly "splitoffs"

MTR 1047

TABLE A1.12

Averages for First and Fifth Year of Two Measures of Economic Status, by Change in Family Composigion (for independent half sample of all individuals)**

	Family Money Income			Head and Wife's Taxable Income			% of Individuals	# of Cases
	1967	1971	Mean Change 1971-1967	1967	1971	Mean Change 1971-1967		
Same Head and Wife								
No change in others, either	$ 9,313	$12,993	+3680	$ 8,626	$11,092	+2466	42	2687
Some change in others, same number or more in family	8,855	13,267	+4412	8,322	11,463	+3141	21	1731
Some change in others, fewer in family	11,501	15,694	+4193	9,671	12,855	+3184	18	1427
Same Head--Not Same Wife (only for males)								
Head married now	6,858	12,710	+5852	6,431	11,821	+5390	1	82
Unmarried now (widowed, divorced or separated)	8,093	9,619	+1526	7,434	8,031	+ 597	1	102
Different Head								
Wife became head (widowed, divorced or separated previous wife)	7,531	7,325	- 206	6,235	2,589	-3646	4	399
*Some other sample person became head, and is single man	9,573	6,473	-3100	6,870	5,666	-1204	1	76
*Some other sample person became head, and is a woman	9,727	5,174	-4553	7,401	3,280	-4121	2	185
*Some other sample person became head and is a married man, or married a non-sample man	8,080	10,940	+2860	5,702	9,462	+3760	7	397
Head from outside family unit, or a previous female head whose husband returned	9,861	10,200	+ 339	7,496	8,370	+ 874	3	217
All	9,430	12,761	+3331	8,329	10,651	+2322	100%	7303

*These persons are mostly "splitoffs"
**Note: Tables 4-7 are for individuals, not families.
MTR 1047

TABLE A1.13

Averages for First and Fifth Year of Family Income and Hours, by Change in Family Composition
(for independent half sample of all individuals)**

	Family Money Income Relative to Needs Standard*			Total Family Work Hours			Leisure Hours (of main adults)		
	1967	1971	Mean Change 1971-1967	1967	1971	Mean Change 1971-1967	1967	1971	Mean Change 1971-1967
Same Head and Wife									
No change in others, either	2.67	3.46	+ .79	4765	4586	- 179	3331	3685	+354
Some change in others, same number or more in family	2.38	3.06	+ .68	5479	5625	+1046	3003	3285	+282
Some change in others, fewer in family	2.28	3.71	+1.43	5776	5399	- 377	3104	3472	+368
Same Head--Not Same Wife (only for males)									
Head married now	2.41	3.34	+ .93	3457	4910	+1453	3481	3489	+ 8
Unmarried now (widowed, divorced or separated)	2.31	3.33	+1.02	5072	3347	-1725	3342	3255	- 87
Different Head									
Wife became head (widowed, divorced or separated previous wife)	2.02	2.15	+ .13	5202	3322	-1880	3350	3638	+288
*Some other sample person became head, and is single man	2.27	2.63	+ .36	5606	2346	-3260	3145	3422	+277
*Some other sample person became head, and is a woman	2.29	2.16	- .13	5621	2236	-3385	3190	3771	+581
*Some other sample person became head and is a married man, or married a non-sample man	2.06	2.95	+ .89	5269	4951	- 318	3045	3435	+390
Head from outside family unit, or a previous female head whose husband returned	2.15	2.76	+ .61	5967	4763	-1204	2935	3534	+599
All	2.44	3.27	+ .83	5195	4827	- 368	3190	3534	+344

**Needs standard not adjusted for inflation and 1967 not adjusted for farmers.
*These persons are mostly "splitoffs"

MTR 1047

TABLE A1.14

Averages for First and Fifth Year Annual Food Standard Change***,
by Change in Family Composition

(for independent half sample of all individuals)**

	Annual Food Needs		Mean Change 1971-1967	% of Individuals	# of Cases
	1967	1971			
Same Head and Wife					
No change in others, either	$ 1184	$1259	+ 75	42	2687
Some change in others, same number or more in family	1371	1631	+ 260	21	1731
Some change in others, fewer in family	1812	1434	− 378	18	1427
Same Head—Not Same Wife (only for males)					
Head married now	852	1166	+ 314	1	82
Unmarried now (widowed, divorced or separated)	1290	841	− 449	1	102
Different Head					
Wife became head (widowed, divorced or separated previous wife)	1424	1165	− 259	4	399
*Some other sample person became head, and is single man	1558	496	−1062	1	76
*Some other sample person became head, and is a woman	1539	736	− 803	2	185
*Some other sample person became head and is a married man, or married a non-sample man	1399	1269	− 130	7	397
Head from outside family unit, or a previous female head whose husband returned	1682	1138	− 544	3	219
All	1382	1331	− 51	100%	7303

*These persons are mostly "splitoffs"
**Note: Tables 4-7 are for individuals, not families
***Changed questions may affect comparability

MTR 1047

TABLE A1.15

Variables Introduced as Possible Factors Explaining the Trend
in Taxable Income of Head and Wife Relative to the Five Year Average

Overall Importance (Eta^2)**	Variable**
	Forced splits
.032	Change in wife's work status
	First rank:
.046	*Age
.002	Sex-marital status in 1972
.017	*Race
.014	Test score
.007	Grew up on a farm
.027	Education
.001	Other training
.000	Veteran
	Second rank:
.006	Size of largest city in area
.023	*Change in jobs over the period
.012	*Change in residence
.002	Unemployment in the county, average of years 2-5
	Indexes:
	Attitudes and Self-ratings:
.006	Sense of efficacy
.006	Trust in others
.007	Ambition-aspiration
.022	Achievement motivation score
	Behavioral reports:
.003	Real earning acts (do-it-yourself, home production)
.016	*Economizing
.010	Risk avoidance
.006	Planning
.009	Connectedness to sources of information and help
.024	*Money earning acts

* Indicates that that variable can account for 1% or more of the
variance with a single adjustment of the whole initial group. However, money earning acts seemed to work in reverse, and the index
of trust in others only became important in two subgroups; its
effect was opposite to the usual expectations: the trusting ones
did worse. Given the large number of things tried, even this last
result is suspect and we shall examine the components of this index
separately.

**See Glossary for definitions of variables and an explanation of
  eta^2.

TABLE A1.16

Factors Affecting the Trend in Taxable Income of Head and Wife, Relative to Average
(for all families with same head and in labor force in 1968 and 1972)
[Regression analysis with categorical predictions]

	All Working Population		Target Population Only	
	Gross Effect*	Net Effect**	Gross Effect*	Net Effect**
Working wife (or one who quit)	.034	.031	.041	.033
Test score (1972)	.006	.009	.011	.043
Achievement-motivation (1972)	.007	.009	.028	.056
Unemployment in county (4-yr avg)	.002	.001	.015	.023
Matters what others think?	.003	.002	.018	.018
Level of income	.013	.071	.026	.094
Have limitations?	.000	.000	.007	.003
Union member	.011	.015	.023	.054
Age	.032	.032	.026	.030
Race	.007	.011	.013	.002
Education	.010	.012	.026	.046
Sex-marital status	.015	.012	.011	.019
Money earning acts (1968-1969)	.015	.021	.034	.041
Connectedness (1968-1969)	.004	.005	.007	.010
Planning acts (1968-1969)	.002	.001	.006	.002
Risk avoidance (1968-1969)	.004	.016	.018	.028
Economizing (1968-1969)	.006	.012	.048	.050
Low education-high test score	.003	.001	.003	.007

N =	2504	891
R^2(adjusted) =	.147	.282
Mean =	6.95	5.81
Standard deviation =	10.63	17.72

*Eta squared (correlation ratio): see Glossary
**Beta squared: see Glossary

MTR 1080

98

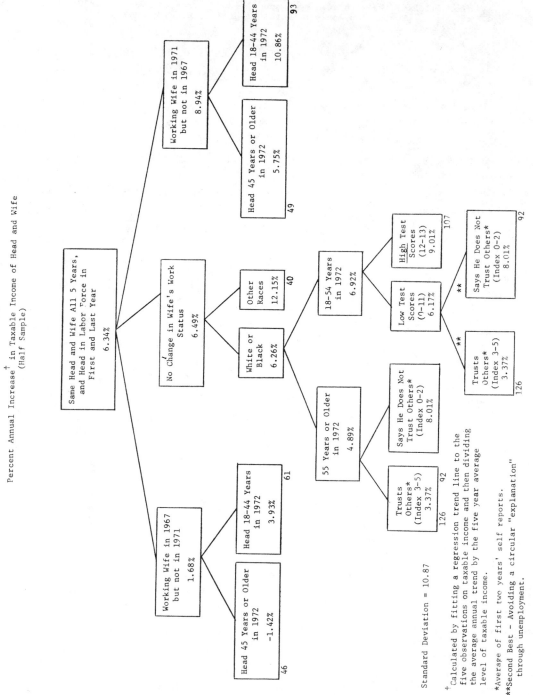

FIGURE A1.1

Percent Annual Increase[+] in Taxable Income of Head and Wife
(Half Sample)

Standard Deviation = 10.87

[+]Calculated by fitting a regression trend line to the
five observations on taxable income and then dividing
the average annual trend by the five year average
level of taxable income.

*Average of first two years' self reports.

**Second Best – Avoiding a circular "explanation"
through unemployment.

MTR 1064A

Chapter 2

FAMILY COMPOSITION

INTRODUCTION

We have seen in Chapter 1 that changes in family composition and the often related changes in labor force participation dominate the changes in a family's economic well-being. There are two ways to look at this. One might argue that they are essentially random events or normal life cycle progressions which can be averaged out, controlled, or otherwise taken care of and are not very interesting in their own right. Or one could argue that at least some of these changes, or their timing, might well be affected by people's purposes, desires, and reactions to their environment. It might then be possible for public policy to have an effect on a family's economic well-being by altering either the environment or people's behavioral responses in such a way that family composition is changed. If it is true that people's economic status in turn affects their decisions about changes in family composition or labor force participation, then we have more than a simple sequence of causation. Figure 2.1 gives an abbreviated representation of these main effects.

There is another more interesting model which might also deserve investigation. It deals with the interrelated set of decisions by which people move toward a satisfactory equilibrium in family, job, and residence. An investigation of the sequences of interrelated decisions is beyond the scope of the present study. It should be remembered that any joint decision can be interpreted, studied, and predicted as though it were a set of conditional decisions, in almost any order. We could, for example, study decisions to change family arrangements and then, given the result of those decisions, we could study decisions about jobs and labor force participation. Given these decisions, we could proceed to study decisions about residential location.

Our purpose in this chapter is more limited -- we merely want to see how the primary influences on change in family composition appear to work. Changes in the lives of most families fall into an expected pattern. Family size in-

FIGURE 2.1

Patterns of Causation – Demographic and Economic

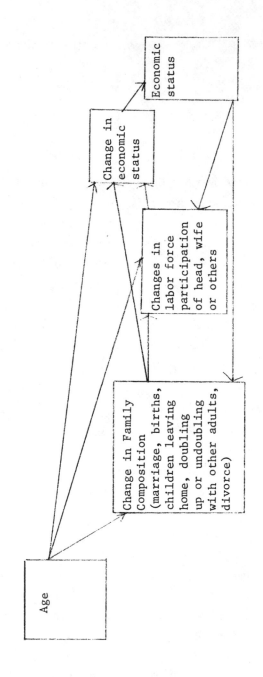

creases as children are born, diminishes as they grow up and leave home. In many families other relatives as well move in and out.

A family's composition and its economic situation are so closely intertwined that the comings and goings of its members can have a more dramatic effect on family finances than changes in earnings or employment. When children leave home, for example, the needs of the parental family, and possibly its income, falls. These changes may, in turn, cause the head of the family or his wife to alter their work effort.

Although many changes in family composition are inevitable or at least customary, their timing may be affected by economic considerations. Children may be pushed into leaving because of overcrowding at home or may stay longer than they want to because they have no job to support them elsewhere.

We will describe the pervasive and complex changes in family composition and see to what extent they occur in response to a family's economic situation or whether they merely reflect the usual processes of a family's life cycle.

During the five years covered by the study, 42% of the families had no change in composition except that growing older altered their needs standard a little. In each of the remaining cases there were changes in family members.

We will try in various ways to classify people according to family changes using some of the categories which, in the previous chapter, explained variations in economic status. Here it is the family changes themselves we want to understand. Later we will shift from families to the individuals within them and look at their changing relationships to the head of the family.

We will begin by looking at a sample of families as they were constituted in 1972 and then examine their histories using the following variation of the change in family composition categories which were used in Chapter 1:

Family Composition	Percent of 1972 Families
Same head and wife and no change in other members since 1968	42%
Same head and wife but more or different others	16
Same head and wife but fewer others (mostly families where children left home)	14
Same head but changed wife -- got married, divorced, remarried, widowed, separated	4
Different head -- wife became head (widowed, divorced, etc.)	6
Different head -- previous female head got married	2
Different head -- some other family member became head (mostly children who left home)	12
Different head -- other (including daughters who left home and got married)	4
	100%

Remember that several families may have originated in the same 1968 family since we have a sample of families as of 1972 and are looking backward.

The usual multivariate methods which account for some variables (like age and marital status), while they examine whether initial economic status affects subsequent changes in family composition, are not available to us unless we look separately at each possible change in family composition. Even then the use of least squares regression procedures to explain low probability events has its problems. We have chosen instead a simpler, more transparent process of dividing the sample sequentially into groups with the largest differences in their distributions according to change in family composition. For this purpose we use a systematic searching program which, given a list of possible explanatory factors, proceeds according to a prestated strategy to search for what matters.[1]

We shall not dwell on the obvious and expected demographic sequences that appear in Figure 2.2. Age, sex, and marital status are associated, of course, with getting married, divorced or widowed, with having children, or with children leaving home. The concept of the family life cycle through which people move is an artificial construct, but most families go through the stages at about the expected ages. What we will look for and report in this chapter are *other* influences on the timing of these events.

Young married people were more likely to have children and were a little less likely to get divorced if they owned their own home. This finding may be correlation, not causation, and is hardly a sufficient basis for a policy encouraging homeownership.

Among families with older heads, more children moved out from homes which were overcrowded in 1968 than from homes with adequate space. It is always possible that families which expected children to start leaving home soon did not expand their housing for the few remaining years. But the question arises of whether less expensive housing, and enough vacancies to encourage moving to more adequate housing, might not encourage families to stay together longer, to educate their children longer, and to delay the formation of new (usually low income) families.

The other differences in Figure 2.2 are well known to demographers. For instance, the longer people had been married, the less likely they were to have more children (enlarge the family) and the more likely the older children were to leave home. Older families were also more prone to be changed by the death of

_____
[1] For a description of the program see THAID in the Glossary and Appendix C or see J. Morgan and R. Messenger, THAID, A Sequential Analysis Program for the Analysis of Nominal Scale Dependent Variables, Institute for Social Research, The University of Michigan, Ann Arbor, Michigan, 1973.

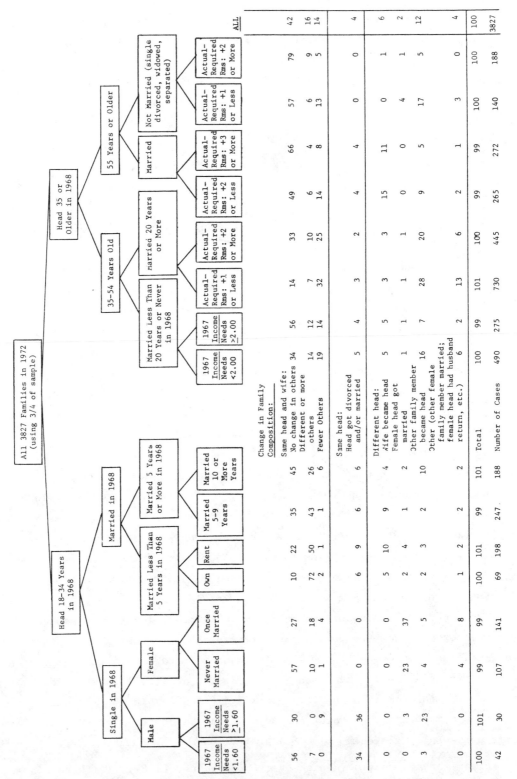

FIGURE 2.2

Change in Family Composition 1968 to 1972 by Condition in 1968

MTR 1040

104

one spouse.

In order to understand better the influence of economics on family composition, we looked at the effects of family economic status in 1968 on the subsequent
pattern of changes in family composition. This was done for each of the eight
main groups of Figure 2.2 according to age, marital status in 1968, sex, and how
long they were married (see Figure 2.3). Among the young single heads, there was
less change of any kind if the initial economic status was poor, but the numbers
are too small to make much of this. Among young married couples, those that had
better initial economic conditions were more likely to have children. Presumably,
this was the result of timing since we have no overall evidence that family size
ends up positively associated with income. There were also more splitoffs (new
heads) leaving intially low income/needs families, even at these young ages (head
18-34 in 1968).

The frequency of divorce was affected by income in intriguingly different
ways depending on how long a young couple had been married. For young couples
married less than five years in 1968, a *low* initial income/needs led to more
divorce, but for young couples married five years or more a very *high* initial
economic status was more often associated with divorce. Perhaps these longer
married couples could only *afford* divorce if they were rather well off, whereas
the younger ones were driven to it by economic difficulties.

Let us turn now to the older families -- those with heads 35 or older in
1968. There was a persistent pattern of more family change, usually from children leaving home, if the initial economic position was poor. The implication is
that economic forces influence at least the timing of this major event -- the
undoubling of families and the formation of new households by the children. Presumably, if the parental income was low the alternative possibilities for the
chidren striking out on their own were better than what they could expect if they
had stayed at home. We can also assume that dropping out of school is connected
with this pattern of leaving home -- low family income makes the temptation of
dropping out of school, getting a job, and leaving home more attractive.

Remember that, although we have done a little selecting of second best predictors, our main results were derived from a flexible search for what affected
changes in family composition. One important advantage of a general search
process like the one we have used is that it can also tell us what does *not* matter. There appeared to be no large racial differences in the frequency of change
in family composition, nor did unemployment in the county seem to inhibit marriage or having children.[1]

_____
[1] In an earlier analysis of change over three years, 1968-1971, there did seem to
be an effect of high local unemployment inhibiting new births; see James Morgan,
Change in Family Composition as a Behavior to be Explained, Working Paper, Survey Research Center, 1972.

FIGURE 2.3

Effects of Initial Money Income/Needs on Change in Family Composition, for Some Subgroups*

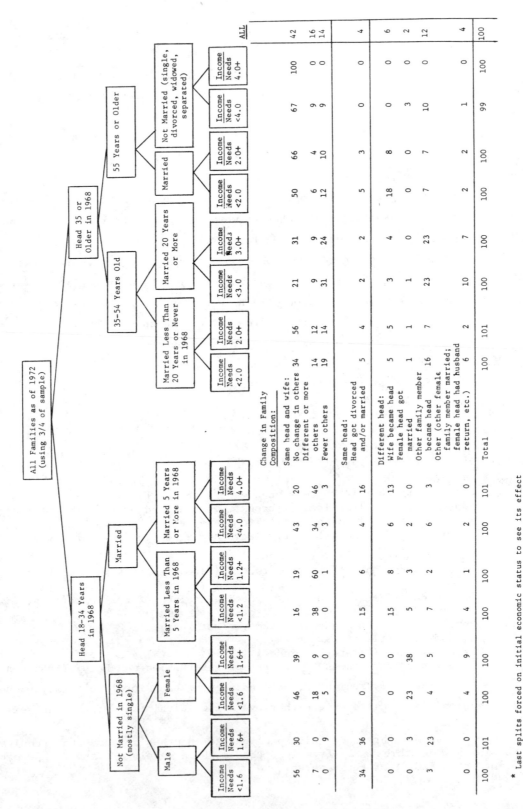

* Last splits forced on initial economic status to see its effect

MTR 1040

ANALYSIS

I. Changes in Family Composition and in Labor Force Participation

Following the general model we presented at the beginning of this chapter, we could look at the effects of changing family composition on changing labor force participation of family members, but that will be part of a more thorough study of work in a later chapter. So we turn here to a brief look at the cat-egories presented in Chapter 1 that combine changes in family with changes in labor force participation where the family head is the same. We do not learn much from describing the 18 groups, certainly nothing beyond the usual demo-graphic relations. Families with changes were younger, better educated, and more likely to have changed residences (see Table 2.1).

To get a clearer picture, we looked only at the families where there had been the same head in all five years and where he had been in the labor force at the beginning and end of the period. There were few enough groups here so that we could use once more a systematic search for things that might matter -- that might increase or decrease the likelihood of a change in family size or a change in the number of other earners (including the wife).[1]

We introduced as possible influences on changes in family size of other earners the following:

Environment
    Unemployment in the county
    Surplus or shortage of rooms in 1968

Attitudes
    Question whether it matters what others think of you
    Sense of personal efficacy (three items averaged over first two years)
    Self-report on planning (three items averaged over first two years)
    Anomie (world is hostile) (two items averaged over first two years)

Behavior Indexes
    Index of "bad habits" or poor record (late to work, skips work, says he
        has a "record")
    Investment in self (schooling, getting training for a better job, first
        two years)
    Real earning acts (index of items, first year)
    Economizing (first year index)
    Planning acts (first year index)
    Index of connectedness to sources of information and help (first year)

None of these environmental, attitudinal, or behavioral factors, however, made any significant difference either overall or within any of the age-sex-

---

[1]Note that we used a broad definition of change in other earners that required crossing a wide threshold, from less than $500 in earnings for wife and others to more than $2000, or the reverse.

TABLE 2.1

Proportions Who Meet Certain Criteria, within Groups
According to Change in Family Composition and in Extra Earners

	1968 Head Was:			Shortage of rooms in 1968	Moved since 1968	1972 Head Was:			Number of cases
	25-34	35-54	Female			18-34	Not high school graduate	Female	
<65, not in labor force 1968-72	11%	50%	51%	12%	50%	17%	67%	63%	285
Entered labor force (same head)	27	37	59	19	68	30	65	60	54
Left labor force	3	12	25	5	28	14	64	26	434
No change in other earners, same members	22	51	15	3	34	20	34	16	1132
No change in other earners, more members	47	23	4	2	57	59	30	4	467
No change in other earners, fewer members	6	81	13	8	35	4	41	14	546
More other earners, same members	21	64	3	7	42	13	28	3	167
More other earners, more members	21	42	22	15	65	51	40	22	84
More other earners, fewer members	4	94	7	3	25	1	40	7	63
Fewer other earners, same members	7	71	17	0	37	15	40	17	32
Fewer other earners, more members	59	11	0	1	57	74	21	0	95
Fewer other earners, fewer members	26	55	11	8	72	31	47	14	53
≥65 not in labor force 1968-72	0	0	39	4	18	0	72	48	278
Different head, single male	7	69	28	12	98	90	26	0	167
Different head, married male	12	65	27	13	95	87	25	0	795
Different head, single female	3	78	19	16	98	96	15	100	150
Different head, widowed female	5	38	6	7	30	5	63	100	96
Different head, divorced female	31	45	11	10	78	58	31	100	207
ALL	17	46	19	7	48	31	48	25	5060

marital status groups. Demographic forces still dominated. This does not mean that the timing of these events cannot be affected by environmental or motivational forces; it means only that it would require a much more detailed analysis of each of the demographic subgroups to uncover the effects. The analysis confirmed the apparent effect of initial housing conditions on subsequent reductions in family size (undoubling).

There were also some suggestive findings that one behavior index and one pair of attitudinal questions might have some effect: among older families, those who exhibited more planning acts in the first two years were more likely to have decreases in family size. Is planning associated with completing one's family earlier and thus having children leave home earlier? Trust also may play a role in family size. Middle aged families who in the first two years said that the life of the average man was getting better, and who said that there were not a lot of people who had good things they did not deserve, had fewer subsequent changes in family size. Perhaps trusting the world helps create family stability or *vice versa*. What really mattered most in determining family size, of course, were age, sex, and marital status as indicated in Table 2.2.

We have not gotten very far beyond the usual demographic forces in explaining changes in labor force participation. But we must keep these changes in mind because they dominate the changes in economic status of families. Insofar as any variations in labor force participation are influenced by public policy, their effects may be much greater than the probably small changes in earnings or in hours of work.

A major difficulty in explaining changes in family composition, other than births, is that information is usually lacking on alternative courses of action. If someone marries, the premarital situation of the non-sample spouse is generally not known. If someone splits off from a panel family, we know his situation before and after the split but we do not know what his alternative opportunities would have been if he had not left home. We can, however, assume that the individual's income, if any, before he left home is some indication of what he could expect if he lived alone. This assumption permits the following analysis of those leaving low income homes.

II. A Separate Look at Those Leaving Low Income Homes

A particular family composition change that merits special study is the departure of adults, other than head or wife, from the household.[1] It is possible

---

[1] Another type of family composition change which is also being analyzed with the Panel data is separation or divorce. Dr. Oliver Moles, formerly of the Office

TABLE 2.2

Change in Family Size and Major Earner Other than Head,
by Age, Sex, and Marital Status (for families with the same
head all five years who was in the labor force in 1968 and 1972)

Family changes	1968 age < 30 and Marital Status			31–40	41–50	>50 in 1968	All
	Single males	Single females	Married couples				
No change in other earners or members	51%	85%	32%	47%	41%	63%	47%
No change in other earners, more members	23	5	45	16	5	5	17
No change in other earners, fewer members	0	1	4	17	36	21	20
More other earners, same members	0	0	4	11	5	4	6
More other earners, more members	22	6	3	1	2	1	2
More other earners, fewer members	0	0	0	3	5	1	2
Fewer other earners, same members	4	3	0	1	2	2	2
Fewer other earners, more members	0	0	9	2	0	0	2
Fewer other earners, fewer members	0	0	4	0	3	3	3
Number of cases	53	78	518	717	670	545	2588

110

to look both at those who left and those who did not leave, whereas with most other doubling or undoubling we do not know the alternatives well. These changes seem likely to be affected by environmental factors and perhaps by public policy. While many of these moves are made by children who leave to set up their own households as a part of the expected life cycle change in families, both the timing of this decision and the decision of other relatives may be motivated by the economic situation of the individual and the family in which he resides.

The particular group of individuals on whom we shall focus are those 17 years of age or older in 1971 who were neither head of the family nor the wife. Since the low income families are of particular relevance to the policy implications of this analysis, we further restrict ourselves to those families whose 1970 income was less than twice the annual needs standard. There are 1008 such individuals. Their relation to the head of the household in 1971 is given in Table 2.3.

Nearly all (90%) of the individuals who split off were sons or daughters of the heads of households. Table 2.3 shows that 26% of all eligible people actually moved out between 1971 and 1972. This proportion varied a little depending upon the relation to the head. Parents of the head and other relatives were less likely to move out than children, grandchildren, and siblings. Age was associated with the probability of moving out, as Table 2.4 confirms: the 22 to 25-year-olds were more likely to move out than older or younger persons.

The probability of moving out varied among different age, race, and sex groups (see Table 2.5). While male-female differences by age groups were not large, black-nonblack differences were substantial. Blacks less than 26 years old were much less likely to move out of the household than nonblacks of those ages, but for those over 26 years old the situation was exactly reversed. Nearly one-quarter of the older blacks moved out while only 5% of the older nonblacks did so.

Several economic factors may be important in the decision to move out. A sufficiently large increase in individual income, a low income/needs level in the original family, and a high income/needs ratio in the new family all are potential predictors. Two additional economic variables which we call "incentives to split" are included. The first is the individual's income relative to his needs (defining his own needs as $1500) in 1971 divided by his family's income/needs in 1971. If the ratio is greater than 1.0, the individual would be economically

of Planning, Research, and Evaluation of the Office of Economic Opportunity and now at the National Institute of Education, is using these data to study marital instability and has produced a working paper entitled Some Social and Economic Background Variables in Marital Instability.

TABLE 2.3

Distribution of Individuals* Eligible to Split Off by Relation to Head

Relation to head (1971)	Number of cases	Proportion of cases	Proportion in group who moved out between 1971 and 1972
Son or daughter	908	90.0%	.27
Brother or sister	26	2.6	.23
Father or mother	24	2.5	.14
Grandchild	15	1.5	.22
Other relative	35	3.4	.11
Total	1008	100.0%	.26

*These individuals were older than 17 in 1971, were neither head nor wife, and were members of families whose 1971 income/needs is less than 2.0.

MTR 1057

TABLE 2.4

Proportion of Individuals* Moving Out by Age Categories

Age in 1972	Proportion Moving Out between 1971 and 1972	Number of cases
18-21	24%	712
22-25	47	157
26 or older	12	139

*These individuals were older than 17 in 1971, were neither head nor wife, and were members of families whose 1971 income/needs is less than 2.0.

MTR 1057

TABLE 2.5

Proportion of Individuals* Moving Out between 1971 and 1972
by Age, Race, and Sex

| | Race | | Sex | | |
Age in 1972	Black	Nonblack	Female	Male	All
18-21	17%	27%	27%	21%	24%
22-25	37	54	50	44	47
26 or older	23	5	14	9	12
Total	28%	22%	28%	24%	26%

---

*Individuals who were older than 17 in 1971 and were neither head
nor wife and were members of families whose 1971 income/needs
ratio did not exceed 2.0.

MTR 1057

TABLE 2.6

Strength of Simple Association between Demographic
and Economic Variables and the Decision to Move Out*

Predictor	Eta^2
Payoff from splitting (before-after)	.157
Change in individual income	.133
Age of individual	.063
1971 incentive to split (pre-split)	.025
1971 total family money income	.020
1971 family income/needs	.010
Race	.008
Sex	.002

---

*For individuals who were older than 17 in 1971, were
neither head nor wife, and were members of families
whose 1971 income/needs ratio did not exceed 2.0.

better off if he or she were living alone, even with his or her present income.
A second measure related to the incentive to split is the "payoff from splitting"
which is the ratio of the 1971 family income/needs to the 1972 family income/
needs.

The variables thought to be important for the decision to move out and a
measure of their simple association (eta^2) with the decision are presented in
Table 2.6.

The two variables most strongly associated with the probability of moving
out are payoff from splitting and the change in individual income. Neither of
these has unambiguous *causal* relationships with the dependent variable. The proportion moving out in different categories of the payoff measure are shown in
Figure 2.4. Groups whose economic status either improved or deteriorated substantially were more likely to include movers. This may only reflect the fact
that those who did not move out lived in families in which there was little
change.

Many people experienced substantial increases in income between 1971 and
1972 and their probability of moving was greater than those without large income
increases (see Figure 2.5). Of course, the increase in income and the decision
to leave home may have been a simultaneous or joint decision, and we cannot be
sure that the income increase actually led to the move.

Turning from the measurement of change in economic status to that of original level of status, it can be seen from Table 2.6 that the "incentive to
split" measure had a stronger association with the proportion moving out than
1971 family money income or 1971 family income/needs. The expected positive relationship between the incentive to split and actually splitting off was strongest for individuals with the greatest incentives to split (see Figure 2.6).

There was no clear relationship between the proportion moving out and
either of the family income measures (family total money income or family income/
needs). It is not useful, then, to think of the decision to move out of poor
families as having a simple association with measures of family status. Race and
sex had no effect either.

This analysis was restricted to changes in a single year, to individuals 17
and older, and to persons who were not the head or wife. There was a substantial number of individuals in the sample in early 1972 who had not been a head,
wife, son, or daughter in 1968, including some children born during the period.
If we exclude those who are not in the sample but merely moved into it, we can
describe the pattern of changes of sample individuals over the period in several
ways.

114

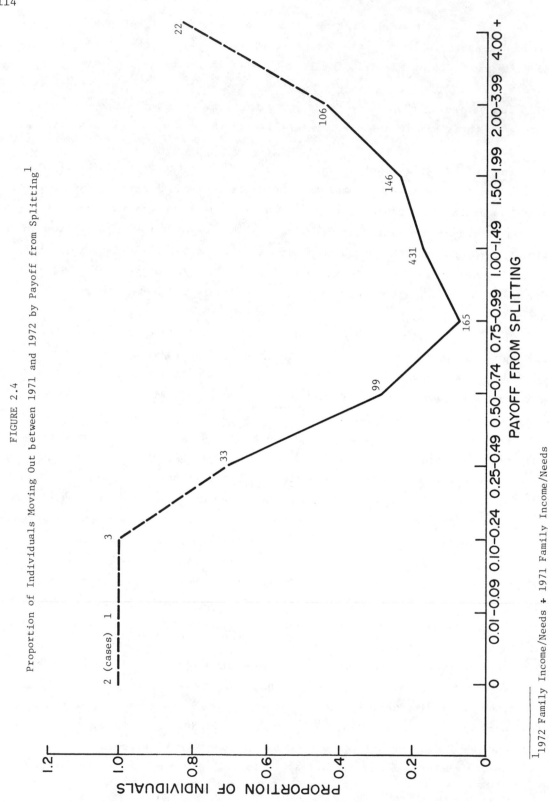

FIGURE 2.4

Proportion of Individuals Moving Out between 1971 and 1972 by Payoff from Splitting[1]

[1]1972 Family Income/Needs ÷ 1971 Family Income/Needs

115

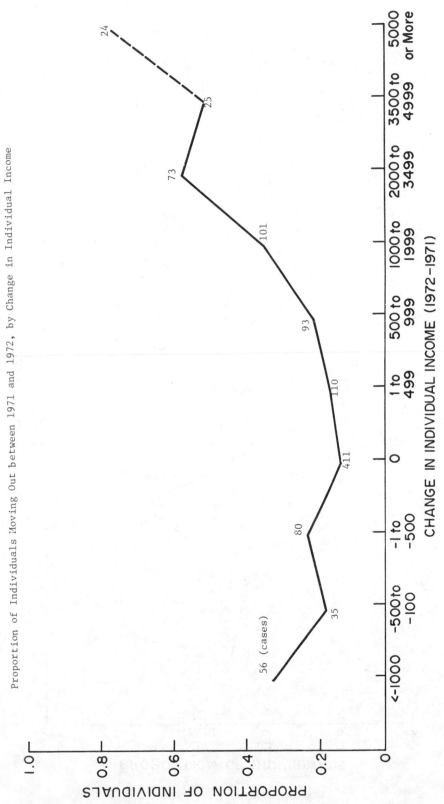

FIGURE 2.5

Proportion of Individuals Moving Out between 1971 and 1972, by Change in Individual Income

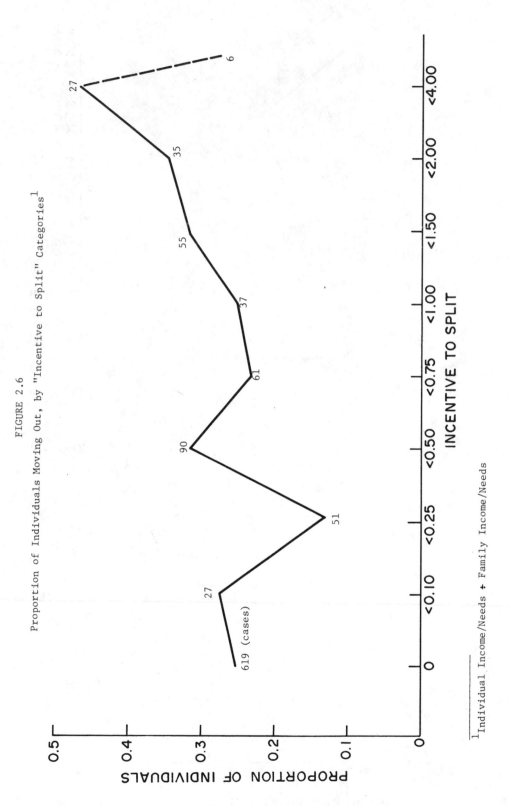

FIGURE 2.6

Proportion of Individuals Moving Out, by "Incentive to Split" Categories[1]

[1]Individual Income/Needs ÷ Family Income/Needs

III.   Changes of Sample Individuals, 1968 to 1972 - Transitions

If we exclude from the sample those individuals not properly in the sample because they married into it or are otherwise not related to the original sample members, then we have 16,140 individuals. Of these, 1532 were not living in the household at the time of the initial interview. Most of these are children born during the period. They represent 7.3% of the sample of individuals, 3.3% of them sons of the head, 3.3% daughters, and 0.7% other relatives such as grandsons and granddaughters.

Table 2.7 gives the transition data showing the joint distribution of each individual's relationship to head and marital status in 1968 and 1972. There are empty cells because people do not change sex, of course. If we notice that some 79.5% are along the diagonal, meaning no change in their relationship to family head, we can introduce for that group a further distinction: whether there was any other change in the family, i.e., in the members other than the head or wife, or in the head or wife themselves. With this additional division, and combining the sexes a bit, we get the transition categories of Table 2.8. It is clear from this table that different age groups had wildly different patterns of change. Cramer's measure of association between age and change in family is .34. Interestingly enough, neither initial economic level nor initial overcrowding had much to do with these changes.

The implications are that changes in the family have a demographic life of their own. Yet Table 2.9 shows that they had profound effects on the individual's economic status, surpassed only by the effects of changes in labor force participation of family members.[1] Individuals who got divorced were usually worse off. Those who got married were much more likely to be better off. The splitoffs were frequently worse off, particularly if they did not acquire a double income family by getting married. Presumably the parental home which they left was in good economic shape with an earner at the peak of his earnings (and perhaps a working wife as well). The patterns would be still more dramatic if the changes in family size and in earners were also distinguished.

We have thus replicated for individuals our findings for families that changes in family structure have profound effects on economic status, and that these changes are relatively frequent.

---

[1]Note that the individual's economic status is measured by the family income relative to family needs of the family he or she is in.

TABLE 2.7

Transitions of Sample Individuals 1968-1972 by Relationship to Head

1968	1972								
	Male married	Single male head	Single female head	Wife	Son	Daughter	Other Male	Other Female	All
Married male head	18.3%	1.0%					0.1%		19.4
Single male head	0.6	1.4							2.0
Single female head			4.9%	0.8%					5.8
Wife			1.9	18.2					20.1
Son	2.4	0.9			18.4%				21.9
Daughter			1.1	2.4		16.5%			20.1
Other male	0.3	0.1			0.4		0.7		1.5
Other female			0.2	0.3		0.2		1.1%	1.8
Not present in 1968					3.3	3.3	0.4	0.3	7.3
All 1968 statuses	21.6	3.5	8.2	21.7	22.2	20.0	1.2	1.4	100.0
Number of cases	2688	464	1435	2734	4172	3871	366	401	16,140

TABLE 2.8

1968-1972 Change in Relation to Head,
and if none, by Change in Family by Age in 1972 (for all individuals)

Change in Individual's Family Situation	Age of Individual in 1972										
	<6	6-11	12-17	18-24	25-34	35-44	45-54	55-64	65-74	≥75	All
No change in relation to head:											
No change	10	44	43	16	30	51	39	62	75	74	39.0
change;same head&wife	14	40	44	35	40	38	51	29	14	11	34.8
change in head/wife	3	13	11	7	5	2	2	1	1	2	5.6
Divorced or widowed				1	5	5	5	5	7	7	2.9
Married				2	5	2	2	1	1	1	1.4
Became a dependent				0	0	0	0	0	0	1	0.2
Son became married head*				11	7	0	0	0	0	0	2.4
Daughter became wife*			1	15	3	0	0	0	0	0	2.4
Son, daughter, other who became head or wife*		0	0	13	6	1	1	1	1	4	3.0
Other dependent with changed family relation	72	3	1	1	0	0	0	0	0	0	8.2
Total	99	100	100	101	101	99	100	99	99	100	99.9
Percent of sample	11	12	13	14	12	11	10	8	6	3	100
Number of cases	2133	2466	2569	2257	1747	1628	1436	1046	567	291	16140

*Mostly splitoffs.

TABLE 2.9

Change in Family Income/Needs, for Individuals by Change in Individual's Relation to Head, or Change in Family Composition (for all sample individuals)

Change in Income/Needs	No Change in Individual Relation to Head		Change; head/ wife	Change; Di- vorced/ widowed	Got married	Being a depen- dent	Son became husband	Dau- ghter became wife	De- pendent became head/wife	Ap- peared	All
	No change in family	Change; not in head/ wife									
-2.00 or less	2	1	4	6	2	0	8	5	13	4	3
-1.00 - -1.99	4	3	4	8	10	0	7	6	14	6	5
- .50 - - .99	4	3	9	11	2	0	6	8	8	5	4
- .01 - - .49	9	10	13	12	7	29	11	10	11	12	10
+ 0 - + .49	24	24	22	20	12	29	16	10	15	21	23
+ .50 - + .99	21	18	15	13	12	4	13	13	8	17	18
+1.00 - +1.99	23	22	18	18	19	1	21	23	18	22	22
+2.00 - +2.99	7	10	11	6	16	17	11	13	7	8	9
+3.00 or more	6	8	4	6	20	19	8	12	5	5	7
Total	100	99	100	100	100	99	101	100	99	100	101
Percent of sample	39.0	34.8	5.6	2.9	1.4	0.2	2.4	2.4	3.0	8.2	100
Number of cases	5443	6252	1106	387	195	20	291	292	446	1708	16,140

SUMMARY

There is a very large amount of change in family composition and in the number of major earners in the family over a relatively short four-year span. These changes have dramatic effects on economic status. For many individuals, such as children, they are changes resulting from the decisions of others. While much of the change is the expected and regular life cycle process, not all of it is, and the *timing* of the standard changes may well be affected by environmental conditions and individual motives and purposes. Much more needs to be done to sort out these marginal effects, now overwhelmed by the basic demographic changes.

Chapter 3

WAGE RATES OF HEADS AND WIVES

INTRODUCTION

We found in Chapter 1 that nearly 70% of the differences in total family income are a result of differences in the amount that the head of the family earns. The earnings of the wife account for only 8% of the income variation among all families, but for about 16% of the income variation among families where the wife works. Changes over time in the combined earnings of the head and wife account for 75% of the change in a family's income over these five years. Whether or not a family is in poverty, then, is in large part dependent on the amount of these earnings.

The elements that determine differences in earnings have been the subject of many previous studies, especially those focusing on education. Income from labor is a result of two distinct factors: a) the wage rate a person is able to earn and b) the hours a person is willing and able to work. Table 3.1 shows that, for the population of families where the head is employed, differences in earnings result about equally from differences in hours and differences in wage rates. For wives, more of the variation is due to hours since many wives work half time or less.

The nature of the mechanism of income determination is revealed better when we look at wage rates and hours separately. We do so for two reasons. First, some factors may influence only one of these variables. Second, at least for men, higher wage rates are associated with fewer hours worked, so that by looking at earnings we would tend to underestimate the influence of factors affecting only wage rates. For example, if men with greater ability receive higher wage rates but if higher wage rates also mean that men will work somewhat less, the influence of ability on total earnings will appear to be less than it is on wage rates. For these reasons the present chapter deals only with what determines the wage rates earned by heads and wives, while Chapter 4 is concerned with what determines the hours that the family members work and the relationships between

TABLE 3.1

Relative Importance of the Components of Head's Labor Income
for Those Who Worked in 1971

$$\underline{B^2}$$

Hours	.45
Wage rates	.41

Correlation between hours and wage rates .16

Relative Importance of the Components of Wife's Labor Income
for Those Who Worked in 1971

$$\underline{B^2}$$

Hours	.69
Wage rates	.24

Correlation between hours and wage rates .07

MTR1071

wage rates and hours.

In the first section of this chapter we discuss some of the issues to be examined and establish a framework for the analysis. We then study the five-year average wage rates of men and women to determine who receives low wage rates. Although we will ignore year-to-year changes, we shall take advantage of the panel by averaging out random "noise" over the five years so that the true static relationship will be easier to see. In the fourth section, we examine the wage rates of young people who leave home during this period and are just starting to work. The last section looks at the trend in wage rates over time for those who have low, medium, and high wage rates in the middle of these five years; we examine who changes their earning power and whether the mechanisms for change are different for the poor than for the nonpoor. All of the final models tested were formulated by searching with only half of the sample for the most important relationships. Thus, we are much more certain that the effects we estimate using the full sample are not just capitalizing on chance.[1]

---

[1] See Appendix A for a more detailed description of this procedure.

ANALYSIS

I. The Model

One of the most important issues to consider is the role of background in
determining what wage rates a person earns. Intergenerational transmission of
poverty may operate by restricting access to high paying jobs for children of
lower status parents, or by restricting access to the education needed for these
jobs. Another aspect of a person's background is his mental ability. The results of other studies investigating the influence of intelligence on earnings
are contradictory. Some have found no effects while others discovered a small
but significant difference. However, all the previous data have been based on
special groups in the population (veterans, army rejects, geniuses). Although
the test administered to the respondents of this panel study has limitations, it
is the first to measure mental ability for a sample representing the whole population of heads of households where detailed income data have also been collected.

The role of education in the determination of income is also important to
investigate. A great deal of emphasis has been placed on education as a means of
getting out of poverty through programs ranging from Head Start to the Job Corps.
Several recent studies have questioned this strategy and have pointed to the fact
that while education has become more equal in recent years, the distribution of
income has not. Some authors, such as Jencks (1972), have gone so far as to say
that the equalization of education would have no appreciable effect on equalizing
earnings and that chance has determined much of the current inequitable distribution of income. A further hypothesis presented by Thurow and Lucas (1972) con-
tends that the U.S. economy is not characterized so much by wage-competition as
by competition for specific jobs. The employers use education as a screening
device to ration the high paying jobs. The increase in the number of college
workers, it is argued, has resulted in employers requiring college credentials
for jobs formerly available to high school graduates. This chapter attempts to
discover what effect education has on hourly earnings and to determine if there
are some interactions with other variables which might explain why more equal
education has not been observed to be associated with more equal earnings over
time. We also investigate whether education has any independent effect or
whether its apparent influence is simply due to its high correlation with background or with occupation.[1]

---

[1] Recent work by Duncan, Featherman, and Duncan (1968) has indicated that the effect of education is more than that of background and that background has no
direct effect on wages, but Bowles (1972) disagrees and concludes that the

Much of the discussion of earnings has centered on the determinants of the supply side of labor. The effects of education and IQ are believed to increase the marginal productivity of labor. Wage rates also reflect varying demand conditions both for labor itself and for the resulting products. Much of the work in the Fifties did look at the effects of demand: specifically the relative importance of industry concentration and unionization since these represented deviations from the classic competition theory. A recent article by Wachtel and Betsey (1972) renews interest in demand conditions and shows that they do have a substantial influence on wage rates. The effects of demand conditions are very important to explore since the varying conditions in different geographic areas are at least in part subject to change by public policy.

The model we shall test in this chapter is based on the following set of hypotheses:

a) The amount of education a person obtains depends on his background, intelligence, and motivation.

b) These same three variables plus education determine what occupation a person works in.

c) Background, intelligence, motivation, education, occupation, and local demand conditions finally determine what wage rate a person receives.

This model can be represented by three equations:

Education = f (Background, intelligence, motivation)

Occupation = g (Background, intelligence, motivation, education)

Wage Rates = h (Background, intelligence, motivation, education, occupation, demand)

The direction of causation is fairly clear for the education and wage equations. The choice of education may depend upon occupational aspirations, however, so the recursiveness is suspect for this equation. However, the main effect is probably the one specified in this system.

We shall not try to estimate all three of these relationships; Chapter 7 is concerned with the exact determinants of educational attainment. Instead, we can infer the mechanism described by the full model by first estimating the wage equation using only background variables. Education is then added, then occupation, and finally, the demand conditions. If growing up in the South, for example, affects wage rates when we are considering only other background measures, but does not have an effect when education is also controlled for, this indicates that having a southern background influences wage rates only insofar as it determines how much education a person receives. We might then conclude that

education effect only reflects social class and that social class has a strong independent impact on earnings.

TABLE 3.2

Simple Correlations with Five-Year Average Wage Rate and Regression Variables –
Male Heads of Households[a]

Background

Age	.05
Age$_2$	.02
Age less than or equal to 30	-.15
Grew up on farm	-.25
Grew up in city	.23
Father's occupation	.22
Father's education	.18
Veteran	.17
Race	-.14
Motivation	.18
Low test score	-.22
High test score	.25

Education

Education	.44
Education, High Test Score	[b]
Education, Veteran	[b]
Education, Grew up in city	[b]
Sibling has less education	.16
Education, age less than or equal to 30	[b]

Occupation

Professional	[c]
Managers	.25
Self-employed	-.04
Clerical, Sales	-.04
Craftsmen	-.04
Operatives	-.14
Laborers	-.20
Farmers	-.19
Misc., Armed services	-.03

Demand

Tenure	.16
Large city	.25
Small town	-.24
Union	.02
County wage	.18
Industry	
Agriculture, Mining	-.21
Manufacturing, non-durables	.02
Manufacturing, durables	[c]
Construction	.01
Trade	-.06
Finance	.08
Services	.07
Government	-.0004
North East	[c]
North Central	.04
South	-.17
West	.02
Education, union	[b]
Education, large city	[b]

[a]The sample used includes males who were heads of households from 1968 to 1972 and who worked at least 250 hours each year. There are 2186 such cases

[b]The simple correlation with an interacted variable is not meaningful and so is not presented here.

[c]Other categories were expressed as deviations from this variable so it was not explicitly included in the regression.

MTR6027

if people from the South had the same education as those from other regions, they would not receive lower wages than others with similar characteristics.

The measure of wage rate that will be used is generated by dividing total annual labor income by annual hours worked. This variable contains a certain amount of measurement error resulting from errors in reporting either hours worked or income earned, but errors in the dependent variable should not bias the estimates of the mechanism of wage determination. This average wage rate is, of course, a combination of those received on a person's main job, for overtime, and on any second jobs. The relationships between the sizes of these different wage rates will be considered in the next chapter. Historically, women have faced a very different labor market than men and, although there have been changes in recent years, many variables still have different effects for men than for women. Therefore, the determinants of wage rates will be estimated separately for male heads of households and for wives and female heads.

II. Average Wage Rates for Male Heads of Households

Table 3.2 contains the explanatory variables we shall consider along with their simple correlation with five-year average wage rate.[1] Taken together, they explain 43% of the variation among the wage rates that men earn. Further, each of the four categories of variables -- background, education, occupation, and demand -- seems to have an important and independent impact on earning capacity. The following table shows the fraction of the variance explained and the net contribution of the categories as they are added to the regression.

TABLE 3.3

Fraction of the Variance in Wage Rates Explained
by the Recursive System - Male Heads of Households[a]

	R^2	Partial R^2
Background	.22	
Adding Education	.32	.13
Adding Occupation	.37	.08
Adding Demand	.43	.10

---

[a]The sample used is males who were heads of households from 1968-1972 and who worked at least 250 hours each year.

---

[1]The correlations among some of the important predictors are given in Appendix 3.1.

BACKGROUND

A man's background is very important in determining what wage rate he receives: background variables alone explain over a fifth of the variation observed. Some of this effect, of course, is due to the fact that background determines both how much education a man has and what occupation he works in, but much of the effect is independent of these factors.

Of all the background characteristics which determine who has high wages and who has low wages, race is the most significant and has the largest effect (see Table 3.4). Blacks have less education than whites, even considering the other background variables, and they also tend to work in lower paying occupations than whites with similar educations. Beyond the lower wage rates that could be expected because of lower education and occupation, we would still estimate that blacks earn about $.40 less per hour than similar whites. But the fact that many blacks live in large cities where wages tend to be higher means that not accounting for local demand conditions leads to an understatement of the true black-white differential. Controlling on background, education, occupation, industry, as well as local area conditions, we estimate that a black man on the average earns $.51 an hour less than a white man in similar circumstances. If they both worked an average number of hours during a year, the black family would receive about $1100 less from the head's earnings than the white family for no other reason than the difference in race.

This does not mean that the efforts of the past decade to alleviate the racial differentials have been useless. Indeed, there is evidence that wage rates of young blacks have been rising faster in recent years than wage rates of whites.[1] It does mean, however, that this success must be viewed with the knowledge that there is still a very large gap and that we are still far from the goal of eliminating racial discrimination.

The area where the head grew up also has an important effect on his wage rate. Those who grew up in a rural area earn an average of $.55 an hour less than those from large cities, even controlling for the fact that they tend to have less education and work in lower paying occupations (such as farming).[2] Growing up in the South was originally included as a background variable but it has no independent effect on wage rates when we control education and current location.

---

[1]See Sections IV and V of this chapter.

[2]Lansing and Morgan (1967) found evidence that moving to the city leads to improvement but not to catching up with those who grew up in the city.

TABLE 3.4

Regression Coefficients on Average Wage Rates for
Background, Motivation and Test Scores - Male Heads of Households

	Alone		Adding Education		Adding Occupation		Adding Demand	
	Coefficient	t-ratio	Coefficient	t-ratio	Coefficient	t-ratio	Coefficient	t-ratio
Black	-.84	(4.4)	-.54	(3.1)	-.41	(2.3)	-.51	(2.9)
Grew up on Farm	-.50	(3.9)	-.53	(4.4)	-.40	(3.4)	-.28	(2.4)
Grew up in City	.74	(6.2)	.50	(4.5)	.49	(4.5)	.27	(2.5)
Father's Occupation	.07	(2.6)	.01	(0.5)	-.005	(0.2)	-.005	(0.2)
Father's Education	.18	(5.2)	.05	(1.6)	.06	(1.7)	.07	(2.1)
Age	.27	(6.7)	.31	(8.2)	.30	(8.1)	.22	(6.1)
Age^2	-.003	(6.6)	-.003	(7.9)	-.003	(7.8)	-.002	(5.8)
Whether under 30	-.24	(1.0)	.20	(0.9)	.03	(0.1)	.09	(0.4)
Veteran	.20	(1.9)	.03	(0.3)	-.12	(1.2)	-.11	(1.2)
Motivation	.09	(4.4)	.03	(1.8)	.03	(1.8)	.01	(0.7)
High Test Score	.92	(7.3)	.26	(2.6)	.31	(2.6)	.38	(3.5)
Low Test Score	-.58	(4.4)	-.29	(2.3)	-.21	(1.7)	-.24	(2.0)

$$R^2 = .22$$

There has been a great deal of discussion about the effect of the father's status on the economic success of his children and the extent to which there is intergenerational transmission of poverty by virtue of a class structure. The two variables measuring characteristics of the father in this model -- his education and his occupation -- produce different results. The father's education does exert a significant effect on his son's wage rate over and above the son's own educational attainment. There is evidently some extra amount of learning which occurs in better educated homes which is useful later on in the market place although the effect may also be a result of differing attitudes and values. This result suggests that compensatory programs for children, such as Head Start, may well help to narrow the earnings gap for children with less educated parents. The father's occupation, however, has no observable effect on the son's wage rate. Although these variations probably contain reporting errors which bias the estimates downward, the relative sizes of their effects suggest that the intergenerational transmission of earning capacity operates by imparting more productivity to children of more highly educated parents rather than by imparting advantages to children with fathers in more prestigious occupations.

The age profiles implied by these regressions are presented in Figure 3.1. The line representing the age effects in the third equation looks like the profile observed in other studies: wage rates increase with age but at a declining rate and, finally, the older groups earn less. The fourth equation, however, shows an important difference. After demand conditions are added to the regression, the slope for the oldest workers remains positive, indicating the older workers are less mobile geographically or less likely to leave unprofitable industries. Because this immobility is associated with age, inadequately controlling for these effects biases the age profile downward. This finding helps reconcile the typical cross-section observation that wages decline after 55 with the longitudinal observation that even older workers experience income increases on the average, although this difference can also be explained by different growth rates for various age groups. We have also included a measure of whether or not the head is under 30, because there is a different effect of education for the young which will be discussed later. However, there is no significant difference in the age profile for those having recently entered the labor force.

Being a veteran is expected to have two opposing effects on wage rates. The time spent in the armed services subtracts from experience in civilian jobs and this is expected to decrease wages. However, the training given to veterans may be useful in other jobs. Although there is some evidence that veterans tend to get into higher paying occupations, relative to others with similar education,

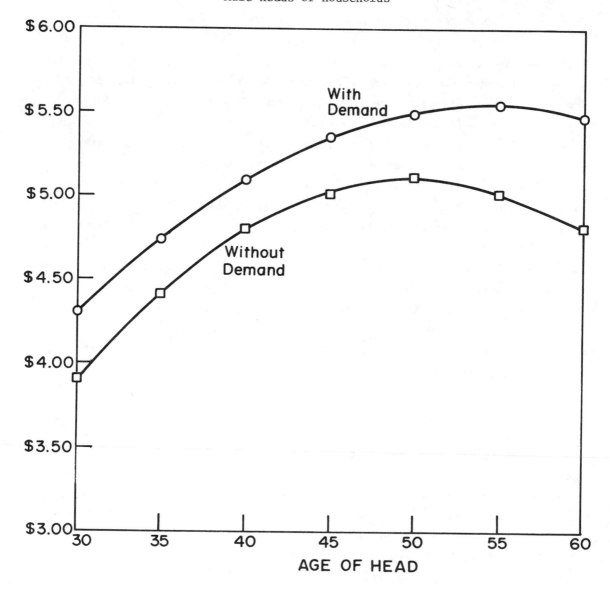

FIGURE 3.1

Age Profiles With and Without Demand Conditions,
Male Heads of Households

within those occupations they tend to earn about $.11 an hour less than non-veterans.

Achievement motivation is included as a background measure because it is a permanent personality trait, at least in theory. However, our measure is taken at the end of this period and may to some extent reflect the results of education and economic success or failure. The motivation scale combines measures of power-autonomy, mastery, and future orientation which have a fairly consistent pattern across heterogeneous populations.[1] Among those who are of similar background and ability, we have found evidence that the more highly motivated attain more education. Beyond that, motivation does not seem to make any difference in what wage rates a man earns. We shall see later, in Chapter 7, Volume II, that a man's motivation does make a difference in other, nonmoney aspects of his job.

The cognitive ability measure administered to this sample is a sentence completion test. Although it is primarily a verbal measure, it correlated well with perceptual performance measures. Differences in these test scores indeed explain a significant amount of the variance in wage rates, controlling for the fact that those with lower scores also tend to have less education. Those who scored in the lower fifth on the test earn over $.60 an hour less than those in the top fifth who have similar backgrounds, education, occupations, and live in similar areas.

It was originally hypothesized that cognitive ability would have an influence on the effect of age. It seemed likely that early wage rates might not reflect ability differences but that the more able would be more efficient in acquiring new skills and would increase their productivity more rapidly than those with lower ability. Such an age-ability relationship was found in other studies.[2] However, the estimated effects were very small and the variation around the pattern was large, so this interaction was not included in the final model.

EDUCATION

Education is very important in determining the wage rate a person earns. It explains an additional 13% of the variance beyond that explained by background, much higher than that found in other studies.[3] It was from observing

---

[1]See Appendix F for a detailed description of this measure.

[2]See Hause (1972).

[3]Griliches and Mason (1972), for example, found a partial R^2 of .07 for education and Bowles found this to be even smaller at .02. Our measure includes the effects of the background-education interactions but their additional explanatory power legitimately belongs to education since the full detail of background was

another data source where education did not have an additional influence on earnings that Bowles concluded:[1] "most of the impact of years of schooling on earnings appears to be a direct transmission of economic status from one generation
to the next." This strong conclusion is simply not borne out by the panel data
in this study.[2] Education does have an impact on the wage rate a man earns, and
it does represent a mechanism for changing his status from that of his father.

The overall effect of education in the full model is $.40 an hour for each
category of education attained.[3] The ratio of this coefficient to its standard
error is 11, making it by far the most significant variable in the model. However, this overall effect is an average of varying payoffs. Some background
variables influence not only the *amount* of education a person receives but also
the *effect* of his education on his earning capacity. There appear to be many
interactions between education and other variables that modify the role of education in determining wage rates (see Table 3.5).[4]

It is often assumed that there is an interaction between education and mental ability. In fact, human capital theory states that there must be. Hause
(1972) pointed out that if ability and education had simply additive effects on

---

given in equation 1 and the only new information added is education. Nevertheless, the partial R^2 of education, without interactions, is about .10, still
very substantial.

[1] See Bowles (1972). Bowles' data had been adjusted for differences in measurement errors in background and education and this adjustment may account for some
of this discrepancy.

[2] Although the dependent variable used here is wage rates and Bowles was looking
at annual earnings, education also has a positive effect on work hours, as will
be shown in Chapter 4. Thus, it seems very unlikely that the negative covariance between wage rates and hours is large enough to account for the difference
in partial R^2s.

[3] Education is measured by the amount of schooling the head attained, but the absolute number of years of education is a poor scale of educational attainment
since the difference between ten and eleven years, for example, has a smaller
impact on earning ability than the difference between eleven and twelve. Education has been rescaled, therefore, as follows:

0. Less than 6 grades and cannot read
1. Less than 6 grades
2. 6-8 grades
3. 9-11 grades
4. High school graduate
5. Non-academic training beyond 12 grades
6. Some college
7. College degree
8. Graduate degree

[4] These have been specified as dummy interactions, where the variable takes on the
level of education if the person is a union member, for example, and zero if he
is not. The coefficients obtained can then be interpreted as deviation from the
general education coefficient which represents the payoff to education for the
excluded group. For further descriptions of dummy variable interactions, see
Appendix D.

TABLE 3.5

Regression Coefficients on Average Wage Rates
for Education and Education Interactions - Male Heads of Households

	With Background		Adding Occupation		Adding Demand	
	Coef-fi-cient	t-ratio	Coef-fi-cient	t-ratio	Coef-fi-cient	t-ratio
Education	.39	(8.7)	.30	(6.6)	.34	(6.6)
Education, high test score	.29	(4.5)	.27	(4.2)	.24	(4.0)
Education, veteran	.08	(1.6)	.07	(1.5)	.08	(1.8)
Education, grew up in city	.15	(2.7)	.14	(2.6)	.18	(3.3)
Education, less than 30	-.43	(5.6)	-.39	(4.7)	-.37	(4.7)
Sibling has less education	-.23	(2.1)	-.20	(1.9)	-.22	(2.2)
Education, union member					-.27	(4.7)
Education, lives in large city					.04	(0.8)

$$R^2 = .32$$

wages, then those with lower ability would have the greatest incentive to acquire
more education since the payoff to education would be the same for all, but the
foregone earnings of those with higher ability would be greater. The estimated
effect of education for those with highest test scores is $.24 more per hour per
category of education than men with medium scores, or a total of $.58. Those
with the lowest scores, however, do not appear to have an appreciably different
payoff to education than those with medium scores. Thus, while it is true that
the greatest return to education is to those with greatest ability, men with
lower ability still benefit from increased education.

Veterans also have a different payoff to education: they earn an additional $.80 an hour for each category of education they have compared to non-veterans.
This may be a result of the training they have received which augments their productivity or a result of employers' requiring veteran status as an additional
credential, where the combination of high education and being a veteran is particularly desirable.

It is sometimes argued that being in the armed services helps the poor by
giving them training they would not ordinarily receive. These data show, however,
that those who already have some advantages are helped more. We found earlier
that veterans experience a decreased wage, but this interaction means that those
with a great deal of education more than make up this difference while those with
only average education do not.

We estimate different returns to education depending on the size of the
place where the head grew up. Urban and rural backgrounds partially reflect differences in the quality of education and partially reflect sociological differences. Growing up in a large city does have a significant influence on the effect of education: the education coefficient is $.18 more per hour for each
category of education attained.

Age is also often assumed to have an effect on the benefit of education.
There are fewer college graduates among older workers so their earnings may be
proportionately greater than those of the more numerous graduates of today.
Also, from a human capital approach, the more highly educated, as they have more
experience in the labor force, may be more efficient at acquiring skills. We do
not find such an interaction across all age groups: men who are forty-five, for
example, do not have a different payoff to education than those who are fifty-
five. Men who are under thirty, however, do not experience any benefit from
education. This is probably a result of the more educated having less labor
force experience at these young ages and also of the young not being permanently
settled in a serious career. It indicates that studies investigating the payoffs

to such programs as Job Corps, by looking at their immediate impact on earnings, may underestimate their longer run effects. It is not until the person has more experience in the labor force that educational differences show up.

Having less education than his oldest brother (or sister, if he had no brother) was included as a measure of a person's motivation. It was originally hypothesized that those who achieve more education than their siblings would also tend to earn more. The opposite appears to be the case. Those who have more education than their siblings earn $.22 an hour less than those whose education is equal to or less than that of their siblings.

We have so far been looking at how background influences the effectiveness of a person's education. Two measures of current status also were tested for their interaction with education. Union membership has a very interesting effect. Although union members with a high school education earn about $.30 an hour more than non-union members, those with more or less education have only slightly different wage rates. Essentially, those working in union jobs do not experience any benefit to education.

There has been conflicting evidence as to whether wage differentials between skill levels are higher or lower in depressed areas. Some studies have found compression of earnings in areas where jobs are scarce and others have found that the lower education groups are hurt more. The size of the city in which one currently resides has a fairly large positive effect on wage rates and thus serves as a good proxy for the presence of job opportunities. However, we do not find any significant effect of city size on wage differences between skill levels.

We originally investigated the possibility that education had a different effect for whites than for blacks. Harrison (1972) found that the payoffs for blacks acquiring education was significantly less than for whites. These data do not confirm this. The estimate of the difference was very small and the variation around the pattern very large.

OCCUPATION, TENURE, AND DEMAND CONDITIONS

The occupation a man works in is a major determinant of his wage rate. The net contribution of these occupational variables is substantial, even controlling for differences in education.[1] Farmers are the worst off, earning $1.17 an hour less than the average, and, at the other extreme, managers earn $1.03 an hour more than average (see Table 3.6). Originally it was thought that occupation

---

[1] The correlation between education and occupation treated as a scale is .56, but this is not so large that we cannot distinguish their independent effects.

TABLE 3.6

Regression Coefficients on Average Wage Rate for Occupation,
Tenure, and Demand Conditions - Male Heads of Households

Occupation	With Background and Education		Adding Demand	
	Coef-fi-cient	t-ratio	Coef-fi-cient	t-ratio
Professionals	.43	a	.49	a
Managers	.96	(5.7)	1.03	(6.1)
Self-employed	-.46	(2.2)	-.27	(1.3)
Clerical, Sales	-.51	(2.8)	-.39	(2.1)
Craftsmen	.14	(0.8)	-.04	(0.2)
Operatives	-.14	(0.7)	-.25	(1.3)
Laborers	-.94	(4.1)	-.74	(3.2)
Farmers	-1.59	(5.8)	-1.17	(3.2)
Misc., Armed Services	-.35	(1.0)	-.01	(0.03)
Tenure			.03	(5.3)
County Wage for Unskilled Labor			.17	(3.1)
Large City			.45	(3.8)
Small Town			-.21	(1.5)
Northeast			-.04	a
North Central			.14	(1.2)
South			-.06	(0.5)
West			-.08	(1.8)
Union			.30	(2.7)
Industry				
Agriculture Mining			-.19	(0.6)
Manufacturing Durables			.19	a
Manufacturing, Nondurables			.07	(0.4)
Construction, Transportation			.41	(2.9)
Trade			-.33	(2.1)
Finance			.27	(1.1)
Services			.23	(1.5)
Government			-.45	(2.1)

$$R^2 = .37 \qquad R^2 = .43$$

_____

[a]Other categories were expressed as deviations from this variable so its
standard deviation is not available.

would affect how wage rates change with age, with the lower occupations offering less opportunity to learn new skills so that experience would be less valuable than in the better paid occupations. We find no significant effect however.

Experience as a determinant of income does not fit neatly into the categories of variables we are examining. Age, representing overall labor market experience, can be thought of as a background measure but seniority on a specific job cannot. We include seniority with the demand variables for convenience, but it does not alter the results if it is included with the occupation measures. The influence of seniority on wage rates is statistically very significant, but the size of the effect is smaller than might be expected. We estimate that those who have had their job less than a year earn about $.10 an hour less than those who have been working six or seven years in the same job. Most of the benefit from experience comes from overall labor force experience rather than from time spent in a specific job.

The conditions which affect the demand for labor in different sections of the country are represented by several local measures and by institutional factors. The wage rate for unskilled labor in the county[1] is the most direct measure of geographic variations in economic conditions we include, and it has a significant effect in explaining differences in wage rates for all workers, not just the unskilled. Other local variables, such as the county unemployment rate, the labor force composition of the county, or the percent of poor living in the area, do not have an effect and are not included in the final regression.

City size and region represent geographical differences in job opportunities and in the cost of living. City size has a large positive effect: men living in large cities (100,000 or more) earn over $.60 an hour more than men with similar qualifications who are living in small towns of less than 25,000 people. The regional differences are fairly large but there is also a great deal of variation so the effects are not statistically significant.

Union membership and industry are the two institutional factors included. They are considered demand conditions on the theory that a person chooses an occupation which can be practiced in several industries, which may or may not be unionized depending on the jobs available. This is not always true, of course, and some occupations may be industry specific, for instance, even within our broad categories. Men who belong to a union earn about $.30 an hour more than those who don't, but this benefit is accompanied by a loss of any education related differentials, as we discussed earlier. The industry in which one works

[1]This measure was collected by a separate mail questionnaire sent to state unemployment compensation officials for the counties in which the respondents live.

has less effect on wage rates than does occupation, but there are some important differences: those working in the construction industry are the best paid while the trade and government industries are paid the least.

CONCLUSIONS

What factors determine who earns a low wage rate and who earns a high one? All four factors that we considered are important. Background has an impact on wage rates independent of its influence on the amount of schooling a person has and on his occupation. Race has a particularly large effect with blacks earning $.51 an hour less than whites in similar circumstances. We also find large differences in earning capacity that are associated with differences in mental ability. Motivation, on the other hand, does not make much difference.

Education is the most important determinant of a person's wage rate, but the effect of education is modified by other characteristics such as ability, urban background, age, and whether the person belongs to a union. These interactions may provide some explanation of the fact that incomes are not becoming more equal as more people become better educated. If those groups who have recently received more education are the groups that have a lower payoff to schooling, then the disparity in incomes would not decrease as rapidly as the overall effect would predict. However, almost all of the groups receive some benefit to education so we cannot dismiss it as a means for increasing income and reducing inequality.

Occupation is also an important determinant of a person's wage rate, as are the characteristics of the area in which he lives, the industry in which he works, and whether he has a union job.

The question remains of how well we can explain who has low wage rates. Table 3.7 shows the actual wage rate a person earns compared to the wage rate we would expect on the basis of his background, education, occupation, and place of residence. A large part of the poverty population is predictably poor. On the

TABLE 3.7

Average Wage Rate by Predicted Average Wage Rate,
Male Heads of Households

Predicted Wage Rate	Low: (Less than $3.25)	Medium: ($3.25–$4.74)	High: ($4.75 or more)
Low	55%	14%	2%
Medium	35%	48%	20%
High	10%	38%	78%
	100%	100%	100%

basis of factors we have studied, 55% of those within the low wage rate group could be expected to be there. They are, for example, young, poorly educated, black, or have a combination of these characteristics. On the other hand, 45% of the low wage population would be expected to earn medium or even high wage rates. How can we account for this disparity? Other aspects of ability or background may play a role. It is also very likely that a large component of chance determines who earns low wage rates and who does not. Nonetheless, if everyone were equal in characteristics such as education and if the effects of other variables such as race were eliminated, over 40% of the variation in wage rates among men would be eliminated.

III. Average Wage Rates for Wives and Female Heads of Households

Most studies on earnings have dealt primarily with males or have included only single females. This panel study has collected earnings data for both female heads and wives, so we are able to combine them to investigate the labor market that most women face. We have included women who were either heads or wives for all five years and women who changed marital status during the interviewing period. We have restricted our investigation (as we did for men) to those who worked at least 250 hours each year. In doing so we eliminate those only marginally in the work force on the grounds that their wage rates may be quite different.

Very few background measures are available for wives. We have not collected data on their parental families, nor were the motivation or ability tests administered to them.[1] The location where a wife grew up and her father's education, however, are generally quite similar to the parental location and status of her husband, since people tend to marry those with like backgrounds. Thus, we substitute the husband's background information for these variables, although doing so obviously introduces a great deal of measurement error.[2] Since the number of variables used to predict wage rates of women is restricted, we also calculated the regressions on male wage rates using this same set of variables so direct comparisons can be made. Table 3.8 lists the variables used, along with their simple correlations with the wage rates of female heads and wives.[3]

---

[1]As this study continues, it would be wise to interview the wife one year to obtain this information.

[2]For young women who split off and got married during this period, the correlation between father's and father-in-law's education is .37.

[3]The correlations among some of the important predictors are given in Appendix 3.5.

142

TABLE 3.8

Simple Correlation With Five Year Average Wage Rate and Regression Variables –
Wives and Female Heads of Households[a]

Background		Education		Occupation		Marital Status	
Age$_2$	-.06	Education	.55	Professionals	c	Whether Single	.07
Age	-.07	Education, less than or equal to 30	b	Managers	.12		
Less than or equal to 30	-.02			Self Employed	-.06	Demand	
Grew up on Farm	-.22			Clerical	-.01	Large City	-.16
Grew up in City	.22			Craftswomen	-.01	Small Town	.16
Father's Education	.18			Operatives	-.12	Male Wage in County	.08
Race	-.18			Laborers	-.37	Female Wage in County	-.01
						Northeast	c
						North Central	.03
						South	-.18
						West	.04
						Industry	
						Agriculture, Mining	-.04
						Manufacturing, durables	.06
						Manufacturing, nondurables	c
						Construction	.11
						Trade	-.18
						Finance	.003
						Services	.09
						Government	.10
						Education, large city	b
						Education, small town	b

[a] The sample used includes women who were either wives or heads of households from 1968 to 1972 and who worked at least 250 hours each year. There are 1031 such cases.

[b] The simple correlation with an interacted variable is not meaningful and so is not presented here.

[c] Other categories were expressed as deviations from this variable so it was not explicitly included in the regression.

BACKGROUND AND EDUCATION

Background alone explains as much of the variation among wage rates for women as for men (see Table 3.9). However, for a woman background mainly influences her wage rate by affecting the amount of education she receives, the occupation she works in, and the area in which she lives. After these variables have been accounted for, a woman's background is less important than a man's in determining the wage she earns. This is especially true of her father's education and the size of the place where she grew up.[1]

Age has an important effect on wage rates but a women's wage increases much more slowly with her age than a man's. For example, a forty-year old man earns $.70 an hour more than a similar man 10 years younger. A forty-year old woman earns only about $.18 more per hour than a woman who is thirty. There are at least three reasons why this might be so. First, age may not be as good a proxy for experience for women since they may have been out of the labor force for several years due to family responsibilities. This is less true for the single women in the sample, however, and all the individuals considered have been working at least five years. Second, it is possible that women tend to be in more "dead-end" kinds of jobs where they have less opportunity to acquire new skills and be promoted. Third, there have been changes in the labor market in recent years which may have benefited younger women more than the older women workers. Without more information on job history for women, these three possibilities cannot be distinguished.

There appears to be the same amount of racial discrimination for women as for men. Blacks recieve wage rates which are about 10% less than whites with the same education, in the same occupation, and living in the same place. The most important influence of a woman's education is on which occupation she works in. Within occupations, differences in wage rates associated with education are considerably less for women than for men: a woman earns $.22 an hour for each education category she has attained, a payoff which is 55% of the benefit education has for men. Education has an even smaller effect for women under thirty, although it is much larger than that for young men. Evidently, young women get settled into serious jobs more quickly than young men do, so the benefit to their education shows up earlier. Education, nonetheless, is the most important variable in distinguishing women who earn high wage rates from those who earn low wage rates.

---

[1]These variables are less well measured for women than men, but as we shall see in Section IV, more direct measures also have little independent influence.

TABLE 3.9

Regression Coefficients on Wage Rates for Background and Education
for Wives and Female Heads of Households

	Background		Adding Education		Adding Occupation		Adding Demand	
	Coef-ficient	t-ratio	Coef-ficient	t-ratio	Coef-ficient	t-ratio	Coef-ficient	t-ratio
Age	.08	(2.2)	.07	(2.2)	.07	(2.4)	.06	(2.1)
Age^2	−.001	(2.6)	−.0007	(2.4)	−.0007	(2.4)	−.0006	(2.1)
Less than or equal to 30	−.17	(0.8)	−.17	(1.0)	−.10	(0.6)	−.09	(0.6)
Grew up farm	−.30	(3.1)	−.26	(3.1)	−.24	(3.1)	−.14	(1.9)
Grew up city	.48	(5.0)	.30	(3.6)	.27	(3.5)	.05	(0.6)
Father's education	.13	(5.4)	.003	(0.1)	−.005	(0.3)	−.003	(0.2)
Race	−.68	(5.8)	−.38	(3.7)	−.25	(2.5)	−.30	(3.1)
Education			.43	(18.4)	.28	(10.9)	.22	(7.0)
Education, less than or equal to 30			−.06	(0.8)	−.08	(1.4)	−.10	(1.7)

$$R^2 = .14 \qquad R^2 = .36$$

OCCUPATION AND DEMAND

A woman's occupation is also an important determinant of her hourly earnings. The set of occupational variables explains 13% more of the difference in wage rates than are explained by background and education. The predicted wage rates in various occupations for women along with the corresponding predictions for men are shown in Figure 3.2.[1] There is a fairly consistent male-female differential within each of the broad occupational categories. Professional women experience the least difference, but their wage rates are still on the average only 73% of those of men with similar qualifications.

The pattern of sex discrimination which this suggests is different from the racial discrimination mechansim which Bergmann (1971) found. She discovered that there were large racial differences among occupations and that blacks were much less likely to be in the higher paying jobs, but that there was not much discrimination on the basis of race *within* occupations. Women, however, seem to face both among-occupation and within-occupation differentials.

Marital status does not fit neatly into any one of the categories in the recursive model but may have an impact on wage rates. It is sometimes argued that women earn less because they are marginally attached to their jobs: that they enter the labor force if their husbands have a temporary decrease in income and leave when economic conditions improve, or that they leave because of family responsibilities. Since these arguments apply mostly to married women, it might be expected that single women would have relatively higher wage rates. This hypothesis is borne out by these data although the effect is small: single women earn about $.14 an hour more than married women and there is a large variation in this pattern.

The impact of conditions which influence demand is greater on a woman's wage rate than a man's. City size is particularly important. Not only do women do better in general in large cities, but the benefit to education is also increased. Figure 3.3 shows the predicted wage rates by various education levels for those living in medium and large cities. Women with college degrees can increase their wage rate by almost a dollar per hour by moving to a large city, while those with a high school diploma can only expect to make an additional $.50 an hour. Thus, the average college educated woman living in a large city earns about $3.75 an hour. This is still less than the $4.75 the average male high school graduate earns in these cities, but it appears that discrimination is less in the large metropolitan areas than elsewhere.

---

[1]These predicted wage rates control for differences in education, background, and demand conditions.

TABLE 3.10

Regression Coefficients on Wage Rates for Occupation, Marital Status,
and Demand Conditions – Wives and Female Heads of Households

	With Background and Education		Adding Demand	
Occupation	Coef-ficient	t-ratio	Coef-ficient	t-ratio
Professionals	.86	a	.93	a
Managers	.56	(3.0)	.65	(3.6)
Self employed	−.49	(1.9)	−.41	(1.6)
Clerical, Sales	−.09	(0.9)	−.13	(1.3)
Craftswomen	−.21	(0.7)	−.40	(1.5)
Operatives	−.04	(0.3)	−.20	(1.3)
Laborers	−.59	(4.9)	−.47	(4.3)
Whether Single			.14	(2.0)
Large City			.52	(3.3)
Small Town			−.24	(2.7)
Education, Large City			.12	(6.6)
Education, Small Town			−.003	(0.1)
Male Wage in County			.04	(1.1)
Comparison of Female Wage in County			−.04	(1.7)
Northeast			.16	a
North Central			.03	(0.3)
South			−.08	(0.8)
West			.09	(0.9)
Industry				
Agriculture, Mining			−.31	(1.1)
Manufacturing, Durables			.39	(3.0)
Manufacturing, Nondurables			.13	a
Construction			.68	(3.4)
Trade			−.28	(2.0)
Finance			.10	(0.5)
Services			−.09	(0.6)
Government			.27	(1.5)
	$R^2 = .45$		$R^2 = .52$	

---

[a] Other categories were expressed as deviations from this variable so its standard deviation is not available.

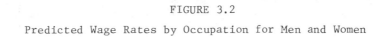

FIGURE 3.2

Predicted Wage Rates by Occupation for Men and Women

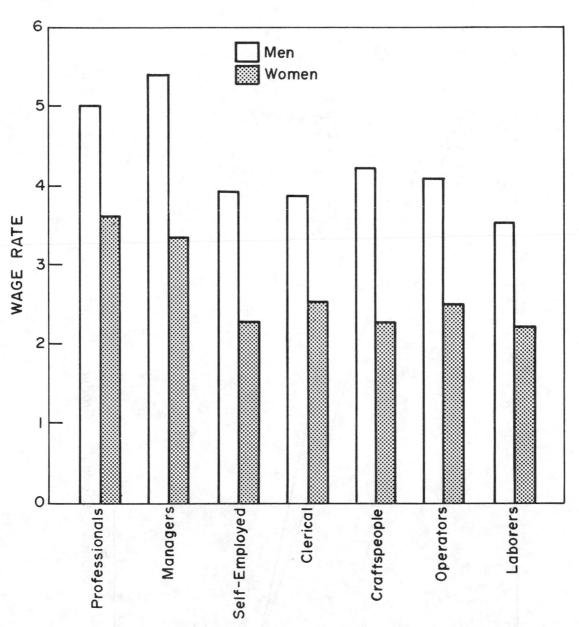

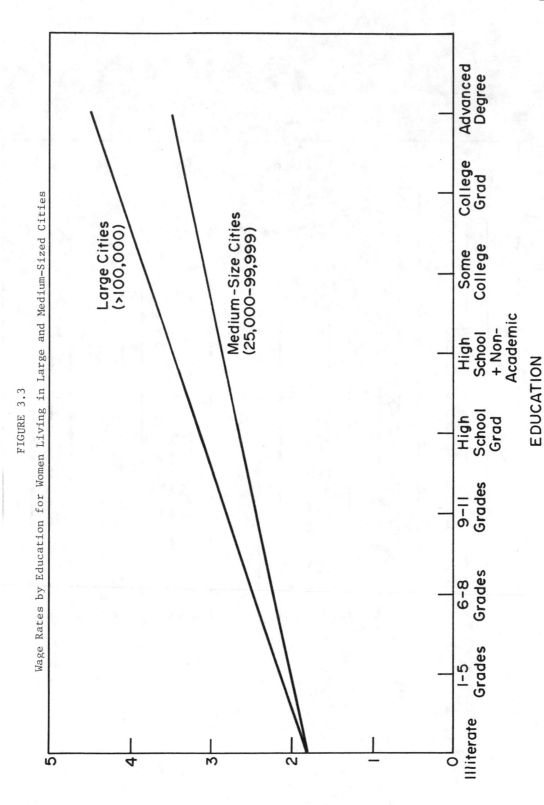

FIGURE 3.3

Wage Rates by Education for Women Living in Large and Medium-Sized Cities

We have included a measure not only of wage rates for unskilled men in the county but also of the extent to which the market for unskilled women is different. Neither of these measures has a significant influence on wage rates for women. As was true for men, there also do not appear to be important regional differences in wage rates.

The industry in which a woman works makes a large difference in the wage rate she earns. The patterns are nearly the same as they are for men, with construction industries paying best and agriculture and trade the worst. The absolute differences, however, are larger for women than for men.

CONCLUSIONS

In general, the mechanism that determines wage rates operates in the same way for women as it does for men. The difference occurs in the size of the benefits that women with various characteristics receive. Thus, women earn more as they acquire more experience, but at a much slower rate than do men. Similarly, although it is positively and statistically significant, the economic payoff to education for wives and female heads is 55% of the corresponding payoff for male heads of households. The predicted occupation wage rates show that women in higher status jobs are paid more than those in lower status occupations. But not only are there fewer women in these jobs, they are also paid less than men with similar characteristics.

The average wage rate for women is $2.70 an hour while men average $4.35 an hour. Some of this differential is due to the fact that women work in lower paying occupations, live in areas where jobs pay less, or have other characteristics that would mean lower wages for both men and women. However, much of the difference is simply due to the fact that women are paid less than men with similar qualifications in the same jobs. If women received the same wage as comparable men, their average wage rate would be about $3.75 an hour.[1]

Since many of the families who have experienced poverty during these five years are headed by women, it is useful to examine what effect sex discrimination has on the poor. Of course, many families are poor because the head does not have a job. Of those families whose average income/needs ratio is less than 1.5, only 20% of the female heads were employed for all five years. But 55% of these families would not be in poverty if the women had been paid wages comparable to

---

[1]This figure was arrived at by running similar regressions for both men and women. The actual wage received can be thought of as the sum of a predicted wage plus the unexplained deviation from that prediction. We have substituted the predicted male wage for the predicted female wage for each individual, but have retained the original unexplained portion from the regression for females.

men. About the same proportion of families with working wives would not be poor if there were no sex discrimination. Efforts to eliminate discrimination would not only tend to increase wages for those already working, but also would make it profitable for other women to find jobs. Equal pay for women would indeed have an important impact on the poverty population.

IV. Wage Rates of Splitoffs

Children who left home during this period were also interviewed. By studying the wage rates they received in 1971, we can investigate the following issues:

a. What determines the earning capacity of those workers just starting out in the labor market?

b. What effect does the quality of education have on wage rates? Most of these splitoffs are young (we restrict our investigation to those under 30) so that current measures of county expenditures per pupil and the average teacher salary are, in most cases, fairly good measures of the quality of education when they were in school.

c. What are the effects of background measures not ordinarily available on earning capacity? We found earlier that education has an important influence on wage rates over and above background differences. However, we may not have measured background as adequately as education. Since we have a great deal of information on the parental family for splitoffs, we can investigate the extent to which we must modify our earlier conclusions when we measure background more thoroughly. The additional background variables to be included are the parents' ability test score, motivation score, and the parental income in 1967. We also have, in most cases, the father's own report of his education and occupation.

For a young man, we find that experience is a very important determinant of the wage rate he receives (see Table 3.11).[1] Both age, which measures overall experience, and tenure on a specific job have larger effects for the young man than for all working men. We estimate, for example, that a person working at the same job for three years earns around $1.25 an hour more than a man with similar characteristics but three years younger and just starting out.

There is much less evidence of racial discrimination among younger men.

---

[1]The correlations among some of the important predictors are given in Appendix 3.3.

TABLE 3.11

Wage Rates for Male Splitoffs in 1971[a]

Background	With Old Background Variables		Adding New Background Variables and Quality of Education	
	Coefficient	t-ratio	Coefficient	t-ratio
Age	.18	(4.9)	.17	(4.5)
Grew up City	-.01	(0.1)	.03	(0.1)
Grew up Farm	.04	(0.2)	.06	(0.3)
Father's Education	-.03	(1.2)	-.04	(1.6)
Father's Occupation	.04	(0.7)	.002	(0.05)
Veteran	.03	(0.1)	-.17	(0.9)
Black	.63	(0.8)	.68	(0.8)
Motivation	.12	(3.5)	.11	(3.0)
Black, Motivation	-.10	(1.2)	-.09	(1.1)
Trust Index	.15	(1.9)	.13	(1.7)
Test Score	.02	(0.5)	.02	(0.4)
Education				
Education	.03	(0.5)	.01	(0.1)
Sibling less Education	-.31	(1.9)	-.25	(1.5)
Education, veteran	-.14	(1.8)	-.11	(1.5)
Occupation	.12	(2.7)	.13	(2.9)
Demand				
Tenure	.25	(3.7)	.23	(3.2)
City size	.10	(2.2)	.08	(1.7)
Union member	.73	(3.8)	.73	(3.9)
Northeast	.35	b	.36	b
North Central	.08	(0.4)	.10	(0.4)
South	-.25	(1.0)	-.25	(0.8)
West	.07	(0.3)	.04	(0.1)
Wage rate for unskilled labor in county	-.06	(0.7)	-.08	(0.8)
New Background Variables				
Parents' Motivation			.02	(0.6)
Parents' Test Score			-.01	(0.2)
Family Income in 1968			.0000	(3.2)
Quality of Education				
Expenditure per pupil			.0000	(0.1)
Average teacher salary			-.0000	(0.1)

$$R^2 = .37$$
$$\text{adjusted } R^2 = .32$$

$$R^2 = .39$$
$$\text{adjusted } R^2 = .32$$

[a] The sample consists of sons aged 18 to 30 who left home between 1969 and 1971 who are not currently in school or the armed forces and who worked at least 250 hours in 1971. There are 287 such cases.

[b] Other categories were expressed as deviations from this variable so its standard deviation is not available.

There is a very large variation in how blacks are paid relative to whites, but our best estimate is that young black men earn slightly more than whites with similar characteristics. This suggests that the efforts to increase opportunities for blacks have been successful in raising the wage rates for young black men.

Another striking difference between the determinants of wage rates for young men and those for all men is the role that attitudes play. In Section II we found that motivation had no independent influence on a man's wage rates, and, although they were not included in the final model, indexes measuring trust, efficacy, and planning were tested and also made no difference. However, for young men who have recently left home, motivation and trust are important predictors of wage rates. Evidently, the more highly motivated or trusting individuals are likely to start out in a serious career. Those who are less motivated or more hostile are more likely to work in lower paying jobs when they are young, but eventually they too settle into higher paying careers. Consequently, these differences in attitudes have little effect on wage rates for older workers. This conclusion must be modified for blacks. Although, again, the pattern varies greatly, there is some evidence that motivation score makes no difference in the wage rates of young blacks.

Ability differences are not reflected in different wage rates for young men. Nor do veterans earn significantly less than non-veterans, although being a veteran does influence the payoff to education. There is actually a negative payoff to education for young veterans but this is probably a result of loss of labor force experience. Veterans with a college education lose about six years of work experience while veterans with only a high school diploma lose about two years. Eventually, this loss of experience is more than made up for since veterans benefit more from education when all age groups are considered.

Education itself has almost no effect on the wage rates young men earn.[1] This is consistent with our finding from studying all working men that educational benefits do not show up until a man is over thirty. It is not surprising, then, that the *quality* of education, as measured by expenditure per pupil and the average salary of teachers in the county, does not appear to make a difference either.

Of the additional background measures we have included, only the parental family income makes a significant difference in the son's wage rate. The inclusion of this variable does not significantly change our estimates of the effects

---

[1]The overall education effect, without interactions, is −.03 with a standard error of .05.

of other variables. In particular, the effect of education is very small to begin with and falls only slightly when differences in family income are taken into account.

The determinants of wage rates for young women are different than those for young men (see Table 3.12).[1] Age has a smaller effect for young women. This was also true in our earlier analysis of all women, but, since we did not have job histories for all women, we could not be sure if this smaller age effect was a result of women sometimes being out of the labor force for many years. However, for young splitoffs, age is as good a measure of experience for women as for men. A smaller age effect for these women lends support to the hypothesis that women are working in "dead end" jobs where they have less chance to acquire new skills or be promoted.

We found some evidence that young black men were doing better than comparable whites, but this does not seem to be the case for young black women. Our estimate is that young black women earn about $.25 less than similar white women, although there is a large variation around this pattern.

Education pays off well for young women and the estimate of this effect is not modified by considering the quality of schooling. Neither the expenditure per pupil nor average salary for a teacher in the county significantly affects wage rates. Further, none of the better measured background variables change the estimated benefit of education for young women. Thus, we can be fairly certain of the size of the education effect we found earlier for all working women.

In summary, then, we find that the young workers who have recently left home face a different labor market than those who are more established. For men we find that experience is the most important determinant of their wage rates, while education makes no difference. There is hopeful evidence that racial discrimination is less among young men. The attitudes that a person expresses also make a difference in how much he earns. Those young men who are more motivated and less hostile receive significantly higher wage rates, at least for whites.

Young women who have recently split off benefit less from labor force experience than men. There is also evidence of more discrimination against young black women than against black men. However, there is a substantial benefit to education for all young women and our estimate of its size does not vary when we also control for differences in quality of education or for better measured background characteristics.

---

[1]The correlations among some of the important predictors are given in Appendix 3.4.

TABLE 3.12

Wage Rates for Female Splitoffs in 1971[a]

Background	Full Model with Old Background Variables		Adding New Background Variables and Quality of Education	
	Coefficient	t-ratio	Coefficient	t-ratio
Age	.10	(3.0)	.08	(2.4)
Grew up City	−.20	(0.8)	−.25	(1.0)
Grew up Farm	.39	(2.1)	.35	(1.8)
Black	−.23	(0.9)	−.32	(1.2)
Father's Education	−.04	(0.7)	−.01	(0.2)
Education	.16	(3.3)	.18	(3.7)
Occupation	−.04	(1.1)	−.03	(0.8)
Demand				
Male Wage in County	.03	(0.2)	−.01	(0.1)
Comparison of Female to Male Wage in County	.02	(0.3)	.02	(0.4)
City Size	.11	(2.1)	.11	(2.1)
Northeast	.17		−.02	
North Central	.07	(0.3)	.07	(0.3)
South	−.02	(0.1)	.05	(0.1)
West	−.26	(1.0)	−.18	(0.6)
New Background				
Parents' Motivation			−.04	(1.6)
Parents' Test Score			−.05	(1.2)
Family Income in 1968			.0000	(0.7)
Quality of Education				
Expenditure per Pupil			.0008	(1.2)
Average Teacher Salary			.0000	(0.3)

$$R^2 = .25 \qquad\qquad R^2 = .28$$
$$\text{Adjusted } R^2 = .20 \qquad\qquad \text{Adjusted } R^2 = .21$$

---

[a]The sample consists of daughters aged 18 to 30 who left home between 1969 and 1971 and who worked at least 250 hours in 1971. There are 235 such cases.

V. Change in Wage Rates Over Five Years

We have so far concentrated on what determines the level of wages and what leads to low wages. There is a substantial amount of change in wage rates over five years, and it is important to investigate the dynamic process involved, particularly to see if there are systematic factors which enable people to increase low wage rates.

From 1967 to 1971 the Gross National Product rose an average of 8% per year. Part of this increase was due to inflation since prices rose about 5% annually, but part was also due to real growth. The average wage rate for male heads of households at all levels kept up with inflation and shared in the growth: the average increase was about 7 3/4% per year.[1] Table 3.13 shows that there are important differences in the distribution of these changes. For those who had low wage rates in the middle of this period, only a fifth maintained their relative income position. Forty percent had increases greater than the average while, on the other hand, 20% experienced increases less than the rate of inflation and another 20% actually experienced a decline in wage rates. Of the families with medium or high wage rates, relatively few had extreme changes and about a third simply had average increases. Thus, it is quite possible that the determinants of change are different for the low wage group, so we stratify and look separately at the predictors of trend in wage rates as a percent of the average for those with low, medium, and high wage rates in the middle year (1969).[2]

There are three reasons that we should expect characteristics to be systematically related to changes in wage rates. Some variables which were related to level of wage rate can be changed; a person's occupation, for example, can be changed and his wage rate would be expected to change from the prevailing rate in his old occupation to the rate in his new occupation. Many characteristics of an individual, however, cannot change, but these stable characteristics can be associated with varying wage rates if their effects are changing over time. Although race is obviously a stable characteristic, if racial discrimination were reduced during this period, we would expect blacks to have relatively larger changes in wage rates than whites. Other stable characteristics can affect changes if they have different impacts on wage rates for different ages. For example, if ability differences show up only for older workers, then we would

---

[1] The trend is expressed as a percent of the five-year average wage rate.

[2] The middle year was chosen since it does not appear as a term in our measure of trend. This equation is as follows: $2 \times Wage_1 + Wage_2 - Wage_4 - 2 \times Wage_5$. Thus, errors in measurement in the stratified year are not correlated with change over the period.

TABLE 3.13

Changes in Wage Rates by Level of Wage Rate in 1969 –
Male Heads of Households

	Low Wage Rate (less than or equal to $3.00)	Medium Wage Rate ($3.01 to $4.25)	High Wage Rate (greater than $4.25)
Decreased	19.6%	12.5%	11.0%
Increased by less than inflation (0-4%)	20.7	20.1	18.8
Increased about average (5-9%)	19.6	32.3	35.2
Increased more than average (10-14%)	17.7	20.6	22.2
Increased substantially (15% or more)	22.4	14.5	12.6
	100.0%	100.0%	100.0%
Average Annual Percent Change	7.6%	7.7%	7.7%

expect the more able to have greater increases as the whole population grows older during the five years.

Table 3.14 shows the variables included in these analyses, along with their relative importance in explaining annual percent changes in wage rates for the high, medium, and low wage categories.[1] We cannot explain change as well as we did level, in part because there is relatively more measurement error. However, there are some systematic relationships that emerge.

Age is important in explaining changes for all groups, and the pattern we find is consistent with the cross-sectional age profiles we found earlier. All age groups experienced positive changes, but the youngest had the largest increases and the size of the changes declined with age for the medium and low wage groups. The high wage older workers, however, had the same change in wage rates as much younger workers. This indicates that the disparity in wage rates among those over fifty increased over this period: the older poor not only have lower wage rates but also had smaller percent increases.

Neither ability nor motivation, as we measure them, had any impact on the change in wage rates for men. Ability did imply large differences in levels of wage rates but these differentials remained constant over time. Only those who scored very low on the test had less than normal increases.

There is some evidence that racial discrimination was reduced between 1967 and 1971, but only for the middle income levels. Figure 3.4 shows that low and high wage blacks had increases equal to similar white workers but that the middle wage blacks experienced a 10% annual change compared to a 7 1/3% change for whites. This does not imply that blacks earned more than whites, but only that they were earning an estimated .54 less in 1967 and .48 less in 1971. The fact that blacks with lower wages did not experience a change in their relative position suggests that they did not have the necessary resources to take advantage of increased opportunities that the middle wage blacks did.

Although education is very important in determining levels of wage rates, it is not important in determining how wage rates change over time for the middle and high wage workers. For those who earned low wages in 1969, we find that those with more education actually had *smaller* changes over this period. There is some evidence that this is especially true of those who work as professionals and managers. Perhaps the factors that lead people to have low wage rates despite the fact they have a good education and work in higher status occupations also lead to their having smaller increases. An attempt was made to

---

[1]The full details of this MCA are given in Appendix 3.5.

TABLE 3.14

Relative Importance of Predictors
Explaining Change in Wage Rates –
Male Heads of Households

	Low Wage Rate		Medium Wage Rate		High Wage Rate	
	β^2	Rank Order of Importance	β^2	Rank Order of Importance	β^2	Rank Order of Importance
Age	.032	(2)	.067	(1)	.015	(4)
Race	.004	(8)	.013	(7)	.015	(3)
Ability	.009	(6)	.004	(10)	.004	(9)
Motivation	.0004	(11)	.008	(9)	.003	(8)
Education	.054	(1)	.018	(6)	.009	(7)
Occupation	.022	(3)	.031	(4)	.013	(5)
Job Mobility	.021	(4)	.045	(2)	.023	(1)
Union Status and Change	.005	(7)	.003	(11)	.001	(10)
City Size	.010	(5)	.021	(5)	.016	(2)
Change in County Wage	.004	(9)	.038	(3)	.010	(6)
Residential Mobility	.001	(10)	.008	(8)	.0006	(11)

$$R^2 = .12 \qquad R^2 = .17 \qquad R^2 = .10$$
$$\text{Adjusted } R^2 = .06 \qquad \text{Adjusted } R^2 = .09 \qquad \text{Adjusted } R^2 = .03$$

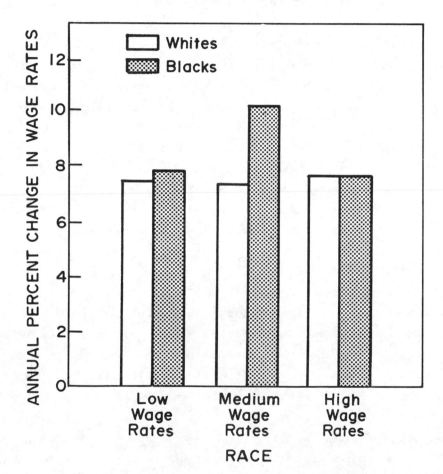

FIGURE 3.4

Change in Wage Rates by Race for Males
with Low, Medium, and High Wage Rates

test this hypothesis by including a person's expected wage as a predictor of change, but the anomalous education effect persisted.

There were very few occupation-related differences in change among blue collar workers. The white collar workers had a more varied pattern but in general experienced larger increases in wage rates during this period. Controlling for these occupational differences, we find that seniority on a specific job had an important impact on the rate of change in wage rates, but that the effects differed across the strata. The high wage workers who kept the same job during this period had substantially greater increases than those who changed jobs (see Figure 3.5). Gaining experience and seniority in one's job, however, was not the best means to economic improvement for those with low or medium wage rates. Moving to another job was, in general, associated with greater increases for these workers. This suggests that government programs should encourage job mobility among low wage workers. But unemployment compensation as currently administered does not do this. There is generally a one to two month period when no aid is given if the worker voluntarily left his previous job. Some early results from the Income Maintenance Experiment suggest that such a program did encourage mobility which resulted in higher wage rates (see Watts, 1971).

Union members had somewhat greater increases in wage rates over this period than nonunion workers. The average union wage rate increased 8% annually, just equal to the growth rate of the economy, while nonunion wage rate increased about 7.6%. There is some evidence that the low wage workers benefited the most from union membership, but the variation in the pattern is large. The results of changing one's union membership reflect the fact that union wage rates are generally higher. Those who joined unions, therefore, had greater than normal increases while those who quit had smaller changes. In fact, the low wage workers who quit unions had changes which were slightly less than the rate of inflation.

The local conditions had a relatively small impact on changes in wage rates for men. There was not a systematic relationship between city size and change in wage rates even though the large cities experienced relatively more unemployment during this period. There is some evidence that those either moving to a county with a higher wage rate for unskilled labor or living in a county where this wage rate improved had greater than average changes. Residential mobility, per se, however, had little effect.

The change in wage rates for wives and female heads is greater than the change for men. Women averaged 8% increase, about equal to the growth rate of the economy as a whole, while the average man had an increase of 7.75%. This

FIGURE 3.5

Change in Wage Rates by Job Mobility for Males
with Low, Medium, and High Wage Rates

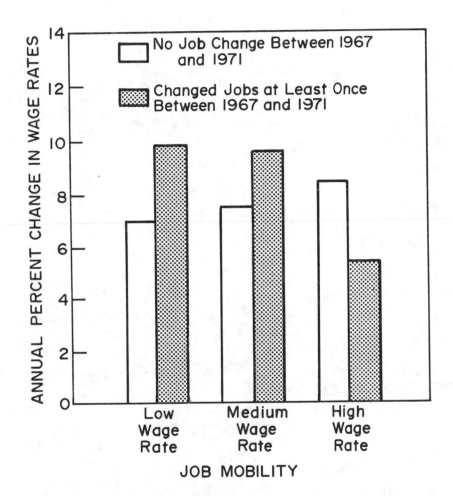

TABLE 3.15

Changes in Wage Rates by Level of Wage Rates in 1969 –
Wives and Female Heads of Households

	Low Wage Rate (less than or equal to $3.00)	Medium to High Wage Rate (greater than $3.00)
Decreased	13.9%	4.8%
Increased by less than inflation (0-4%)	24.5	22.6
Increased about average (5-9%)	22.3	38.6
Increased more than average (10-14%)	22.1	20.6
Increased substantially (15% or more)	17.2	13.3
	100.0%	100.0%
Average Annual Percent Change	7.8%	8.3%

suggests that there have been changes in recent years in the job market which women face and that sex discrimination, while still widespread, has decreased somewhat from 1967 to 1971.

The distribution of changes by strata are shown in Table 3.15. (Very few women had wage rates over $4.25 an hour, so we have combined the medium and high wage groups.) The main differences in these distributions and the comparable ones for men are that fewer women experienced actual declines during this period and that more women had average (5-9%) increases.

Table 3.16 contains the variables included and their importance in explaining change in wage rates for women.[1] Since we did not measure motivation or ability for women, these variables were omitted from this analysis.

Age is less important in explaining changes in wage rates for women than for men. This is especially true of young women, for whom age is a good measure of experience, and provides more evidence that women do not work in jobs where they can gain skills with experience.

In both the low and medium wage groups black women have improved their relative position with annual increases of over 9.7%. We found for men that only the middle wage blacks experienced greater than normal increases and hypothesized that low wage workers did not have the resources to take advantage of increased opportunities. Because of sex discrimination, however, women with low wage rates in general have more qualifications than similarly paid men, so it may be that low paid black women did have enough education or other skills to move into better paying jobs while the men did not.

More education was associated with greater increases in wage rates for women in both the medium and low wage groups, which was not the case for men. This suggests that decreases in sex discrimination have occurred mainly among the higher status women. The changes associated with occupation further support this, since it is only in the white collar jobs that women had increases larger than the men (see Figure 3.6). This was true for both the medium and low wage groups. There did not appear to be any relationship between change in wage rates and change in occupation for women.

The size of the area in which a woman lives was important in determining her rate of economic improvement during these five years, but the direction of this effect differs across strata. Women with low wage rates had the greatest improvement in rural areas and small towns of less than 25,000. These workers are generally among the lowest paid and may have been benefited most by changed

---

[1] The full details of this MCA are given in Appendix 3.6.

TABLE 3.16

Relative Importance of Predictors
Explaining Change in Wage Rates —
Wives and Female Heads of Households

	Low Wage Rate		Medium to High Wage Rate	
	β^2	Rank Order of Importance	β^2	Rank Order of Importance
Age	.011	(5)	.023	(5)
Race	.007	(6)	.062	(1)
Education	.018	(4)	.028	(4)
Occupation	.035	(1)	.042	(2)
Change in Occupation	.002	(8)	.008	(7)
City Size	.014	(3)	.028	(3)
Change in County Wage	.029	(2)	.019	(6)
Residential Mobility	.002	(7)	.006	(8)

$$R^2 = .10$$
$$\text{Adjusted } R^2 = .05$$

$$R^2 = .22$$
$$\text{Adjusted } R^2 = .08$$

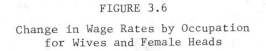

FIGURE 3.6

Change in Wage Rates by Occupation
for Wives and Female Heads

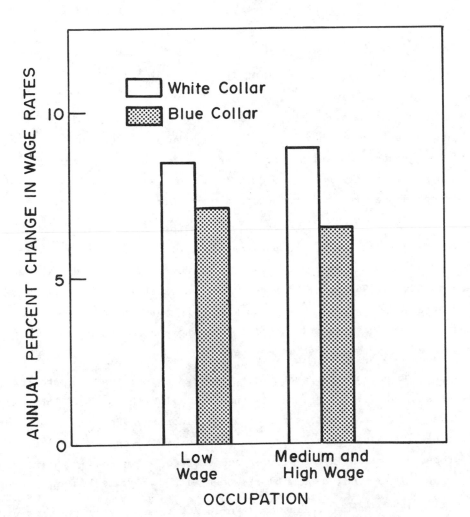

minimum wage legislation. Among the medium and high wage workers, however, those living in large metropolitan areas had the largest changes. We found evidence when looking at the determinants of level of wage rates that there was less sex discrimination in these areas. This result indicates that sex discrimination has been decreasing more rapidly in large cities as well. Neither changes in the county wage nor residential mobility had any further effect on changes in wage rates.

SUMMARY

This chapter has examined the determinants of wage rates for men, women, and young people just after they left home. We have looked at the relative importance of background, education, occupation, and demand conditions and found that each has an important and independent impact on earning ability. The following are a set of general conclusions that emerge from this study:

1. Women are paid about $1.00 an hour less than similar men, and the impact of sex discrimination on the poverty population is substantial since many poor families have a woman as head. There is evidence that this discrimination has decreased between 1967 and 1971 since women had slightly larger percentage increases over this period than men. The women who made the largest gains, however, appeared to be those in white collar jobs who had a good education and not those who were earning the lowest wage rates.

2. Race also has an important effect on wage rates: we estimate that a black man earns about $.50 per hour less than a similar white man. There appears to be some change in the amount of racial discrimination. For young men just starting out there are no significant race differences in the amount they earn per hour. Those black men in the middle wage group also increased their relative position during this period, as did black women with low or medium wage rates.

3. The ability measure which was developed for this study explains significant differences in wage rates. Those with greater ability also benefit more from education although even those who score lowest on the test have a positive benefit to education.

4. A person's attitudes have very little to do with the amount he earns. Only for those just starting out do we find that the more motivated and more trusting do better. For the working population as a whole, there is no such systematic pattern.

5. The education of a person's father has a significant effect on his wage rate, over and above the person's own education or ability. This suggests that compensatory programs for children of less well educated parents may be useful independent of the effects such programs may have on a child's cognitive ability.

6. Education is the most important variable included in the analysis, but the benefit to education varies according to other characteristics. Those who have high test scores or urban backgrounds, or who are veterans have benefits greater than average, while those who are young or belong to a union generally experience smaller benefits. For men, educational differences in wage rate remain stable over time while more highly educated women improve their position. In general, we can conclude that increasing education does seem to be a useful means of increasing income.

7. Experience, as measured by age and seniority on the job, also makes a large difference in both the level and in the changes in wage rates over time for men. The level of wage rates increases with age, but at a declining rate. High wage workers who did not change jobs during this period had larger increases. Stability on one's job is not, however, related to increased wage rates for low and medium wage workers. Rather, those who find new jobs do relatively better. This suggests that public policy should encourage job mobility among low wage workers. Experience is much less important in determining wage rates for women. Age may not be a good proxy for work experience for older women who may have been out of the labor force for many years; but we find the same small age effect on the level of wage rates among women just starting out and in the changes in wage rates among younger women. It seems reasonable to conclude that many women are working in "dead end" jobs.

8. Local area conditions have a large impact on the level of a person's wage. These differences in part reflect differences in the cost of living, but they also reflect real differences in employment opportunities. Public policy can affect these opportunities by placing publicly funded projects in areas where the private sector is slack.

References

Bergmann, Barbara, "The Effect on White Incomes of Discrimination in Employ-
    ment," Journal of Political Economy, (March/April) 1971.

168

Bowles, Samuel, "Schooling and Inequality from Generation to Generation, Journal of Political Economy, 80 (May/June) 1972.

Duncan, Otis D., Featherman, David L., and Duncan, Beverly, Socioeconomic Background and Occupational Achievement: Extensions of a Basic Model. Project No. S-00/4 (EO-919). U. S. Department of Health, Education and Welfare, May 1968.

Griliches, Zvi, and Mason, William M., "Education, Income and Ability," Journal of Political Economy, 80 (May/June) 1972.

Harrison, Bennett, "Education and Underemployment in the Urban Ghetto," American Economic Review, December 1972.

Hause, John C., "Economic Profile: Ability and Schooling," Journal of Political Economy, 80 (May/June) 1972.

Jencks, Christopher, et al, Inequality. New York: Basic Books, 1972.

Lansing, John B., and Morgan, James N., "Effects of Geographic Mobility on Income," Journal of Human Resources, (Fall) 1967.

Thurow, Lester C., and Lucas, Robert E. B., "The American Distribution of Income: A Structural Problem," Joint Economic Committee, U. S. Government Printing Office, Washington, D.C., March 1972.

Wachtel, Howard M., and Betsey, Charles, "Employment at Low Wages," Review of Economics and Statistics, LIV (May) 1972.

Watts, Harold W., "Mid-Experiment Report on Basic Labor-Supply Response," 1971, mimeograph.

APPENDIX 3.1

Correlations Among Some Important Predictors of Five Year Average Wage,
Male Heads of Households

	Mean	Std. Dev.	1	2	3	4	5	6	7	8	9	10	11	12	13	14	15	16	17	18	19	20	21
1 Age	45	12	1.00																				
2 Age²	2147	1139	.99	1.00																			
3 Father's Occupation	5.9	2.2	.10	.10	1.00																		
4 Father's Education	2.7	1.5	-.16	-.15	-.35	1.00																	
5 Veteran	.49	.5	.004	-.05	-.07	.00	1.00																
6 Black	.08	.27	-.03	-.03	.15	-.09	-.08	1.00															
7 High Test Score	.21	.41	-.05	-.05	-.19	.18	.06	.05	1.00														
8 Low Test Score	.20	.40	.08	.09	.12	-.17	-.14	.22	-.26	1.00												
9 Education	4.4	2.0	-.19	-.19	-.34	.37	.15	-.18	.32	-.35	1.00											
10 Managers	.14	.34	.002	-.01	-.14	.11	.13	-.10	.06	-.12	.20	1.00										
11 Self-employed	.07	.26	.07	.06	-.01	.01	-.05	-.04	-.02	.00	-.02	-.11	1.00									
12 Clerical	.11	.31	-.01	-.001	-.05	.06	.04	.01	.05	-.02	.09	-.14	-.10	1.00								
13 Craftsmen	.23	.42	.02	.01	.08	-.09	.06	-.04	-.10	.02	-.21	-.22	-.15	-.19	1.00							
14 Operatives	.16	.36	-.04	-.04	.10	-.15	-.05	.11	-.12	.15	-.29	-.17	-.12	-.15	-.23	1.00						
15 Laborers	.08	.27	.09	.09	.10	-.10	-.12	.22	-.10	.17	-.25	-.11	-.08	-.10	-.16	-.12	1.00					
16 Farmers	.04	.19	.04	.05	.16	-.03	-.12	-.05	-.04	.04	-.10	-.08	-.06	-.07	-.11	-.09	-.06	1.00				
17 Misc., Government	.02	.14	-.08	-.07	-.02	.02	-.04	.02	.06	-.03	.02	-.06	-.04	-.05	-.08	-.06	-.04	-.03	1.00			
18 Union Member	.30	.46	-.04	-.06	.05	-.16	.05	.08	-.14	.08	-.20	-.16	-.13	-.02	.23	.22	.03	-.12	-.02	1.00		
19 Large City	.56	.50	-.03	-.04	-.15	.05	.06	.06	.04	-.02	.14	.03	-.01	.03	.04	-.06	-.05	-.18	.03	.13	1.00	
20 Small Town	.25	.43	.04	.04	.16	-.08	-.05	-.07	-.08	.05	-.18	-.02	.03	-.04	-.02	.03	.01	.21	-.03	-.15	-.65	1.00
21 Average Wage	4.35	2.59	.05	.02	-.22	.18	.17	-.14	.25	-.22	.44	.25	-.04	-.04	-.04	-.14	-.20	-.19	-.03	.02	.25	-.24	1.00

MTR 6022

APPENDIX 3.2

Correlations among Important Predictors of Average Wage Rate,
Wives and Female Heads

	Mean	Std. Dev.	1	2	3	4	5	6	7	8	9	10	11	12	13
1 Age	45	12	1.00												
2 Age^2	2186	1095	.99	1.00											
3 Black	.13	.33	-.009	-.02	1.00										
4 Education	4.4	1.68	-.21	-.20	-.16	1.00									
5 Managers	.03	.18	.05	.05	-.06	.06	1.00								
6 Self-employed	.02	.13	.03	.03	-.02	-.01	-.02	1.00							
7 Clerical	.36	.48	-.01	-.01	-.11	.03	-.14	-.10	1.00						
8 Craftswomen	.01	.12	-.02	-.03	-.04	-.02	-.02	-.02	-.09	1.00					
9 Operatives	.16	.37	-.04	-.05	.01	-.29	-.08	-.06	-.32	-.05	1.00				
10 Laborers	.23	.42	.15	.16	.24	-.31	-.10	-.07	-.41	-.07	-.24	1.00			
11 Large City	.05	.22	.18	.19	.13	-.36	-.04	-.01	-.11	-.03	.05	.21	1.00		
12 Small Town	.18	.39	-.05	-.05	-.06	.27	.08	.01	.14	.03	-.15	-.05	-.11	1.00	
13 Average Wage Rate	2.71	1.35	-.06	-.07	-.18	.55	.12	-.06	-.01	-.02	-.12	-.37	-.16	.55	1.00

MTR 6022

APPENDIX 3.3

Correlations among Important Predictors of Wage Rate,
Male Splitoffs

	Mean	Std. Dev.	1	2	3	4	5	6	7	8	9	10	11	12	13	14
1 Age of Head	23	2.7	1.00													
2 Father's Education	9.6	3.9	-.03	1.00												
3 Black	.12	.33	-.08	-.08	1.00											
4 Splitoffs Motivation	9.3	2.6	.02	.25	.05	1.00										
5 Splitoffs Test Score	9.7	2.2	.21	.30	-.26	.12	1.00									
6 Parent's Test Score	9.3	2.3	.10	.53	-.09	.28	.37	1.00								
7 Family Income (1967)	10,765	6285	.12	.35	-.25	.21	.21	.30	1.00							
8 Education	12.4	2.3	.22	.52	-.11	.35	.34	.30	.32	1.00						
9 Occupation[a]	5.8	2.2	.14	.39	-.07	.17	.25	.24	.13	.46	1.00					
10 Seniority on Job	2.0	1.2	.24	-.08	-.04	-.13	-.0002	-.09	.12	-.03	-.21	1.00				
11 City Size[a]	7.2	1.9	.10	.19	.06	.09	-.007	.11	.22	.20	.18	-.01	1.00			
12 Union Member	.25	.43	-.19	.07	-.02	.002	.06	-.02	.03	-.03	-.25	.08	.09	1.00		
13 Average Expenditure per Pupil	945	215	.02	.21	-.12	.11	.08	.16	.19	.21	.14	.04	.34	-.003	1.00	
14 Wage Rate	3.19	1.51	.37	.12	-.10	.23	.18	.09	.35	.24	.16	.25	.24	.14	.18	1.00

[a]This variable is scaled as 10 minus the documented code.

MTR 6023

APPENDIX 3.4

Correlations among Important Predictors of Wage Rate,
Female Splitoffs

	Mean	Std. Dev.	1	2	3	4	5	6	7	8	9	10
1 Age	23	2.6	1.00									
2 Father's Education	10.5	3.7	-.13	1.00								
3 Black	.12	.33	-.02	-.27	1.00							
4 Parent's Test Score	9.5	2.3	-.17	.52	-.28	1.00						
5 Family Income (1967)	11,438	6569	.11	.30	-.28	.26	1.00					
6 Education	13	2.0	.18	.34	-.20	.27	.32	1.00				
7 Occupation[a]	6.1	2.2	.05	.29	-.07	.26	.17	.44	1.00			
8 City Size[a]	7.5	1.7	.03	.17	.02	.05	.23	.09	.19	1.00		
9 Average Expenditure Per Pupil	994	227	.35	.03	.03	-.08	.22	.04	.16	.30	1.00	
10 Wage Rate	2.48	1.31	.28	.02	-.08	-.09	.14	.26	.11	.25	.27	1.00

[a]This variable is scaled as 10 minus the documented code.

MTR 6023

APPENDIX 3.5

MCA on Annual Percent Change in Wage Rate for Male Heads

	Low Wage Rate in 1969				Medium Wage Rate in 1969				High Wage Rate in 1969			
	N	Percent	Mean	Adjusted Mean	N	Percent	Mean	Adjusted Mean	N	Percent	Mean	Adjusted Mean
AGE OF HEAD												
<25	29	3.9	12.6	14.9	9	0.9	16.6	20.4	3	0.2	25.4	28.3
25-34	224	26.1	9.0	9.5	182	32.0	9.6	9.8	110	14.6	9.0	9.1
35-44	222	20.7	8.3	7.9	154	26.5	7.5	6.8	238	32.6	7.6	7.4
45-54	207	19.4	5.6	5.4	118	20.8	6.9	6.9	250	33.9	7.7	7.6
55-64	173	19.5	7.8	6.8	77	15.5	4.4	4.0	99	15.2	6.9	7.1
65-74	46	9.0	3.5	4.2	16	4.3	8.6	12.1	21	3.4	5.9	7.3
75 or older	7	1.4	8.9	10.2	---	---	---	---	1	0.1	15.0	14.2
RACE												
White	495	81.9	7.2	7.4	395	88.4	7.5	7.3	643	94.8	7.6	7.6
Black	368	13.6	8.4	7.8	136	7.7	9.6	10.2	63	3.5	8.7	7.6
Spanish American	38	4.3	13.3	11.1	19	3.1	8.5	11.2	8	0.9	18.0	19.3
Other	7	0.2	7.2	5.1	6	0.8	13.0	13.2	8	0.8	9.9	9.7
TEST SCORE												
0- 6	186	12.8	6.6	4.7	52	4.7	6.6	8.9	26	2.3	3.5	4.0
7- 8	193	18.3	7.3	7.1	117	18.5	8.2	8.4	70	8.9	7.7	8.2
9-10	320	38.6	8.1	8.3	212	41.2	7.5	7.9	246	33.1	7.7	7.8
11-13	209	30.4	7.6	8.2	175	35.7	7.9	7.0	380	55.7	7.9	7.7
MOTIVATION												
0- 7	321	33.2	7.8	7.9	144	25.8	7.5	7.7	162	20.7	7.3	7.4
8- 9	271	29.7	7.6	7.4	141	24.6	6.3	6.5	181	24.8	7.4	7.3
10-12	264	32.2	7.5	7.5	212	37.8	8.5	8.7	296	41.8	7.7	7.8
13-16	52	4.9	6.7	7.0	59	11.8	8.6	7.2	83	12.6	9.0	8.9
EDUCATION OF HEAD												
<6 grades	70	4.4	12.7	14.9	5	0.7	0.4	4.2	4	0.2	-7.6	-6.1
6-8 grades	85	5.4	8.5	11.0	19	2.1	7.4	8.8	9	1.0	11.0	11.9
9-11 grades	244	25.5	8.6	10.5	103	17.5	5.3	5.8	58	6.9	7.1	7.1
12 grades	186	19.8	7.0	6.8	120	16.9	8.8	9.1	90	11.8	7.1	7.5
12 grades + non-academic	136	17.6	6.3	6.0	138	27.3	7.7	6.9	144	19.8	8.1	8.2
Some college	52	7.3	7.7	6.4	58	12.1	8.0	8.6	84	11.2	8.3	8.5
College degree	100	14.5	7.3	5.1	69	14.0	9.3	8.6	133	20.0	7.8	7.7
College degree + some graduate	27	3.8	3.7	1.9	30	6.1	8.5	8.1	118	17.4	7.2	6.9
N.A.	8	1.7	8.3	3.6	14	3.2	6.9	10.2	82	11.9	8.1	7.8
OCCUPATION												
Professional	37	6.2	9.4	12.1	47	10.6	6.3	5.6	192	27.7	7.6	7.7
Manager	23	3.9	9.2	9.8	43	10.3	8.0	8.5	113	17.8	8.2	8.0
Self-employed	65	11.3	6.7	8.9	18	4.5	12.0	12.7	22	3.0	7.7	9.0
Clerical, sales	67	10.5	6.1	6.6	68	14.1	8.0	8.0	78	10.8	7.4	7.3
Craftsmen	139	16.3	7.0	7.0	140	26.0	6.8	7.1	186	25.6	7.1	7.4
Operative	216	19.2	6.8	5.5	147	23.1	8.0	7.3	83	10.3	7.6	7.4
Laborer	252	18.7	8.5	7.4	72	8.1	7.5	7.6	27	2.4	9.2	7.6
Farmer	80	10.9	6.2	7.3	5	1.1	5.5	6.7	4	0.4	19.9	22.7
Miscellaneous	29	3.1	14.7	12.9	16	2.2	12.3	14.8	14	2.0	10.4	8.3
CITY SIZE												
>500,000	219	20.0	9.6	9.5	206	29.3	6.5	5.6	329	48.2	7.5	7.7
100,000-499,999	143	14.8	7.7	7.4	118	24.3	8.9	8.7	178	24.3	7.8	7.7
50,000- 99,999	106	12.3	6.9	6.8	70	13.9	7.3	8.5	74	10.1	9.0	9.5
25,000- 49,999	69	7.1	9.4	9.8	30	6.7	6.5	7.9	33	4.2	4.5	3.5
10,000- 24,999	136	18.6	6.6	6.0	56	11.6	8.0	8.8	46	5.8	7.4	7.3
<10,000	235	27.2	6.6	7.2	76	14.2	8.9	8.8	62	7.4	8.9	9.2

APPENDIX 3.5

MCA on Annual Percent Change in Wage Rate for Male Heads (continued)

	Low Wage Rate in 1969				Medium Wage Rate in 1969				High Wage Rate in 1969			
	N	Percent	Mean	Adjusted Mean	N	Percent	Mean	Adjusted Mean	N	Percent	Mean	Adjusted Mean
FIVE YEAR CHANGE IN OCCUPATION												
Not always employed	167	19.8	5.9	5.3	50	9.2	6.1	3.7	46	6.0	5.2	5.2
No changes; same employer 10 yrs+	132	11.4	6.7	7.4	128	23.3	6.7	8.2	252	36.1	7.8	8.5
No changes; same employer 4-9 yrs	91	8.8	8.0	7.8	76	12.4	6.9	7.1	106	15.1	9.2	8.4
No changes; same employer 1-3 yrs	218	27.6	6.1	6.7	122	22.7	7.7	6.9	142	19.3	8.8	8.4
Changed job once	160	17.8	10.8	11.0	103	19.9	9.1	9.2	110	14.1	6.3	6.2
Changed job more than once	136	14.2	9.6	8.4	74	11.8	10.1	10.4	60	8.5	5.7	5.3
N.A.	4	0.4	2.1	2.4	3	0.6	-4.1	-6.5	6	0.8	14.2	13.7
CHANGE IN UNION MEMBERSHIP												
Quit union	59	6.4	5.0	4.7	49	8.1	6.9	6.6	38	5.5	5.9	6.6
Joined union	80	8.7	10.1	9.3	50	7.4	9.6	8.4	36	4.5	8.6	8.2
Never belonged to a union	690	76.2	7.4	7.5	268	51.9	7.8	7.5	432	60.6	7.8	7.7
Always belonged to a union	79	8.7	8.8	8.5	189	32.7	7.3	8.2	216	29.4	7.6	7.8
FIVE YEAR CHANGE IN RESIDENCE												
No moves; lived same place 5 years before 1968	303	37.0	6.5	7.6	176	34.0	7.0	8.7	314	44.6	7.4	7.5
No moves; into original place between 1964 & 1968	173	17.9	7.3	7.0	122	22.3	6.5	6.8	155	22.4	7.6	7.6
Moved once	231	22.4	7.2	7.4	134	22.8	8.9	8.0	144	20.0	8.8	8.1
Moved more than once	201	22.8	10.0	8.2	124	20.9	8.9	6.7	109	13.0	7.5	7.8
CHANGE IN COUNTY WAGE												
Decreased more than $.50/hour	5	0.7	11.1	8.2	3	0.5	10.8	12.1	2	0.3	4.8	7.8
Decreased $.50/hour	7	1.3	14.6	13.0	10	2.1	9.6	11.8	32	4.3	5.0	4.9
Same	369	37.5	7.0	7.2	189	31.9	8.8	9.3	226	30.4	7.0	7.4
Increased $.50/hour	410	44.6	7.3	7.4	234	43.4	5.9	5.6	296	41.9	7.8	7.5
Increased more than $.50/hour	117	15.9	9.3	8.5	120	22.0	9.5	9.1	166	23.0	9.1	9.1

APPENDIX 3.6

MCA on Annual Percent Change in Wage Rates for Wives and Female Heads

| | Low Wage Rate in 1969 | | | | Medium to High Wage Rate in 1969 | | | |
	N	Percent	Mean	Adjusted Mean	N	Percent	Mean	Adjusted Mean
AGE								
<25	27	4.0	6.3	6.1	4	0.7	9.7	11.5
25-34	153	19.1	8.4	8.0	73	23.9	9.1	9.3
35-44	208	23.2	8.2	8.1	64	24.3	8.5	8.2
45-54	219	26.8	8.7	8.9	61	26.3	7.9	7.6
55-64	145	22.4	6.5	6.7	52	22.8	8.3	8.6
65 or older	22	4.5	6.5	6.3	4	2.0	5.3	4.2
RACE								
White	406	80.2	7.6	7.4	217	93.3	8.4	8.3
Black	341	16.5	8.2	9.6	39	5.6	9.0	10.4
Spanish American	20	2.8	8.9	9.8	1	0.5	13.1	12.5
Other	6	0.5	4.1	4.4	1	0.6	-18.4	-14.0
EDUCATION								
<6 grades	31	2.3	3.3	2.2	2	1.0	6.5	5.7
6-9 grades	152	15.6	7.9	8.2	5	1.2	7.7	8.2
9-11 grades	200	21.2	7.4	7.0	25	8.8	7.2	7.6
12 grades	188	27.3	8.2	8.1	61	23.4	9.4	8.5
12 grades + non-academic	101	17.0	7.2	7.7	45	18.3	7.2	8.3
Some college	60	9.7	8.1	8.7	41	16.1	7.1	6.8
College degree	26	5.0	11.0	10.2	42	16.6	10.1	10.3
College degree + some graduate	5	0.6	12.4	11.5	34	13.0	7.9	7.5
N.A.	10	1.2	6.0	6.5	3	1.6	11.2	12.7
OCCUPATION								
Professional	36	6.8	9.0	7.8	88	35.3	8.7	8.2
Manager	5	1.0	11.5	11.5	10	4.7	6.8	8.4
Self-employed	6	1.2	7.0	6.3	4	1.9	13.8	10.8
Clerical, sales	223	36.8	8.3	8.5	100	37.6	9.3	9.5
Craftsmen	18	3.0	4.3	4.1	7	3.4	5.9	6.0
Operative	132	17.3	5.9	6.0	26	9.9	8.0	8.5
Laborer	321	29.6	7.6	7.2	19	5.3	14.1	3.9
Farmer	2	0.4	4.8	3.3	--	--	--	--
Miscellaneous	30	4.1	12.8	14.0	4	1.9	6.5	4.2
CITY SIZE								
≥500,000	285	30.0	7.0	7.1	117	44.4	7.3	7.2
100,000-499,999	175	21.0	8.4	7.7	67	26.9	10.2	10.0
50,000- 99,999	87	14.0	6.4	6.6	20	8.5	9.3	10.0
25,000- 49,999	48	7.0	7.3	7.6	6	2.2	6.6	8.0
10,000- 24,999	62	11.0	8.9	9.1	22	8.2	7.9	7.8
Less than 10,000	116	17.0	9.2	9.4	26	9.9	7.4	7.5
RESIDENTIAL MOBILITY								
Lived in same place 10+ years	267	38.1	8.1	8.2	97	43.4	8.3	8.2
Lived in same place 5 years	156	21.3	7.0	7.6	54	22.3	8.6	8.8
Moved once since 1968	200	21.3	7.3	6.8	61	22.0	8.6	8.7
Moved 2+ times since 1968	150	19.4	8.9	8.6	46	12.3	7.3	7.1
CHANGE IN OCCUPATION								
No change since 1968	535	69.5	7.7	8.1	196	79.0	8.3	7.9
Changed since 1968	238	30.5	8.1	7.4	62	21.0	8.3	9.7
CHANGE IN COUNTY WAGE								
Decreased more than $.50	3	0.5	24.6	24.4	1	0.5	9.8	12.4
Decreased $.50	12	1.6	-0.3	0.1	7	2.3	15.9	14.0
Same	268	33.1	8.4	8.2	81	31.4	8.7	8.9
Increased $.50	358	43.0	7.6	7.9	101	38.9	8.1	7.7
Increased more than $.50	138	21.8	7.8	7.4	68	27.0	7.5	7.9

$R^2 = .10$
Adjusted $R^2 = .05$
Mean=7.8
Standard Deviation=.10

$R^2 = .22$
Adjusted $R^2 = .08$
Mean=8.3
Standard Deviation=.10

Chapter 4

LABOR SUPPLY OF FAMILY MEMBERS

INTRODUCTION

The analyses in the previous chapter have dealt with factors which determine wage rates. In this chapter we consider the determinants of labor force
participation and hours of work of important groups of workers in the population.

It is useful to distinguish three basic sources of differences in labor
supply within the broad spectrum of work effort. The first, on which most studies of labor supply have focused, are the behavioral changes which occur in response to variables which may be altered by public policy. Response to differences in wage rate or to income supplements are chief among these. The second
is the result of simple differences in preferences among individuals who have
equivalent resources and opportunities. The third major component encompasses a
multitude of effects lumped under the heading "institutional factors." Unemployment is prominent among these but there are numerous other important constraints
and discontinuities in the employment opportunities available to many workers in
the population.

These three general influences on labor supply are not independent in their
effects, and it is one of the major theses of this paper that it is important to
take account of institutional factors and variations in personal preference in
estimating behavioral effects which may be influenced by policy.

In the first three sections of this chapter we consider various aspects of
the labor supply of male heads of families. The first is an analysis of factors associated with the incidence of unemployment and the resulting involuntary
loss of work time. In the second section we review the basic economic theory of
voluntary variations in work effort and consider the effects of a number of institutional factors which limit workers' flexibility to make the theoretically
expected adjustments in their work hours. In the third section we estimate the
parameters of a conventional labor supply model and make a number of tests of
their sensitivity to measures of institutional factors.

A model of the labor force participation and hours of work of married women
is presented in Section IV. A similar model for single women with children is
estimated in Section V.

ANALYSIS

I. Five Year Unemployment Experience of Male Heads of Families

What is the economic impact of involuntary loss of work hours? Who is affected most severely by unemployment? We investigate this problem in terms of the
incidence of unemployment over five years in order to gain an accurate picture of
infrequent unemployment as well as that which is recurrent. The measure used is
total unemployment time experienced over five years scaled at 40 hours per week.
The analysis sample includes all males who were heads of families for all five
years and who worked or were looking for work at least half time each year.

These men averaged 216 hours or roughly 5½ weeks of unemployment over the
five-year period. Behind this average value is a broad distribution of problems
experienced by different individuals. In Figure 4.1 we see that 67% of stable
male family heads were not unemployed at all during the five years, and 12% were
unemployed less than five weeks. The remaining 21% of workers experienced widely
varying amounts of unemployment ranging from 5.8% who lost 5 to 9 weeks during
the five years to 4.1% who had very serious losses of 40 or more weeks.

Figure 4.2 furnishes a useful perspective on the incidence of unemployment
among heads of families at various levels of economic status. Clearly the causal link does not run from economic status to unemployment, but the incidence of
unemployment at different economic levels helps us to put the relative impact of
unemployment on economic status into context.

First, it is striking that the proportion of workers experiencing at least
one week of unemployment during a five-year span is quite large at all economic
levels. Even among heads of families with incomes 3 times their needs, 30% experienced some unemployment during the five years and 15% of those with income
more than 4½ times needs were unemployed at least one week.

The incidence of unemployment in the broad middle range -- 1 to 30 weeks
in five years -- falls only gradually with economic status: 26% of workers whose
income is 3 times their needs experience unemployment in this range as compared
with 37% of those at very low income levels. The distribution of actual number
of weeks of unemployment within this broad range is quite similar at different

FIGURE 4.1

Five Year Unemployment Experience of Stable Male Family Heads
in the Labor Force all Five Years

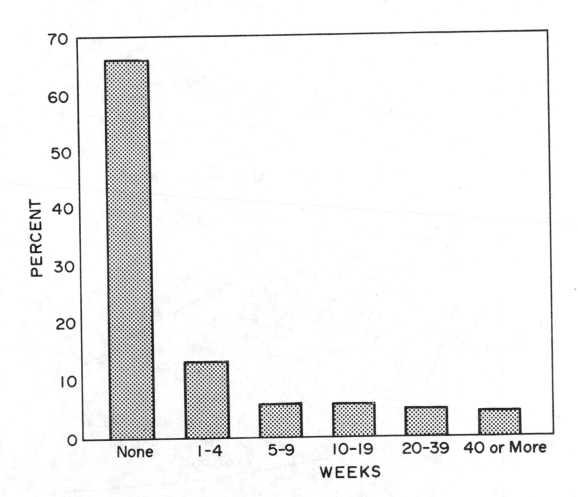

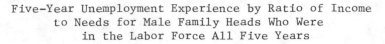

FIGURE 4.2

Five-Year Unemployment Experience by Ratio of Income
to Needs for Male Family Heads Who Were
in the Labor Force All Five Years

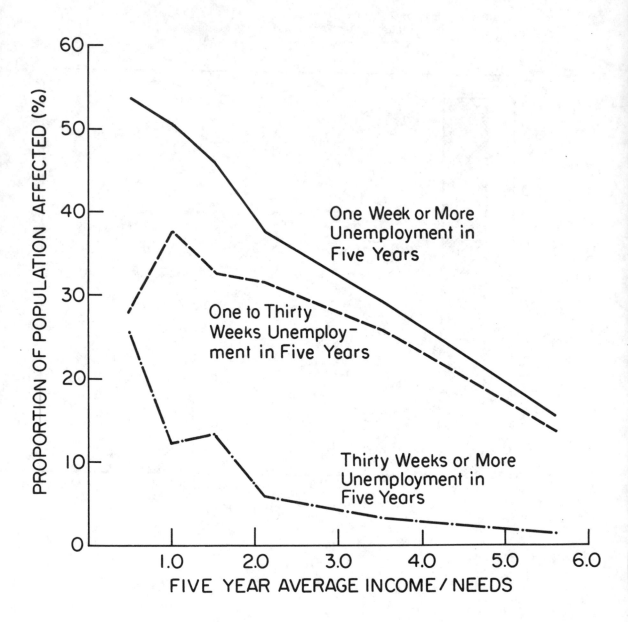

economic levels.

The comparative incidence of very serious unemployment is much more strongly related to economic status: the proportion of poor and near poor workers who face 30 or more unemployment weeks is more than double the proportion of middle status workers with similar problems. But the proportion of working males who experience such serious unemployment is not large in an absolute sense at any economic level. It ranges from 25% for the very poor to below 5% at middle levels and above.

How, then, do we view the importance of unemployment for male family heads as it affects their economic status? On the one hand, unemployment and the resulting income loss represent a serious economic problem which falls most heavily on low income workers and also affects substantial proportions of workers in middle and higher income ranges. On the other hand, income loss directly attributable to unemployment cannot be viewed as the major cause of poverty. Even if it were possible to devise a policy which utterly eliminates unemployment but which leaves relative wage rates unchanged, only one in four of the very poor male workers and one in eight of the near poor would gain more than 12% in work time over a five-year period. Another 30% to 40% of such workers would experience significant but smaller gains in work time.

Unemployment, then, emerges as a problem which compounds but is not the root cause of the economic difficulties of low income workers. There is also a large element of chance involved. Middle income workers had an 18% to 25% chance of five or more weeks of unemployment during the five years while even at the lowest income level 46% of workers experienced no unemployment at all.

Given this perspective on the impact of unemployment, we turn to an analysis of characteristics of workers and their economic environments which are associated with unemployment problems. The following variables are included in the analysis:

> Average hourly earnings
> Education
> Occupation
> Age
> Union membership
> Race
> Unemployment rate in county of residence
> Relative labor market conditions for nonwhites
> Number of children
> Disability

The wage rate of the family head is the primary determinant of the economic status of the family if the head is fully employed. Wage rate is also presumed to reflect the level of a worker's skills, representing the payoff to education,

occupational choice, job training, accumulated experience, good fortune, and so
forth.

Since workers with limited skills are likely to be the last hired and the
first laid off, we would expect a very strong relationship between wage rate and
the incidence of unemployment. The analysis does indeed show such a relationship, but it also shows that other aspects of a worker's qualifications, particularly education and occupation, have important payoffs in terms of reduced unemployment which are over and above their effects on earnings rates.

The effects of hourly earnings on the expected level of unemployment are
shown in Figure 4.3. The simple average of unemployment, represented by the
dashed line, falls very smoothly with wage rate. The independent effect of wage
rate, after controlling for the effects of other variables in the analysis, is
stronger than the simple effect at low wage levels, but essentially disappears
at wage levels above $3.50 per hour. The more serious problems associated with
low wages in the multivariate model reflect the experience of low wage workers
who are not farmers, while farmers' relative freedom from unemployment is accounted for by the occupation coefficients. On the other hand, the less serious
employment difficulties at high wages shown by the simple averages are more
closely attributable to the higher education levels of such workers and do not
appear as an independent effect of wage rate in the multivariate model. Thus, a
worker with little education earning $5.00 or more per hour was no less likely to
experience unemployment than a similarly educated counterpart earning $3.50 per
hour.

The relationship between education and the incidence of unemployment is
very strong and remains so even when other indicators of success in the labor
market are included in the model. Of the various steps of educational attainment
the completion of high school has the greatest payoff in reduced unemployment.
Both the simple and the multivariate relationships illustrated in Figure 4.4
show that the expected work loss of roughly 400 hours in five years for workers
who did not finish high school is nearly three times the expected work loss for
high school graduates. The pattern at low education levels is somewhat erratic:
those who completed less than 6 grades of schooling suffer the greatest work loss
but those with 6 to 8 grades experience a work loss some 100 hours smaller than
do high school dropouts. Even this odd middle group, however, has an expected
loss more than twice that for high school graduates. The simple means show a
further decline in employment problems for workers with college educations. This
effect is largely channeled through access to professional and managerial occupations and does not show up as an independent effect of education in the multi-

183

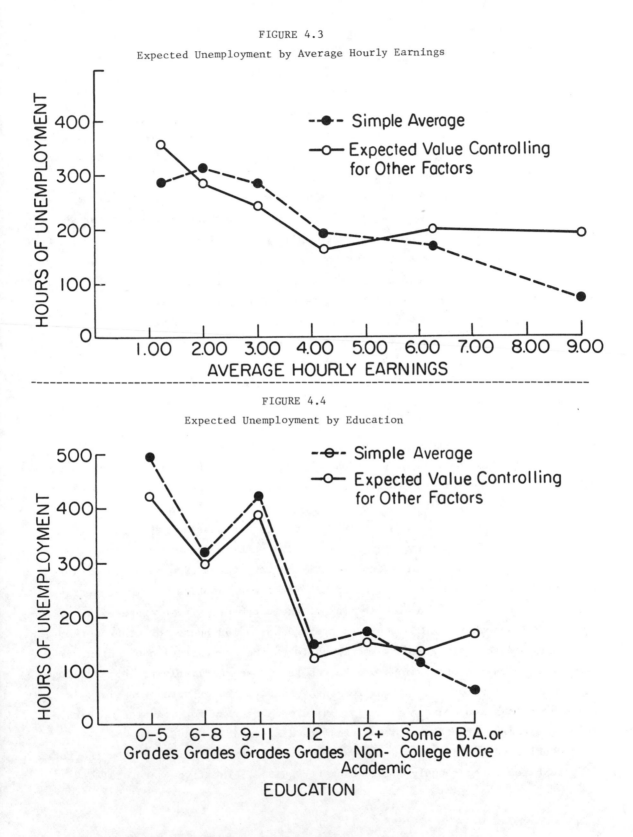

FIGURE 4.3

Expected Unemployment by Average Hourly Earnings

FIGURE 4.4

Expected Unemployment by Education

variate relationship.

The occupational effects on labor market problems referred to above fall into three broad categories -- self-employed businessmen and farmers, white collar workers, and blue collar workers. Self-employed workers have the lowest incidence of unemployment with an average work loss some 150 hours less than would be expected on the basis of their other characteristics. It should be noted, however, that no shortage of work does not necessarily imply no shortage of money for these workers whose incomes are especially vulnerable to the vagaries of weather or market conditions.

As might be expected, white collar workers experience significantly less serious employment difficulties than do blue collar workers. White collar workers lose an average of 75 hours of work, while blue collar workers lose an average of 366 hours. A substantial portion of the difference between the two groups is attributable to differences in education, wage level, and other characteristics, but even after controlling for these factors, the expected work loss for blue collar workers is more than 150 hours greater than for white collar workers.

Age is often included in models of earnings to represent skills gained through labor market experience. The relationship of age to expected unemployment indicates that such skills contribute to the reduction of unemployment among older workers. The expected level of unemployment for workers under age 35 is about 275 hours in five years as compared with 150 hours for workers over age 55 with intermediate values for those in the middle age range.

For the most part the wage, eduation, occupation, and experience effects discussed above reflect the fact that workers who are worse off with respect to income are also likely to be worse off with respect to employment difficulties. Farmers are an exception to the rule in that they are substantially free of unemployment despite their low wage rates. Union members are another prominent exception. While union members command higher wage rates than nonunion workers with equivalent characteristics, expecially at lower eduation levels, this increase is accompanied by a greater risk of unemployment. The average of work lost by union members is 353 hours as compared with 153 hours for other workers. About half of the difference is attributable to the concentration of union members in blue collar occupations and to the fact that relatively few have college educations, but after controlling for these factors the expected work loss is still more than 100 hours greater for union members than for nonunion members. This result is consistent with the findings discussed in Chapter 7, Volume II.

Published monthly statistics on unemployment rates typically show the rate for nonwhites to be roughly double that for whites. The five-year total of unemployment hours or weeks experienced by stable male heads exhibits a similar though somewhat smaller differential. Nonwhites lost an average of $8\frac{1}{2}$ weeks of work to unemployment during the period from 1967 through 1971 as compared to the average of 5 weeks lost by white workers during the same period.

The relative differential is slightly larger in the proportion of workers who were unemployed for 30 weeks or more. Ten percent of nonwhites were so affected as compared with 5.4% of whites and a large part of the racial differential in the incidence of very serious unemployment persists when we control for education as can be seen in Figure 4.5. The largest differential incidence occurs among high school graduates. While the completion of high school very significantly reduces the risk of prolonged unemployment for both whites and nonwhites, the proportionate reduction is several times as great among whites.

In the full multivariate model, race no longer shows an independent effect on expected unemployment. This result does not indicate that nonwhites are essentially free of disproportionate employment problems, but rather that the effects of labor market discrimination occur at another level. Nonwhites are more likely to find employment in low wage jobs and blue collar occupations than are whites with the same education. Once given this employment situation, nonwhite workers do not experience significantly more serious employment difficulties than the smaller proportion of whites in similar jobs.

Almost by definition we would expect unemployment experiences of individuals to be related to differences in the unemployment rates in counties where they live. The data do show the expected relationships but they are not at all strong. Workers who fared best were those living in areas where the unemployment rate bucked a rising trend in the country as a whole and remained below 4% in 1971. The average unemployment for this group was about 65 hours less than the mean unemployment for all workers but only 14% of the population lived in such areas. Another 2% of the population lived in areas where the unemployment rate was below 2% in 1968 but about 4% in 1971 and they experienced unemployment about 70 hours less than the mean. Average unemployment levels for workers in areas with higher unemployment rates in 1968 and 1971 fall within 30 hours of one another and slightly above the mean.

Local employment conditions for blacks and other racial minorities often are not accurately represented by the overall unemployment rate, which usually reflects the experience of the predominant white population. In questionnaires sent to local employment security departments, information was solicited on the relative employment opportunities for low skilled nonwhites. About 31% of nonwhites lived in areas where the employment opportunities were characterized as

FIGURE 4.5

Proportion Experiencing 30 or More Weeks of Unemployment
in Five Years by Education and Race

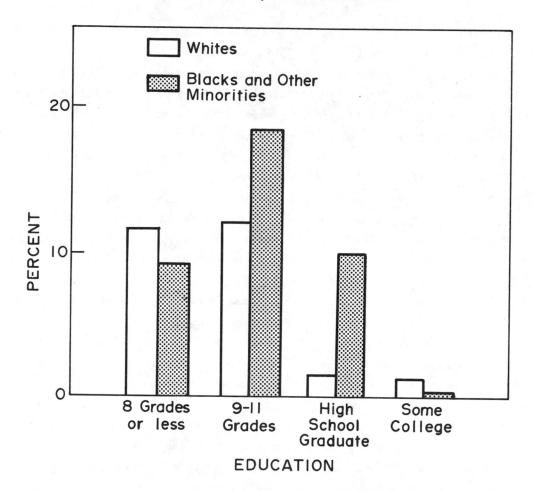

"about the same" as for whites and 55% lived in areas with "worse" opportunities. The latter group experienced about 75 hours more unemployment than the former, but only a third of this differential appears as an independent effect in the multivariate relationship. About 7% of nonwhites lived in areas with "much worse" relative employment conditions and they experienced an average of 165 hours more unemployment, but the differential in the multivariate context is only 40 hours.

The number of children in the family was included as the variable in the analysis because the economic status of a family depends on the number of mouths to be fed as well as total family income. It can also be hypothesized that family responsibilities would pressure a worker to find another job sooner and thus have less unemployment. Among workers with less than a high school education we find an unfortunate tendency for higher incidence of unemployment among heads of large families. The average work loss rises from 331 hours for heads of families with one or two children, to 422 hours for those with three or four children, and 479 hours for those with still larger families. Part of the relationship is due to lower skill levels among heads of large families, but a 100 hour differential remains as an independent effect. The overall result is a compounding of economic difficulties in those families for whom even full employment income may be thinly spread. The relationship between unemployment and family size is much weaker among workers who completed at least high school, but there is still an estimated differential of 35 hours.

Disability is the major cause of reduced labor force participation among male family heads below retirement age. Disabled workers who do participate in the labor force face an increased incidence of unemployment for closely related reasons. For some, unemployment may result from interruption of employment due to a period of full disability, while for others it results from difficulty in finding work which they are able to perform. Expected unemployment was 313 hours for those who reported a limiting disability in both the initial and final years and 291 hours for those with a disability in one of the end years which did not persist through the full period, as compared with 204 hours for workers with no reported disability. Workers with transitory disability reported in one of the middle years showed no difference in unemployment experience.

Unemployment is an economic problem which rests most heavily on workers of low economic status but which also affects a substantial minority of workers at middle income levels and above. The factors related to the incidence of unemployment are much the same as those which determine earning rates, but even when wage rate is included in the analysis, worker characteristics such as education and occupation exhibit important independent effects on the expected level of unemployment. The education effect shows a particularly large payoff to the completion of high school, with graduates having expected unemployment about half that of dropouts. According to bivariate analysis, the relative reduction in extensive unemployment for nonwhite high school graduates, though still substantial, is not nearly as large as the reduction for whites. The multivariate analysis, however, shows a negligible race effect indicating that effects of discrimination on the incidence of unemployment are not greater than would be expected given the other characteristics of jobs in which nonwhites find employment.

Membership in a union or in a self-employed occupation has an effect on unemployment which is opposite to the respective effects on wage rates, indicating a possible tradeoff between employment security and earning capacity.

Five-year unemployment experience of family heads is related to measures of local employment conditions as might be expected, but the relationship is not strong.

Among family heads with low education, the economic difficulties of those with large families are compounded by greater expected unemployment. Similarly, the disabled who are able to work experience significantly more unemployment than non-disabled workers.

II. Institutional Factors Relating to Work Hour Choices

Reductions in work effort below standard full-time work are largely the result of involuntary work loss due to unemployment or illness. Overall, however, unemployment and illness account for only about 30% of the interpersonal variance in work hours among male heads of households over the five-year period. A much larger portion of the variance in work hours among such workers is the result of a distribution of work effort which extends well above the standard 40 hours a week, 50 weeks a year.

The established pattern of research in the area of policy-relevant work hours behavior has involved the estimation of the "income" and "substitution" effects. In the basic economic theory a worker is conceptualized as trading off the satisfaction or utility derived from earned income for the utility he could get from the leisure which must be given up in order to earn income. He is then presumed to adjust his work hours to get that combination of income and leisure which yields the greatest overall satisfaction. If other factors are equal, the point at which this equilibrium level of work effort is reached is determined by two offsetting forces. The income effect reflects the fact that a low income worker has a greater need for additional income to meet basic material needs than does a higher income worker. If two workers with different incomes but the same work hours were given the chance to work additional hours at the same wage rate, the low income worker would be expected to work a greater number of additional hours than the high income worker who could afford to enjoy relatively more leisure.

The substitution effect, on the other hand, reflects the fact that a worker with given income and work hours would be more likely to work additional hours if he were offered a high wage rate for those additional hours. Conversely, if the worker had a very low marginal wage rate he might choose to reduce his work hours because he could enjoy more leisure at only a small cost in lost income.

In our society where a very large part of income is earned from work, most variations in one of these effects are accompanied by similar variation in the offsetting effect. Low-wage workers have low incomes at standard work hours and consequently there is a strong income effect which motivates them to increase work hours. But the same low wage results in a substitution effect which discourages a worker from additional work effort because it brings in so little income per hour. At the other extreme, high wage workers are unlikely to have a pressing need to work more than full time but are encouraged to do so because it pays so well.

Thus, estimates of the effects of differing or changing wage rates on hours of work yield only the net result of the two countervailing effects. It is necessary to obtain separate estimates of the response of labor supply to nonwage income in order to distinguish the income effect. Given an estimate of this effect, we can then estimate the substitution effect from the response to wage rates.

The necessity for estimating the separate effects arises because proposed public policies such as a negative income tax or other income supplementation programs break up the usual correspondence between wage rates and income and alter the balance between income and substitution effects. On the one hand, an income supplement reduces the need for extra income and the pressure for extra work hours. On the other, the provisions which reduce the supplement if earnings increase have the effect of reducing a worker's marginal wage rate, and cause an additional work-inhibiting substitution effect. Thus, theory gives an unambiguous prediction that the income supplementation proposals would result in reduction of work effort by eligible workers who were in equilibrium before the onset of the program. And the amount of the work reduction should be estimable given estimates of the separate income and substitution effects.[1]

---

[1]If a worker is assumed to have optimized his work hours at a given constant wage rate and level of nonwage income, his expected response to a small change in

Many researchers, beginning with Kosters (1966), have elaborated this simple model to apply to a household in which two or more workers optimize their work hours at different wage rates. In the elaborate models, as in the simple ones, responses to nonwage income are interpreted as measures of the income effect while responses to wage rates represent combinations of income and substitution effect with the additional complexity that one worker responds to others' wage rates as well as his own.

A basic difficulty with research based on the theoretical income-substitution model is that the conditions which must be assumed in order to derive the mathematical relationships do not correspond to the conditions faced by a majority of workers in the U.S. labor market. Of all employed male heads of households in 1971 *less than 13%* held jobs in which they were free to vary their work hours at well defined marginal wage rates and nearly half of those gained their flexibility of work hours by taking a second job. The employment conditions faced by the remaining 87% of employed males differ from the theoretical assumptions for a variety of reasons, ranging from constraints on work hours to the absence of a defined marginal wage.

It can be argued that constraints on the number of hours worked on one's main job are not critically important because the worker has the option of taking a second job. But under many circumstances, a second job will require the overhead costs of job search and perhaps training. It will often pay lower wages than his regular job and will involve disproportionate travel costs. In short, while an opportunity to vary work hours exists there is a substantial discontinuity and the potential net income per hour to be realized from taking a second job is not well represented by the wage on the primary job.

Over a longer period a worker might change main jobs so that, even if he doesn't have freedom to vary his work hours in the short run, the constrained hours are close to those hours which he prefers to work. But job changes involve costs, often very substantial ones, ranging from lost seniority or pension rights to relocation costs. And it is not at all clear that in changing jobs to get more or fewer work hours a worker would retain his current wage rate.

---

wage may be decomposed into income and substitution effect according to the following basic relationship:

$$\frac{dh}{dw} = \frac{\partial h}{\partial w_y} + H\frac{\partial h}{\partial Y}$$

where $\frac{dh}{dw}$ is the change in work hours resulting from a small change in wage rate for all hours worked; $\frac{\partial h}{\partial w_y}$, the pure substitution effect, is the expected change in work hours due to a small change in marginal wage rate holding income level constant. H is the equilibrium level of work hours, and $\frac{\partial h}{\partial y}$ is the expected change in work hours from a change in income with wages held constant.

Two basic questions must be dealt with in assessing the impact of institutional complexities in the labor market on the labor supply behavior predicted by economic theory. First, is it possible to obtain reasonable estimates of the economic parameters from statistical studies of interpersonal differences and temporal changes in labor supply occurring naturally in the population? Second, given estimates of those parameters, do the constraints and discontinuities which characterize most employment opportunities modify the labor supply responses which may be expected to result from a policy change?

We turn first to a more detailed analysis of the nature of employment opportunities and their differences from theoretical assumptions. It is important to understand how institutional factors are related to the basic economic variable whose effects we wish to estimate.

JOBS WITHOUT MARGINAL PAY

Salaried positions and other jobs for which the relationship between marginal work hours and income is indeterminant represent a major institutional departure from the assumed conditions of the theoretical model. In the absence of a defined rate of pay for variations in work effort a worker cannot make the marginal choices between income and leisure which are assumed in the theory. It should be emphasized that the returns to marginal work in these jobs are not necessarily zero. A salaried worker's overtime may increase his chances of promotion, more cultivation may increase crop yields, and longer business days probably generate more sales. The essential point is that the returns can be estimated only with substantial error by even the worker himself and are quite sure to be poorly measured by averaging his total earning over total hours of work. Further, it is clear that long run decisions embodied in the choice of such a job are relatively much more important in determining income and leisure choices than would be the case for workers who are free to vary hours at a given rate of pay.

Of all male household heads employed in 1972, an estimated 45.7% held jobs in which they would not have been paid for overtime work. A small fraction of these workers did have hourly wage rates for their regular work time which can be interpreted as their marginal wage for a reduction in work hours, but 42.8% of workers did not have defined marginal wage rates for either expansion or contraction of work effort.

The proportion of workers holding jobs without marginal pay varies widely across types of jobs. Even casual observation of the labor market indicates that such jobs are much more prevalent at higher wage levels. A simple descriptive analysis of who it is that is likely to have a job without marginal wages sustains this impression in part and furnishes useful insights into the complexities of labor market opportunities as well. The major factors associated with the frequency of such jobs are shown in Figure 4.6.[1]

A salaried position is the most common example of a job without marginal wages and given the popular association of salaried jobs with white collar occupations, the large differential between white and blue collar occupations is not surprising. Nearly two-thirds of white collar workers hold jobs without marginal wages as compared with less than one-fifth of blue collar workers. And proprietors and farmers as a group are still less likely than white collar workers to receive a well-defined rate of pay for marginal variations in work hours.

Among white collar workers, the proportion in salaried positions generally increases with job status ranging from 41.9% for sales and clerical personnel to 80% for managers. The popular image of salaried professions is apparently based on those with college degrees and particularly those in education, government, and professional service industries of whom 90% hold salaried positions. Among professional and technical personnel with less education, fewer than 40% are paid on a salaried basis. Salaried positions are also less universal among managers at lower education levels but the differential is smaller than for professionals. Union membership is low in white collar occupations and is concentrated among sales and clerical personnel where it is associated with a much greater prevalence of hourly pay for regular hours and overtime.

Among blue collar workers, the prevalence of hourly pay rates does not differ much by occupation, but there are substantial differentials by union membership and industry. Hourly wages are almost universal among unionized blue collar workers with more than 19 out of 20 workers so paid. And nonunion workers in the manufacturing and construction industries are paid by the hour in 5 out of 6 cases. Nonunion workers in other industries, however, are much more likely to hold jobs in which they are not paid for marginal variations in work; nearly 40% work under such conditions. The absence of marginal wages and resultant effects on the behavior of these workers is the more important for policy purposes because of the disproportionate numbers of low wage workers in this sector. The lower incidence of jobs without marginal pay among nonwhites (in nonunionized industries other than manufacturing and construction) is not easily interpreted. In the absence of an independent half sample for testing the model, the differential might have been dismissed as a statistical artifact uncovered by the search algorithm. However, given that a large race differential was also evident

---

[1] The categorization used is based on a search analysis using the AID algorithm. The search was conducted on a half sample and the resulting model was tested and confirmed on the other half. The percentages shown are based on the full sample.

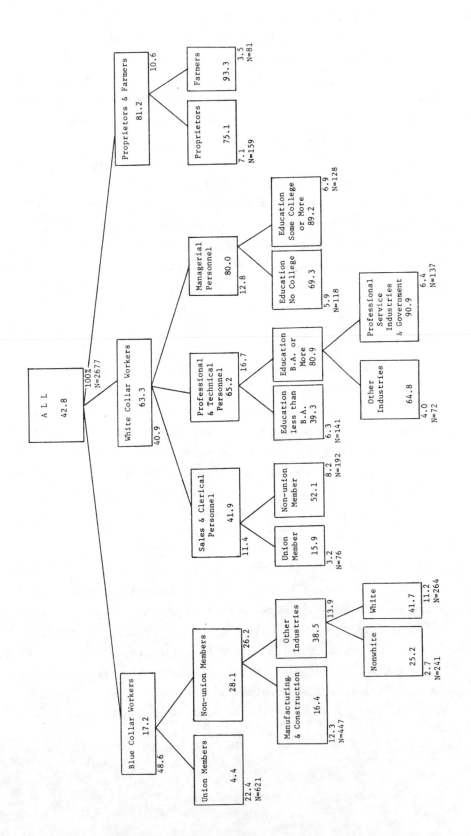

FIGURE 4.6

Proportion of Males in Jobs Without Marginal Pay

MTR 5533

194

in the test sample -- 15% as compared with 18% in the search sample -- the likelihood that it is a chance result is very low.

One of the problems of interpretation is that the benefits of such jobs are
not clear cut. A blue collar job which does not pay for marginal work does not
carry the same image of prestige that is associated with a salaried white collar
position. And as shown in Figure 4.7, the higher frequency of such jobs in the
higher pay ranges occurs only among white collar workers. Except for the high
frequency of non-marginal wage jobs at the very lowest average wage levels, the
incidence of such jobs is nearly neutral with respect to wage rate among blue
collar workers. On the other hand, there appears to be a slightly higher incidence of such jobs among blue collar workers with more education and/or higher
scores on the sentence completion test. An hypothesis which will be explored
subsequently is that jobs of this sort offer opportunities for greater earnings
through longer work hours than are generally available in the conventional sector. Restricted access to such nonwage opportunities may be a subtle form of
discrimination experienced by nonwhites. It is consistent with expectations that
such discrimination would be more severe among the small local firms which characterize the nonunionized, nonmanufacture sector.

In overview then, jobs without marginal pay are the predominant form of
employment for upper level white collar workers and for proprietors and farmers,
while such jobs are very much the exception for unionized blue collar workers.
For nonunionized blue collar workers and lower level white collar workers, jobs
without marginal pay constitute a significant minority of employment situations.
Workers in these jobs do not have an opportunity to make marginal changes in
income and leisure at their present jobs, but their choice of such jobs may reflect a long run accommodation of their work-leisure preferences.

CONSTRAINTS ON WORK HOURS

Jobs which do not pay a worker for marginal variations in work effort effectively constrain the worker from adjusting his combinations of earnings and
leisure in the short run. Many workers on jobs which do pay for marginal work
face similar constraints in that additional work is often not available on their
main jobs and because reductions in work effort are frequently not optional. A
sequence of four questions was asked of heads of families in each survey year to
determine the extent of such constraints on work effort and the extent to which
workers were dissatisfied with their work hours when constrained.[1]

[1] See Panel Study of Income Dynamics, Volume I, for the exact questions asked.

FIGURE 4.7

Proportions of Workers in Jobs without Marginal Pay
by Average Hourly Earnings and Occupation

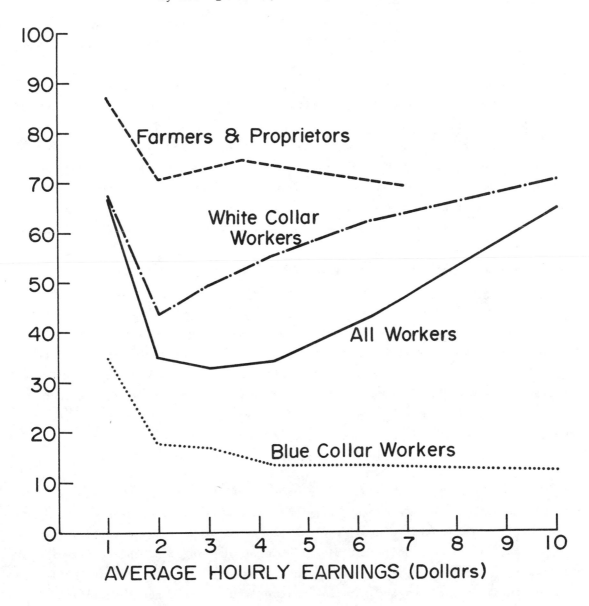

The distributions of combinations of constraint -- satisfaction responses for workers with a single job paying marginal wages in 1971 -- are shown in Table 4.1. The distributions are remarkably similar across major wage-occupation groups, especially in contrast to the wide variation across these groups in the proportion of workers who are paid for marginal variations in work hours.

The most striking feature of the distributions is that fewer than one in five workers in such jobs are fully free to optimize their work hours at this given wage rate as assumed in the basic economic theory. Another 25% to 30% of workers had some opportunity to vary work hours but chose satisfactory work hours at the upper or lower limits of the available range. White collar workers were more likely than blue collar workers to choose the lower limit of available work hours. About one-fifth of high wage blue collar workers and one-fourth of workers in other groups were fully constrained in their work hours but found these hours acceptable. Eighteen to twenty-five percent of white collar workers and 30% of blue collar workers said they wanted more work than was available on their jobs and 5% to 9% of workers reported that they would have preferred to work less and accept the loss of income.

Constraints on work effort are not generally such a stable feature of a job as is the mode of payment, since the amount of work available often varies with the economic conditions faced by the employer. Also individual preferences vary over time as a function of unusual needs for income and numerous other factors so that a worker may choose work hours within the available range in one period but against a limit in another. Overall, the fact that a very large proportion of workers face a variety of constraints on their hours of work is consistently observed in all five survey years. There are also persistent differences among jobs in the amount of work hour flexibility available which workers might be expected to consider when making job choices.

MOONLIGHTING

A second job provides another possible solution to inadequate work hours on one's main job and may allow greater flexibility and cause less disruption than changing main jobs. A significant minority of workers do avail themselves of moonlighting opportunities, but even second job holders face employment conditions quite different from the assumed conditions underlying the calculation of income and substitution effects. As shown in Table 4.2, between one-fifth and one-third of workers in the different occupation wage categories had second jobs in 1971 with the higher proportion among white collar workers and at lower average wage rates. The proportion of blue collar moonlighters who are free to vary

TABLE 4.1

Freedom to Vary Work Hours by Occupation* and Wage Level
for Employed Males with One Job which Paid Wages for Marginal Work.

Male Heads of Families in 1971

	Blue Collar		White Collar	
	Low Wage (Under $3.50 per hour)	High Wage ($3.50 or more per hour)	Low Wage (Under $3.50 per hour)	High Wage ($3.50 or more per hour)
Free to increase or decrease	14.5%	17.9%	16.6%	17.2%
Free to increase, not free to decrease but satisfied	8.8	9.3	17.7	16.6
Free to decrease, not free to increase but satisfied	16.4	18.3	14.4	10.4
Not free to vary but satisfied	24.5	19.6	23.3	24.3
Wanted more work than was available	30.9	29.1	18.9	25.8
Would have preferred to work less even if earned less	4.9	5.7	9.2	5.5
	100.0%	100.0%	100.0%	100.0%

Proportions of Workers in Occupation-Wage Categories
Holding One Job which Pays Marginal Wages

Blue Collar		White Collar	
Low Wage	High Wage	Low Wage	High Wage
59.4%	68.5%	30.0%	24.7%

*Blue Collar -- Craftsmen, foremen, operatives, laborers and service workers.

White Collar -- Professional and technical, managerial, and sales and clerical personnel.

Farmers and proprietors have been excluded because of very small sample size.

TABLE 4.2

Effective Constraints Among Second Job Holders
by Occupation* and Wage Level --
Male Heads of Families in 1971

	Blue Collar		White Collar	
	Low Wage	High Wage	Low Wage	High Wage
Free to vary at given marginal wage	29.4%	33.1%	12.8%	14.7%
Some or full constraint	29.8	29.9	20.3	11.7
No marginal wage	16.3	11.6	47.4	56.8
Want more work	24.4	25.4	19.4	16.9
	100.0%	100.0%	100.0%	100.0%

Proportions of Wage-Occupation Groups Holding Second Jobs

	Blue Collar		White Collar	
	Low Wage	High Wage	Low Wage	High Wage
	25.4%	19.3%	33.8%	25.7%

*Blue Collar -- Craftsmen, foremen, operatives, laborers and service workers.

White Collar -- Professional and technical, managerial, and sales and clerical personnel.

Farmers and proprietors have been excluded because of very small sample size.

their work hours at a defined marginal wage is roughly double the percentage of those with only one job but is still under one-third. Another 30% still face some constraints but are satisfied with their hours, while fully one-quarter of blue collar workers wanted more work than they could get, even with their second jobs. The proportions constrained and/or wanting more work are lower but far from negligible among white collar second job holders.

The proportion of second job holders who are not paid definite marginal wages is only slightly lower than the proportion for all workers, and there is a very similar pattern across wage and occupation groups ranging from 11.6% for high wage blue collar workers to 56.8% for high wage white collar workers. The absence of a defined marginal wage rate is less of a theoretical problem in the case of second jobs, however, since a worker's average rate of pay on his second job serves as the effective marginal rate for his total work effort so long as work on the second job is a relatively small fraction of total work effort.

CHOICE OF EMPLOYMENT MODE

There are two different perspectives from which a researcher may view the widespread constraints, discontinuities, and absence of marginal wages which characterize the employment opportunities in the current U.S. labor market. At one extreme, one may interpret them as evidence that a majority of workers have very little to say about the amount they work, and that the variations in hours of work which are observed in the population are largely a function of employers' choices and workers' good or bad luck for having found particular jobs. At the other extreme, one might acknowledge the existence of complexities in labor market opportunities but presume that a worker can make long run job choices from a sufficiently broad and well understood variety of alternatives so that his resulting work hours are not significantly different from those he would have chosen under the simpler conditions assumed in economic models. In the following section we investigate the variety of different job characteristics for which we have measures in an attempt to get a better understanding of the set of employment opportunities from which a worker makes job choices which may optimize his long run labor supply.

We first consider some simple theoretical aspects of constraints. If a worker has a choice between two jobs which are similar in all respects except that one has fixed work hours and the other allows him to choose how much he wants to work, he would presumably prefer the latter except in the special case where the fixed work hours happen to coincide with those he would have chosen. This result is illustrated on the preference diagram shown in Figure 4.8.[1] Thus,

---

[1] Both income and leisure provide satisfaction for a worker and the points on an indifference curve -- C_1 or C_2 -- represent different combinations of income and

FIGURE 4.8

The Effects of Constraints on Work Hours

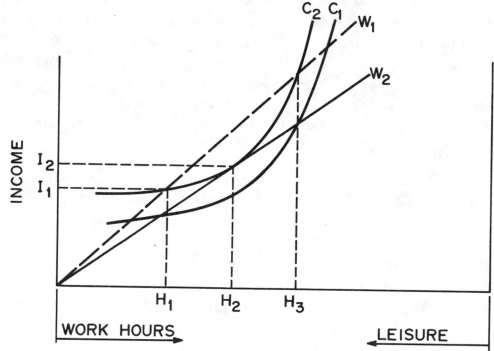

if a worker's hours are fixed at non-optimal levels his total satisfaction is lower than if he were free to optimize at the same wage rate. However, if a worker were paid a premium wage rate in a constraining job, he might choose it over one which allowed freedom to optimize. In the figure, a job paying the higher wage rate W_1 with hours constrained at H_1 or H_3 would give the same level of satisfaction as one paying wage W_2 and allowing choice of work hours.

Thus, in a competitive labor market with workers of equivalent skills and preferences, and jobs which were similar in other respects, firms which didn't offer choice of work hours would need to pay premium wages relative to those firms offering choice in work hours in order to attract and keep a labor force. The premium would be necessary for constrained work hours either greater or less than those generally preferred and would need to be larger the more divergent they were from preferred hours. With a diversity of preference among workers the fixed hour premium would be relatively small over the range of more common preferences but would not be expected to drop to zero because of the search costs of finding workers whose preferences exactly matched the hours offered.

The fact that we observe such a large proportion of jobs in which work hours are fixed or restricted, despite the expected wage premium, leads us to the presumption that there are gains in efficiency which make such premiums worthwhile to the firm. And we would expect just such gains in efficiency from coordination of multiple production stages by assembly line work and shift work which optimize the utilization of a highly capital intensive plant. Both of these factors reduce the flexibility of workers' hours. On the other hand, we would expect firms offering fixed or restricted work hours to attempt to minimize the wage premium by adapting their production schedules so that the work hours offered correspond as much as possible to the preferences of a majority of workers.

Given the predominance of constraining jobs but the expectation that they will tend to accommodate majority preferences, we might expect interesting differ-

---

leisure which yield the same total level of satisfaction. The level of satisfaction represented by curve C_2 is higher than that for C_1 since the worker has more income at any given level of leisure or more leisure at any given level of income. The line W_2 represents the combinations of income and work hours which are possible if the worker earns a constant wage rate given by the slope of the line. The highest level of satisfaction which the worker can reach at that wage rate occurs when the worker supplies H_2 hours and earns income I_2. If he were to work more hours his total satisfaction would decrease because he values the remaining leisure more highly than the money he could earn by giving it up. Conversely, the extra leisure which he would gain by decreasing work hours is worth less than the income given up, so fewer work hours would also reduce satisfaction.

202

ences to be evident among workers with atypical income-leisure preferences as Figure 4.9 demonstrates.[1]

In a labor market where the prevailing wage is set by large firms offering a restricted range of work hours which satisfies a majority of workers, the opportunity may exist for small firms with suitable technology to cater to (or exploit) the divergent preferences of a minority of workers by offering unrestricted work hours at a lower wage rate. In theory we might expect such jobs to attract workers with work hours preferences at either extreme. However, among male family heads in the U.S. labor force, we observe that most of those who are free to vary their work hours work more rather than fewer hours.

The above discussion does not give clear implications as to the expected work hours characteristic of jobs which do not pay marginal wages. We would, however, expect such jobs to play a distinctly different role in the market faced by blue collar workers as compared with white collar workers. In the latter group such jobs are the predominant form of employment. They are also associated with a variety of job characteristics such as the level of responsibility and sense of achievement from work. The relative importance of such factors poses very substantial problems for analysis of job choices of white collar workers in the simple income and work hours dimensions. Thus, while there are many interesting issues to be explored in this area, the subsequent analysis is restricted to blue collar workers. In so doing, we retain a great majority of the working population which might be affected by income supplementation policies.

Among blue collar workers we observe that the minority who hold jobs without marginal pay have a distribution of work hours quite similar to that of workers who are free to vary hours. This suggests that the two kinds of jobs occupy a similar niche in the labor market, offering more satisfactory combinations of income and work hours to a minority of workers who would be dissatisfied with the restricted work hours available in the dominant sector. The hypothesis we wish to test is that workers in such jobs command a lower wage rate than they

---

[1]The income-leisure indifference curves of two typical workers are represented by C_1 and C_2. If free to vary their work hours at wage rate W_1, they would choose H_1 and H_2 work hours, respectively. At the premium wage W_2 both would accept constrained work hours in the range between H_3 and H_4 and their separate ranges of acceptance are somewhat broader. Indifference curves of a worker with an atypically high preference for income relative to leisure are represented by C_3 and C_3'. Curve C_3 represents the level of satisfaction he could attain if he were free to choose his work hours at wage W_1, while curve C_3' represents the level attained if he holds a job paying wage W_2 with hours fixed at H_1. He could also attain the satisfaction level of C_3' if he were free to vary his work hours at the lower wage W_3. He would thus prefer a job paying slightly more than W_3 and allowing choice of work hours to the constraining job paying wage W_2.

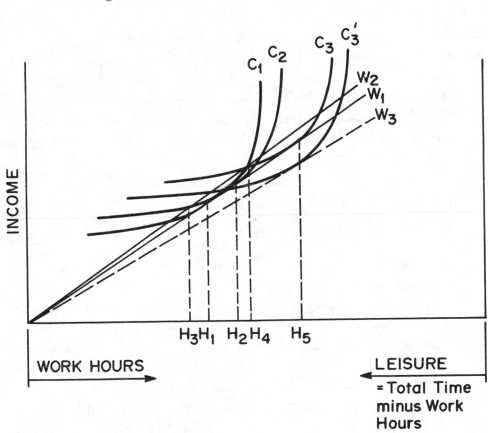

FIGURE 4.9

Divergent Preferences, Work Hours, and Wage Rates

would if they held jobs with more restricted work hours.

To investigate the possibility that jobs allowing unusual work hours also offer lower wages, we classify workers' employment situation into 12 employment modes which differ in the extent to which they accommodate divergent work hours. The classification is made on the basis of constraint or variability of work hours, presence or absence of marginal wages, and whether single or multiple jobs. We then estimate the effects of the various employment modes on a worker's expected average hourly earnings using a model which also controls for more traditional determinants of earning capacity. The expected deviations from average work hours associated with the various employment modes are also estimated. The use of the same predictive model serves to control for the dependence of work hours on expected wage level. The number of weeks of unemployment and illness are also included as control variables allowing us to observe the effects of employment mode independent of these factors which are taken to be exogenous in this analysis.

The employment mode classification used in this analysis is shown in Table 4.3 along with the estimated coefficients for average hourly earnings and annual work hours. The control variables included in the model are listed below the table.

The joint effects of the various employment modes on hourly earnings and work hours are more easily observed in the graphical presentation of Figure 4.10. The employment mode points are distributed quite consistently in a diagonal pattern with lower wages for those modes with high annual work hours and higher wages for the modes with low work hours. For the most part, the wage deficit for the higher hour modes is of a size that might be voluntarily accepted by a worker with a high preference or need for additional income.

If we focus on the employment modes representing single-job holders who were satisfied with their work hours (group numbers 1, 3, 4, 5, 6) we have a picture of the average opportunities available to a worker who wishes to adjust his work hours by changing jobs. The dashed line fitted to the points for these employment modes provides an estimate of the reduction in wage rate associated with an increase in work hours by switching modes. A blue collar worker with average qualifications in a job with constraints on work hours had an expected hourly wage of $4.27 in 1971 and predicted annual work hours of 2013 for an expected annual income of $8596.[1] A worker with the same qualifications in the

---

[1] Based on the average of wage and work hours coefficients for the three constrained but satisfied modes -- groups 4, 5 and 6 -- added to the sample mean values for wage rates and work hours.

TABLE 4.3

Net Effects of Employment Mode on Average Hourly Earnings
and Annual Work Hours for Employed Blue Collar Male Family Heads
in 1971 Coefficients

	Effect on Average Hourly Earnings	Effect on Annual Work Hours	Unweighted N	Percentage of Population
No Second Job, No Marginal Wage				
Satisfied with work hours	$-.02	117	116	9.4%
Want more work	.24	-190	38	1.9
No Second Job, Paid for Marginal Work				
Full freedom to vary hours	.03	30	125	9.8
Freedom to increase only	.16	-123	94	6.5
Freedom to decrease only	.19	- 79	126	11.6
Fully constrained but satisfied	.04	- 95	226	14.8
Want more work	.06	-156	329	19.6
Want less work	.70	10	54	5.0
Second Job				
No marginal wage, satisfied	-.80	324	33	2.9
Paid for marginal work, free to vary	-.22	225	77	6.9
Part or full constraint, satisfied	-.22	226	75	6.1
Want more work	-.67	230	83	5.5
			1376	100.0%
Mean value	$4.16	2108 hrs.		
Beta^2 for mode classifications	.022	.073		

Control Variables Included

Education	Education of father
Verbal test score	Race
Age	Size of place grew up
Job tenure	Size of largest city in current county
Whether veteran	Whether enjoy job
Occupation	Weeks of unemployment
Industry	Weeks of illness
Union membership	Wage level for unskilled labor in county

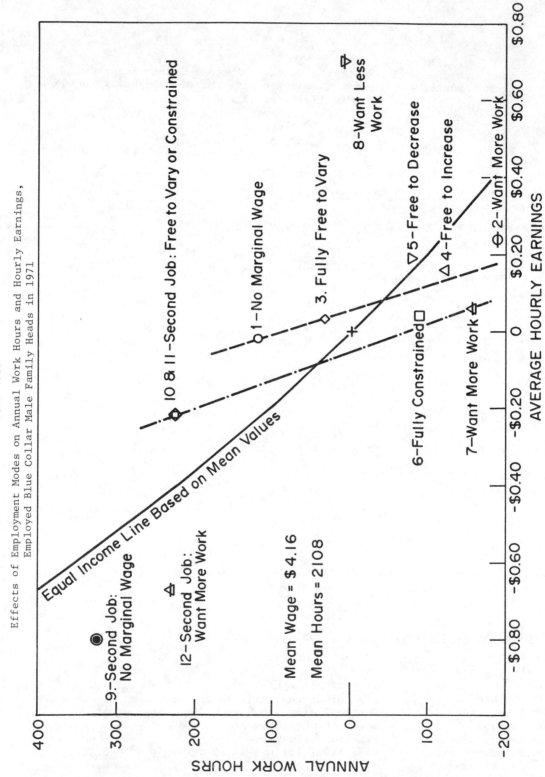

FIGURE 4.10

Effects of Employment Modes on Annual Work Hours and Hourly Earnings,
Employed Blue Collar Male Family Heads in 1971

employment mode without marginal wages would have expected wage rates and work hours of $4.14 and 2225, respectively, for an income of $9212. A worker switching from a typical constrained job to one without marginal wages would earn $616 more income for 212 additional hours of work. His effective marginal wage from switching jobs would thus be $2.91 or 68% of his initial average hourly earnings.

We place more confidence in the result that the effective marginal wage to be expected from switching jobs is lower than a worker's average hourly earnings than we do in the specific estimate of the magnitude of the deficit. The various employment modes as we have defined them are still very broad. Workers with preferences for long work hours are expected to be more heavily represented in jobs with freedom to vary work hours and in those without marginal wages but certainly not to the exclusion of workers with more typical preferences who find employment in such jobs for other reasons. And similarly, some jobs with constraints on work hours offer sufficient range to satisfy quite divergent preferences. The estimated wage-work hours trade-off is thus based on relatively small shifts in the overall distributions of work hours.

Another difficulty is that we have not been able to control specifically for the presence of workers who would prefer to work *less* than standard work hours. Such workers would also be expected to prefer jobs with freedom to vary work hours and their disproportionate presence in that work mode would bias the average work hours of that group downward. However, the comparative distributions of work hours show that, while there is substantial variation of work effort within modes, the major differences among single job employment modes are in their accommodation of higher than standard work hours.[1]

The moonlighting employment modes include a much heavier preponderance of workers with preferences for high work hours than do any of the single job modes we have defined. A minority of second job holders may take the extra job because they enjoy the variety, want to gain a new skill, or want to do a favor for a friend, but a large majority do so in order to earn more money than they could on their main job alone. Reasons for taking a second job were not asked in this study but responses reported in a Bureau of Labor Statistics study -- Perrella (1970) -- indicated that 61% of male moonlighters in May 1969 said they held second jobs for such financial reasons as meeting regular expenses, paying off debts, and saving for the future. Still other financial motivations such as

---

[1]The 17.3% of "free to vary" workers who worked less than 1800 hours in 1971 is very closely matched by the 16.8% of constrained but satisfied workers with those hours. By contrast, 51.7% of the "free to vary" workers worked more than 2100 hours as compared with 34.3% of constrained workers.

needing money for extras were coded together with miscellaneous non-financial responses in an "other" category comprising another 30% of male moonlighters.

We have estimated a marginal wage for *changing* jobs and now turn to the estimation of an effective marginal wage rate for second jobs, but this requires some presumption about the moonlighters' hours and wages on their primary jobs. If we presume that those moonlighters who received marginal wages and were satisfied with their work hours held primary jobs similar to those single job holders who wanted more work, this yields an estimated marginal wage[1] of $2.51 per hour for an average worker or 59% of his expected average wage on the primary job.[2] This estimate is quite comparable to the earlier estimate of the effective marginal wage from changing jobs.

If we make the same presumption for the other moonlighting modes, however, we obtain estimated marginal wage rates of approximately zero. Such an estimate may be partially accurate for those moonlighters who were not paid a specific hourly wage (mode 9) inasmuch as the small group includes a number of part-time farmers and basement businessmen. It is unlikely, however, that those second job holders who want still more work would have chosen to work their present moonlight hours for nothing. Rather, we must infer that the primary jobs held by workers in this group pay substantially less than the expected wages for workers of the same measured qualifications in typical constraining single jobs.

The fact that these workers did not fare well in the primary job market and were also not able to find as much work as they needed or wanted in the extra job market points up again that workers who are disadvantaged in one sector are likely to suffer disadvantages in others as well. In an earlier section of this chapter is was shown that low education, which has a well-documented effect on earning capacity, is also very strongly associated with a higher incidence of unemployment. The rate of second job holding shows a similar, though somewhat weaker, relationship to education. An estimated 43.7% of stable male heads of households held a second job in one or more of the five years covered by this study. As shown in Figure 4.11, the proportion holding a second job is 10 to 15 percentage points below the mean for workers with no secondary education. For those with intermediate levels of education up to some college the proportion of moonlighters is relatively constant at about 45% and then rises above 50% for college graduates.

---

[1] As with the earlier example we add the wage rate and hours coefficients to the sample mean values and calculate expected earned income for a worker of average qualifications in the various modes. Modes 10 and 11: hours = 2333, wage = $3.94, income = $9192. Mode 7: hours = 1952, wage = $4.22, income = $8237. The $955 income difference when divided by the work difference of 381 hours yields the marginal wage of $2.51.

[2] See the dotted line between modes 10, 11 and 7 in Figure 4.11.

FIGURE 4.11

Effect of Education on Second Job Holding,
Stable Male Heads of Families in the Labor Force

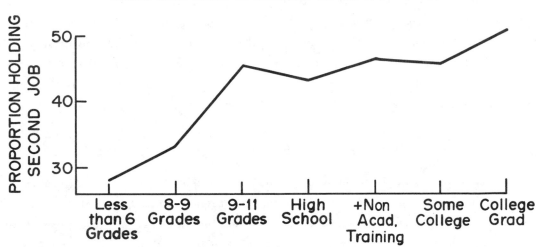

The effect of local labor market conditions for nonwhites which was observed in the unemployment analysis is also evident in the market for extra jobs,
and is considerably stronger. Overall, the proportions holding second jobs are
very similar for whites and nonwhites, but in areas where employment conditions
were characterized as "about the same" for all races, 56% of nonwhites held
second jobs as compared with 43.8% of whites. Among the larger number of nonwhites in areas with "worse" employment conditions the moonlighting rate falls
to 38% and it falls still further to 17% for nonwhites in "much worse" areas.

These lower rates of second job holding among disadvantaged workers
strongly suggest that the relative moonlighting opportunities available to them
are significantly less favorable than would be inferred from the positions of
typical satisfied second job holders. And, as we have seen, even the latter
workers achieved their extra work hours at effective marginal rates less than
would have been explained on the basis of their average hourly earnings.

The analysis presented here provides a useful perspective on the extent to
which workers are able to optimize their labor supply in a complex labor market.
The central finding is that while workers in constraining jobs do have opportunities to change their work hours by taking a second job or switching jobs, there
are substantial costs involved in such changes and the income to be expected is
notably less than proportional to the change in work hours. A significant minority of workers have sufficiently strong preferences or needs for additional
income to choose the employment modes which offer higher hours despite the

limited payoff. Another substantial minority of workers express a desire for
more work if it were available but have not chosen to switch modes to get it.
Many of these workers presumably predicate their desires for additional work on
a marginal wage equal to or greater than their average wage but do not consider
the more limited opportunities to be worthwhile. However, given the evidence of
more limited second job holding among disadvantaged workers, we infer that some
workers who expressed a desire for more work than they find do not take second
jobs because their opportunities are significantly more limited than those of the
typical moonlighters.

IMPLICATIONS FOR ESTIMATION OF LABOR SUPPLY RESPONSES

If we wish to predict the reduction in labor supply which might result from
an income supplementation policy, the consideration of institutional factors is
very important. The most obvious factor to consider is that a large proportion
of the affected workers would not have the option of decreasing their work hours
on their current jobs. Some 35% of male blue collar workers in 1971 held jobs in
which they were not free to decrease their work hours. Another 27% wanted more
work than they were able to find and thus would be expected to decrease their
work hours only if the decreased desired labor supply resulting from the supplement was less than the amount they currently work.

Among those workers who would be more likely to reduce work hours in
response to an income supplement, a substantial number are second job holders
whose effective marginal wages are lower than their hourly earnings on their main
job. Their work reduction would be expected to come from the low paying second
job rather than their main job. Similarly, workers with single jobs in the low
wage long hours sector might switch to a job with shorter hours but a higher wage
rate. In both cases the productivity loss to the economy, as measured by the
reduction in earned income, would be less than proportional to the reduction in
hours.[1]

Workers in constraining jobs at standard work hours who wish to reduce
their work hours do have the option of finding other jobs which accommodate their
wishes. We do not have data on the nature of employment opportunities which
offer less than standard time work. The theory suggests, however, that such
jobs may also pay lower than standard wage. If this is the case, the result
would be a *higher* effective marginal wage rate for reductions in work hours
below standard time. For example, if a worker earning $3.00 per hour for a 40
hour week could make only $2.70 per hour for a 35 hour week, he would lose $25.50

---

[1] Such behavior might be one of the factors underlying the effects observed in
early analysis of the New Jersey Negative Income Tax experiment (Watts, 1971).

per week in income for an effective marginal wage rate of $5.10 per hour. Such a structure of employment opportunities facing workers in standard jobs might thus largely offset the disincentive substitution effect of the recapture provisions of income supplementation policies.

The institutional factors not only affect the labor supply response to changes in wage rates but also may imply biases in the traditional estimates of cross-section parameters. The next section will investigate this issue.

III. The Determinants of Labor Supply for Male Heads of Families

Numerous researchers have used a variety of data sets to estimate a "conventional" labor supply model. The most important parameters of the model are the income and substitution effects and efforts have focused on quantifying these effects into dollar magnitudes. As stated in the previous section, these effects have considerable public policy value. Income supplement programs may affect the labor supply of the recipient and estimates of the income and substitution effects are needed to estimate the probable labor supply responses.

In the previous section, we have discussed numerous aspects of short run constraints on labor supply. To estimate better the long run equilibrium aspects of an individual's labor supply position and to minimize problems with constraints, the five years of observation on labor supply that the data provide are averaged and treated as a single observation. This average will then be related to average levels or other summary measures of important independent variables.

Much of our attention is focused on the relationship between wage rates and labor supply since this relationship is expected to reflect the combination of income and substitution effects. A majority of previous studies have found significant negative relationships or "backward bending" labor supply curves indicating that the need for income among low wage workers tends to outweigh the discouraging substitution effect of low marginal earnings. We find a similarly backward bending relationship and also find significant differences in the slope of the relationship for different subgroups of workers.

In order to investigate the extent to which the cross-sectional wage-hours relationships may be a function of institutional factors rather than worker preferences, we expand the model to include a number of measures of important institutional factors and observe the effects on the overall slope and on the differences between different groups. We then look for evidence of differential income effects among workers in different subgroups which might account for the observed differences in wage slopes.

The variables included in the basic model are shown in Table 4.4 along with

TABLE 4.4

Basic Variables Included in Labor Supply Model[a]

	Mean	Standard Deviation	Simple Correlation with Work Hours
Annual work hours -- 5-year average	2321	470	1.00
Average hourly earnings	$4.51	2.66	-.118
Wife's labor income	$1547	2175	-.111
Unemployment and workmen's compensation	$ 47	173	-.174
Other transfer income of family	$ 159	621	-.085
Other nontransfer income	$2572	3007	.098
Education index[b]	4.42	1.96	.152
Achievement motivation index	9.16	2.66	.137
Age of individual in 5th year	44.2	11.0	-.119
Age squared	2081	1014	-.127
Number of children in family[c]	1.69	1.63	.083
Whether not married	0.044	0.207	-.111
Job tenure index 5th year[d]	4.08	1.54	-.017
Unemployment rate in county[e]	11.0	2.43	-.099
Wife did not work (and not farmer, proprietor or manager)	0.46	0.50	.053
Non white	0.10	0.30	-.062
Farmer, proprietor or manager	0.22	0.41	.314
Employed in trade, transport or service (and not farmer, proprietor or manager)	0.23	0.43	-.018
Union member	0.37	0.48	-.214
Annual weeks of unemployment (average)	0.98	2.57	-.312
Annual weeks of illness (average)	0.94	1.53	-.261

[a]Sample includes male heads of households who were interviewed in each of five years, who did not change marital status, and who worked at least 250 hours in each year. Number of cases = 1853.

[b]1 = < 6 grades, 2 = 6-8, 3 = 9-11, 4 = 12, 5 = additional non academic training, 6 = some college, 7 = college graduate, 8 = graduate work.

[c]truncated at 7.

[d]1 = <12 months, 2 = 12-18 months, 3 = 1½-3½ years, 4 = 3½-9½ years, 5 = 9½-19½ years, 6 = over 19½ years.

[e]5-year sum -- each year scaled 0 = < 2%, 2 = 2-5.9%, 3 = 6-9.9%, 5 = over 10%.

their means, standard deviations, and simple correlations with five-year average annual work hours. The rationale for the inclusion of particular variables is discussed in conjunction with the interpretation of estimated effects.

It is one of our basic concerns in this analysis that involuntary variations in work hours which happen to be correlated with wage rates or other important independent variables should not be interpreted as behavioral adjustments. Variations in work time due to unemployment or illness are the most obvious instances of such involuntary variation. One traditional approach to the problem is to use hours of labor supplied rather than hours of work as the dependent variable in the analysis. Labor supplied is defined as the sum of time actually worked and time unemployed but seeking work. Cohen, Rea, and Lerman (1970) follow this method and use hours per week when working as the measure of a worker's labor supply during a week of unemployment.

In this analysis we follow an alternative approach, suggested by Rea (1971), in which unemployment is included as an independent variable in the analysis. The other estimated parameters in such a model are essentially equivalent to those from a model with labor supplied as the dependent variable but we also are able to observe possible behavioral responses to unemployment. Hours worked subsequent to a period of unemployment are expected to be increased by the income effect of earnings lost during unemployment, so that annual work hours would not be reduced in proportion to weeks of unemployment. The reduction in hours of work due to unemployment will also be less than proportional if the worker considers unemployment time to be a substitute for vacation or other desired leisure time.[1]

Another factor affecting the cross-sectional estimate of the effect of unemployment on work hours is that some workers who suffer unemployment are also unusually prone to other less drastic difficulties in the labor market such as short work days or restricted access to overtime. If such is the case, unemployment will serve as a proxy for these other difficulties and the apparent reduction in hours worked could be more than proportional to unemployment.

Illness time is treated in the same way as weeks of unemployment, and the behavioral responses are expected to be similar. But there are differences. Many workers receive sick pay so that the income incentive to offset time that is

---

[1] The size of the observed effects will also be affected by the relationships between the observation period and the worker's implicit accounting period. If unemployment occurs late in the observation period, the observed work hours may not reflect full adjustment to that unemployment and, conversely, observed hours may reflect adjustment to unemployment before the observation period. Except for very severe periods of unemployment, the worker's adjustment period is unlikely to be much longer than one year so that the five-year observation period in this study should minimize end effects.

lost due to illness is missing. Also, time lost due to illness may be correlated with poor health while working, which would tend to reduce the work hours. These factors combined lead us to expect a greater reduction in work time for a week of illness than for a week of unemployment.

The regression equations presented in Table 4.5 show estimates of parameters of the basic model of five-year average annual work hours with and without the inclusion of illness and unemployment time as independent variables.

The estimated work loss of 48.9 hours per week of unemployment is greater than the average weekly work hours for the sample. This indicates that unemployment time is serving as a proxy for employment problems beyond the direct loss of work. Similarly, the estimated work loss of 60 hours per week of illness indicates associated work-reducing ill health in addition to time fully lost from work.

We now turn to estimates of other important parameters in the basic labor supply model and note any differences in estimates resulting from the inclusion of unemployment and illness time in the model. The estimated wage coefficient of average annual work hours is strongly negative. Controlling for other variables in the model, workers with average hourly earnings of $2.00 average about 212 more work hours per year than those with hourly earnings of $6.00. Somewhat surprisingly, this estimate is negligibly affected by the inclusion of unemployment and illness in the model. One reason for the small change is that the education variable served to control for the differential incidence of unemployment.

The education coefficient of work hours is 46.9 in the model without unemployment and 29.3 after involuntary losses of work time are explicitly controlled for.

If the wage coefficient is to be decomposed into separate income and substitution effects, a separate estimate of labor supply response to nonwage income is necessary. Ideally we would like to estimate this response on the basis of a source of income which is not itself affected by workers' labor supply preferences and choices and which is also free of institutional correlation with labor supply. Unfortunately, none of the significant sources of income other than a worker's own earnings which occur naturally in the population fully meet these criteria.

The effects of income other than the head's earnings have been estimated for four separate components of family income: 1) wife's labor income, 2) income from unemployment insurance or workmen's compensation, 3) other transfer income and 4) a residual component including capital income, income of others than head and wife, and imputed rental income from home ownership.

TABLE 4.5

Regression of Five-Year Average Work Hours of Married Men

	Simple Model		Unemployment and Illness Added	
	Coef-fi-cient	Standard* Error	Coef-fi-cient	Standard* Error
Constant	1874		1974	
Average hourly earnings	-53.9	(4.3)	-52.7	(4.1)
Wife - labor income	-.034	(.006)	-.029	(.006)
Unemployment benefits	-.341	(.056)	.118	(.06)
Other transfer income	-.070	(.016)	-.061	(.015)
Other family income	.018	(.004)	.017	(.003)
Education	46.9	(5.9)	29.3	(5.8)
Achievement motivation index	16.4	(3.7)	15.3	(3.6)
Age in 5th year	27.2	(6.2)	30.3	(5.9)
Age squared	-.34	(.067)	-.35	(.064)
Number of children	-1.4	(6.8)	4.0	(6.5)
Whether unmarried	-295	(48)	-265	(45)
Job tenure index	-4.9	(6.7)	-24.2	(6.6)
Local unemployment rate index	-12.6	(3.9)	-10.1	(3.7)
Wife did not work	-4.3	(25.5)	12	(24)
Nonwhite	16.4	(32.2)	-3.3	(30)
Farmer, proprietor or manager	290	(25.7)	257	(24)
Trade, transport or service	63.3	(23.3)	40.7	(22.2)
Union membership	-77.5	(21.3)	-62	(20.2)
Weeks of unemployment annual average			-48.9	(4.3)
Weeks of illness annual average			-60.5	(6.2)

$$R^2 = .27 \qquad R^2 = .35$$

*Not corrected for sample design effect. See Appendix B.

In using wife's income in the model we assume that the husband's expected
response to a given amount of income is essentially independent of whether the
wife worked a few hours at a high wage or more hours at a lower wage. There is
also a source of bias in that the amount of wife's income is to some extent a
result of the level of husband's work hours. A husband's long work hours result
in higher income which would tend to reduce the wife's work hours and hence her
income. The true effect of wife's income on husband's work hours is thus exag-
gerated by the inclusion of some effects which operate in the other direction.
This bias is not expected to be large, however.

On the other hand, a working wife has less time to engage in productive
activities in the home so that her money income from market work overstates the
increase in total family real income relative to families in which the wife does
not work. This effect would tend to reduce the effect of wife's income relative
to that of nonwage income from other sources.

We do not know the net effect of these opposite biases. However, the estimated coefficient indicating approximately 30 hours reduction in annual hours per
thousand dollars of income can certainly be taken as a good estimate of the order
of magnitude of the income effect.

Income from unemployment insurance or workmen's compensation is clearly a
result, not a cause, of work lost due to unemployment or injury. The estimated
coefficient of -341 hours per thousand dollars of such income obtained in the
simple model thus clearly cannot be interpreted as an estimate of the income
effect. However, in the model which controls for the direct work loss due to
these factors, responses to differences in unemployment compensation might be
expected to reflect the simple income effect. This does not prove to be the case
since the estimated coefficient in the latter model is positive. It is possible
that workers who are unemployed but do not receive unemployment compensation are
more likely to have poor jobs when employed and thus work fewer hours than those
with unemployment benefits.

Other transfer income includes income from such varied sources as social
security, armed forces pensions, welfare, help from relatives, and support of
spouses' children from other marriages. Most of these sources are not directly
related to the individual's work hours as were unemployment benefits, and controlling for unemployment and illness helps eliminate such spurious correlation. However, some sources, such as social security, are accompanied by an increased marginal tax rate with its additional work inhibiting effect. The estimated coefficient of -61 hours per thousand dollars of transfer income should thus be regarded as an upper limit of the magnitude of income effect.

The fourth income component which includes capital income, income of others in the family, and imputed rental income, provides the least satisfactory estimate of the income effect. If accepted literally, the significant positive coefficient would imply the implausible conclusion that higher income leads to lower consumption of leisure. It is likely that those preference characteristics which lead an individual to accumulate income producing investments and equity in a home are also strongly associated with high annual work hours, thus producing a spurious positive correlation. It was hoped that such variables as education and the index of achievement motivation would control for these preference differences, but they are apparently insufficient.

We are thus left with two estimates of the income effect which have the theoretically expected signs and are significantly different from zero. As indicated, neither estimate is to be regarded as unbiased, but together they strongly suggest an income effect in the range of -30 to -60 hours per thousand dollars of income.

The substitution effect implied by a wage slope of -50 and a range of income coefficients from -.030 to -.060 evaluated at 2300 hours per year are shown below:

Substitution Effects Corresponding to a Range of Income Effects
Given a Wage Coefficient of -50

Income Coefficient (hours per dollar)	Substitution Effect (hours per dollar of hourly earnings)
-.030	19
-.040	42
-.050	65
-.060	88

As an illustration of the reduction in labor supply which these values would imply, consider a worker earning $2.00 per hour and working 2400 hours per year who becomes eligible for a base supplement of $4000 which is reduced by $.50 for each $1.00 of his earnings. At his old work hours he is eligible for a supplement of $1600 and his effective marginal wage rate is reduced from $2.00 to $1.00 per hour. An estimated income effect of -.030 would imply a desired work reduction of about 48 hours and a further reduction of 19 hours due to the corresponding substitution effect for a total reduction of about 2.7% of original work hours. A larger estimated income effect also implies a larger substitution effect so an income effect of .060 would be expected to result in a total work reduction of 184 hours or about 8% of the original equilibrium value.

Different estimated wage slopes would, of course, imply different corresponding pairs of income and substitution effects. Before we turn to the consideration of a model with different wage slopes for various subgroups, we briefly note interesting effects of other control variables in the model.

As noted earlier, education has a large positive effect on hours of work, a substantial portion of which operates through the avoidance of unemployment by more highly educated workers. Achievement motivation also has a significant positive relationship which is primarily related to voluntary variations in work effort. The quadratic age profile peaks between ages 40 and 45 and is about 115 hours lower at ages 25 and 60. The number of children in the family has a significant positive relationship to hours of work if the age variables are not included in the model but those effects are apparently accounted for by the age peak at child rearing ages. Unmarried males have an estimated annual labor supply of 65 hours lower than their married counterparts.

The estimated effect of job tenure changes quite substantially when unemployment and illness are controlled for. After accounting for the more serious unemployment among workers who have recently changed jobs and for age effects, the estimated tenure coefficient indicates that employees with 1 to 4 years of job tenure work an average of 100 hours more per year than those with more than 20 years' job tenure. Longer job tenure generally increases the monetary and fringe benefits on a worker's current job relative to those he might receive if he changed jobs. Recognition of such differential benefits and the increased implicit costs of changing jobs may lead to acquiescence to lower work hours by longer tenured workers.

The estimated effect of differences in local unemployment rates is significantly negative though not particularly strong. A large part of the effect persists after accounting for the direct work loss due to unemployment. Based on the standard deviation of the unemployment rate index, the 20% of workers in the areas with most favorable employment conditions work roughly 50 more hours per year than the 20% in areas with most serious unemployment

The five categorical variables -- wife did not work; nonwhite; occupation of farmer, proprietor, or manager; employment in trade, transport, or service industries; union membership -- define population subgroups which differ in the estimated wage slope of the cross-sectional labor supply curve as discussed in the next section. We turn now to a discussion of those differences.

DIFFERENCES IN WAGE SLOPES OF LABOR SUPPLY CURVES

In earlier sections of this chapter we have argued that institutional complexities in employment opportunities may limit the interpretability of estimated labor supply responses in terms of the simple income and substitution effects of economic theory. As one way of investigating the implications of institutional factors for estimates of theoretical labor supply parameters, we have used a search-test procedure[1] to identify population subgroups which differ in the wage slopes of the cross-sectional labor supply curves. Some of these groups are defined in terms of characteristics such as occupation, industry, and union membership which are associated with differences in work hours opportunities or employment modes. The way in which these differences might affect estimated wage and income effects is not immediately self-evident. We attempt to understand more about possible institutional effects by expanding the model to include measures of constraints on work hours and mode of employment and looking for changes in the wage and income coefficients estimated in the expanded model.

The estimated coefficients for the basic model allowing for different wage slopes are given in the first column of Table 4.6. Those control variables whose coefficients are essentially similar to the estimates in Table 4.5 have been omitted for the sake of simplicity. The model as specified incorporates additive categorical interactions on the hourly earnings variable to allow different slopes for various groups.[2] The base group wage coefficient of -52 hours per dollar of hourly earnings is the slope estimated for white, nonunion workers under age 55 whose wives work and who are not farmers, proprietors, or managers and are not employed in the trade, transport, or service industries. The coefficients of the wage interaction variables are then interpreted as the *differences* in wage slope associated with the interacted characteristic. Thus, the estimated wage slope for union members is more negative than that for nonunion members by 40 hours per dollar of hourly earnings and the estimated slope for nonwhite workers is less negative than that for whites by 22 hours per dollar. The estimated value of the wage slope for workers with some combination of characteristics is given by the sum of the base group coefficient and the appropriate interaction coefficients. The estimated slope for a nonwhite union member would thus be:

$$
\begin{array}{lr}
\text{Base} & -52.7 \\
\text{Nonwhite} & 22.3 \\
\text{Union} & \underline{-39.8} \\
\text{Estimated slope} & -71.2
\end{array}
$$

All characteristics apply to a minority of the sample, and with the exception of union members with nonworking wives less than 10% exhibit any given pair of characteristics.

The dispersion of estimated wage slopes is quite striking. The character-

---

[1] This procedure is described in Appendix A.

[2] See Appendix D for a more complete explanation of this method of specification.

TABLE 4.6

Estimated Differences in Responses to Wage Rate
and the Effects of Constraints and Institutional Factors
on Five-Year Average Work Hours of Stable Male Heads of Families

	1. Basic Model with Wage Interactions		2. Adding Constraint and Payment Mode Variables		3. Adding Second Job Holding	
	Coeffi-cients	Std. Dev.	Coeffi-cients	Std. Dev.	Coeffi-cients	Std. Dev.
Wife's income	-.027	(.005)	-.026	(.005)	-.025	(.005)
Unemployment benefits	.106	(.06)	.102	(.058)	.094	(.057)
Other transfer income	-.059	(.014)	-.053	(.014)	-.055	(.014)
Other family income	.017	(.003)	.012	(.003)	.012	(.003)
Education	29.1	(5.7)	14.6	(5.6)	8.3	(5.6)
Motivation	15.6	(3.4)	11.2	(3.3)	10.0	(3.2)
Basic wage slope	-52	(8.8)	-50	(10)	-37.7	(10)
Wife does not work						
level*	4.0	(23)	-5.8	(22)	-1.7	(22)
wage slope difference	26.2	(9.2)	26.0	(8.8)	23.0	(8.8)
Nonwhite						
level*	-11	(30)	-2.8	(29)	4.0	(28)
wage slope difference	22.3	(10.8)	19.2	(11.2)	26.0	(11)
Farmer, proprietor or manager						
level*	303	(90)	210	(25)	228	(25)
wage slope difference	-39	(9.9)	-27.2	(9.8)	-27.8	(9.6)
Trade, transportation or service industries						
level*	54	(21)	34	(21)	43	(20)
wage slope difference	-36	(11.0)	-37	(10.6)	-37	(10.5)
Union member						
level*	-39	(20)	-10	(20)	-22	(20)
wage slope difference	-40	(9.9)	-47	(9.7)	-50	(9.6)
Age 55 or older in 1968						
wage slope difference	40	(8.0)	43	(7.7)	45	(7.7)
Weeks of unemployment	-47.8	(4.2	-44.4	(4.1)	-42.9	(4.0)
Weeks of illness	-59.6	(6.1)	-57.5	(5.9)	-56.0	(5.7)
Free to increase work hours			32.5	(32)	16	(32)
Want more work			-120	(42)	-150	(42)
Free to decrease work hours			255	(33)	220	(33)
Want less work			228	(65)	265	(65)
No marginal wage						
level			107	(24.9)	101	(24.4)
wage slope difference			-10.9	(8.1)	-11.8	(7.9)
Second job holding						
level					345	(38)
wage slope difference					-15	(4.7)
Constant	1825		1816		1766	
R^2 =	38.3		43.6		46.4	

Number of observations = 1853

Standard errors are given in parentheses.

Note: Coefficients of age, age^2, number of children, whether unmarried, job tenure,
    and unemployment rate have been omitted. They are stable and essentially
    similar to values in Table 4.5.

*Differences in level of wage curves for different subgroups are evaluated at $4.00 per hour.

istics of union membership, employment in the trade, transport, and service industries, and occupation of farmer, proprietor, or manager are each associated with
wage slopes 70% to 80% more steeply negative than the base group. The combination of union membership and industry or occupation characteristics implies a yet
more negative estimated slope, though we might suspect that the effect of the
combined characteristics is not as strong as is implied by the additivity assumption. On the other hand, the estimated slopes for nonwhite workers, those 55 or
older, and those whose wives don't work are reduced in magnitude by 45% to 80%
relative to the base slope of -52 hours per dollar of hourly earnings. For small
groups with combinations of these characteristics the estimated slopes are close
to zero or slightly positive, but again these combined estimates may be exagger-
ated by the additivity assumption.

Two basic questions arise from these results. First, to what extent do the
various parameter estimates represent real differences in the population as
opposed to peculiarities of the sample? Second, if the differences are real, is
it possible to infer more basic underlying mechanisms which might also be subject to study?

In tests on the independent half sample, the interaction coefficients show
considerable variation in magnitude but are all sustained in direction. The
union, occupation, and age interactions all have estimated coefficients in the
test sample which are more than double their conventional standard errors. The
test sample coefficients of the industry and nonworking wives interactions are of
the order of one standard error. The interaction for nonwhites is quite weak in
the search sample but is included because the results of Hill (1970) have shown
near zero wage slopes for nonwhites. The interaction coefficient for this group
proves to be substantially stronger in the test sample, and the full sample coefficient is slightly more than double its conventional standard error.

The characteristics which are associated with wage slope differentials are
much the same as those characteristics which were earlier shown to be associated
with differences in mode of payment for work. Union members are paid almost exclusively on an hourly wage basis, while the large majority of farmers, proprietors, and managers do not receive well defined hourly wages. For blue collar
workers, jobs in trade, transport, and service industries offer the greatest
choice of payment modes. On the basis of the earlier analysis of mode choices
we would have expected higher labor supply at low wages in those groups where
large number of jobs did not pay hourly wages. The wage slopes for the occupation and industry groups are consistent with this expectation but union members
have a very similar wage slope and yet are at the opposite end of the payment

mode spectrum. Thus, if there is a relationship between this institutional characteristic of employment opportunities and estimated labor supply responses, it
is unlikely to explain the differences for all groups.

In regression 2 of Table 4.6, a direct measure of payment mode is introduced into the model along with a wage interaction for those workers who are not
paid hourly wages for marginal variations in work. Measures of freedom to vary
or constraints on work hours are also included. These variables are quite powerful determinants of the level of labor supply, contributing almost as much to the
explanatory power of the model as did direct measures of work lost due to unemployment and illness. However, the changes in estimates of economic parameters
in the expanded model are not large. The wage interaction coefficient for workers not receiving hourly pay has the expected sign but is quite weak. The magnitude of the interaction for farmers, proprietors, and managers is decreased by
some 25%, approximately the amount attributable to the payment mode interaction,
but the larger part of the occupational interaction is not explained by the added
factors. And the interaction coefficient for union members is 20% larger in the
expanded model indicating that their labor supply differences are certainly not
attributable to constraints and payment mode factors. The other interaction
effects are essentially unaffected.

The effects of the added variables on the level of labor supply are of some
interest in themselves. Workers in jobs without marginal pay average 10% more
hours per year than workers paid by the hour. Somewhat paradoxically, the variable among the measures of constraints on work hours which is most powerfully
associated with higher work hours is the freedom to decrease work hours. Workers
who were free to decrease work hours in all five years averaged some 250 hours
more per year than those who were never free to decrease them. In interpreting
this effect it is important to remember that the coefficient of this variable
represents its effect independent of other variables. As such, it distinguishes
workers who chose the upper limit of a range of work hours and workers with full
freedom to vary from those who were fully constrained or who chose the lower
limit of an available range. It is thus partly a proxy for interpersonal differences in preferences for work hours.

The mode choice analysis in the previous sections indicated that workers
taking second jobs generally do so at some sacrifice in hourly earnings. In
equation 3 of Table 4.6, the model is expanded to account explicitly for second
job holdings. The negative wage interaction coefficient for second job holders
is not large but has a tight confidence interval. More interestingly, the base
wage coefficient which now applies to workers without second jobs decreases in

magnitude by about 25%. It is evident, then, that second job holding exaggerates the backward bend of the labor supply curve relative to that which would be observed if all workers optimized their work hours on single jobs at given wages.

The only interaction coefficient notably affected by the inclusion of second job variables is that for nonwhites. The positive interaction coefficient becomes larger for this group and when combined with the reduced negative slope of the base group, nearly eliminates the backward bend of the supply curve for nonwhites with a single job. Again, the change is not large but it suggests that second jobs play a relatively more important role for nonwhites seeking longer work hours than they do for whites.

A further observation of interest on the estimates of equation 3 is that the education coefficient has fallen to less than one-fifth the size of the coefficient in the basic model. The benefits of education for labor supply behavior thus appear to operate largely through avoidance of unemployment and work-reducing constraints and through increased access to second jobs and other modes offering higher work hours.

The expansion of the model to include the institutional factors discussed above has suggested some ways in which these factors affect parameter estimates. The effects are relatively small, however, and offer only limited understanding of the observed subgroup differences in wage slopes.

Another more conventional hypothesis is that observed differences in wage slopes result from differences in income and substitution effects in the various population subgroups. To test this hypothesis, we have estimated a model including income interactions parallel to the wage slope interactions discussed above. Stronger estimated income effects for the groups with more backward bending supply curves would tend to confirm that the observed differences are due to variations in this classical economic determinant of labor supply.

The interactions were specified for the wife's income variable since this is the only component with a plausible basic coefficient which is sufficiently widespread in the population. We have indicated earlier the possible problems of bias in estimates of the income effect from this variable. The major part of the estimated coefficient is presumed to reflect the true income effect, however, and important differences in the income effect should be evident in the estimated interaction coefficients.

The results of the test of different income effects are mixed. In initial tests on the search half sample the income interactions were not particularly strong, but the rank ordering of the size of the estimated income effects for different population groups was the same as the order of increasingly negative estimated wage slopes. This was encouraging because the income interactions were not themselves a direct product of the search process. In estimates on the test half sample, however, four of the five income interaction coefficients were reversed in sign with the net result for full sample estimates that two coefficients are weakly in the expected direction, one is reversed and two are essentially zero. In short, there is very little consistent evidence that differences in estimated wage slopes of labor supply are due to variations in the classical income effect.

We are left with the possibility that differences in the substitution effect account for wage slope differences. This hypothesis cannot be tested directly, however, because the substitution effect can be estimated only by use of the estimated income effect.

In the preceding analyses of labor supply responses we have succeeded in demonstrating the existence of numerous complexities and some implications of those complexities. The overall pattern of labor supply responses to wage rates and other income remains basically unchanged. While we do not understand many of the internal complexities of the structure of responses we conclude that the basic estimates provide reasonable population values of the effect of changes in economic variables on desired labor supply. But the presence of constraints and other institutional factors is expected to cause important modifications in the actual labor supply effects of public policies.

IV. LABOR SUPPLY OF WIVES

The labor income of wives accounts for a major portion of the family income of married couples. While differences in the labor income of male heads of families are predominantly a function of differences in wage rate, variations in labor supply account for a much larger proportion of the interfamily differences in wives' income. The great majority of able-bodied male spouses work full time or more and most supply within 20% of the average annual work hours. The dispersion of wives' labor supply is much greater. Among nonaged wives who were stably married over the five-year study period 37.1% did not participate in the labor force or worked only a very small fraction of the time. Among the 62.9% of wives who worked at least 200 hours during the five years, the average hours of work for the full period was 4975 hours or almost exactly half of standard full-time work of 2000 hours per year. The standard deviation of five-year work hours for these working wives was 3440 hours indicating a range of typical work hours extending from part time in a single year to essentially full time in all years.

As we study factors which affect the labor supply of wives and the resulting impact on the economic well-being of families, it is useful to distinguish
separate effects on participation and on the amount worked by those who do participate in the labor force. It is also important to the understanding of the distribution of income that we know the proportion of families who receive no income
from this source as well as the expected amount of income for those families in
which the wife does work.

The income and substitution effects which were discussed in the analysis of
male labor supply are very much in evidence as determinants of wives' labor supply, and the separate effects are rather more easily distinguishable. The husband's wage rate is the most important variable in determining the level of family income, and while his labor supply response is a mixture of opposing income
and substitution effects, a wife's labor supply response to her husband's wage
rate is almost wholly an income effect. Measures of income from capital and
transfer income are also included in the model to provide further estimates of
the income effect.

The effects of wives' wage rates or potential wage rates are conceptually
different for labor force participation and for hours of work among those who
work. Variations in wives' potential wages have no effect on family income if
they do not work, thus the incentive to enter the labor force due to a high potential wage is not offset by an income effect. Among wives who do work, a higher wage is expected to create incentive to work more, but it also results in
higher income which reduces the need for additional work. However, the work
reducing income effect of wives' wages is expected to be relatively weaker than
the own-wage income effect for males because wives' labor income is a smaller
part of total family income. On the other hand, the positive substitution effects associated with wives' wages are expected to be stronger than for males
because their alternative activities are typically concentrated in productive
activities in the home, while the nonwork time of men is predominantly spent in
leisure activities.

Wives' potential wage rates, the appropriate variable for the participation
model, are obviously not known for those wives who do not work. Variables which
are related to earning capacity are thus included in the model as proxies. Education is the most important of these and other variables included are measures
of local wage levels for unskilled workers, local unemployment rates, and relative employment opportunities for women. Race and age are related to potential
wage levels but reflect other influences as well.

All of the above variables are also included in the model for the number of hours worked by wives. The latter model is estimated both with and without a direct measure of wives' average hourly earnings while working.

The importance of wives' alternative productive activities in the home is strongly related to the number of children in the family and their ages. Control variables for these family composition characteristics as well as for births during the study period are thus included in both models.

A number of other variables related to preference effects and possible interactions of husbands' and wives' labor supply decisions are also included in the estimated models. We cover those effects in the context of the discussion of the estimated responses of wives' labor supply to the three major sets of variables to which we now turn.

We first consider the income and substitution effects on the model of work hours of wives in the labor force for which a more complete specification is possible. A striking feature of this model is the very powerful positive relationship between wives' average hourly earnings and hours of work during the five-year period. As shown in Figure 4.12, wives who earned between $1.50 and $2.50 per hour worked an average of 1969 more hours during the five-year period than those who earned less than $1.50 per hour. The positive differential in work hours for the next higher wage interval is nearly as large and the average wage slope over this range is 1726 hours per dollar of hourly earnings. At wage levels above $3.50 per hour and especially above $5.00 per hour, the curve turns down but the steeply rising portion of the curve represents some three-quarters of the working wives. If the estimated relationship can be presumed to be a reasonably unbiased estimate of the average response of wives' work hours to a change in wage rates, it indicates a remarkably strong substitution effect which completely outweighs the income effect.

A similarly high positive wage elasticity at low wages was estimated in the income and welfare study done by Morgan, et al (1962) for spending unit wives who worked in 1959. However, the results of Rea (1971) using 1967 CPS data showed annual work hours to be lower for wives with wages between $1.00 and $2.50 per hour than for those with wages under $1.00 per hour. Rea's results show positive wage slopes above $2.50 per hour but the differentials are of the order of 100 hours per year, about one-third the magnitude of our estimates when expressed in annual terms. Our use of total labor supplied over five years picks up variations in long run labor supply which are the result of intermittent participation as well as those due to variations in annual hours of work when in the labor force; the former may be particularly sensitive to wage effects. Single-year regressions on the current data set show a positive wage effect about two-

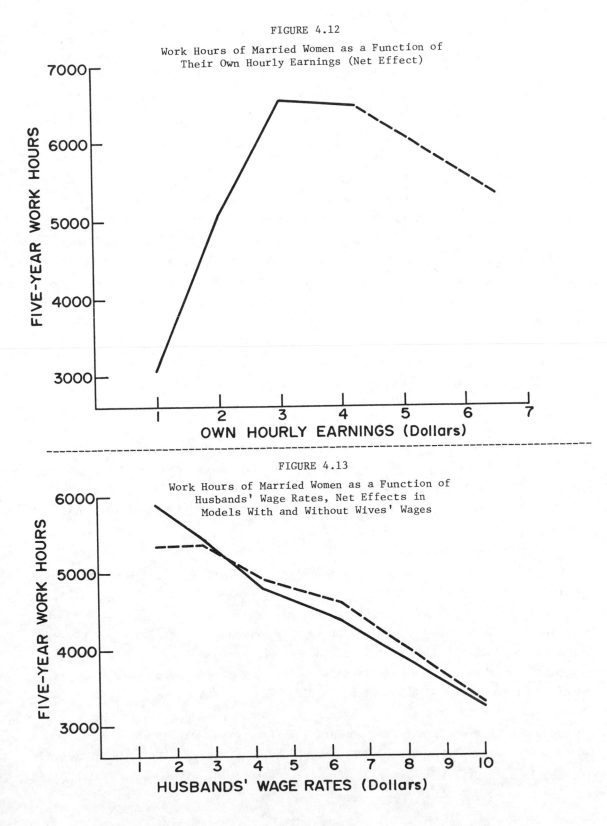

FIGURE 4.12

Work Hours of Married Women as a Function of
Their Own Hourly Earnings (Net Effect)

FIGURE 4.13

Work Hours of Married Women as a Function of
Husbands' Wage Rates, Net Effects in
Models With and Without Wives' Wages

thirds the size of the five-year effect.

An alternative possibility is related to the hypothesis raised in the mode choice analysis for males. Wives who wish to work intermittently or only a small fraction of full time may be able to find such employment only at low wage rates. In such a case the estimated wage effect would exaggerate the expected response to exogenous change in wage rates.

The estimated relationship of wives' work hours to husbands' wage rates permits an estimation of the income effect which can then be used to determine the substitution effect. The relationship is shown by the solid line in Figure 4.13. Over the range of husbands wage rate below $5.00 per hour the curve is essentially linear with a slope of -440 hours per dollar wage difference. Under the assumption of a negligible cross substitution effect and using 2300 hours for the husbands' mean annual work hours this translates into an income effect of -172 hours per thousand dollars of annual income. Note that we continue to express wives' hours in terms of five-year totals, although the income variables are expressed in annual terms. The estimated means effect implies a reduction of 3.4% of the mean total hours per $1000 of annual income. The substitution effect implied by the wage and income terms as evaluated at 5000 total hours is 2586 hours per dollar change in marginal wage rate. If this figure is reliable, it predicts a very major reduction in work effort by wives facing increased marginal tax rates under an income supplementation program.

The relationship of wives' work hours to husbands' wage rates as estimated in the model excluding wives' own wage but including education and other proxies illustrates an important estimation problem. This relationship, shown by the dashed line in Figure 4.13, is significantly less steeply sloped at low wage rates than that estimated in the full model.

We interpret this result as an indication that spouses' abilities are highly correlated. Education and other variables included in the model partially control for the wife's wage and its effects but there are substantial residual variations in wives' wage rates which are correlated with variations in husbands' wage rates. Since the two wage variables have opposite effects on wives' work hours the estimated effect of the husbands' wage rate is biased toward zero when the wife's wage rate is omitted from the model. The bias in the work hours model is of the order of 30% over the middle range of the curve.

This problem may well carry over to the participation model in which it is not possible to measure the true potential wage of wives who do not work. The education effect in the participation model shown in Figure 4.14 is quite similar to that in the hours model without the direct measure of wives' wages which leads to the inference that potential wage has a similar strongly positive effect on participation.

FIGURE 4.14

Labor Force Participation of Married Women
as a Function of Education

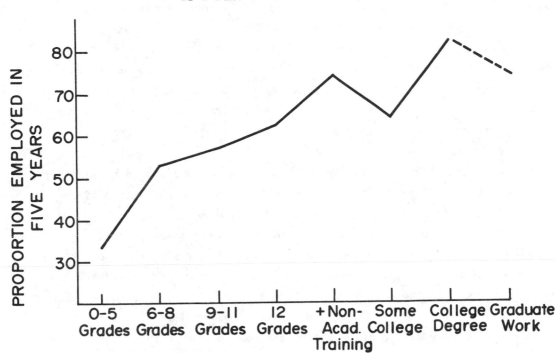

The estimated relationship of wives' labor force participation to husbands' wage rate is only slightly weaker than that estimated for work hours in the complete model. The curve shows a 4.1% reduction in rate of participation per dollar of hourly earnings above $2.00 per hour. Translated into an income effect and expressed as a percentage of the mean participation rate, the reduction is 2.8% per $1000 as compared with 3.41% for work hours. If we allow for possible bias in the participation estimate, the two are very similar.

It would be desirable to corroborate the estimate of the income effect based on the husband's wage with estimates based on other income sources. The alternative estimates are not very satisfactory. The transfer income slope for working wives is roughly -1000 hours per $1000 of annual income, which is large enough to indicate an institutional rather than a behavioral relationship. Participation, on the other hand, rises slightly over part of the range of transfer income. The relationship of capital income to both participation and hours is weak and irregular.

Local market conditions are expected to influence the labor supply of married women through effects on potential wages and on ease of finding a job. The estimated effects of the available measures of local conditions are not strong but show a number of interesting effects. The wage level in the county of residence is represented by the typical wage for unskilled males and a male-female differential. There is a slight negative effect of higher male wage levels on wives' participation and most of the effect is the result of larger male-female differentials in areas where unskilled males earn higher wages. Roughly two-thirds of married women in areas with typical male wages above $2.50 per hour faced a wage deficit of more than $.50 per hour, and their participation rates were about 10% lower than wives facing more favorable relative conditions. Local wage levels showed very little effect on hours of work for those wives in the labor force.

Local unemployment rates were included in the model as a combination variable representing the pattern of local unemployment levels in the first and last years of the period. Rates of participation were about 10% above the mean for the small proportion of wives in areas with initial unemployment rates below 2%. Subsequent rises in unemployment rates in these areas had little effect on participation but were associated with a 10% reduction in total work hours. More than half of the sample lived in areas with initial unemployment rates between 2% and 4%. Participation rates and work hours are close to mean levels for this group and also show very little effect of variations in unemployment rate at the end of the period. In areas with higher initial unemployment levels which subsequently remained relatively stable, participation rates were 3% to 6% above the mean, but participation was 7% to 12% below the mean in areas with high and rising unemployment. The local unemployment differentials in this range had little effect on hours of work for wives in the labor force.

The unemployment rate figures used apply to the total labor force and do not necessarily reflect market conditions for women. But the subjective measure of relative employment conditions for unskilled females obtained from local employment security officials does not show an important effect on either the labor force participation or the work hours of married women.

The expected wage rates of nonwhite women are lower than for white women with equivalent characteristics. On that basis, we would expect lower labor force participation by nonwhite wives after controlling for family income factors. However, previous studies have shown higher participation rates among nonwhite wives and our results are similar. The estimated participation rate for nonwhite wives was 74% as compared with 62% for white wives. Other analyses of annual hours for wives in the labor force have shown negative differentials for nonwhites. In this analysis of total work hours over five years, which includes labor supplied by intermittent participation, we find that total work hours for nonwhites are about 400 hours higher than for whites.

In earlier sections, the unemployment experience and second job holding of nonwhite males was seen to be sensitive to relative employment conditions for nonwhites. This effect is not significant for the labor supply of nonwhite married women. Their rate of participation is lower -- about the same as for whites -- in areas where relative employment conditions were characterized as "much worse" for nonwhites but the estimate is based on only 36 observations.

The expected wage rates of women in the labor force rise with age but the relationship of age to wives' labor supply appears to be much more representative of life cycle effects and historically rising labor force participation. Expected labor force participation falls quite monotonically with age from 77.4% for wives under age 25 to 41.5% for wives over age 55. The work hours of those in the labor force are about 12% below the mean for young wives and rise to a slight peak in the age range between 35 and 45 and then fall off slightly for older wives.

The control variables for family composition have very powerful effects on both wives' participation and hours of work which are quite consistent with expectations.

The rate of participation for married women with children under age three at the beginning of the period was some 12% lower than the mean and participation among those with additional births during the period was still lower by a similar amount. Those women whose first child was born during the study period had a participation rate some 10% above the mean. Among wives who worked the presence of a young child did not appreciably reduce hours of work, but the birth of a child during the period reduced work hours by 1000 to 1500 hours. The number of children in the family had a larger proportional effect on hours of work than on participation rates. The work hours of wives with three of more children were 20% lower than the hours for wives with one or two children, while the differential in participation rates was approximately 12% of the mean rate.

A number of hypotheses have been advanced concerning the role of wives' labor supply in offsetting unexpected losses of income from other sources, particularly husbands' income. In an analysis based on data from the first three years of this study (Dickinson and Dickinson, 1970), very little evidence was found to support the hypothesis that wives' labor force participation is responsive to annual variations in husbands' income. An alternative hypothesis tested in this chapter is that wives whose husbands are frequently unemployed are more likely to enter and remain in the labor force, thus providing an income buffer for the family. Both the total unemployment of the husband during the five years and the number of different years with unemployment were entered in the model in test of this hypothesis. The estimated effects of both variables are quite weak, however, and do not provide consistent support for the hypothesis.

V. Labor Supply of Single Women with Children

Single women with children face many of the same labor market opportunities as do married women and their labor supply decisions involve many of the same factors. There are also very important differences attendant on the absence of husbands and the income they provide. The more limited potential labor resources of families headed by single women make this group particularly important in the poverty population. The labor supply decisions of these women have an important influence on the economic status of their families, as is shown by the distributions of labor force participation and average work hours given in Table 4.7.

In this analysis, as in that for married women, we study the separate effects of major factors on rates of participation in the labor force and on the number of hours worked for those who do participate. We study the effects of variables representing the potential wage rate and employability of the individual, local conditions, family characteristics, race, and motivation. The measured wage rate is included in the work hours analysis. We do not attempt direct estimates of income and substitution effects because of the general absence of income sources which are free of institutional correlation with labor supply.

The variables included in this analysis are presented in Table 4.8, along with a measure of their relative importance in explaining labor force behavior of single women with children in the year 1971.

Wage and employability characteristics are the most important determinants of differences in labor force participation. Education is the strongest proxy for a woman's potential wage rate and is the most important single determinant of whether a woman works. Among women with some high school education, 63% worked as compared with 69% of high school graduates and 88% of those with some college. This relationship is similar to that estimated for wives though the overall participation rate is higher for single women. The ability measure, which was not available for wives, is also expected to be positively related to potential wages but, surprisingly, bears a negligible relationship to labor force participation.

Almost one-quarter of the single women with children say they have a health problem that limits the kind or amount of work they can do; of those, only 50% have a job. These health problems may not be permanent disabilities and some may

TABLE 4.7

Proportion of Single Women with Children Who Worked in 1971
and Their Average Hours of Work by Income/Need

Income/Needs	% Employed	Average Hours Worked For Those Employed	% of Population
Less than .80	40	295	16.9
.80 - 1.19	62	714	17.0
1.20 - 1.59	64	931	15.8
1.60 - 1.99	72	1172	11.9
2.00 - 2.39	84	1523	9.2
2.40 - 2.99	96	1493	10.6
3.00 - 3.99	91	1578	9.9
4.00 or more	84	982	8.7
Total	70	1030	100.0

Sample size = 717

TABLE 4.8

Relative Importance of Predictors of Labor Force Behavior
of Single Women with Children

	Whether Employed		Hours Worked for Those Employed	
	β^2	Rank Order	β^2	Rank Order
Family Characteristics				
Age of head	.017	(11)	.030	(9)
Marital status	.067	(2)	.066	(3)
Number of children	.023	(9)	.072	(2)
Age of youngest child	.036	(7)	.047	(7)
Local Conditions				
Region	.036	(6)	.021	(11)
City size	.022	(10)	.052	(5)
Unemployment in county	.052	(4)	.014	(12)
AFDC per recipient in county	.044	(5)	.009	(14)
Employability of Head				
Education	.073	(1)	.044	(8)
Test score	.012	(12)	.056	(4)
Disability	.058	(3)	.025	(10)
Race	.007	(13)	.012	(13)
Motivation	.033	(8)	.048	(6)
Wage Rate	--	--	.121	(1)
Mean	.70		1469	
Standard deviation	.46		802	
R^2	.42		.58	
Adjusted R^2	.36		.49	

be psychological. Nevertheless, health does seem to play an important role in the economic well-being of these women.

The local employment conditions also have a great deal to do with whether a woman works. In areas which local employment security officials characterized as having "many unskilled workers unable to find jobs," only 62% of single women with children held jobs in 1971 as compared with 73% of those in areas with "most workers able to find jobs."

The average AFDC payment per recipient is included as a measure of the adequacy of alternatives to working. The estimated effects indicate that women are less likely to be employed in areas where these payments are larger. Single women with children living in states where payments are less than $35 per recipient had estimated participation rates of 82% as compared with 60% for those in areas with payments of more than $55. The direction of this effect is quite clear, but the estimated magnitude is somewhat suspect because of the correlation between level of payments and region. The simple proportion of female family heads who work is 6% lower in the Northeast than in the South but in the multivariate model the estimated rate is 20% higher. It is difficult to understand why there is such a large differential attributable to the true independent effects of region of residence, and we suspect that part of the result is due to multicollinearity problems. The size of largest city in the area which was expected to represent the availability and variety of jobs does not have an important effect on participation rates for female heads of families.

The estimated effects of family characteristics on the employment of female heads with children are modest but largely in the expected direction. The estimated participation rates decline smoothly from 75% for women with one child to 59% for those with four children. The presence of a child under age 3 results in an estimated participation rate of 55% as compared with an average of 73% for women with all children over age 6. The woman's age has only a small effect, showing a small decline for older women. Marital status, however, is quite important. It was hypothesized that women who were never married would be more likely to work since they would have fewer alternative means of support than widows or divorcees. But we find that divorced women are more likely to work. This may be because they have become accustomed to a higher standard of living than the single women and are working more to maintain this standard. These women may also have less reliable alternative incomes than widows who are likely to receive pensions and insurance benefits.

Overall, we find that black women are less likely to work than white women, but this difference is not attributable to race, per se, but rather to the fact that blacks have less education and live in less advantageous areas. When we control for all the other characteristics, no race effect remains. Motivation also has no systematic effect on whether a female family head works.

Among working single women with children, differences in hourly earnings have by far the strongest relationship to hours of work of all variables included in the model. The relationship is similar to that for female heads in that work hours rise steeply with increases in wage rate over the lower range of the distribution. The rising portion of the curve for single women, however, peaks in the wage range between $1.50 and $2.00 per hour, while that for married women rises over the range up to $3.50 per hour. Apparently the absence of adequate alternative financial resources means that even quite low wage rates are sufficient to induce a large proportion of single women to work close to full time while a majority of married women are induced to work full time only at substantially higher wages.

Other measures of the employability of female heads have quite different effects on hours of work than they do on whether a woman works. Controlling on the other characteristics, education has no effect on the amount a woman works while it is the most important predictor of whether she is employed. This contrasts with the estimates for married women in which education retained a significant positive effect on work hours even in the presence of measured hourly earnings. The key to the difference is in the estimated effect of the measure of verbal ability which was not available for wives. The effect of ability on the work hours of single women with children is strongly positive with those in the top quarter of the distribution of scores on the measure working nearly 400 more hours per year than those in the bottom half. The reasons why education and ability have different effects on participation and work hours are not entirely clear. It is possible that the formal qualifications represented by education are more important for finding a job while basic ability has more influence on success in coping with the combined demands of work and family once employed.

The effect of disability on work hours is similar to, though smaller than, its effect on work participation. Women with limiting health problems work about 350 hours less than those who do not report such problems.

The work hours of single female heads in the labor force are strongly affected by the number of children in their family. Women with three children or less tend to work about 1500 hours a year but the amount of work drops precipitously for women with larger families; those with five children average only 640 hours, for example. The age of the youngest child has relatively little influence. Both of these effects are similar to those for married women. Marital status again has a large impact: divorced women work the most. A woman's age makes little difference in the number of hours she works.

Local conditions are relatively unimportant as determinants of the hours a woman with children works. The size of the city and the availability of unskilled jobs have little effect.

High levels of AFDC payments are associated with somewhat reduced hours of work when only that variable is considered, but the effect disappears in the multivariate estimates. This may again be influenced by multicollinearity with region. Women in the Northeast are estimated to work some 290 fewer hours per year than those in the South. Neither of these effects is as strong as those in the participation model.

The estimated effects of race are small with black female heads of families working an estimated 160 more hours per year than whites. The measure of achievement motivation is essentially unrelated to the work hours of single women with children.

SUMMARY

1. In the analysis of involuntary work losses due to unemployment we find the expected result that unemployment is more serious among workers with low wage jobs. There are also strong independent effects of education and occupation. The education effect is particularly striking. High school dropouts experience unemployment levels approximately double those of high school graduates. The reduction in risk of unemployment resulting from completion of high school is not as great for nonwhites as for whites.

2. The economic theory of labor supply assumes that workers are able to adjust their work hours to optimal levels in response to changes in wage rates or other sources of income. We find that more than 85% of employed men work under conditions different from those assumed in the theory. One major departure from the assumed conditions occurs in jobs which pay a given total wage for a given amount of work. While salaried positions in high wage white collar occupations are the most common example of such jobs, jobs without marginal pay constitute a significant minority of employment opportunities for nonunion blue collar workers in local industries. These jobs offer longer work hours with somewhat higher earnings but lower average wage rates than the typical job with marginal pay. As such, they also offer an alternative mode of employment for those with preferences for long work hours. There is some evidence that access to these jobs is restricted for nonwhites.

3. Jobs which pay hourly wages often restrict the number of work hours available. A majority of workers report that they are satisfied within these constraints. However, a substantial proportion of workers would prefer to work more than they are able to on their main jobs. Second jobs are an option available for these workers but they generally pay less than the worker's main job.

4. Economic theory predicts that an income supplementation program would result in reduction in work effort. However, in an economy characterized by widespread constraints on work hours with alternative opportunities for longer work hours at lower wage rates, we expect important modifications of these responses. More than a third of workers potentially affected are not free to work fewer hours and 37% actually want *more* work than is currently available. We might expect reductions in work hours among those who have chosen long work hours at low wage rates but the loss in productivity to the economy would be less than proportional to the reduction in work hours if they switch to jobs with higher wage rates.

5. We estimate a conventional model of labor supply and find, as other studies have found, that lower wage rates result in higher work hours. We find important differences in the wage response for different subgroups of the population. Union members and those employed in trade, transportation, and service industries work relatively longer hours at low wage rates while the hours of older workers and nonwhites are less strongly related to wage levels. If we had been able to relate the observed differences in wage responses to the presence of constraints on work hours and the variety of alternative employment modes, we might have been better able to estimate the quantitative impact of these factors. While we find that these institutional factors have a large direct impact on hours of work in the population, we find little evidence that they affect our estimates of desired labor supply responses to economic variables. The observed differences in wage responses thus remain as further complexities in the expected responses of labor supply to public policy.

6. For married women who work we find a very strong positive relationship between their wage rates and the number of hours worked. The contrast between the wage responses of men and married women is in large part due to wives' greater involvement in productive activities at home. The strong positive wage response for wives implies that those facing a high marginal tax rate under an income supplementation program would be expected to make very substantial reductions in work hours. On the other hand, it indicates that progress in eliminating sex discrimination in wage rates can be expected to result in large

increases in wives' labor supply. The labor force participation of married
women increases strongly with education level which leads to the inference that
their decision of whether to work is similarly related to potential wage rate.

Wives' labor force participation and hours of work are both negatively
related to the husbands' wage rate. We hypothesized that the wife's labor
supply might be higher if the husband was prone to frequent or extensive unem-
ploymemt because her income could serve as a buffer when he was out of work.
We find no appreciable effects of either the number of years in which the husband
was unemployed or of the total duration of his unemployment.

7. The labor force responses of single women with children are similar
to those of wives in many ways, but there are important differences. Among the
70% of single women who work, hours of work increase sharply with wage rate up
to $2.00 per hour. The hours of working wives rise to a similar level only at
wage rates of $3.50 per hour. The absence of substantial alternative incomes
apparently induces many single women to work essentially full time even at quite
low wage rates. The level of AFDC payments in the county, included as a measure
of adequacy of alternatives to working, has quite a strong effect on labor force
participation with lower participation observed in areas with more adequate payment levels. The payment level does not affect the work hours of those in the
labor force.

The verbal ability measure which is available for female heads but not for
wives is expected to be related to potential wage rate and thus to the probability of being employed. Somewhat surprisingly, ability has a negligible effect
on participation rates but quite a strong positive influence on the number of
hours worked. We hypothesize that while formal educational qualifications are
more important for finding a job, basic ability is more important for success
in holding a job and managing a family at the same time.

References

Cohen, Malcolm S., Rea, Samuel A. Jr., and Lerman, Robert I., A Micro Model of
    Labor Supply, U. S. Bureau of Labor Statistics, Staff Paper 4, U. S. Govt.
    Printing Office, 1970.

Dickinson, Katherine P. and Dickinson, Jonathan G., "Labor Force Participation of
    Wives: The Effects of Components of Husbands' Income," Surveys of Con-
    Sumers, 1971-72 - Contributions to Behavioral Economics, Lewis Mandell, et
    al, ed., Survey Research Center, University of Michigan, 1973.

Hill, C. Russell, "The Economic Determinants of Labor Supply for the Urban Poor,"
    presented at the Econometric Society Meetings, Dec. 30, 1969; Revised 1970.

240

Kosters, Marvin, Income and Substitution Effects in a Family Labor Supply Model, Rand Corporation, 1966.

Morgan, James N., et al, Income and Welfare in the United States, McGraw Hill, 1962.

Perella, Vera C., "Moonlighters: Their Motivation and Characteristics," Monthly Labor Review, August 1970.

Watts, Harold W., "Mid-Experiment Report on Basic Labor Supply Response," mimeograph, 1971.

APPENDIX 4.1

MCA Results for Wives' Labor Supply

Wife's Education	Whether Wife Worked More than 200 Hours in 5 Years:				Hours of Work for Those Who Worked:			
	Unweighted N	% of Population	Unadjusted Mean	Adjusted Mean	Unweighted N	% of Population	Unadjusted Mean	Adjusted Mean
0-5 grades	120	2.9	.40	.34	50	2.4	4529	4149
6-8 grades, grade school	301	10.4	.55	.53	172	9.1	4785	4759
9-11 grades	467	19.0	.63	.58	295	18.9	4250	4472
12 grades	627	34.0	.63	.62	406	33.8	5205	5317
12 grades plus non-academic training	232	13.1	.72	.74	168	15.0	5587	5460
Some college, no degree	197	11.4	.62	.64	130	11.4	4928	4655
College, bachelor's degree	105	6.4	.72	.83	77	7.4	4931	4783
Graduate work	27	1.8	.71	.75	19	2.0	5906	5651
Husband's Average Wage								
Less than $2.00	407	12.4	.59	.73	251	11.6	5009	5875
$2.00-3.49	715	30.0	.71	.70	497	33.9	5215	5402
$3.50-4.99	547	30.2	.67	.64	359	32.2	5021	4785
$5.00-7.49	303	20.0	.56	.53	169	17.7	4800	4368
$7.50-9.99	65	4.7	.42	.41	28	3.2	3529	3283
$10.00 or more	39	2.8	.32	.31	13	1.4	3399	3146
Age of Wife								
Under 25	307	14.1	.79	.77	238	17.7	3986	4289
25-34	556	25.0	.64	.69	362	25.5	4652	4882
35-44	623	29.2	.65	.66	400	29.7	5156	5363
45-54	400	20.4	.59	.55	234	19.2	5794	5167
55+	190	11.3	.44	.42	83	7.9	5568	4893

APPENDIX 4.1
(continued)

Numbers, Ages and Births of Children	Whether Wife Worked More than 200 Hours in 5 Years:				Hours of Work for Those Who Worked:			
	Unweighted N	% of Population	Unadjusted Mean	Adjusted Mean	Unweighted N	% of Population	Unadjusted Mean	Adjusted Mean
No children and none born	450	26.6	.59	70.1	272	25.2	6320	6091
Child born during period:								
No children before birth	80	4.8	.93	73.0	73	7.1	4848	5055
One child before birth	111	6.0	.63	46.1	69	6.1	3222	3428
Two or three children before birth	149	6.4	.53	42.2	85	5.3	2737	3533
Four or more children before birth	80	2.3	.41	35.1	35	1.5	3732	3508
One or two children and none born during period:								
Youngest under 3 in 1968	104	5.1	.68	54.0	72	5.5	4692	4668
Youngest 3-5 in 1968	90	4.7	.73	66.5	64	5.5	5067	5199
Youngest 6 or older in '68	381	20.2	.67	72.8	246	21.4	5419	5314
Three or four children and none born during period:								
Youngest under 3 in 1968	211	6.9	.54	48.5	130	5.9	4061	4583
Youngest 3-5 in 1968	202	7.3	.63	61.3	135	7.4	3976	4009
Youngest 6 or older in '68	218	9.6	.60	63.2	136	9.1	4326	4125
Typical Male Wage								
Unskilled male wage <$2.00:								
Female wage about the same	400	18.0	.68	.64	263	19.4	5282	5404
Female wage $.10-.49 lower	483	19.1	.69	.66	331	20.8	5037	5210
Female wage lower by $.50 or more	21	0.4	.72	.88	14	0.4	2314	3219
Unskilled male wage $2.00-$2.49:								
Female wage about the same	79	4.9	.55	.59	43	4.2	4921	4779
Female wage $.10-.49 lower	766	38.6	.63	.64	486	38.5	4915	4704
Female wage lower by $.50 or more	54	3.2	.57	.56	30	2.9	5132	5209
Unskilled male wage >$2.50:								
Female wage within $.50	78	4.2	.58	.62	45	3.9	4864	5034
Female wage lower by $.50 or more	195	11.6	.53	.55	105	9.8	4572	4746

APPENDIX 4.1
(continued)

	Whether Wife Worked More than 200 Hours in 5 Years:				Hours of Work for Those Who Worked:			
Change in Unemployment Rate	Unweighted N	% of Population	Unadjusted Mean	Adjusted Mean	Unweighted N	% of Population	Unadjusted Mean	Adjusted Mean
Under 2% in 1968, under 4% in 1971	85	4.8	.78	.73	66	5.9	5649	5435
Under 2% in 1968, 4% or more in 1971	76	2.1	.82	.71	59	2.8	4372	4564
2-3.9% in 1968, under 4% in 1971	177	8.6	.68	.60	122	9.2	5175	4890
2-3.9% in 1968, 4-5% in 1971	544	26.0	.61	.63	329	25.4	4956	5023
2-3.9% in 1968, 6% or more in 1971	394	21.7	.59	.61	230	20.3	4832	5050
4-5.9% in 1968, under 6% in 1971	382	15.1	.68	.66	260	16.2	4994	4860
4-5.9% in 1968, 6% or more in 1971	204	11.3	.51	.56	113	9.2	4734	5044
6% or more in 1968, under 10% in 1971	157	8.3	.71	.69	112	9.3	5030	4674
6% or more in 1968, 10% or more in 1971	57	2.2	.49	.49	26	1.7	5408	5337
Unskilled Female - Male Labor Market Comparison								
More women able to find jobs	346	20.0	.57	.60	199	18.0	5294	5222
About the same	577	31.1	.63	.65	365	31.2	4571	4645
Fewer women able to find jobs	915	42.2	.67	.64	615	44.7	5140	5093
Many fewer women able to find jobs	238	6.7	.58	.54	138	6.2	4906	5084
Race and Relative Job Opportunities								
White	1476	90.1	.61	.62	903	88.0	4951	4936
Nonwhite by market conditions:								
"same" employment opportunities	176	2.8	.76	.71	124	3.4	5025	5344
"worse" employment opportunities	388	6.2	.78	.76	272	7.6	5177	5220
much worse opportunities	36	1.0	.65	.64	18	1.0	5422	5382

APPENDIX 4.1
(continued)

	Whether Wife Worked More than 200 Hours in 5 Years:				Hours of Work for Those Who Worked:			
	Unweighted N	% of Population	Unadjusted Mean	Adjusted Mean	Unweighted N	% of Population	Unadjusted Mean	Adjusted Mean
Annual Transfer Income of Head and Wife								
None	1189	59.0	.62	.62	751	58.4	5247	5261
<$500	507	23.2	.66	.62	346	24.3	4839	5015
$500-999	140	6.4	.68	.66	92	6.9	4122	4278
$1000-1999	120	5.8	.66	.75	78	6.1	4515	4171
$2000-3999	89	4.0	.53	.57	40	3.4	4127	3063
>$4000	31	1.6	.35	.46	10	0.9	3877	3412
Annual Capital Income of Head and Wife								
None	1066	39.0	.69	.63	721	42.6	4892	5156
<$500	550	32.4	.64	.66	350	33.0	4956	4815
$500-999	147	9.1	.58	.63	82	8.4	5310	4965
$1000-1999	112	6.9	.59	.63	66	6.4	5288	5209
$2000-3999	116	7.3	.48	.51	56	5.6	5228	5156
$4000-5999	52	3.2	.50	.60	27	2.6	3736	3158
>$6000	33	2.1	.45	.59	15	1.5	5796	4948
Achievement Motivation of Husband								
Index Score:								
<5	116	4.7	.62	.62	72	4.7	4936	5139
5-6	282	12.7	.56	.56	156	11.3	5278	5168
7-8	492	22.5	.65	.67	325	23.2	4776	4909
9-10	602	29.3	.63	.62	385	29.2	5047	4936
11-12	411	21.5	.64	.64	262	21.8	4953	4965
>13	173	9.4	.66	.66	117	9.8	4957	4979

APPENDIX 4.1
(continued)

Occupation of Husband	Whether Wife Worked More than 200 Hours in 5 Years:				Hours of Work for Those Who Worked:			
	Unweighted N	% of Population	Unadjusted Mean	Adjusted Mean	Unweighted N	% of Population	Unadjusted Mean	Adjusted Mean
Head not in labor force	61	2.4	.46	.59	27	1.8	5639	6444
Professional, technical	235	15.1	.62	.63	146	14.9	4343	4542
Managers, officials and proprietors	165	11.1	.57	.63	94	10.0	4998	4881
Self-employed businessmen	100	5.9	.52	.54	56	4.9	5621	5545
Clerical and sales	201	11.4	.70	.68	136	12.6	5682	5059
Craftsmen and foremen	447	23.3	.62	.63	278	22.9	4907	4945
Operatives	421	16.6	.70	.67	293	18.4	4771	5009
Laborers and service workers	305	8.1	.70	.64	202	9.1	5310	5219
Farmers, farm managers	86	3.9	.45	.41	42	2.7	3710	3675
Miscellaneous, armed services, protective workers	55	2.3	.72	.63	43	2.6	5640	5899
Trend in Husband's Hourly Earnings (per year)								
Decline of $.50 or more	169	8.3	.49	.60	82	6.5	4954	5262
Decline of less than $.50	294	12.9	.69	.70	201	14.1	4506	4463
Increase less than $.25	564	24.5	.65	.62	367	25.2	5225	5058
Increase $.25-.49	554	26.9	.67	.64	370	28.7	5477	5160
Increase $.50-.99	381	20.4	.61	.61	236	19.8	4691	5065
Increase $1.00 or more	114	7.1	.51	.61	61	5.7	3532	4325
Husband's Total Unemployment in 5 Years								
None	1332	69.1	.61	62.9	826	66.6	5100	4877
Less than 200 hours	250	11.3	.74	64.0	182	13.2	4652	5311
200-799 hours	256	10.4	.61	56.0	153	10.1	5313	5517
800 or more hours	238	9.2	.70	69.3	156	10.2	4253	4650

APPENDIX 4.1
(continued)

	Whether Wife Worked More than 200 Hours in 5 Years:				Hours of Work for Those Who Worked:			
Number of Years Unemployed	Unweighted N	% of Population	Unadjusted Mean	Adjusted Mean	Unweighted N	% of Population	Unadjusted Mean	Adjusted Mean
None	1332	69.1	.61	61.8	826	66.6	5100	5100
One	377	16.3	.70	67.8	256	18.2	4862	4667
Two	177	6.8	.70	66.1	120	7.6	4683	4568
Three	98	3.7	.69	65.9	61	4.1	4050	4402
Four or five	92	4.0	.57	53.7	54	3.6	4932	5755
Wife's Average Hourly Earnings								
<$1.50					434	25.5	3209	3054
$1.50-2.49					527	40.1	5000	5018
$2.50-3.49					210	19.8	6573	6508
$3.50-5.00					107	10.7	6319	6448
≥$5.00					39	3.9	4501	5299

APPENDIX 4.2

MCA Results – Labor Supply of Single Women with Children

| | Single Female Heads with Children | | | | | | | |
| | Whether Worked in 1971: | | | | Hours Worked if Employed: | | | |
	Unweighted N	% of Population	Unadjusted Mean	Adjusted Mean	Unweighted N	% of Population	Unadjusted Mean	Adjusted Mean
Education								
Cannot read, write; has trouble reading, writing	21	2.6	.06	.20	5	0.2	506	589
0-5 grades	22	2.2	.49	.61	9	1.6	982	1690
6-8 grades, grade school; DK but mentions could read, write	130	13.4	.52	.69	66	9.8	1054	1664
9-11 grades, some high school	253	27.7	.64	.64	151	25.3	1384	1409
12 grades; high school	155	24.4	.78	.70	106	27.2	1574	1432
12 grades plus non-academic training	53	10.5	.76	.73	39	11.3	1571	1450
College, no degree	50	10.4	.90	.88	43	13.4	1547	1537
College degree	14	5.7	.87	.86	12	7.1	1607	1433
Not ascertained	19	3.2	.91	.84	14	4.2	1580	1365
Test Score								
0-5	92	9.4	.41	.67	36	5.5	1126	1049
6-7	138	15.5	.63	.73	82	13.9	1273	1463
8-9	238	27.8	.74	.76	155	29.5	1303	1283
10	128	23.0	.76	.68	85	25.0	1569	1539
11	76	14.9	.76	.70	54	16.1	1594	1675
12	35	6.6	.79	.57	25	7.4	2006	1771
13	10	2.7	.67	.64	8	2.6	1838	1677
Whether Has Disability Limiting Kind of Work Head Can Do								
Has disability	225	24.6	.42	.51	82	14.7	905	1164
Does not have disability	492	75.4	.79	.76	363	85.3	1566	1521

APPENDIX 4.2
(continued)

Single Female Heads with Children

Male Labor Market Conditions in Local County	Whether Worked in 1971:				Hours Worked if Employed:			
	Unweighted N	% of Population	Unadjusted Mean	Adjusted Mean	Unweighted N	% of Population	Unadjusted Mean	Adjusted Mean
More jobs than applicants	28	7.3	.90	.98	22	9.3	1416	1501
Most men able to find jobs	121	14.1	.75	.73	88	15.0	1528	1297
A number of unskilled workers unable to find jobs	273	39.3	.72	.72	180	40.5	1451	1478
Many unskilled workers unable to find jobs	260	33.9	.58	.62	131	28.2	1431	1478
Not ascertained	35	5.4	.90	.80	24	7.0	1659	1691
Average Amount of Aid to Families with Dependent Children per Recipient for State of Residence								
$0-24	133	12.6	.67	.75	92	12.0	1408	1362
$25-29	80	6.9	.74	.90	60	7.3	1547	1467
$30-34	54	8.7	.77	.86	38	9.6	1652	1466
$35-44	124	19.2	.85	.64	77	23.2	1596	1471
$45-54	185	26.0	.64	.71	104	23.9	1466	1410
$55-69	99	14.8	.58	.55	48	12.1	1322	1616
$70 or more	42	11.8	.71	.68	26	12.0	1241	1544
Current Region								
Northeast	103	23.4	.63	.84	49	21.0	1228	1308
North Central	174	24.6	.75	.72	107	26.3	1355	1388
South	324	31.3	.70	.63	218	31.0	1631	1597
West	116	20.8	.73	.63	71	21.7	1606	1538
Size of Largest City in Area								
500,000 or more	414	43.7	.63	.68	221	39.5	1330	1322
100,000-499,999	143	20.6	.82	.81	111	24.2	1510	1511
50,000-99,999	57	8.8	.70	.70	38	8.7	1651	1724
25,000-49,999	19	6.2	.77	.66	15	6.8	1300	1342
10,000-24,999	29	7.7	.86	.77	23	9.4	1340	1367
Less than 10,000	55	13.0	.62	.60	37	11.4	1961	1851

APPENDIX 4.2
(continued)

Single Female Heads with Children

	Whether Worked in 1971:				Hours Worked if Employed:			
	Unweighted N	% Population	Unadjusted Mean	Adjusted Mean	Unweighted N	% of Population	Unadjusted Mean	Adjusted Mean
Number of Children								
One	209	37.1	.75	.75	144	39.7	1573	1537
Two	187	32.4	.72	.69	125	33.4	1512	1525
Three	108	12.8	.64	.65	65	11.7	1619	1525
Four	103	11.0	.57	.59	57	8.9	1200	1357
Five	53	3.7	.78	.89	28	4.1	612	639
Six	25	1.4	.59	.67	14	1.2	592	699
Seven	20	1.0	.38	.46	5	0.5	541	783
Eight or more	12	0.6	.66	.89	7	0.6	1373	2025
Age of Youngest Child								
Less than 2 years old	131	14.1	.60	.64	80	12.1	1172	1453
2 years	76	8.8	.53	.49	38	6.7	1866	1577
3 years	40	5.5	.74	.77	22	5.8	1395	1244
4 years	41	6.0	.79	.82	24	6.8	1323	1323
5 years	54	7.5	.69	.66	31	7.3	1306	1266
6-8 years	126	19.4	.73	.72	83	20.1	1523	1514
9-13	158	24.0	.77	.77	109	26.3	1413	1361
14-17	91	14.6	.71	.70	58	14.8	1733	1816
Marital Status								
Married (spouse absent)	10	2.0	.51	.58	5	1.4	1189	1486
Single	132	11.6	.66	.61	80	10.9	1293	1455
Widowed	135	20.8	.53	.56	77	15.7	1155	1057
Divorced	197	42.7	.86	.84	154	52.5	1685	1632
Separated	243	22.8	.60	.64	129	19.5	1258	1367
Age of Head in 1972								
Less than 25	112	14.5	.72	.74	72	14.9	1315	1346
25-34	180	27.4	.77	.71	112	29.9	1663	1573
35-44	213	29.8	.74	.67	138	31.3	1477	1397
45-54	136	16.4	.66	.73	88	15.6	1339	1495
55-64	65	8.2	.53	.66	32	6.2	1225	1385
65 and over	11	3.7	.40	.70	3	2.0	1347	1941

APPENDIX 4.2
(continued)

Single Female Heads with Children

	Whether Worked in 1971:				Hours Worked if Employed:			
	Unweighted N	% of Population	Unadjusted Mean	Adjusted Mean	Unweighted N	% of Population	Unadjusted Mean	Adjusted Mean
Race								
White	178	63.7	.76	.71	129	68.9	1519	1418
Black	520	33.0	.62	.70	310	29.0	1347	1580
Spanish-American	14	3.0	.47	.50	5	2.0	1524	1631
Other	5	0.3	.14	.50	1	0.1	40	-95
Achievement Motivation Score								
0-4	72	11.0	.44	.54	29	6.9	1120	973
5-6	142	19.0	.75	.77	90	20.2	1541	1545
7-8	220	28.4	.75	.77	142	30.5	1401	1483
9-10	180	26.6	.72	.68	123	27.3	1427	1427
11-12	80	11.6	.67	.59	48	11.2	1567	1503
13-16	23	3.5	.81	.80	13	4.0	2222	2019
Head's Average Hourly Earnings								
Less than $1.00					62	12.2	942	1053
$1.00-1.49					87	19.1	1340	1487
$1.50-1.99					85	11.5	1614	1674
$2.00-2.49					67	15.4	1555	1649
$2.50-2.99					44	12.1	1583	1359
$3.00-3.99					56	13.8	1751	1732
$4.00-5.99					27	9.7	1942	1647
$6.00 or more					17	6.2	824	749

Chapter 5

TRANSFER INCOME

INTRODUCTION

The previous two chapters have dealt with the determinants of the earnings of various family members. However, the distribution of incomes earned by current productive effort would leave many people unable to meet even the most basic needs. Society has a variety of mechanisms for redistributing income more equitably. The most ancient method of redistribution, of course, is accomplished within the family where some members contribute earned money and others expend their time and effort. The young and old usually receive transfers from the middle-aged.[1]

A second method is saving and dissaving. People accumulate reserves when they are earning and use them up when they retire. Private pensions and social security are the two main examples of this mechanism. Various forms of insurance such as unemployment, workmen's compensation, and private insurance redistribute resources according to prior agreement from the protected premium-paying population to those who need help because of misfortune covered by the insurance. We can call these *contributory* or *funded* transfers because insurance is only a transfer in time.

A third redistribution mechanism is the *non-contributory* transfer. Government programs of this type include Aid to Families with Dependent Children, General Assistance, and other categorical assistance programs. These are generally referred to as "welfare." Private philanthropy is a private-sector non-contributory transfer.

This chapter investigates the several aspects of transfer income. The first section describes the relationship between transfers and other sources of income. The second studies the adequacy and equity of non-contributory transfers, and the third looks at the dynamics of who got on and who got off welfare.

---

[1] For an analysis of the impact of within-family transfers, see Baerwaldt and Morgan (1972).

The analyses in this chapter by no means exhaust the uses of these data. In particular, this panel study is useful for simulating various plans for welfare reform, since it contains information not only about the family but also about the individual family members. A transfer system may have an important effect on the composition of the family itself, and these data can shed light on what might happen to families under various rules.

ANALYSIS

I. Relationship between Transfer Income and
    and Income from Other Sources

Transfers do redistribute incomes and make them more equal, but the amount of redistribution on the average is not large. For example, families whose incomes just equal their need standards receive an average of $1480 from transfers while those whose incomes are three and one-half times their needs receive about $1000.[1] Of course, the type of transfer changes as income rises. Low income families primarily receive non-contributory transfers and social security while high income families receive more from private retirement pensions and insurance.

The number of families that would be in poverty without transfers is large. Table 5.1 shows that only 10% of the total population have incomes less than their needs, but this number would double if there were no transfers. If we consider those with incomes less than 1.5 of needs as poor, again an additional 10% of the families would be in poverty without transfer mechanisms.[2] Thus, transfers do compensate somewhat for low incomes.

It is also important to investigate the dynamics of this process to see how transfers respond to changes in other income. Considering families who received some transfer income in both 1967 and 1971, nearly 60% of those with decreases in other income had a substantial increase in transfer income (see Table 5.2a). Similarly, of those with increases of 10% or more in other income, 40% had reductions in the amount of transfers they received. There are important exceptions to this compensating pattern. Eighteen percent of the families with decreases in other income also experienced decreases in transfers. Over half of the families who had increases in non-transfer income less than the rate of inflation were

---

[1] For details on the composition of income at different levels of well-being, see Appendix G.

[2] For a more detailed description of which families benefit most from transfers, see Okner (1973).

TABLE 5.1

Distribution of Total Income/Needs for Families
with Non–Transfer Income/Needs Less than 1.50 in 1971

Total Income Needs	Non-transfer Income/Need					Percent of Population
	0	.01-.29	.30-.59	.60-.99	1.00-1.49	
0	1.3	0	0	0	0	0.1
.01 - .29	2.2	4.2	0	0	0	0.4
.30 - .59	15.9	12.9	18.3	0	0	2.6
.60 - .99	31.6	28.4	23.4	34.8	0	6.8
1.00 - 1.49	32.4	24.9	28.3	30.5	51.0	10.8
1.50 or more	16.5	29.5	30.1	34.8	49.0	79.8
TOTAL	100%	100%	100%	100%	100%	100%
Percent of Population	6.3	5.9	4.6	6.0	8.2	

% of population with total income/needs <1.50 = 20.7%

% of population with non-transfer income/needs <1.50 = 31.0%

TABLE 5.2a

Percent Change in Non-Transfer Income by Percent Change
in Transfers for Families Receiving Transfers in 1967 and 1971

Annual Percent Change in Transfer Income	Annual % Change in Non-Transfer Income				
	Decreases	Increases less than Inflation	Small Increases	Substantial Increases	Percent Population
Decreases	17.8	31.5	30.9	40.7	32.3
Increases less than inflation (1-4%)	15.8	21.3	29.0	19.6	21.0
Small increase (5-9%)	6.9	5.8	6.7	9.2	7.6
Substantial Increase (>10%)	59.4	41.6	34.4	30.4	39.1
TOTAL	100%	100%	100%	100%	100%
Percent Population	20.6	18.7	19.7	41.0	

TABLE 5.2b

Percent Change in Non-Transfer Income/Needs by Percent Change
in Transfer Income/Needs for Families Receiving Transfers in 1967 and 1971

Annual Percent Change in Transfer Income/Needs	Annual % Change in Non-transfer Income/Needs				
	Decreases	Increases less than Inflation	Small Increases	Substantial Increases	Percent Population
Decreases	50.6	21.7	7.1	9.3	19.6
Increasess less than inflation (1-4%)	9.3	7.6	4.0	7.8	7.4
Small increases (5-9%)	4.0	6.6	7.7	8.9	7.2
Substantial Increase (>10%)	36.2	64.1	81.2	74.0	65.8
TOTAL	100%	100%	100%	100%	100%
Percent Population	21.1	16.3	18.9	43.6	

worse off: thirty percent had declines in transfers and another 20% had in= creases in transfers which were also less than the rate of inflation.

We found in Chapter 2 that changes in the composition of the family had a very important impact on the changes in well-being of its members, so we have also considered the changes in transfer and other income relative to the family's needs standard (see Table 5.2b). There is very little evidence that transfer income mechanisms, as a whole, make allowances for these important family changes. Of those with decreases in other income relative to their needs, 50% also had declines in transfer income relative to their needs; 74% of those with substantial increases also had substantial increases in transfers relative to their needs.

Transfers reduce the inequality among families by redistributing income more equitably. An additional 10% of the population would be in poverty if there were no transfers. However, the compensatory nature of transfers is less evident when we look at the relationship between changes in transfer income and changes in income from other sources. This is especially true when we also consider the changes in the composition of families.

II. Adequacy and Equity of the Non-Contributory Transfer System

The purpose of non-contributory transfers, or welfare, is to help make up the difference between the income a family has and the amount it needs to maintain some minimum standard of living. Welfare may not make up this entire difference. In fact, many states' payments are set by law at some specified fraction of the family's needs. Further, the amount of the benefits may not decrease, dollar for dollar, with the amount of income: the federal government requires, for example, that payments should decrease by $.67 for each dollar the family earns above $30. The amount of welfare a family receives can be represented, generally, by the following equation:

$$\text{Welfare payments} = a(\text{Needs}) - b(\text{Other Income}) \text{ or, equivalently,}$$

$$\frac{\text{Welfare}}{\text{Needs}} = a - b \ \frac{\text{Other Income}}{\text{Needs}}$$

That is, the percentage of the family's need standard that welfare pays is equal to a constant amount minus some fraction of the percentage of needs that the family has from other sources of income.

This single equation does not describe the transfer system that every household in the United States faces. There are large differences in state AFDC laws both in the definition of a family's needs and in the amount of income a family can earn before all benefits are cut off.[1] There are also differences in the adequacy of benefits depending on which welfare program a family can qualify for, and this depends on the age of the head and on the presence of children in the family.

In order to describe the variations in the adequacy of benefits in the welfare system as a whole, we have regressed the ratio of welfare to needs on the ratio of other-income to needs and on characteristics of the place where the family lives and of the family itself. This shows the average relationship between income and the amount of welfare received and how the benefits differ for various groups in our society, controlling on any differences in income. We consider only families whose income from sources other than welfare is less than or equal to one and one-half times their need standard, since almost no one with income greater than that receives any welfare. We consider the 1971 income year, and both income and the welfare payments have been adjusted for geographical differences in the cost of living.

Table 5.3 shows the estimated transfer/needs ratios for various levels of other-income/needs ratios controlling for locational and family characteristics. (That is, the average transfers/needs we estimated that these families would receive if they were alike on all other characteristics except other income.)

TABLE 5.3
Relationship between Welfare Payments
and Income from Other Sources

Income Other than Welfare/Needs	Estimated Welfare/Needs	Estimated Total Income/Needs
0	.74	.74
.10	.45	.55
.30	.27	.57
.58	.18	.76
.87	.07	.94
1.12	.06	1.18
1.37	.03	1.40

Families with no other income have an estimated welfare/needs ratio of .74, indicating that the government will give families, on the average, about three-quarters of their need standard if they have no other income. A very large inequity exists for those families who have very low but positive income. The welfare system leaves them less well off than those with no other income at all. Table 5.4 shows how this operates.

A family on welfare with an other-income/needs ratio of .30 will receive an

_____
[1]See Heffernan (1973).

TABLE 5.4

Relation between Welfare Payments and
Other Income for Those Receiving Welfare

Other Income/Needs	Estimated Welfare/Needs [1]	Estimated Total Income/Needs	Percent Receiving Welfare
0	.74	.74	100%
.10	.62	.72	81
.30	.58	.88	55
.58	.58	1.06	33
.87	.36	1.23	19
1.12	.34	1.46	10
1.37	.38	1.75	6

_____

[1]The standard deviation of the estimated means for all income groups is about .30.

additional 58% of its needs from the government so its total income will be 88% of its needs. But even at this low income only 55% of the families receive any welfare at all. The rest are left with very inadequate income/needs ratios of .30. Thus, there is an enormous disincentive for families with no other income to seek additional sources of income. Since there is only a 55% chance that a family with a small amount of other income will stay on welfare, these families can expect, on the average, to be much worse off. Put another way, there is a marginal tax rate of over 150% in the lowest income/needs group.

There is some evidence that welfare recipients perceive this large marginal tax rate. In 1972 we asked those who were receiving welfare the following two questions:

"How much money can a person earn before they start to cut his welfare?"
"If a person earns $10 more than that amount, how much is his welfare cut?"

Not one person responded to the second question with an amount less than $10, even though many were on AFDC where, by law, the marginal rate is 67%. Of those giving an answer, 70% said that welfare would be cut by the full $10 and the rest said that all the welfare would be cut off. It is also revealing that half of the respondents answered that they didn't know how much welfare would be cut, indicating that there is a great deal of ignorance and uncertainty as to exactly what the rules are.

The other characteristics included in the regression are listed in Table 5.5 in order of their relative importance in explaining the variation in the relationship of welfare to a family's needs. By including these characteristics additively, they can explain how the average payments for all income levels vary according to these characteristics, but do not imply any variation in the basic

TABLE 5.5

Relative Importance of Predictors in Explaining Welfare/Needs

	β^2
Income other than welfare/needs	.283
Age of youngest child	.054
Age of head	.020
Region	.014
Number of children	.012
City size	.009
Race	.005
Mobility	.005
Sex-Marital status	.005
Imputed rent from owning own home	.005

$R^2 = .43$

relationship between income and welfare payments. We have searched for characteristics which do effect this relationship and found only two of importance:
region and city size. These will be discussed later.

By looking at the effects of the two variables representing the presence of
children in the family, we estimate that, on the average, families without children receive 9% less from welfare in relation to their needs than similar families
with children. This results primarily from the fact that families with no children are 21% more likely to receive no welfare. For those who do receive payments
the families without children fare about the same as those with children.

The adequacy of welfare is not affected by the age of the youngest child in
the family, but it does have an interesting relationship to the number of children. Figure 5.1 shows how for those families receiving welfare the amount of welfare in relation to the need standard varies according to the number of children
in the family, other things (including income) being equal. The average family
with two children receives welfare equal to 58% of its needs while a family with
five children receives welfare equaling only 37% of its needs. While the need
standard used here closely approximates the one developed by the Social Security
Administration which is used widely by other government agencies, these data
indicate that this need standard bears little relationship to the realities of
the welfare system. By law, each state defines the needs standard to be used in
administering AFDC. These data show that the level of support that such laws
imply is not only lower than the federal guidelines, but also does not have the
same relationship to family size. Large families receive much less per child
than small families, even taking into account "economies of scale" in feeding,
clothing, and housing a larger number of children. The stereotype of welfare
mothers deliberately having more children in order to increase their welfare payments is difficult to maintain considering that having more children means the

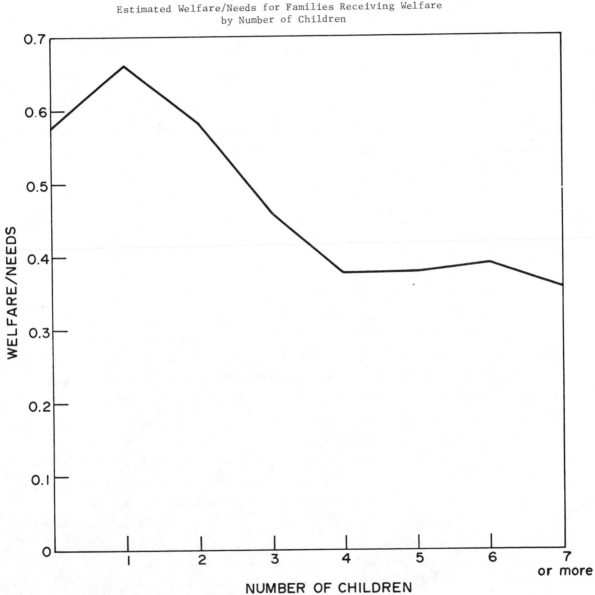

FIGURE 5.1

Estimated Welfare/Needs for Families Receiving Welfare
by Number of Children

entire family will be living in greater poverty.

The age of the head is another very important predictor of the amount of welfare a family receives. This is a result of both families with older heads having a greater probability of being on welfare and, if they are, of receiving more in relation to needs than other families. This relationship exists across the entire age spectrum and is not just a function of the very old being eligible for Old Age Assistance and others not. For example, families with heads 45 years old have, on the average, an 85% greater probability of receiving some welfare than families with heads 25 years old, controlling for income and for the presence of children.

The race of the family also makes a difference in the adequacy of the welfare they receive. Black families have an estimated 28% probability of being on welfare compared to 24% for white families in the same situation. Further, for those families on welfare, blacks receive 20% more than whites. Spanish Americans have a different pattern: while they are the least likely of all the races to receive welfare, those who do receive benefits average more than either black or white families. Even if we estimate the basic relationship between income and welfare payments differently for the South and for large cities, these race effects still persist.

The geographic mobility of the family was originally included to control for any residency requirements that still might remain. We find, however, that movers receive more welfare than non-movers. This is probably a result of the fact that welfare recipients move relatively often. When they do move, the welfare agency often pays the expenses so the amount they receive would indeed be higher. For a discussion of the causes of moving, see Chapter 2, Volume II.

The sex and marital status of the head also affect the adequacy of welfare payments. Single men and married men receive about the same average benefits. However, single men have a higher probability of receiving welfare but lower payments if they are on welfare. Single women on welfare receive only slightly higher payments relative to their needs than do married men but have a 33% higher chance of receiving benefits, even controlling for income adequacy and the number of children in the family.

The last family characteristic included in the analysis is the amount of imputed rent a family earns by owning its own home. It was hypothesized that if a family owns a home, they would have decreased housing costs and the welfare agency would take this into account in determining the level of benefits. The cost savings would directly relate to the amount of equity the family has and the imputed rent is assumed to be 6% of this equity. Contrary to our expectations,

there does not appear to be any relationship between this imputed rent and welfare adequacy. This is a result of two offsetting factors. The estimated percent of families receiving welfare declines sharply with the amount of imputed
rent, but the benefits increase just as sharply. Larger equity probably means
the family owns a larger house with correspondingly higher utility bills and
maintenance costs. Welfare agencies often pay these costs so the total benefits
would indeed increase with imputed rent. Owning a large home, on the other hand,
might also be a proxy for having other assets and welfare agencies might well
take these into account in determining eligibility. They also might be more
reticent to accept owners of large homes on welfare since the agency is indeed
incurring a greater responsibility in terms of paying out larger benefits.

Since welfare is administered by the states and since state laws differ, we
would expect that characteristics of different locations would have an effect on
the percent of its needs a family can receive from welfare. Region and the size
of the largest city were included in this analysis in an additive fashion (as
were the family characteristics). We also estimated the basic relationship
between income adequacy and welfare adequacy separately for large cities and for
the southern states since a search procedure indicated that these might be important interactions. We find that city size does not usually affect the size of
benefits, except that in cities greater than 100,000 the very poor do better than
elsewhere. The eligibility rules appear to be easier since a larger portion of
very poor people are on welfare in the big cities, and the benefits are larger
relative to the families' needs. However, these benefits and the percent of
families eligible to receive them decrease sharply with income. Those whose incomes equal their need standards are worse off in the large cities than elsewhere
in terms of aid from welfare.

There are also large regional differences in the adequacy of welfare as
shown in Table 5.6. On the average, a larger fraction of the families in the

TABLE 5.6

Regional Differences in Welfare Received

Region	Estimated percent of Families Receiving Welfare with other Income/Needs less than 1.5	Estimated Average Wel-fare/Needs for Families Receiving Welfare
Northeast	.28	.67
North Central	.24	.64
South	.23	.39
West	.27	.54

Northeast and West are on welfare than in the North Central and South, other
things being equal. If we estimate the relationship between eligibility and

income separately for the southern states, we find that for the very lowest income group the probability of receiving welfare is greater in the South than elsewhere, but that eligibility declines very sharply with income. Families with incomes greater than 80% of their needs have a much lower chance of receiving aid in the South than in other regions.

More important regional differences occur in the average payments to those on welfare. If we compare families on welfare who are alike in all characteristics except the region in which they live, those living in the South receive on the average 40% less than do families living in the Northeast. The data have been adjusted for differences in the cost of living, so these families experience real differences in their total resources. This regional difference in the average benefits is fairly consistent across all income groups.

What, then, can we say about the adequacy and equity of the non-contributory transfer system? In general, for those with no other income, welfare makes up only three-quarters of the money the family needs to feed, house, and clothe itself. Not even this inadequate level of support is afforded to those who have some small amount of income. Their total income, including any welfare received, averages to just over one-half of their need standard. A large fraction of these families receive no welfare at all.

Given the basic relationship between income adequacy and welfare adequacy, other characteristics of the family imply differences in the average amount of welfare it receives relative to its needs. Some of these differences reflect deliberate policy decisions, others do not. Specific welfare programs have been set up for families with children and for the very old, so it is not surprising that families with children receive about 10% more than other families, or that the elderly fare better than younger people. However, the adequacy of welfare increases directly with age, even for those under 65.

In an effort to provide incentives for birth control, some states will increase welfare payments for each additional child only up to a specified number of children. Our data show that the adequacy of welfare payments declines significiantly with *each* additional child, not just for very large numbers of children. We also find that on the average white families receive less in relation to their needs than families of other races. Households with women as heads are likely to receive more adequate benefits than families with similar incomes where the head is male.

The geographic location of the family also determines the level of welfare it receives. Regional differences reflect variations in state laws, but differences due to city size probably reflect variations in the local administration of these laws. We find that families in the South, on the average, receive far less than those elsewhere but that the very poor in the South are more likely to receive some benefits than they are in other regions. Large cities are also more likely to give welfare to the poorest families and less likely to do so for families that are somewhat better off.

III. Changes in Welfare Status

The number of families **receiving** welfare rose dramatically between 1967 and 1971 and the data from the study reflect this trend. If we consider the families in the target population where either the head or wife was in the sample for all five years, about 40% had some welfare experience. Of these, nearly twice as many went on **welfare as got off** (27% compared to 15%), 46% of the families were on welfare in both 1967 and 1971, and the remainder received benefits at some point but not at the beginning or end of the study.[1]

The question we now turn to is what types of families went on welfare and what types were able to get off welfare during this period? We look at the relative importance of several characteristics: local conditions, background of the family, the family composition, employability of the head, and the attitudes the head expressed in the first year.

WHO GOES ON WELFARE?

When we compare families in the target population who went on welfare to those who did not, we find that the most important characteristic that distinguishes these two groups is the composition of the family (see Table 5.7). The sex of the head is particularly important. Among families with the same head for all five years, women are only an additional 2% more likely to go on welfare than men.[2] However, women whose husbands left during this period and who had three or more children are much more likely to turn to welfare for assistance than families with a male head for all five years. Women who become divorced or separated but have small families are only somewhat more likely to go on welfare than women who remain unmarried. Families where a female head gets married are the least likely to go on welfare.

The characteristics of the children are also important. Families with children are more likely to go on welfare, reflecting the existence of specific

---

[1]We have excluded those over 65 from this analysis since they have little change in welfare status.

[2]Barbara Boland (1973) also finds that the participation rates for women did not change during this period.

TABLE 5.7

Probability of Getting on Welfare between 1967 and 1971
for Families in the Target Population

	Getting on Welfare		Adjusted
	Coefficient	t-ratio	Partial R^2s
Local Conditions			.01
Unemployment rate	.007	(0.8)	
Large city	.007	(0.3)	
Small town	−.005	(0.2)	
Northeast	.11	_a	
North Central	0	(0)	
South	−.06	(1.5)	
West	.04	(1.3)	
Average Welfare per Recipient in County	−.02	(2.4)	
Background			.02
Grew up on farm	.03	(1.3)	
Grew up in city	.03	(1.4)	
Race	.12	(4.9)	
Family Composition			.07
Male head all 5 years	0	_a	
Female head gets married	−.09	(1.6)	
Female head all 5 years	.02	(0.3)	
Wife becomes head:			
3≥ children	.26	(6.5)	
<3 children	.08	(2.4)	
Age of head, female	−.003	(1.9)	
Age of head, male	−.001	(1.2)	
Whether children, 1968	.14	(3.8)	
Number of children, 1968	.004	(0.6)	
Age youngest child, 1968	−.02	(3.5)	
Child born between 1968 and 1972	.02	(1.1)	
Employability			.01
Disability, 1968	.08	(3.8)	
Education	−.01	(1.7)	
Test score	−.004	(1.1)	
Attitudes			.002
Efficacy	−.004	(0.6)	
Planning	−.002	(0.3)	
Trust	.01	(1.4)	

Fraction of variance explained $R^2 = .14$

Adjusted for degrees of freedom   adjusted $R^2 = .12$ Number of cases   n=1288

---

[a] The coefficients for related categories were obtained as deviations from this category so no standard deviation is available.

programs to aid these families, but the total number of children in the family does not have any effect. What *does* increase the chances of a family going on welfare is the presence of young children and, to a lesser extent, the birth of a child during this period. Families with older children may have more options for work since the need for child care is less of a constraint, and older children may be able to contribute financially. The age of the head makes some difference: the probability of getting on welfare declines slightly with age for both men and women.

Background is the next most important set of characteristics in explaining who goes on welfare. Race is particularly significant. Blacks are twelve percentage points more likely than whites to go on welfare. This is partially due to the fact that even within the target population black families have lower average incomes than whites and, as we said earlier, to the greater percentage of black families receiving welfare even controlling for income. Families where the head grew up on a farm or in a large city seem to have a slightly greater chance of going on welfare than those where the head grew up in a small town. We do not have available all the relevant background variables for these families, but we will investigate the effects of other background characteristics in analyzing the welfare status of splitoffs.

It was expected that counties with high unemployment rates would have more families turning to welfare for support, but this does not seem to be the case. Nor does it make any difference whether the family is living in a large city or in a rural area. There are, however, large differences in the probability of receiving welfare depending on the region in which the family lives. Those living in the Northeast are an additional 11% more likely than the average to go on welfare while those living in the South are six percentage points less likely. These differences probably reflect the regional variations in eligibility for welfare that we discussed earlier. The average welfare payment per recipient in the county was included in this analysis because it was expected that families living in areas where the average level of support is highest would have a greater incentive to go on welfare. The opposite seems to be true: the probability of going on welfare declines as the size of the average benefit increases. This variable may be serving as a better proxy than the unemployment rate for the economic conditions of the county.

The employability of the head is measured by three variables: whether she or he is disabled, the education of the head, and the score on the ability test administered to the head in the 1972 interview. Of the three, only disability shows any significant relationship. Those families who were not on welfare in

1967 and whose head reported a disability severe enough to limit work were more likely to be on welfare in 1971. The education of the head may have some small effect: our best estimate is that the probability of going on welfare declines by one percentage point for each category of education, but this relationship is not very certain. The test score, which does affect other elements of economic well-being, has no effect on whether the family goes on welfare. The attitudes expressed by the head are the least important set of characteristics in explaining who does and who does not go on welfare in the target population. Neither efficacy nor planning nor trust show any significant effect.

WHO GOES OFF WELFARE?

When we look at the non-aged population on welfare in 1967, we find that 38% were no longer receiving it by 1971. The factors determining which families get off welfare operate in a more systematic fashion than those determining which get on: we are able to explain almost half of the variation among families by the characteristics of local conditions, background, family composition, employability, and attitudes.

Family composition is again the most important characteristic in explaining changes in welfare status. Families who were on welfare in 1967 and have a female head by 1972 are an additional 95% less likely to get off welfare than families with a male head for all five years. This group includes both families with the same female head during the period and families where the husband left. They both have the same high probability of remaining on welfare. Women who marry are still an additional 50% less likely than male heads to be off welfare by 1971.

When we look at the effects that the sex of the head have on both types of changes in welfare status, an interesting pattern emerges. We found earlier that women are about 20% more likely to *be* on welfare than men. However, women who are off welfare are not more likely to get on. The difference lies in the fact that women who are on welfare are much more likely to stay on. The principle paths of change between these two groups involve change in marital status. It is the women whose husbands leave them with large numbers of children who are more likely to go on welfare, and it is the women who marry who are more likely to get off.

In considering who gets off welfare, we find that the effects of age are different depending on the sex of the head. Older men on welfare are more likely to remain there than younger men while the reverse is true for women. Evidently, if a man is unable to find an adequate job when he is young, it is even less likely that he will find one as he grows older. Women, on the other hand, are

TABLE 5.8

Probability of Getting off Welfare between 1967 and 1971
for Families Receiving Welfare in 1967

	Getting off Welfare		Adjusted
	Coefficient	t-ratio	Partial R^2s
Local Conditions			.09
Unemployment rate	-.07	(2.9)	
Large city	-.11	(1.8)	
Small town	-.07	(1.0)	
Northeast	.02	$-^a$	
North Central	.05	(0.7)	
South	-.06	(0.6)	
West	-.01	(0.2)	
Average Welfare per Recipient in County	-.07	(3.1)	
Background			.004
Grew up on farm	.04	(0.8)	
Grew up in city	.01	(0.2)	
Race	-.07	(1.7)	
Family Composition			.24
Male head all 5 years	0	$-^a$	
Female head gets married	-.50	(3.4)	
Female head all 5 years	-.95	(6.4)	
Wife becomes head	-.95	(9.7)	
Age of head, female	.006	(2.3)	
Age of head, male	-.01	(6.4)	
Whether children, 1968	-.04	(0.4)	
Number of children, 1968	-.03	(3.1)	
Age youngest child, 1968	-.008	(0.7)	
Child born between 1968 and 1972	-.05	(1.2)	
Employability			.02
Disability, 1968	-.08	(1.7)	
Education	.02	(1.4)	
Test score	.007	(0.8)	
Attitudes			.02
Efficacy	.008	(0.5)	
Planning	.05	(2.4)	
Trust	.05	(2.2)	

Fraction of variance explained $R^2 = .46$

Adjusted for degrees of freedom   adjusted $R^2 = .42$ Number of cases n=404

---

[a]The coefficients for related categories were obtained as deviations from this category so no standard deviation is available.

for the most part unable to work because they have children and the effect of this "handicap" decreases with time.

The variables representing the characteristics of the children in the family have different relationships to getting off welfare than to going on. It appears that only the absolute number of children is what matters and not the age composition. The age of the youngest child has no effect on the family's probability of getting off welfare, and whether a child is born during this period may have only a slight influence. However, the probability of a family getting off welfare declines by 3% for each child.

Local area conditions are relatively more important in explaining who gets off welfare than who goes on. Families living in counties where there are many more applicants than jobs among unskilled laborers are 14% less likely to get off welfare than those who live in areas where the number of jobs about equals the number of applicants. There is some evidence that those living either in large cities or in small towns are less likely to get off welfare than those in medium sized cities, but the variations from this pattern are too large to say this with much certainty. Welfare payments average higher in the Northeast than elsewhere, so it is not surprising that families in the Northeast have less incentive to get off welfare and are much less likely to do so. However, if we control for the higher payments, the regional pattern changes: families in the Northeast and North Central states are more likely to get off welfare than those in the South and West. These differences most likely reflect regional variations in employment conditions.

Although attitudes expressed by the head have no effect on who goes on welfare, they do show an important relationship to which families get off welfare. People who express future orientation by saying that they plan ahead, would rather save for the future, and think a lot about the future are more likely than others to get off welfare, as are those who trust most people, care about other people's opinions, think the life of the average person is getting better, and do not believe that there are a lot of people with good things they don't deserve. High scores in personal efficacy, however, do not help in getting off welfare.

Over 40% of the heads of welfare families report that they have a disabilith sever enough to limit work, but there is only a suggestion that the disabled are less likely to get off welfare. Our best estimate is that they are about eight percentage points less likely, but this is not statistically significant. Of the other employability characteristics, neither the education of the head nor the test score makes any difference in who gets off welfare.

The background variables are the least important set of characteristics. The size of the place where the head grew up makes no difference whatever. We discovered a very definite race effect for getting on welfare, but the pattern for getting off is inconclusive. We cannot say with any certainty that black families are more likely to stay on welfare than white families.

SPLITOFFS

In investigating changes in welfare status, we have so far looked only at the behavior of the same family over five years. Another aspect of the dynamics of welfare is the extent to which the parental family's being on welfare has an effect on the next generation. About 10% of the splitoffs in the target population were on welfare in 1971. We can compare these families to newly formed families that were not on welfare to determine whether several characteristics of the original family make any difference in the splitoff's welfare status.

Table 5.9 shows the results of a regression on whether the family was on welfare in 1971 using the variables representing family composition, local conditions, and employability of the head that we used earlier, plus an expanded set of background characteristics (attitudes were not included in this analysis since we only have concurrent measures and including them as predictors of current status would be circular). Whether or not the main family was on welfare in 1967 has only a slight effect on the splitoff's probability of being on welfare in 1971, and the variation in this pattern is so great that we cannot say with certainty that there is any effect at all. Controlling for the other characteristics, including parental income, our best estimate is that while only 10% of all the splitoffs in the target population are on welfare, about 15% of splitoffs from welfare families are receiving benefits. We are quite certain this estimated probability is not as high as 25% and it may not differ from the average. Thus, the stereotype of large numbers of families living from generation to generation on welfare is not borne out by these data, but there is some evidence that if one's family was receiving welfare, then the individual's chances of being on welfare are increased by 5%.

Interestingly, for the target population, variations in the parental income do not have any effect on the splitoffs chances of being on welfare, and neither does the education of the head of the original family. There is, again, only a suggestion that the probability of the splitoff family receiving welfare increases if the head of the original family was a woman or if there were large numbers of siblings.

The other variables have much the same effects on splitoffs as they do on

TABLE 5.9

Probability of a Splitoff Being on Welfare in 1971

	Coefficient	t-ratio
Local Conditions		
Unemployment rate	.02	(1.3)
Large city	.04	(1.3)
Small town	−.02	(0.5)
Northeast	.06	_a
North Central	0	(0)
South	−.07	(1.4)
West	.05	(1.2)
Average welfare per recipient in county	−.02	(2.2)
Background		
Grew up farm	.04	(1.4)
Grew up city	.01	(0.4)
Race	.05	(1.5)
Family on welfare in 1967	.05	(1.4)
Family income in 1967	.00	(0)
Family head female	.04	(1.5)
Number of siblings	.01	(1.5)
Parents' education	.00	(0.1)
Family Composition		
Male head:		
Son	−.03	_a
Daughter married	−.03	(1.0)
Female head	.06	(2.4)
Age of head	.002	(1.7)
Number of children	.04	(3.0)
Age youngest child	−.004	(0.6)
Employability		
Disability	.08	(2.2)
Education	−.04	(4.7)
Test score	.00	(0.7)

$$R^2 = .18$$
$$\text{adjusted } R^2 = .15$$

Number of cases n=704

---

[a]The coefficients for related categories were obtained as deviations from this cateogry so no standard deviation is available.

the main families, although local conditions have a little more influence on splitoffs, especially the unemployment rate. Family composition is somewhat less important, but we still find women much more likely to be on welfare. The number of children, rather than their age composition, has the greatest effect for splitoffs, probably because there is much less variation in the age of the children in these young families.

The most important difference between splitoffs and main families lies in the effect education has on the probability of getting on welfare. For splitoffs this probability declines by four percentage points for each category of education attained, and this estimate is very statistically significant. For main families the estimate is much lower and the variation around that pattern is much greater. For newly formed families, the most important characteristic that distinguishes those who are on welfare and those who are not is the education of the head. This is further evidence that the emphasis in the sixties on education for the children of the poor as a means of breaking the "cycle of poverty" was not misplaced.

In conclusion, we find that the factors that are most important in determining who goes on and who gets off welfare are characteristics of the family itself. A pattern seems to exist where there are some family structures that imply a much greater chance of *being* on welfare. As families move into these critical structures they are more likely to change status by going on welfare. Families which had already attained these "high-risk" compositions by 1967 and were not then on welfare did not have a greater chance of getting on welfare by 1971. For example, we found earlier that families with female heads are more likely to be on welfare. Families which change from a male head to a female head during this period indeed had a higher chance of going onto welfare, but families which already had a female head and were not on welfare did *not* have a greater chance of changing their status. Similarly, families with children are more likely to receive aid, but families that had a large number of children, but who were not on welfare in 1967, were not the ones most likely to need help. Whether they had a young child is what made the difference. Those families just moving into this "high-risk" family structure in 1967 and having young children were the most likely to go on welfare during the next five years.

Once families with children or with female heads are on welfare, however, there is a much greater chance that they will stay on. Women are less likely to get off welfare than men by 95 percentage points, and the chance of getting off welfare does not change as the children grow older. The only characteristic of the children that matters here is the number of children in the family.

What then are the characteristics other than family composition that determine whether a family changes its welfare status? Local conditions, which are most easily changed by public policy, do not make much difference in who goes on welfare, except for a regional difference probably reflecting variations in eligibility rules. Living in a county with low unemployment, however, affects a family's chances of getting off welfare. Background, particularly race, also is an important predictor. Blacks are more likely to go on welfare by 12 percentage points, but are only slightly more likely to stay there than similar white families. No statistically significant reason for splitoffs being on welfare can be traced to characteristics of the parental family. Those families whose parents were on welfare may be an additional 5% more likely to receive welfare, but this relationship is quite uncertain.

Employability exerts an influence on changes in welfare status mainly because the disabled are more apt to go on welfare and are slightly more likely to stay there. Only for splitoff families does the education of the head make any difference, but the young are the only group whose amount of education is at all subject to current public policy.

No attitudes expressed by the head in 1968 have anything to do with the family going on welfare, but families already on welfare are more likely to get off it if the head of the family trusts others and looks toward the future. These attitudes are a more important influence than objective variables such as disability and education.

SUMMARY

We have investigated three aspects of the welfare system: the relationship between transfer income and income from other sources, the adequacy and equity of the non-contributory transfers, and the determinants of getting on and off welfare. The following are major conclusions from this study.

1. Transfer income does serve to redistribute income more equitably. An additional 10% of the population would be poor without the transfer mechanisms. Changes in the amount of other income a family has, however, are often not accomplished by opposite changes in the amount of transfers they receive. Nearly 20% of those with decreases in other income also had decreases in transfer income. When we consider changes in the family's need standard as well, there is even less evidence of a compensating pattern.

2. When we consider non-contributory transfers, or welfare, we find that virtually all families with no other income receive welfare, and their benefits average to about 75% of what the family needs to feed, house, and clothe itself. There is, however, a large inequity for families with some very low income from other sources: a large fraction of these families receive no welfare at all, and on the average, they have a total income equal to just half of their need standard.

3. Aside from the amount of money the family has, other characteristics determine the adequacy of welfare payments. Specific programs exist to aid the very old, but we find the adequacy of welfare increases with age for all age groups, not just for those over 65. Families with children also benefit from specific programs, but the level of support for the whole family declines consistently with each additional child.

4. There are important regional variations in the welfare system, with families on welfare in the South receiving about 40% less than those in the Northeast. The very poor are more likely to receive support in the South than elsewhere.

5. In studying which families change welfare status, we find evidence of a transition crisis. Families where a woman *becomes* head of the family or where there are *young* children are the most likely to go on welfare. Families that were already headed by a woman or had older children and had managed to stay off welfare are no more likely than other families to turn to welfare for assistance. Once women with children are on welfare, though, they have a high probability of staying there until the children grow up or until the woman gets married.

6. A higher proportion of black families are on welfare than are white families but the dynamic pattern is important. Blacks are more likely than whites to go on welfare but no more likely to stay there.

7. When we consider which of the newly formed families are on welfare, there is no significant evidence that children from welfare families are themselves more likely to go on welfare.

8. The employability of the head has surprisingly little to do with which families changed welfare status. Only disability makes much difference. Neither education nor our measure of cognitive ability has any effect for the main families, but for splitoffs education is very important.

9. The attitudes the head expressed have no effect on which families go on

welfare, but of those who are receiving benefits, the more trusting and those who plan ahead are more likely to get off.

References

Baerwaldt, Nancy, and Morgan, James, "Trends in Intra-Family Transfers," _Surveys of Consumers, 1971-1972,_ Lewis Mandell, ed., Survey Research Center, Institute for Social Research, University of Michigan, 1973.

Heffernan, W. J., "Variability in Negative Tax Rates in Current Public Programs: An Example of Administrative Discretion," Institute for Research on Poverty, Reprint Series 94, University of Wisconsin (1973).

Okner, Benjamin, "Transfer Payments: Their Distribution and Role in Reducing Poverty," Brookings Reprint 254, The Brookings Institution, Washington, D.C. (1973).

Boland, Barbara, "Participation in The Aid to Families with Dependent Children Program," Working Paper, The Urban Institute, Washington, D.C. (1973).

APPENDIX 5.1

MCA on Welfare/Needs and Whether on Welfare in 1971

	Welfare/Needs for all Families with Other Income/Needs less than 1.5				Whether Received Welfare		Welfare/Needs for Families Receiving Welfare			
	N	Percent	Mean	Adjusted Mean	Mean	Adjusted Mean	N	Percent	Mean	Adjusted Mean
OTHER INCOME/NEEDS										
0	133	3.8	.82	.74	100.0	90.2	133	15.3	.82	.74
.01- .19	120	5.2	.52	.45	80.7	70.7	108	16.9	.64	.62
.20- .39	124	5.0	.31	.27	55.0	50.3	81	11.1	.56	.58
.40- .74	345	20.7	.17	.18	32.8	32.9	122	27.4	.51	.58
.75- .99	298	21.0	.06	.07	18.6	18.6	63	15.7	.37	.36
1.00-1.24	297	19.6	.04	.06	10.2	13.3	43	8.0	.40	.34
1.25-1.50	329	24.6	.02	.03	5.7	7.8	26	5.6	.41	.38
AGE OF HEAD										
<25	282	16.7	.12	.06	18.5	12.2	75	12.4	.66	.46
25-34	271	13.7	.19	.11	27.0	14.9	118	14.8	.70	.62
35-44	325	14.7	.18	.13	33.9	20.0	137	20.1	.54	.52
45-54	297	12.7	.18	.14	34.7	27.6	111	17.7	.51	.48
55-64	243	11.7	.13	.16	24.8	30.0	83	11.7	.53	.54
65-74	124	15.4	.09	.20	19.1	36.4	30	11.8	.46	.66
75+	104	15.0	.08	.17	19.0	34.6	22	11.5	.41	.60
NUMBER OF CHILDREN IN FU										
0	623	55.9	.08	.15	15.2	24.9	129	34.2	.53	.58
1	230	11.8	.21	.18	34.5	23.0	80	16.3	.62	.66
2	205	10.4	.20	.14	34.2	26.5	97	14.2	.59	.58
3	158	6.2	.20	.09	35.4	21.8	65	8.9	.57	.46
4	166	6.6	.29	.15	52.6	33.8	80	13.9	.56	.51
5	114	4.4	.12	.05	27.4	19.2	46	4.9	.45	.38
6	64	2.4	.13	.01	27.5	12.0	28	2.6	.47	.39
7	46	1.4	.25	.10	50.2	29.2	29	2.9	.50	.41
8	20	0.4	.12	.04	48.9	34.5	11	0.9	.25	.35
9+	20	0.5	.19	.04	63.8	43.1	11	1.2	.30	.24
AGE OF YOUNGEST CHILD										
No Children	623	55.9	.08	.08	15.2	15.2	129	34.2	.53	.53
01	238	9.4	.19	.20	32.0	34.6	92	12.0	.58	.55
02	112	4.3	.31	.27	51.0	46.9	60	8.7	.60	.60
03	69	2.9	.13	.15	31.2	31.7	29	3.7	.41	.47
04	62	3.1	.26	.29	35.4	42.5	28	4.4	.72	.80
05	78	3.0	.17	.16	37.3	35.3	39	4.5	.46	.43
06-08	180	8.2	.25	.24	41.2	39.9	80	13.6	.61	.60
09-13	196	9.3	.18	.19	35.5	35.5	83	13.3	.51	.55
14-17	88	3.9	.15	.14	34.7	31.8	36	5.5	.44	.39
SEX-MARITAL STATUS										
Married Couple	670	40.5	.07	.11	17.3	21.3	123	28.2	.41	.54
Single Man	173	14.2	.09	.12	17.5	25.5	32	10.0	.53	.42
Single Woman	803	45.3	.21	.16	34.0	27.9	421	61.8	.61	.57
LARGEST CITY										
≥500,000	679	28.0	.23	.16	35.3	28.4	344	39.7	.65	.57
100,000-499,999	297	17.8	.15	.15	25.1	26.1	99	17.9	.58	.56
50,000- 99,999	166	12.9	.07	.09	16.9	20.5	36	8.8	.39	.47
25,000- 49,999	74	5.9	.11	.07	20.4	21.1	12	4.9	.56	.58
10,000- 24,999	138	11.9	.12	.15	28.7	31.9	38	13.7	.43	.50
<10,000	289	23.3	.07	.12	15.8	19.8	46	14.7	.43	.57
N. A.	3	0.2	.51	-.22	39.6	-12.3	1	0.3	1.29	.24

APPENDIX 5.1

MCA on Welfare/Needs and Whether on Welfare in 1971 (continued)

	Welfare/Needs for all Families with Other Income/Needs less than 1.5				Whether Received Welfare		Welfare/Needs for Families Receiving Welfare			
	N	Percent	Mean	Adjusted Mean	Mean	Adjusted Mean	N	Percent	Mean	Adjusted Mean
5 YEAR CHANGE IN RESIDENCE										
Lived in same place 10+ years	439	34.4	.10	.13	21.4	25.4	117	29.5	.45	.50
Same place 5 years	246	13.5	.12	.11	27.5	24.1	94	14.9	.45	.49
Moved once since 1968	459	23.9	.16	.13	25.6	21.3	172	24.7	.63	.57
Moved 2+ since 1968	499	28.0	.17	.17	27.5	27.8	193	30.9	.62	.60
N. A.	3	0.3	.00	.08	0.0	11.4	-	-	-	-
RACE										
White	604	70.8	.09	.12	18.6	23.8	120	53.0	.49	.49
Black	973	24.6	.25	.17	42.0	28.3	427	41.5	.59	.61
Spanish American	56	4.0	.24	.16	31.2	22.4	24	5.1	.75	.65
Other	13	0.5	.10	.13	20.9	23.6	5	0.4	.47	.64
CURRENT REGION										
Northeast	187	17.1	.22	.17	35.4	28.4	94	24.3	.63	.67
North Central	360	28.2	.14	.16	20.5	23.8	136	23.3	.68	.64
South	842	36.8	.08	.10	22.4	23.0	235	33.1	.37	.39
West	254	17.7	.15	.15	26.7	27.1	110	19.0	.57	.54
Foreign	3	0.2	.51	.52	39.6	39.7	1	0.3	1.29	1.41
IMPUTED RENT										
$ 0	1139	58.5	.18	.15	30.8	28.6	477	72.3	.60	.56
$ 1- 99	79	4.7	.12	.12	30.8	27.7	27	5.9	.40	.45
$ 100- 299	120	7.9	.08	.11	25.0	25.4	29	7.9	.32	.41
$ 300- 599	149	11.3	.07	.12	17.7	21.0	25	8.0	.39	.51
$ 600- 899	90	9.5	.06	.12	10.7	16.2	10	4.1	.56	.69
$ 900-1199	35	3.7	.02	.08	4.1	11.8	6	0.6	.53	.77
$1200 or more	34	4.4	.05	.09	6.6	10.7	2	1.2	.72	.79

Chapter 6

INCOME INSTABILITY

INTRODUCTION

Annual money income is, by far, the most commonly used measure of economic well-being. Some economists, however, have argued that annual incomes may yield erroneous representations of well-being and have, therefore, advocated the use of a longer run income concept such as "permanent" income. The use of longer run income concepts reduces the likelihood of classifying individuals on the basis of an unusual income year. Even permanent income, however, does not provide a complete picture of economic well-being. Individuals with the same permanent income levels may be at different levels of well-being depending on their temporal income uncertainty. That is, unless individuals can readily borrow and lend in response to unexpected income fluctuations, those individuals with high uncertainty about their future incomes will be at a lower utility level than other individuals with the same permanent incomes but no uncertainty.[1] Thus, in order to describe an individual's welfare position more completely, we must consider not only the level of his income but also the uncertainty associated with that level.

The implications of income uncertainty on individual behavior have, in recent years, received increased attention in economic literature.[2] Empirical investigation of the impact of uncertainty, however, has lagged far behind the theoretical development. This lag is in large part due to the absence of adequate longitudinal data. The lag may also be due in part to the difficulty in developing an empirically useful measure of income uncertainty.

---

[1] Drèze and Modigliani (1972).

[2] Sandmo (1969) and (1970), Leland (1968), Block and Heineke (1973).

In this chapter we develop a measure of temporal income uncertainty. We assume that each individual has an expected income level as well as an expected trend. Deviations from these individual expectations are then employed to estimate an individual's income uncertainty. In our discussion we often refer to this estimate of income uncertainty as income instability.

In Section I we present a brief discussion of the rationale used in deriving our measure of temporal income uncertainty. A more complete development of this rationale and the procedure used to derive the instability measure are presented in an appendix to this chapter.

The income instability measure we develop is based on head's annual labor income. The use of annual incomes, however, may yield misleading results if individuals with relatively stable annual incomes experience substantial within-year income instability. While the data are not available for a complete analysis of the potential bias resulting from our use of annual incomes, we are able to examine the relationship between inter- and intra-year income instability. Specifically, we compare our measure of annual income instability with the responses to the question, "Does your family's income change from month to month...?" The results of this analysis are discussed in Section II.

The major part of the empirical analysis is devoted to an investigation of the determinants of income instability. The determinants include: family money income, occupation, education, race, sex, and the local labor market conditions. These results are presented in Section III.

If fluctuations in head's labor income are initiated by a family's other income sources, then instability of head's labor income may exaggerate a family's income uncertainty. That is, the tax and transfer systems are designed to reduce a family's temporal income fluctuations. In addition, other family members may respond to variations in head's labor income by adjusting their labor supply. The importance of these factors in reducing a family's income fluctuations is examined in Section IV.

Since income instability may result from voluntary changes in employment status, which do not reflect income uncertainty, we restrict our empirical analysis to those family heads who were in the labor force "full time" throughout the analysis period. An individual is assumed to be in the labor force full time if his hours worked plus his hours missed due to unemployment and/or illness exceed 1500 hours each year.

ANALYSIS

I. A Measure of Income Instability

In order to capture an individual's unexpected income fluctuations, we must first remove that portion of an individual's income variability that is anticipated. Since a direct measure of each individual's anticipated earnings is not available, we assume that individuals form their earning expectations *partly* on the basis of their cohort income movements. Cohort income movements are determined by cross-section regression of earnings on race, sex, years of schooling, and years of work experience. Thus, we obtain different cohort income patterns for males and females, whites and nonwhites, and so forth. In effect, our procedure assumes that if, for example, middle-aged white males experience a 5% earnings growth during our analysis period, an individual with these characteristics anticipates this pattern.

An individual's expected earnings pattern is not determined by cohort income movement alone. Individuals with exceptional ability, for example, are likely to expect higher earnings' growth than their cohorts. To capture this variation across individuals we examine each individual's deviations from his cohort's income pattern. If an individual's earnings level differs consistently from his cohort's, these deviations are assumed to be anticipated and, therefore, are not included in our measure of income instability.

Our instability measure, therefore, considers only that portion of an individual's income variation not explained by either his cohort income movements or his consistent deviations from the cohort income pattern. What remains is a measure of unanticipated income fluctuations.

II. Impact of Accounting Period

An analysis of income instability based on annual incomes may yield erroneous results if individuals with relatively stable annual incomes are subject to substantial income uncertainty over shorter accounting periods (e.g., monthly). To examine the relationship between annual income instability and monthly income instability we present in Table 1 the distribution of the responses to the question, "Does your family's income change from month to month...?" Overall, nearly 22% of the sample responded that their income varied from month to month. Among those with the highest annual instability levels, more than one-third had month to month income instability; among those with the lowest annual instability levels, approximately 15% reported monthly income instability. The positive relationship between annual income instability and monthly variability of income

TABLE 6.1

Proportion of Families with Monthly Instability
by Annual Instability Levels
(same head and in the labor force at least 1500 hours all five years)

Annual Instability S.E.E.	All			Same Job		
	(1)	(2)	(3) Proportion with Monthly Instability	(4)	(5)	(6) Proportion with Monthly Instability
	N	Per- cent		N	Per- cent	
<.02	127	7.3	.166	95	10.0	.126
.02 - .029	172	9.7	.137	122	12.8	.102
.030 - .039	199	10.5	.148	134	13.3	.131
.040 - .049	234	11.5	.150	163	14.6	.129
.050 - .059	230	11.0	.187	149	12.8	.148
.060 - .079	364	16.2	.210	216	16.0	.172
.080 - .109	358	13.9	.263	182	12.2	.254
.110 - .149	255	8.9	.322	99	5.7	.296
.150 - .199	143	4.9	.393	35	1.6	.275
≥.200	193	6.2	.349	24	0.9	.306
Total	2275	100.0	.219	1224	100.0	.164

is encouraging inasmuch as it suggests that varying the accounting period is not likely to significantly affect the results on instability. While the evidence is not overwhelming, it does suggest that our results on annual income instability may yield similar results to an analysis of instability over a different accounting period.

One difficulty with the above comparisons of monthly and annual income instabilities is that the monthly instability question refers to the family's circumstances in 1968, while the annual instability refers to events over a five-year period. The impact of this discrepancy may be reduced by examining only those families whose income source remained relatively constant throughout the analysis period. We, therefore, present in Table 6.1 the distribution of families where the head did not change jobs since 1968. For these families the comparison of monthly instability with annual instability is more appropriate since the source of the two instabilities is similar.[1]

Among the families where the head did not change jobs since 1968, approximately 16% responded that their incomes fluctuated from month to month (as compared with 22% for the entire sample). The relationship between annual and monthly instability remains the same. Those with low annual instability levels are least likely to have monthly fluctuations, and those with high annual instability levels are most likely to have monthly fluctuations.

III. The Determinants of Income Instability

To describe a family's economic well-being we must consider not only its income level but also the uncertainty associated with that level. To examine the relationship between income level and income uncertainty we present in Table 6.2 the distribution of our instability measure by five-year average income levels. The results indicate that the poor are subject to greater relative income instability than the middle and high income groups. In fact, relative instability declines monotonically as average head's labor income rises to $15,000. Above this income level, relative instability increases slightly.[2] This result suggests that income level alone underestimates the difficulties of the poor. Their

---

[1] However, the source of the two instabilities is not identical since the 1968 question refers to family money income and the annual instability measure is based on head's labor income. Since head's labor income is the dominant component of family money income, this discrepancy is not likely to be significant.

[2] Mirer found a similar pattern using a slightly different measure of instability. See Thad W. Mirer, Chapter 12 in Volume II.

TABLE 6.2

Annual Income Instability by Five-Year Average Income Level

(same head and in labor force at
least 1500 hours all five years)

Average Head's Labor Income	N	Percent	Instability Level (S.E.E.)
Less than $2000	80	1.6	.221
$ 2000 - 3999	325	7.6	.140
$ 4000 - 5999	462	15.1	.106
$ 6000 - 7999	471	19.8	.080
$ 8000 - 9999	360	19.1	.065
$10000 - 11999	235	13.9	.062
$12000 - 14999	181	11.6	.056
$15000 - 19999	94	6.5	.061
$20,000 or more	67	4.7	.078
TOTAL	2275	100.0	.081

difficulties arise not only from their low income levels, but also from the substantial uncertainty associated with their low incomes.

In addition to income level, personal and environmental characteristics such as occupation, education, age, local unemployment rate, and such, may be important determinants of income instability. The expected impact of each of these variables is examined below. Following this discussion we examine their impact in a multivariate regression.

Intuitively one would expect substantial variation in income instability by occupation and education. For example, the self-employed and farmer groups are likely to exhibit high instability, while the instability of professional and other salaried occupations is likely to be low. Although education and occupation are highly correlated, education may exhibit some independent effect on income instability. Within each occupational group, those with more education are likely to experience less instability since employers may be more reluctant to lay off workers with substantial human capital.[1] As a result, we expect to observe an inverse relationship between education level and income instability.

It is also expected that the young experience greater income instability than their older counterparts. This expectation is due in part to their greater mobility, uncertainty over careers, and greater willingness to take risks (since they may not have family responsibilities). In addition, the young have less to lose in terms of on-the-job training and job tenure by changing jobs. For all these reasons, we expect them to exhibit relatively high income instability.

The queuing theory of labor suggests that blacks are last to be hired and first to be fired. As a result, they are likely to experience more frequent and longer periods of unemployment than whites. The theory, therefore, suggests that blacks experience greater income instability than whites.

The effect of sex on head's labor income instability is ambiguous. Female headed families are likely to have only one major earner. As a result, any loss of earnings is likely to create severe economic hardships. To avoid these, female heads are more likely than male heads to avoid risk and choose stable jobs. This reasoning suggests that female heads are likely to exhibit lower income instability than male heads. Counteracting this tendency is the fact that the welfare laws make it easier for female headed families to receive public assistance.[2] Thus, income downturns are more likely to be mitigated by transfer

---

[1]See Oi (1962).

[2]For an analysis of transfer payments see Chapter 5.

payments for female heads than for male heads. The welfare system may be thought
of as compensating, to some extent, for the frequent absence of a secondary
earner among female headed families and may, therefore, encourage risk taking
and greater labor income instability.

The most powerful factor likely to affect females' income instability is
employment discrimination. Females, like nonwhites, are often among the first
to be laid off during economic downturns. As a result, females are likely to
experience more income instability than their male counterparts. Thus, the
overall effect of sex on income instability is ambiguous.

In addition to the personal characteristics discussed above, environmental
conditions such as the local unemployment rate may affect income instability.
In areas of full employment, for example, an individual is less likely to experience unemployment. When unemployment does occur, its duration is likely to be
relatively short as a result of the tight labor market conditions. On the other
hand, those who live in areas of substantial unemployment are more likely to
experience unemployment and when it occurs its duration may be longer
than for individuals in low unemployment areas. These factors lead us to
expect a positive relationship between the local unemployment rate and income
instability.

The impact of each of these environmental and personal characteristics on
income instability may be examined in a multivariate regression. Not wishing to
assume that the explanatory variables are linear in their effect, we employ a
dummy variable regression technique (MCA).[1] To employ this technique each continuous variable must first be converted into a set of dummy variables which are
then included in the regression as independent variables. The results of this
regression are presented in Table 6.3.

Using the square of the beta coefficient[2] we obtain the following ordering
of the predictors in terms of their explanatory power:

    1. Average income
    2. Occupation
    3. Age
    4. County unemployment rate

---

[1] Rather than use the standard dummy variable regression technique, which requires
that one category from each predictor be omitted, we employ the Multiple Classification Analysis (MCA) technique. For details, see Andrews, Morgan, and
Sonquist (1967).

[2] The square of the beta coefficient is equal to the "sum of squares attributable
to the predictor (after 'holding other predictors constant') relative to the
total sum of squares." Ibid., p. 118.

TABLE 6.3

MCA on Income Instability[*]
(same head and in the labor force at least 1500 hours all five years)
N=2275; $\overline{R}^2$=.189

Predictor	Gross Effects (η^2)	Net Effects (β^2)	Percent	Unadjusted Mean	Adjusted Mean
Age of Head (1968)	.015	.007			
Less than 25			8.3	.098	.098
25-34			23.8	.077	.082
35-44			30.7	.076	.079
45-54			24.8	.077	.075
55-64			11.5	.098	.087
65 and over			1.0	.116	.068
Race	.012	.001			
White			89.2	.078	.080
Black			10.8	.105	.089
Sex of Head	.011	.000			
Male			89.9	.079	.081
Female			10.1	.104	.082
Education of Head	.035	.003			
0-5 grades			3.9	.116	.083
6-8 grades			13.9	.103	.085
9-11 grades			16.3	.092	.085
High school			21.3	.073	.074
High school plus			12.1	.078	.083
Some college			15.5	.071	.080
College degree			10.3	.070	.084
Advanced degree			6.7	.063	.083
Average Head's labor income	.156	.107			
Less than $2000			1.6	.221	.209
$ 2000 - 3999			7.6	.140	.128
$ 4000 - 5999			15.1	.106	.098
$ 6000 - 7999			19.8	.080	.078
$ 8000 - 9999			19.1	.065	.068
$10000 - 11999			13.9	.062	.066
$12000 - 14999			11.6	.056	.062
$15000 - 19999			6.5	.061	.068
$20,000 or more			4.7	.078	.084
Occupation (1972)	.098	.039			
Professionals			16.4	.062	.069
Managers			13.4	.061	.073
Clerical and sales			12.8	.076	.076
Craftsmen			21.5	.071	.077
Operatives			15.1	.084	.080
Laborers			9.2	.119	.087
Farmers			3.1	.153	.130
Self-employed			7.0	.121	.119
Miscellaneous			1.6	.069	.079
County Unemployment Rate[a]	.002	.004			
Less than 2%			1.4	.081	.057
2.0 - 3.9%			13.2	.078	.074
4.0 - 5.9%			32.9	.081	.081
6.0 - 10.0%			42.1	.080	.082
Over 10%			8.8	.092	.090
Not ascertained			1.6	.086	.082

[a]Highest unemployment rate experienced in the five year period.

[*]Mean = .081
Standard deviation = .075

     5.   Education
     6.   Race
     7.   Sex

The most powerful predictor of income instability is five-year average income level (B^2=.107). Even after holding constant the effect of the other predictors, we find, as in Table 6.2, that the poor experience substantially higher instability than the non-poor. As before, there is a monotonic decline in instability as average income rises to $15,000. Beyond this income level instability increases.

Occupation is the second most important predictor of income instability.[1] As expected, the farmer and self-employed groups experience the highest instability. Among the remaining occupational groups instability is nearly equal, although blue collar occupations display slightly higher instability levels than white collar occupations.

As expected, income instability is inversely related to age of head. That is, the young experience more instability than the old. The relationship, however, is not monotonic; those in the 55-64 age bracket (in 1968) exhibit a relatively high instability level. This aberration probably reflects the fact that some individuals in this age group reduce their labor force participation as they approach the age of retirement.[2]

The variable likely to be of most interest to policy makers is the county unemployment rate. The unemployment rate in any one year, however, may yield a misleading picture of labor market conditions experienced throughout the five-year period. As a result, we employed in our regression the highest unemployment rate (over the entire period) experienced by the individual. The results indicate that local labor market conditions have an impact on individual income instability. In fact, the relationship between the highest unemployment rate and income instability is monotonic. Those who lived in areas with low unemployment rates throughout the five-year period experience less income instability than others who lived in areas with higher unemployment rates. It appears, therefore, that environmental factors have some impact on individuals' income instability.

After taking account of the other variables in the regression, head's education shows little impact on income instability. Prior to holding constant the effect of other predictors, education displayed a relatively strong inverse relationship with income instability, but, when income and occupation are taken into account, education has little net effect.

---

[1] The occupation variable refers to the head's occupation at the time of the 1972 interview.

[2] However, to be included in the analysis, these individuals remain in the labor force 1500 hours or more.

The difference in income instability between whites and nonwhites is reduced when we hold constant the impact of other predictors, but the difference is
not eliminated. Nonwhites still experience greater income instability
than their white counterparts. In contrast, differences in income instability
between the sexes is nearly eliminated when we consider the impact of the other
predictors.[1]

These results on the determinants of income instability may be summarized
with the observation that differences in income instability among individuals are
accounted for largely by differences in income level and occupation. After controlling for these dominant explanatory variables we find a much smaller impact
for variables such as age, county unemployment rate, education, and race. Sex
of head appears to have virtually no impact on income instability.

IV. Family Income Instability

Variation in head's labor income across the population accounts for nearly
70% of the variation in total family income.[2] Other family income sources
(e.g., wife's income, others' income, transfer income, and capital income) account for much smaller fractions of the variation in total family income. Thus,
head's labor income is the dominant income source in "explaining" interpersonal
variation in total family money income.

If head's labor income is also the dominant source of *intertemporal* variation in total family money income, then our measure of income instability based
on head's labor income serves as a reasonable proxy for family income instability.
If, on the other hand, other income sources account for a substantial portion of
the intertemporal variability of family income, a broader income concept may be
necessary to capture the income instability of a family.

In this section we examine the relative importance of temporal variations
in several income components in explaining the variation of total family income
over time. We also examine the relationship between fluctuations in head's labor
income and fluctuations in other income sources. If fluctuations in head's labor
income are offset by other income sources, head's labor income instability exaggerates the uncertainty associated with total family income. On the other hand,
if all income sources fluctuate coincidentally, head's labor income instability
underestimates total family income uncertainty. To get an accurate picture of
family income uncertainty, then, we must examine the intertemporal variability of

---

[1]This is the reverse of many findings on levels of income, where adjustments for
education, etc., reduce racial differentials far more than they reduce sex differentials.

[2]See Chapter 1.

288

all the components of total family income.

To examine the relative importance of fluctuations in head's labor income in explaining family income fluctuations we decompose total family money income into its components. That is, family money income (FY) is defined as the sum of head's labor income (HY), wife's labor income (WY), others' taxable income (OY), transfer income (TY), and capital income (CY). For each family (i), total family income may, therefore, be written as:

$$FY_i = HY_i + WY_i + OY_i + TY_i + CY_i \qquad (1)$$

By taking the variance of both sides of equation (1), the intertemporal variance of family income may be decomposed into the sum of the variances of each of the components and their covariances:[1]

$$var(FY_i) = var(HY_i) + var(WY_i) + var(OY_i) + var(TY_i) + var(CY_i)$$

$$+ \sum_{\substack{I=1 \\ I \neq J}}^{5} \sum_{J=1}^{5} cov(Y^I, Y^J) \qquad (2)$$

where $Y^1 = HY_i$, $Y^2 = WY_i$, $Y^3 = OY_i$, $Y^4 = TY_i$, and $Y^5 = CY_i$.

For each family equation (2) is an identity. For the sample as a whole, however, we can use this equation to estimate the relative importance of each of the income components in explaining individual differences in intertemporal income variation. Since intertemporal variation in income is likely to be highest for those with high incomes, the results are likely to be dominated by families with high incomes. To reduce this dominance we estimate the relationship separately for low, medium, and high income groups. The groups are defined on the basis of their five year average family money income: low = less than $8000, medium = between $8000 and $15,000, and high = over $15,000.

Since our main concern at this stage is to evaluate the relative importance of intertemporal variation in each of the components, we simplify the analysis by excluding the covariance terms from our regressions. We replace these covariances by a single constant term and estimate the following regression:

$$var(FY_i) = a_o + b_1 \, var(HY_i) + b_2 \, var(WY_i) + b_3 \, var(OY_i)$$

$$+ b_4 \, var(TY_i) + b_5 \, var(CY_i) \qquad (3)$$

The squares of the beta coefficients from each of these regressions are presented in Table 6.4.

As expected, head's labor income is the most important income source in

---

[1] See Goldberger (1964)

TABLE 6.4

Regression Beta-Squares
for the Whole Sample and Three Income Subgroups

	Whole Sample N=2275	Low Income N=873	Medium Income N=984	High Income N=419
var(Head Income)	.424	.417	.247	.438
var(Wife Income)	.009	.052	.088	.006
var(Other Income)	.034	.109	.106	.033
var(Transfer Income)	.004	.000	.009	.000
var(Capital Income)	.120	.156	.150	.126
$\overline{R}^2$	.764	.780	.625	.739

explaining individual differences in family income variation over time. For both
the high and low income groups variation in head's labor income is as important
as the other four income sources combined.

Wife's income variation, on the other hand, has an impact on family income
variation only for the low and medium income groups. For the high income group,
variation in wife's labor income has virtually no impact on family income variation. Variation in others' income behaves similarly with very little impact
within the high income group and substantial impact within the low and medium
groups. Transfer income variation has virtually no impact in explaining individual differences in family income variation. This result holds for each of the
three subgroups.

Capital income variation is second only to head's labor income variation in
explaining family income variation. A *priori* one would expect capital income to
be important only for the high income group, but a close examination of the
components of capital income reveals why it turns out to be important for all
three income groups. Capital income is defined (in this study) as the sum of
income from rent, interest, dividends, as well as the asset part of income from
a farm or business. For the high income group, variation in income from dividends and interest is likely to be important; on the other hand, for the lower
income groups, variation in farm income and business income is likely to be important. Since all of these sources are volatile, we find that variation in
capital income is an important source of family income variation for all income
groups.

We may conclude that fluctuations in head's labor income dominate the
variation of total family income over time. Capital income is also quite important, although it includes some components that are difficult to distinguish
from labor income. In spite of our careful attempts to allocate farm and
business income into labor and capital components, the estimated asset income
from farm or business may partly reflect labor income. The regressions may,
therefore, underestimate the impact of variations in labor income.

As suggested above, income from sources other than head's labor income may
offset fluctuations in head's labor income. If this occurs, family income will
be more stable than head's labor income. In Table 6.5 we examine the correlation
between annual deviations of head's labor income (from its five-year mean) and
annual deviations of other income sources (from their five-year means). A negative correlation between deviations of head's labor income and deviations of
other income sources suggests that deviations from permanent levels are off-

TABLE 6.5

Correlation of Deviations of Head's Labor Income
with Deviations of Other Income Sources[a]
(deviations taken from five-year means)

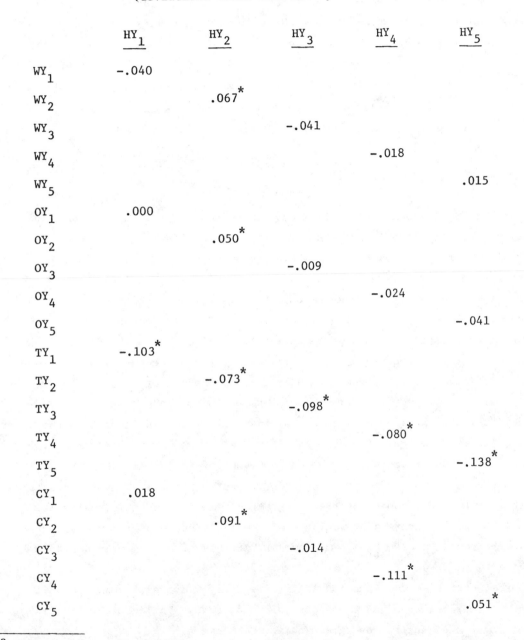

	HY_1	HY_2	HY_3	HY_4	HY_5
WY_1	-.040				
WY_2		.067*			
WY_3			-.041		
WY_4				-.018	
WY_5					.015
OY_1	.000				
OY_2		.050*			
OY_3			-.009		
OY_4				-.024	
OY_5					-.041
TY_1	-.103*				
TY_2		-.073*			
TY_3			-.098*		
TY_4				-.080*	
TY_5					-.138*
CY_1	.018				
CY_2		.091*			
CY_3			-.014		
CY_4				-.111*	
CY_5					.051*

[a]Asterisks indicate significant correlations at the 5% significance
level under an assumption of normality.

setting. The correlations in Table 6.5 indicate that only transfer income has a consistent significant offsetting influence on variations in head's labor income. The other income sources occasionally offset and occasionally reinforce the fluctuations in head's labor income. As a result, we cannot reach a clear cut conclusion about the correlation of these deviations with head's labor income deviations. The evidence presented in Table 6.5 is, therefore, inconclusive. For some families head's labor income may exaggerate family income instability; for others, head's labor income instability may underestimate family income instability. For the sample as a whole it appears that head's income instability is neither offset nor reinforced by variations in other family income.

SUMMARY

Income level, even when it is measured over a long period, presents only a partial picture of economic well-being. That is, individuals may experience vastly different income patterns yet have the same income level. To capture such differences in income patterns, additional parameters such as income trend and instability are necessary. These parameters may serve as additional dimensions of economic welfare, distinct from income level. Clearly, an individual with constant income is in a different welfare position from another individual whose income fluctuates unexpectedly -- even if their average incomes are the same. With stable income, for example, an individual can make long run plans and commitments with confidence that his income level will continue at a steady rate. An individual who experiences substantial instability in his income, on the other hand, is likely to refrain from committing himself to long run obligations.

In this chapter we have developed a measure of income instability which reflects the individual's income uncertainty. Our empirical analysis reveals that those with low incomes experience greater relative instability levels. Income level alone, therefore, yields a misleading picture of individual well-being. *The poor not only have low incomes, but they also have more unstable incomes.*

Other variables that substantially affect individuals' income instability include occupation, age, and county unemployment rate. The last of these is subject to some extent to government policy action.

An examination of the impact of various income sources on the variability of family money income revealed that head's labor income is the most important source of family income variation over time. Fluctuations in head's labor income, therefore, reasonably approximate family income fluctuations. This conclusion is reinforced by the absence of consistent correlations between fluctuations in head's labor income and fluctuations in other income sources (with the exception of transfer income).

In this chapter we have developed an instability measure which is intended to reflect a family's income uncertainty. One indication of its adequacy as a measure of income uncertainty is its effectiveness in explaining economic decisions such as labor force participation, current savings, and so forth. This test will be the subject of a later analysis.

References

Andrews, Frank, Morgan, James, and Sonquist, John, Multiple Classification Analysis. Ann Arbor: Institute for Social Research, 1967.

Block, M.K. and Heineke, J.M., "The Allocation of Effort under Uncertainty: The Case of Risk-Averse Behavior," Journal of Political Economy, Vol. 81, No. 2, 1973, pp. 376-385.

Drèze, Jacques and Modigliani, Franco, "Consumption Decisions under Uncertainty," Journal of Economic Theory, Vol. 5, 1972, pp. 308-335.

Goldberger, Arthur S., Econometric Theory. New York: Wiley and Sons, Inc., 1964.

Leland, Hayne E., "Saving and Uncertainty: The Precautionary Demand for Saving," Quarterly Journal of Economics, Vol. 82, 1968, pp. 465-473.

Oi, Walter Y., "Labor As a Quasi-Fixed Factor," Journal of Political Economy, (December) 1962, pp. 538-555.

Sandmo, Agnar, "Capital Risk, Consumption and Portfolio Risk," Econometrica, Vol. 37, No. 4, 1969, pp. 586-599.

_____, "The Effect of Uncertainty on Saving Decisions," Review of Economic Studies, 37, 1970, pp. 353-360.

APPENDIX 6

A Measure of Income Instability

Income instability is defined in our analysis as an individual's unexpected income variation. In measuring instability we must, therefore, remove that portion of temporal variation in income which is anticipated. One source of anticipated earnings variation is given by the life cycle earnings path. That is, individual earnings are expected to grow faster in early working years than in later years.[1] As a result, we first remove that portion of income variations associated with differences in individual work experience. Failure to take account of this source of anticipated earnings variation may lead to the conclusion that the young experience greater instability when, in fact, their earnings growth may be regular and anticipated.

Another source of anticipated differences in earnings growths are the individual differences in human capital investment.[2] Individuals with relatively large investments in human capital expect their earnings to grow more rapidly than others' earnings. Their observed rapid earnings growth should, therefore, not be interpreted as unexpected earnings variation.

In order to take account of these anticipated sources of income variability we estimate an expected earnings level for each individual from a cross-section earnings regression. In addition to years of work experience and years of schooling we include as predictors dummy variables for race and sex. The cross section earnings function may be written as:

$$\ln y_i = \beta_o + \beta_1 S_i + \beta_2 X_i^2 + \beta_3 X_i^2 + \beta_4 NW_i + \beta_5 F_i + U_i \tag{1}$$

---

[1] See, for example, Gary S. Becker (1964), (1967) and Ben-Porath (1967).

[2] Ibid.

where,

y = head's annual labor income,

S = years of schooling

X = years of work experience

NW = 1 if non-white; 0 otherwise

F = 1 if female; 0 otherwise

i = 1, 2,..., N

Since we do not have a direct measure of work experience, we assume that individuals begin work immediately after completion of schooling.[1] We also assume that work experience does not start until an individual is at least 13 years old. Potential work experience may, therefore, be expressed as:

$$X_i + A_i - S'_i - 5$$

where,

A_i = head's current age

S'_i = 8, when $S_i \leq 7$

  S_i, otherwise

As formulated, equation (1) omits several variables that may enter the determination of expected earnings. For example, such things as tenure on the job, geographic mobility, and local employment conditions are all likely to affect an individual's earnings expectations. The effect of these variables is summarized in the error term (U_i), and may be thought of as determining an individual's relative income position within his cohort. For example, if job tenure seniority is postively correlated with earnings, those individuals with long tenure will exhibit positive residuals and those with short tenure, negative residuals.

Our procedure of obtaining, for each individual for each year, an expected cohort income level as well as a residual reflecting his personal relative income position within the cohort, will later prove useful in our empirical analysis. That is, this procedure makes possible an isolation of instability due to cohort income movement and instability due to personal income movement. The former reflects income variation not subject to individual control while the latter reflects both the effect of individual decisions (i.e., mobility, voluntary changes in labor supplied, etc.) and unexpected events (i.e., unemployment, illness, etc.).

A difficulty arises if the variables omitted from equation (1) are correlated with the included variables. In that case the estimated coefficients in

---

[1]Of course, individuals may increase their schooling after entering the labor force. This effect, however, is likely to be insignificant.

equation (1) will be biased as well as predicted incomes derived from these coefficients.[1] Thus, our approach of first removing the effect of predetermined factors and then analyzing the effect of other variables by examining the residuals
is appropriate if the omitted variables are uncorrelated with the included variables.[2] If the two sets of variables are correlated, the residuals obtained may
be biased. The direction of the bias will depend on the sign of the correlations.
The net effect remains ambiguous.

An examination of the cross-section earnings function reveals that the rate
of return to schooling is restricted to be the same for each year of schooling.
The function also restricts experience to have the same effect on everyone's
earnings. That is, schooling only influences the level of the experience-earn-
ings profile but not its shape. These restrictions may, of course, be relaxed to
allow for changes in the rate of return to schooling as well as for the school-
ing-experience interaction. At this stage, however, we choose not to complicate
the analysis by experimenting with various specifications of the earnings function.

Using the cross-section earnings function given in equation (1), we obtain
an expected cohort earnings level for each individual in the sample. Repeating
this process for each of the five years of the panel we obtain a time series of
expected cohort earnings for each individual (Y_{it}). The difference between an
individual's actual earnings (Y_{it}) and his expected cohort earnings yields a
time series of residuals ($r_{it} = y_{it} - Y_{it}$).

Since these residuals represent both the effects of variables omitted from
the earnings function and random fluctuations, they do not reflect unexpected
income variations exclusively. For example, an individual with superior ability
may well expect to be consistently above his cohort earnings level. On the other
hand, individuals with low motivation levels may expect to earn less than their
cohort. One may, therefore, interpret an individual's five-year *average* residual
level as expected rather than unexpected deviations from cohort income levels.
One possible measure of income instability may, therefore, be the variance of an
individual's income around his mean residual level.

---

[1] A discussion of the coefficient bias resulting from omitted variables may be
found in Theil (1957).

[2] For a discussion dealing with the effect of omitting ability from the earnings
function in the analysis of returns to education, see Taubman and Wales (1972).

The variance around the residual mean may not, however, be entirely unexpected since some individuals may not expect to maintain a constant position relative to their cohort. For example, individuals who begin the period with large residuals may anticipate a reduction in the gap over time. Others may expect an increase in the residuals over time. For these individuals the variance around the mean is an inappropriate measure of unexpected income variability.

To capture the expected pattern of the residuals, that is, whether they are expected to fan out from, or regress back toward, the cohort earnings levels, we estimate each individual's residual time trend. That is, we estimate for each individual the slope in the following regression:

$$r_{it} = a_i + b_i (t) \tag{2}$$

where, r_{it} = i's residual in year t and t = 1, 2,...5. The slopes from these regressions then serve as estimates of individuals' expected residual trends. The individual slopes (b_i) may be estimated by the following equation:

$$\hat{b}_i = \frac{\sum_{t=1}^{5} (r_{it} - \bar{r}_i)(t - \bar{t})}{\sum_{t=1}^{5} (t - \bar{t})^2} \tag{3}$$

However, if we set the origin at the midpoint of the analysis period (i.e., T = -2, -1, 0, 1, 2) the equation for the slope simplifies to:

$$b_i = \frac{\sum_{t=1}^{5} r_{it} T_t}{\sum_{t=1}^{5} T_t^2} \tag{4}$$

$$b_i = \frac{2r_{i5} + r_{i4} - r_{i2} - 2r_{i2}}{10} \tag{5}$$

From equation (5) we see that the end years have twice the weight of the interior years and the middle year has a zero weight. There is a danger, therefore, of substantial bias in the time trends if, for example, initial year incomes were underreported relative to subsequent years (due to initial apprehension about reporting income). However, our use of separate regressions for each year to obtain expected earnings reduces much of the problem. Only if there were differential underreporting in different subgroups of the sample is the problem serious.

Since we employ the time trend of an individual's residuals as his *expected* departure from group norms, variations around this time trend may be interpreted as the individual's *unexpected* income variability. There still remains a question of how these unexpected flucutations should be combined to form an instability measure. One possibility is to sum the absolute deviations from the trend line. Another is to compute the standard error of estimate for each

$$\text{individual (i.e., S.E.E. } = \sqrt{\frac{\Sigma(r_{it} - \hat{r}_{it})^2}{3}}).$$

If we assume, for simplicity, that the cross-section regression remains constant for the five years of the panel, we can easily describe our procedure graphically. In Figure A6.1a, two individuals with identical annual incomes are depicted. Individual A has 10 years of work experience and B has 25 years of work experience. We then calculate each year's deviation from an expected earnings level, where expected earnings are given by the cross-section earnings function. The residuals for individuals A and B are presented in Figure A6.1b.

For each individual we then estimate a residual time-trend by regressing the residuals on "time." The deviations of an individual's residuals from his own trend line are then considered unexpected income fluctuations.

Regression Results

The results of the annual cross-section regressions on log of head's labor income are presented in Table A6.1. The education coefficients indicate that each year of schooling increases earnings by $350-400 per year of schooling. The impact of an additional year of work experience on earnings is less than that of schooling. The negative coefficient on the squared term indicates that the effect of an additional year of experience declines with the level of experience.

The regression results indicate that males earned at least one-third more than females; also, whites earned more than nonwhites. A somewhat surprising result is the unusually high race coefficient in 1967, indicating that whites earned 22% more than nonwhites (holding all the other variables constant). One possible explanation for the large race coefficient in 1967 is that nonwhites underreported their incomes in 1967 relative to whites and to later years. We do not, however, have evidence that such underreporting occurred.

The results of the annual cross-section regressions are depicted graphically in Figure A6.2. A visual examination reveals that the earnings peak occurs at approximately 30 years of experience. There also appears to have been a shift in the peak (to the right) during the analysis period.

FIGURE A6.1

Graphical Presentation of Income Instability Determination
for Two Individuals

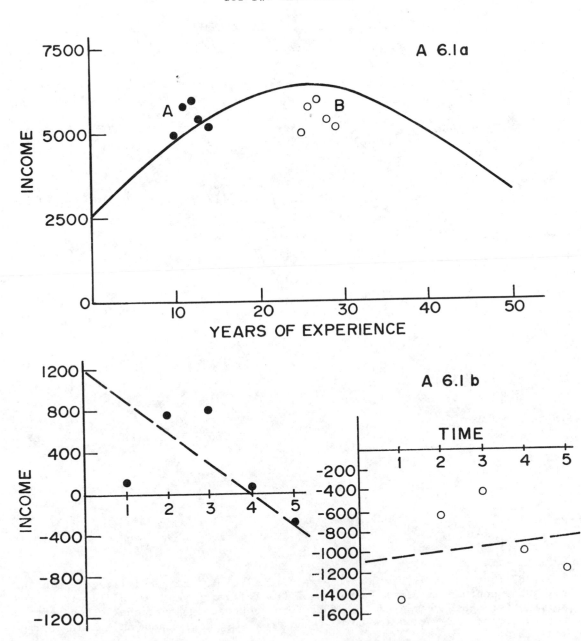

TABLE A6.1

Annual Cross-Section Regressions on Log of Head's Labor Income
(numbers in parentheses are t-ratios)

	Year				
	1967	1968	1969	1970	1971
Constant term	2.5299	2.6363	2.6905	2.6677	2.5985
Years of schooling	.0364 (16.6)	.0399 (18.7)	.0354 (17.7)	.0367 (19.6)	.0381 (15.3)
Work experience	.0256 (13.1)	.0216 (11.7)	.0298 (17.8)	.0311 (20.5)	.0309 (16.0)
Work experience^2	−.0005 (13.0)	−.0004 (11.2)	−.0005 (17.1)	−.0005 (18.9)	−.0005 (14.2)
White	.2188 (9.8)	.1178 (5.4)	.1160 (6.1)	.1353 (7.7)	.0954 (4.1)
Male	.3980 (19.3)	.4052 (20.7)	.3581 (20.6)	.3408 (21.9)	.4246 (21.4)
Standard error of estimate	.3879	.3826	.3615	.3409	.4587
$\overline{R}^2$	.27	.26	.28	.31	.22
Sample size*	3029	3149	3389	3547	3759

---

*The 1967 regression is based on the main families in the panel (i.e., excluding all subsequent split-offs). In each of the following years we add newly formed split-offs. Each year's sample, therefore, represents a national cross section for that year. T-ratios are to be taken at a discount because of sample design effects.

FIGURE A6.2
Annual Experience - Earnings Profiles

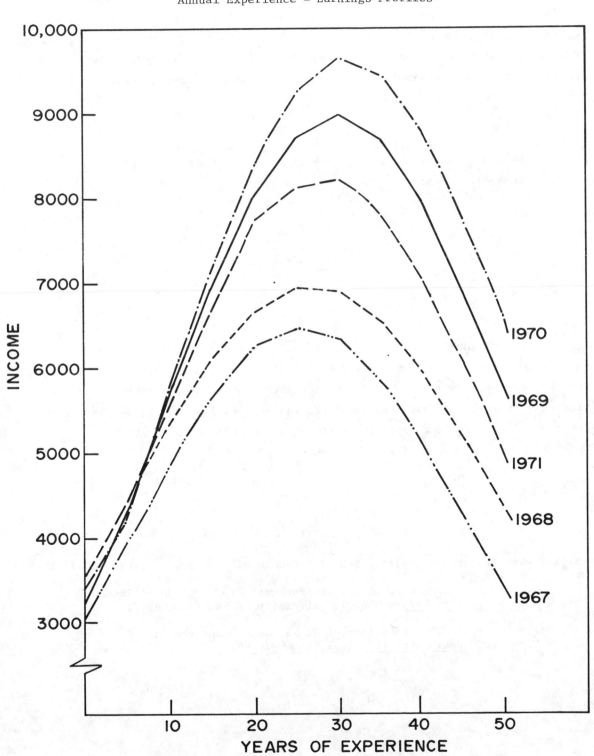

Using the predicted values from the cross-section regression we obtain for each individual a time series of residuals. The persistence of these residuals to remain positive or negative throughout the analysis period is indicated in Table A6.2. Approximately 60% of the sample remained either permanently above or permanently below their cohort income levels. Of these, two-thirds were consistently above their cohort income levels and the remainder consistently below. For a majority of the sample, therefore, cohort income consistently over- or under-estimates permanent income level.

TABLE A6.2

Persistence of Relative Income Position
(same heads and in the labor force at least 1500 hours all five years)

Number of Times Below Cohort Income	N	Percent
0	848	40.9
1	302	11.8
2	233	10.0
3	212	8.9
4	243	9.7
5	437	18.7
Total	2275	100.0

The individual time-series of residuals are then used to calculate a standard error of estimate (S.E.E.) for each individual. Since the S.E.E. is based on the residuals from a regression on the logarithm of head's labor income, it reflects relative, rather than absolute, instability levels. In the analysis portion of this chapter we employed the standard error of estimate as a measure of family income uncertainty.

References

Becker, Gary S., Human Capital. New York: Columbia University Press, NBER, 1964.

_____, "Human Capital and the Personal Distribution of Income," J.S. Woytinsky Lecture, No. 1, University of Michigan, 1967.

Ben-Parath, Yoram, "The Production of Human Capital and the Life Cycle of Earnings," Journal of Political Economy, 1967.

Taubman, Paul and Wales, Terence, "The Inadequacy of Cross-Section Age-Earnings Profiles When Ability Is Not Held Constant," _Annals of Economic and Social Measurement_, Vol. 1, No. 3, 1972.

Theil, Henri, "Specification Errors and the Estimation of Economic Relationships," _Review of the International Statistical Institute_, Vol. 25, 1957.

Chapter 7

EDUCATIONAL ATTAINMENT

INTRODUCTION

Young adults who have recently left home and formed their own households average about 12½ years of formal schooling. That is, they obtain a little additional schooling beyond high school by either going to college, junior college, or vocational school. The educational attainment of children leaving poor homes[1] is 11½ years; the typical child from a poor family does not complete high school.

Given the importance of education in determining occupational opportunities, wages and desirable job characteristics,[2] it can be seen that children forming their own households and beginning careers are at a considerable disadvantage if they come from a poor family.

What causes the inequality in educational attainment? Part of it is undoubtedly due to the fact that poor families cannot afford to finance much of their children's education. The average income of the poor families in the sample is about $6000, compared with the entire population average of over $12,000. Another important factor is the difference in the educational attainment of the

---

[1] In keeping with the practice of several other chapters in these volumes, membership in a poverty or "target" population is defined by being in the lowest quintile of income relative to needs in any one of the five years of the study. The exact population and variables used in this introductory section are explained in Section II.

[2] Several chapters in this volume have documented the pervasive importance of education for various components of economic well-being. Chapter 1 showed that a family's chances of being in the target population or being persistently poor were strongly related to the educational attainment of that family's head. Chapter 3 found that education was the single most powerful predictor of wage rates; Chapter 4 showed that education is strongly associated with unemployment experience, even after occupational and wage differences are taken into account. Finally, Chapter 6, Volume II, provides evidence that when non-pecuniary aspects of jobs (such as flexibility of work hours and choice in work) are added to the wage rate to get a more general measure of work payment, the importance of education *increases*.

parents of these children. Parental education is related to the quality of the
early home environment of the child and to the values and attitudes toward education that are instilled in the child. The parents of poor children average 8.2
years of formal schooling, as compared to the overall population average of 10.4
years.

The list of background variables which could affect educational attainment
can be extended considerably. Rather than make a sequential presentation of
these variables, this chapter will develop and estimate a model of educational
attainment which takes into account characteristics of both the family and the
child and also includes environmental factors. Implications of the estimated
relationships for policies which seek to equalize educational opportunity will
then be discussed.

ANALYSIS

I. Determinants of Educational Attainment

The basic model which will be examined with the data is displayed in Figure 7.1.[1] Educational attainment is taken to be the result of three kinds of
factors: 1) characteristics of the family, 2) characteristics of the individual
himself, and 3) environmental factors that prevail at the time the attainment
decisions are made. Family characteristics such as income level and parental education levels have both a direct effect on the education of the child and an
indirect effect through the intervening variables of the child's cognitive skills
and achievement motivation. These latter variables each have a direct effect on
the amount of education that the child receives. The third set of variables --
environmental conditions -- also influence educational attainment but are not
themselves determined by either family or individual characteristics.

With some additional assumptions, the set of relationships depicted in Figure 7.1 forms a recursive system and the strength of the direct and indirect effects within the model can be estimated. The actual estimation is reported in
Section III. The remainder of the present section will consist of a more complete
specification and justification of the model.

There are several aspects of an individual's family that would be expected
to influence attainment. Education, in part, is an investment decision made on

---

[1]The form and content of the model presented here draw upon the work of the
Duncans (1967, 1972) and Sewell and Shah (1968).

FIGURE 7.1

Schematic of the Determinants of Educational Attainment

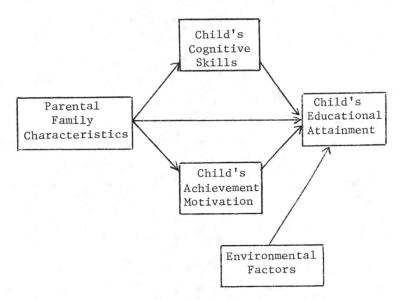

behalf of an individual by his parents. Thus, one would expect that families which are more burdened by the cost of education will be less likely to invest in it. The burden of the cost on a family will depend on available financial resources and on the needs which compete with educational attainment for these resources. Greater resources or fewer competing needs make it easier for the family to invest in additional schooling.

Quite independent of the family's economic situation are the norms, values, and orientations that the parents hold which encourage or discourage educational attainment. A family may have ample resources to send their child through college, for example, but unless they have socialized him to high levels of aspiration and achievement, he may not complete or even attend college.

To better understand the way in which family background characteristics influence educational attainment, it is helpful to specify intervening variables -- in this case characteristics of the individual himself -- which are determined by family background factors and which, in turn, determine educational attainment. Two such characteristics will be considered here -- cognitive skills and achievement motivation.

The exact way in which cognitive skills are formed is a matter of considerable controversy. It is generally agreed that both genetic and environmental components influence cognitive skills. The debate centers on the relative importance of these two components. To the extent that IQ is genetically determined, there will be a positive relationship between the cognitive skill measures of the parents and children. But any measured correlation will not reflect just the pure genetic component. Parental cognitive skill has been determined by both genes and environment, and part of the correlation may be due to the similarity of the parents' and the child's early environments. The environmental component of the child's cognitive skills will depend upon the quantity[1] and quality of the time and goods that parents give to their children. These should be related to some of the structural characteristics of the family. Quality of home environment should be measurable in part by the measured cognitive skills of the parents and by their levels of education. The quantity of goods provided for the child should relate positively to a measure of family resources and negatively to the extent to which other needs compete for these resources.

The relationship between cognitive skills and educational attainment is less ambiguous and there are several reasons why there should be a positive association between the two variables. First, an able person has a better chance of completing an education increment successfully. The investment for him will be more "profitable." Second, since financial aid is often awarded on the basis of ability, the abler person will face lower direct costs of education. Third, it may be that more capable people can translate a given education increment into higher earnings.[2]

There is one argument against this expected positive association between ability and educational attainment. A person who is abler in school is probably also abler in the labor market and the cost of staying in school (in terms of what he could be earning if he dropped out) is higher for him. Ability's effect on education is thus somewhat ambiguous and will depend on the magnitude of these various factors.

Achievement motivation, according to Atkinson's (1966) formulation, "is assumed to be a multiplicative function of the strength of the motive, the expectancy (subjective probability) that the act will have as a consequence the attainment of an incentive, and the value of the incentive: motivation = f(motive X expectancy X incentive)" (p. 13). The motives are further argued to be "relatively general and stable characteristics of the personality which have their origins in early childhood experience" (p. 13). To the extent that motives are formed through early independence training, there will be an association between

---

[1] The quantity of time that parents from different socio-economic strata spend with their children is the subject of an entire chapter in the second volume of this report. See Chapter 11, Volume II.

[2] This ability-education interaction was found to have a statistically significant effect on wage rates in Chapter 3, Volume I.

family structural characteristics and achievement motivation. Factors which help form the achievement motive, such as the number of demands placed upon the child by the parents and the age at which the demands are made, could be related to characteristics such as the education level of the parents or their level of cognitive skills. The level of the child's achievement motivation should be positively related to his educational attainment.

A final set of variables which will influence educational attainment come from outside the family. One cost of staying in school is not being able to earn income from a full-time job. Local labor market conditions should be important in determining this cost. The more easily an individual can get a job and the higher the wages that the job will pay, the greater will be the cost of staying in school.

A second environmental variable which should relate to the quantity of schooling obtained is the *quality* of schooling. Prestigious schools bestow not only prestige on their graduates, but also higher earnings. Additional schooling in a high quality school will appear more attractive for that reason. Higher quality secondary schools may produce indirect benefits to their graduates by placing them in higher quality colleges or by keeping them in whichever college they attend.

II. The Data

The Panel provides unique data with which these determinants of educational attainment can be investigated. Because the study is longitudinal and follows not only main families over the five years but also splitoffs from those main families, it provides a sample of children living in the main family in the first year who became heads or wives in their own households by the fifth year. Information on the attainment, cognitive skills, and achievement motivation of the children is gathered directly from them in the final year, while information on their parents' financial situation, educational attainment, and cognitive skills was obtained from the parents themselves during the five interviewing years. Most other studies of attainment have had to rely upon the child to report the financial and background situation of his parents -- a procedure obviously fraught with recall error.

Because interviews were conducted with *heads* of households and not wives, the important intervening variables of cognitive skills and achievement motivation are not measured for the daughters in the first year who had become wives by the fifth. The models will thus be estimated separately for males and females -- the complete set of variables are available for males, the intervening variables of achievement motivation and cognitive skills are missing for females.

To obtain a reasonably homogeneous age cohort of those recently completing school, the sample was restricted to those between the ages of 18 and 30 as of the fifth year. The educational attainment of the children is reported by them in the last year and is scaled in years. The few that had not completed their schooling at this time were eliminated from the sample.

Several variables will be used to measure characteristics of the child's family. The financial resources available to them are measured by the average total parental family income over the five interviewing years. This income information was obtained each year. The family needs which compete for resources will be measured by the number of siblings of the child. A larger number of siblings should have a detrimental effect on educational attainment. To the extent that measured cognitive skills are environmentally determined, the number of siblings should also have a negative relationship with these skills.

The education level of each parent will also be included as measures of family characteristics and there are several reasons to expect a positive relationship between them and the educational attainment of the child. First, parental education levels are a measure of the quality of the child's early environment and they should influence both cognitive skills and achievement motivation. The relative importance of each of the parents in the formation of these intervening variables should be reflected by the relative importance of their respective educational attainments. While parental education may influence the child's attainment by operating indirectly through cognitive skills and achievement motivation, it is also plausible to expect a direct effect for it. The norms and values that parents hold toward education will be reflected, in part, by their own educational attainment and will be transmitted to their children quite independently of either the child's cognitive skills or achievement motivation. The relative importance of the father and mother in this process will be reflected in the estimated direct effect of parental education levels on the child's attainment.

The final family characteristic variable included is a measure of the cognitive skills of the head of the parental household. It will be called the "parental test score" because it comes from a sentence completion test that was given in the fifth interviewing year. It should have an indirect effect on educational attainment by influencing both the cognitive skills and the achievement motivation of the children.

The measures of cognitive skill and achievement motivation both come from the fifth year of interviews and are reported directly by the children themselves[1]

---

[1] These measures are described in Appendix F and are documented in Veroff, McClelland and Marquis (1971).

Each is measured after the educational attainment process has been completed, and it is possible that a component of each measure was determined by education rather than vice versa.[1]

Various measures of local labor market conditions and quality of education were available. The ones which proved most satisfactory are 1) the typical wage rate for unskilled labor in the 1968 county of residence and 2) the expenditure per pupil in the public schools in the 1968 county of residence. (less aggregate expenditure data were not available). Each of these variables is bracketed; the first has five categories; the second has nine. The county wage information was obtained from state unemployment offices each year. It is expected that higher wages will increase the opportunity cost of education to the child and will have a negative effect on his educational attainment. The expenditure measure is expected to have a positive effect on educational attainment.

The variables which will be used to estimate the model of educational attainment are given in Figure 7.2.[2] Straight lines indicate hypothesized causal paths. The intercorrelations among these explanatory variables are substantial but not so high that the estimated coefficients will be unstable. A complete correlation matrix for these variables is given in the Appendix tables A7.1 and A7.2. The highest correlation is between father's education and mother's education and equals .55. Most other correlations are considerably lower than this.

---

[1] It is impossible to prove that this is not the case with the two measures but some evidence which supports them can be given. First, the sentence completion test has been administered with many different types of intelligence tests and it was found to be significantly correlated with every other test, even when education, age, and race were controlled for. Concerning the achievement motivation measure, it has been found that the least stable component of measured achievement motivation is future orientation. The scores on questions which measured future orientation were subtracted from the overall achievement motivation score and the remainder is used here. Its explanatory power in the empirical results which will be presented in the next section is greater than that of the complete achievement motivation index.

[2] The initial approach to these data was with a much more elaborate attainment model which was composed of many kinds of additional variables and interactions. Race was included as a separate predictor and was interacted with the intervening variables. Sex of head of household was also a separate predictor and it was interacted with parent test score. Other explanatory variables included father's occupation, asset and savings levels of the family, and an occupation-savings interaction. Virtually none of these was statistically different from zero, and coefficients on them rarely even exceeded their standard errors. Their inclusion did not change the estimated effects of the remaining variables to any appreciable degree and the overall *increase* in explanatory power of the entire elaborate set of variables was quite small. It was felt that this smaller set of variables was much easier to present and discuss. More importantly, it was felt that the implications drawn on the basis of these variables would not be appreciably changed if a more elaborate model was presented.

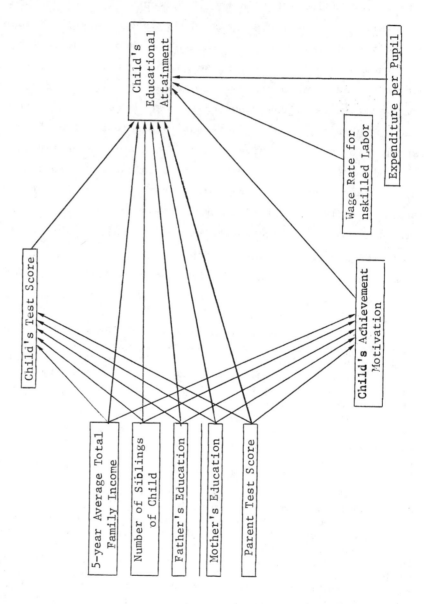

FIGURE 7.2

Model of Educational Attainment
to be Estimated with Data on Males

Another measure of intercorrelation of the predictors is given by their covariance ratio. This is the square of the maximum correlation (R^2) between each predictor and a linear combination of all other predictors. The highest covariance ratio, for father's education, is .48.

III. Results

The model developed in the previous section can be decomposed into three separate equations:[1]

1) Cognitive skills = f_1(parental family characteristics)
2) Achievement motivation = f_2(parental family characteristics)
3) Educational attainment = f_3(parental family characteristics, cognitive skills, achievement motivation, environmental factors)

where f_1, f_2, and f_3 are linear and additive functions. The estimated relationships for the entire model are given for males in Figure 7.3.[2] Only paths which are statistically significant are shown on the path diagram.[3] The full detail of the three estimated equations appears in Table 7.1. The complete correlation matrix of all variables is given in the Appendix in Table A7.1.

In general, the educational attainment model performs well for males. Over one-third of the variance of the education variable is explained by the nine predictors. Less well-explained are the intervening variables of child's test score and achievement motivation.

Almost all of the parental family characteristics have the expected effects. Parental family income, for example, has a significant positive effect on educational attainment. Two children with identical cognitive skills, achievement motivation, parental education levels, and so on, who differ only in that one comes from a family whose average income is $5000 while the other's family income is $15,000, can be expected to differ in their own educational attainments by

---

[1] Each of these equations should also include a residual term and the assumptions need to be made that each residual term is uncorrelated with the explanatory variables of its equation and that they are uncorrelated with one another.

[2] The numbers which appear on the diagram are "beta weights" or standardized regression coefficients. They indicate the relative size of the relationship between the dependent variables and each independent variable, when all other independent variables are taken into account.

[3] Coefficients on arrows to each of the three dependent variables which do not come from the other variables in the system measure the effects of residual factors not in the system. This number is the square root of the proportion of variance in the dependent variable not accounted for by the antecedent variables in the system.

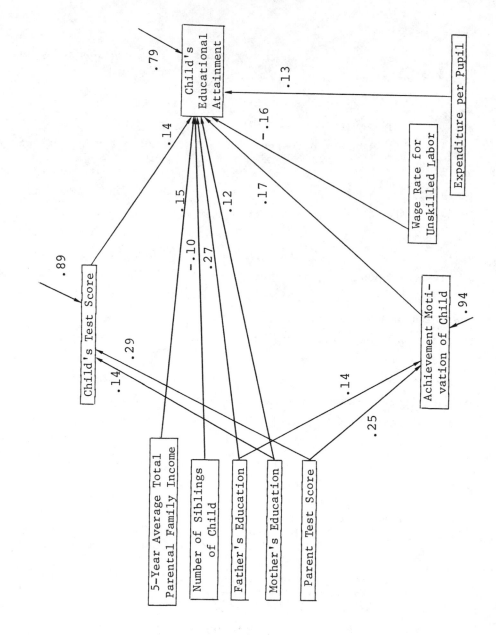

FIGURE 7.3

Estimated Model of Educational Attainment for Males 18-30 Years Old.
Paths which are statistically significant at the 5%
probability level are shown.

TABLE 7.1

Standardized Regression Coefficients (and Standard Errors) for
Explanatory Variables of Cognitive Skills, Achievement Motivation,
and Educational Attainment – Males, 18–30 Years Old

	Dependent Variable		
Predictor	Test Score of child	Achievement Motivation of child	Educational Attainment of child
Five year average total family income	.03 (.05)	.09 (.06)	.15 (.05)
Number of siblings of child	-.07 (.05)	.05 (.05)	-.10 (.05)
Father's education	.06 (.07)	.15 (.07)	.27 (.06)
Mother's education	.13 (.06)	-.11 (.06)	.12 (.05)
Parent test score	.28 (.06)	.25 (.06)	-.09 (.05)
Child's test score			.14 (.05)
Child's achievement motivation			.17 (.05)
Wage rate for unskilled labor			-.16 (.05)
Expenditure per pupil			.13 (.05)
R^2	.195	.112	.369

Number of observations = 353

MTR7055

316

about one-half a year.[1]

Parental education levels have interesting effects on educational attainment and on the intervening variables of cognitive skills and achievement motivation. The mother's education has a much stronger relationship to the cognitive skills of the child than does the father's education. This is consistent with the view that some of the cognitive skills acquired by a child are learned in the home at an early age from the mother. The child's achievement motivation, on the other hand, has a positive, significant relationship with his father's education, but not his mother's.

The indirect effects of parental education are much smaller than their direct effects. The direct effect of father's education is estimated to be .27. The indirect effect of father's education operating through achievement motivation, .02, is the product of the path between father's education and achievement motivation (.14) and the path between achievement motivation and educational attainment (.17). The indirect effect of the education of father through the cognitive skills variable is negligible. The total effect of father's education is the sum of direct effects and indirect effects, which is .29. What this coefficient means in terms of years of schooling is that when cognitive skills, achievement motivation, parental income, mother's educational attainment and all other variables are taken into account, having a college educated father rather than a grade school educated father is associated with, on the average, an additional 1.5 years of schooling for the son.

While mother's education has a strong indirect effect on the child's education by influencing his cognitive skills, its direct effect is considerably less than that of father's education and its overall effect is less than half that of father's education.

The cognitive skill level of the parents (usually the father) has significant indirect effects on educational attainment through both of the intervening variables. That there is a strong positive relationship between the parental test score and the child's test score is expected and it could reflect both genetic and environmental factors. That parental test score should have an important positive effect on the achievement motivation of the child is interesting and suggests that actual parental cognitive skills are much more important determinants of motivation than a measure of formal training.

There are two somewhat surprising results concerning the effect of the test

---

[1]This is calculated from the standardized regression coefficient of total family income (.15) converted to raw score form by multiplication by the ratio of the standard deviation of the educational attainment variable to the standard deviation of the income variable.

score and achievement motivation on educational attainment. First, the estimated impact of test score on education is not as large as some of the parental family characteristic variables (i.e., father's education and family income). The simple correlation between test score of child and his educational attainment (given in Appendix Table A7.1) is .33 which is considerably lower than the .54 correlation used by Duncan and his associates (1972) or the .45 and .41 correlations that Sewell (1968) found between intelligence and college attendance and graduation, respectively. Before the test score measure used here as an intelligence measure is faulted, it should be noted that the test score-education correlation for the *fathers* is .54, a figure entirely consistent with observed correlations in the other studies. The implication of this lower correlation for the 18 to 30 year old males in the present sample is that either admission and performance standards of educational institutions have become less meritocratic recently or that smarter people simply do not attempt or complete as much education as they used to.

The second noteworthy point concerning the intervening variable is that achievement motivation has a slightly *larger* effect on educational attainment than does the test score variable. While it is a plausible proposition that motivation is more important than cognitive skills in determining educational attainment, much more attention has been focused on the determinants and consequences of intelligence than on those of motivation. The results presented here suggest that motivation should be awarded equal time.

Family size has a significantly detrimental effect on the educational attainment of males. Each additional sibling leads to a decrease in schooling of approximately one-tenth of a year. Also of interest is that siblings affect test scores adversely. Less confidence can be put in this relationship, however, because the coefficient of number of siblings on test score is not statistically significant.

The effects of the two environmental measures are consistent with the hypotheses of the last section. Local demand conditions, as reflected in the typical wage for unskilled labor variable, have a significant negative effect for male educational attainment. The higher the wage rate, the more attractive are non-school opportunities and the lower is the educational attainment. The quality of schooling measure of expenditure per pupil is also a significant determinant of educational attainment. The estimated importance of expenditures is quite close to estimates from different, less aggregate data sets. Jencks' (1972) conclusion that "qualitative differences between high schools seem to explain about 2 percent of the variation in students' educational attainment" (p. 159) is supported by our data.

Since measures of cognitive skills and achievement motivation are not available for females, only a reduced form of the educational attainment model discussed so far can be estimated. The form of this model is given in Figure 7.4. From it, the coefficients on family characteristics represent *total* effect of these variables on educational attainment. It is impossible to estimate how much of this **total effect is a direct effect** and how much is an **indirect effect** operating through the intervening variables of test score and achievement motivation.

The estimated reduced form model for females appears in Figure 7.5. As with the full male attainment model displayed in Figure 7.3, the numbers on the diagram are standardized regression coefficients and indicate the relative importance of the various family characteristics and environmental variables in determining the educational attainment of the sons and daughters. The numbers by the arrows to the dependent variables which do not come from the other variables in the system (.87 for females, .84 for males) measure the effects of residual factors. These numbers are the square root of the proportion of variance in the dependent variables not explained by the included variables. Only significant paths are shown. Also shown in that figure for purposes of comparison is the estimated reduced form model for males. The full detail of the regressions for males and females is given in Table 7.2; a full correlation matrix for females appears in Appendix Table A7.2.

The set of variables, taken as a whole, explain one-quarter of the variance of educational attainment of females. This is smaller than the explained variance for males and is probably due to the fact that there are more alternatives to education for females that are not measured by the included variables.

When parental education and family size are taken into account, the effect of total family income on female educational attainment is almost identical to that on males. A $1000 increase in income is associated with an increase of .06 years of schooling.

The effects of parental education levels on educational attainment differ considerably between males and females. Results for males presented earlier showed that while mother's education has a significant direct effect and indirect effect via the child's test score, the total effect of father's education level is almost three times as large as the total effect of mother's educational attainment. Figure 7.5 shows that this is not the case for females. The total effect of father's education on the educational attainment of daughters is negligible -- the estimated coefficient is positive but does not exceed its standard error. The total estimated effect of mother's education on daughter's

FIGURE 7.4

Reduced Form of Educational Attainment Model
Which Will Be Estimated for 18-30 Year Old Females

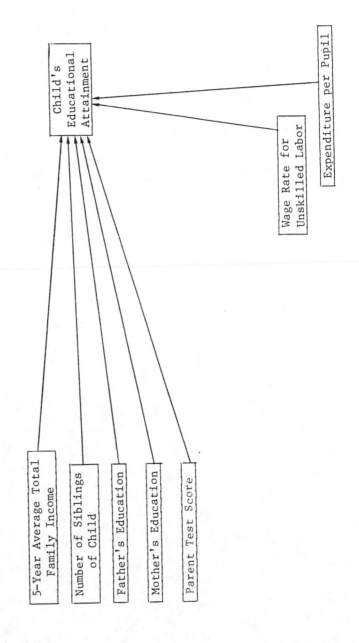

320

FIGURE 7.5

Estimated Reduced Form Educational Attainment Models
for 18-30 Year Old Females and Males*

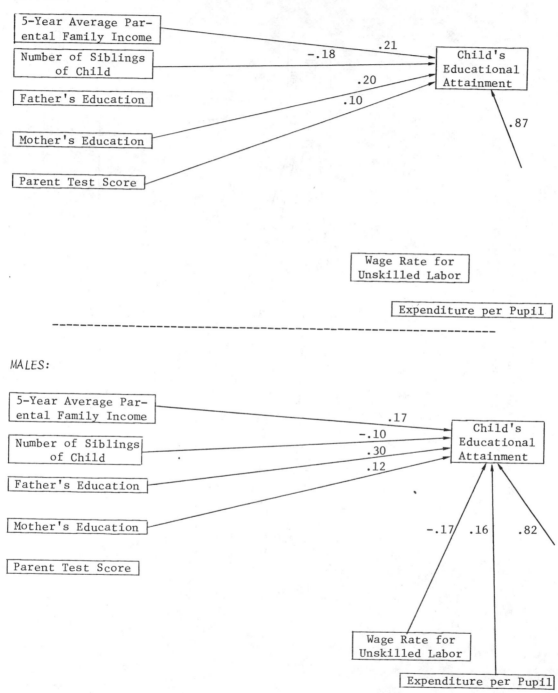

*Only paths which are statistically significant at the 5% probability level are shown.

TABLE 7.2

Standardized Regression Coefficients (and Standard Errors) for
Explanatory Variables of Reduced Form Model
of Educational Attainment – 18-30 Year Old Females and Males

Predictor	Females	Males
Five year total family income	.21 (.05)	.17 (.05)
Number of siblings of child	–.18 (.04)	–.10 (.05)
Father's education	.03 (.05)	.30 (.06)
Mother's education	.20 (.05)	.12 (.06)
Parent test score	.10 (.05)	–.01 (.05)
Wage rate for unskilled labor	–.02 (.04)	–.17 (.05)
Expenditure per pupil	.01 (.05)	.16 (.05)
R^2	.246	.325
N	446	353

education is large and significant. When income, family size, and father's education are taken into account, having a college educated mother rather than a grade school educated mother is associated with slightly more than one extra year of schooling for daughters. The implication of this is that the fathers set standards for sons while mothers set them for daughters.

The effect of family size on educational attainment depends upon the sex of the child. For males, the number of siblings had a small but significant negative effect on educational attainment. For females, on the other hand, family size has large negative effects. When other variables such as income level and parental educational attainment are held constant, each additional sibling leads to one-sixth of a year less of education for daughters.

The variable "parent test score" which measures the cognitive skills of the head of parental household (86% of whom were males) has a significant and positive direct effect on educational attainment of daughters. For sons, it can be recalled, there were important effects of parental test score on the child's achievement motivation and test score, but the total effect of parental test score on the educational attainment of the son was small and insignificant. Since the intervening variables are not measured for females, it is impossible to estimate the direct and indirect effects for them.

The environmental variables of wage rate for unskilled labor and per pupil education expenditures are not significant determinants of educational attainment of females.

IV. Implications and Speculation

The results presented thus far have shown that many factors lead to unequal educational attainment. Family resources and parental education levels are important, independent determinants of the educational attainment of both sons and daughters. Local labor market conditions and quality of schooling are important for sons but not for daughters.

An often stated goal of society is to equalize the *opportunity* for education. A definition of equal opportunity is given by Masters (1968): "Equal opportunity is defined as a situation in which each individual's chances of achieving his goals depend only on his own inherited ability and are unaffected by his parents' income and education" (p. 159). It was shown in the previous section that family income and parental education levels have powerful effects on educational attainment, even when measures of ability and motivation are taken into account. Furthermore, it was seen that the ability and motivation measures themselves were related to parental education levels. The remainder of this section will present a more complete interpretation of these results in light of the goal of equal opportunity for education.

While both income and parental education levels are important determinants of a child's educational attainment, the overall effect of the former is considerably less than that of the latter. An additional $1000 of family income can be expected to increase average educational attainment of either the son or daughter by a little more than one-twentieth of one year.[1] To the extent that education subsidy programs are viewed by families as income their effect on attainment will probably be quite small. Tailoring any such programs not only to the income of the family but also to the needs of the family will have more effect on the education of women than men. This follows from the fact that the number of siblings had twice the detrimental effect on female educational attainment than on male attainment.

The importance for males of the county wage rate for unskilled labor suggests that it is useful to consider the opportunity cost to the student of attending school. With all other variables held equal, a $.50 per hour increase in the unskilled wage rate is associated with an average *drop* in educational attainment of a little more than one-quarter of a year. Young men might be kept in school by a program which lowers the opportunity cost of education, such as a payment to enrolled students

While opportunity cost, family income, and needs have significant effects on educational attainment, the importance of parental educational attainment is as great or greater than any of them. In a sense, this is an unfortunate finding because the effect of the income and needs variables are more amenable to change through public policy. Unfortunate though it may be, the importance of socio-economic background, independent of income, is clearly shown in the statistical analysis of this study. When income and family size are taken into account, the educational advantage to the son of college educated parents over the son of

---

[1] Other studies have used single year income as a measure of family resources. Most have found a similar relationship between it and educational attainment. Masters (1969) does this but argues that a single year income measure may not adequately capture the "permanent income" of a family. He thus includes a housing quality variable as an additional measure of permanent income and finds a very large relationship between it and education. The income measure used in this chapter is a five year average total family income for families in roughly the same life cycle stage (i.e., with children leaving home). That it performs little better than single year measures argues against speculation that the relationship between education and family income is appreciably understated if a single year income variable is used.

grade school educated parents is greater than two and one-half years. To daughters the advantage of these different parental educational levels is a little over one year.

Since parental education levels have such an important effect on educational attainment of the child, independent of income, it is important to understand the way in which these effects operate. Leibowitz (1972) has suggested a human capital framework with cognitive skills as the chief intervening variable. The results presented in the previous section confirm that a measure of cognitive skills for males is systematically related to the "quality" of the home environment as measured by the cognitive skills and education of the parents. But the importance of the indirect effect of parental educational attainment operating through the cognitive skills measure of the child is swamped by the estimated direct effect.[1] The indirect effects are small partly because of the imperfect relationship between parental education levels and the child's cognitive skills, but mainly because of the weak relationship between the child's cognitive skills and his educational attainment. These findings are rather unfortunate from a policy viewpoint. Preschool programs which attempt to reduce the inequality in the distribution of cognitive skills will apparently do little to equalize either educational opportunity or actual attainment. A successful preschool program will have to concentrate on reducing the effects of unequal home environments which are, to a large extent, independent of the cognitive skills of the children.

The additional intervening variable -- a child's achievement motivation -- was included in this study as an attempt to further specify the ways in which parental attainments influence the attainments of their children. Like cognitive skills, it is systematically related to the educational attainment of one of the parents. But even though the effect of achievement motivation on educational attainment is larger than the cognitive skills effect, the relationship is still so imperfect that the indirect effects of parental attainments operating through achievement motivation are quite small.

The child's cognitive skills and achievement motivation fail to explain the relationship between parental educational attainments and the attainment of the child. While part of this may be attributed to measurement error, it seems very unlikely that these are powerful intervening variables. Other variables need to be specified. Sewell (1971) reports on the success of three sets of "social psychological intervening variables: (1) high school performance, (2) signifi-

---

[1] The estimated indirect effect of mother's education was .02, the direct effect was .12; father's education had a negligible indirect effect and a .27 direct effect.

cant others' influence, and (3) educational and occupational aspirations" (p. 799). He finds that these variables mediate about two-thirds of the total association between socioeconomic background and educational attainment. Economic writers speculate on a different set of intervening variables. Bowles (1973) argues that certain characteristics which are developed in the home, such as mode of self-presentation, dependability, and docility, are important in determining both years of education and income. Leibowitz (1973) writes that these and all other human capital investment variables need to be specified.

What emerges from the data analysis undertaken in this and other studies is the fact that there is an important effect of socioeconomic background on educational attainment which is independent of permanent income and family size. Part of this effect operates through the child's cognitive skills while some of it goes through the intervening variable of achievement motivation. Most of it, however, seems to be independent of these two variables. It is important that further research efforts be directed toward the specification and measurement of additional intervening variables so that the way in which status is passed on from parent to child is better understood.

SUMMARY

1. Educational attainment of children was hypothesized to be a function of parental family characteristics (income, family size, parental cognitive skills and educational attainments), characteristics of the child (cognitive skills and achievement motivation), and environmental factors (local labor market conditions and quality of schooling). The characteristics of the child are also a function of the parental family characteristics.

2. The data used to estimate the model come from reports of both the child and the parents over five years of interviews. Measurement of family characteristics should be considerably better than in other data sets.

3. When the relative importance of the various determinants of educational attainment are estimated, there are significant independent effects for parental attainments and family income for both males and females.

4. For males, the intervening variables of cognitive skills and achievement motivation are equally important in determining educational attainment. The former is strongly related to the education of the mother, the latter to the father's education. Neither of these intervening variables explain much of the

total relationship between parental attainments and the education of sons. The total effect of father's education on the education of sons is considerably greater than the effect of mother's education. The local labor market conditions are also important for males and indicate that programs which seek to equalize educational opportunity need to account for the opportunity costs of education.

5. For females, the intervening variables were not measured and only a reduced form of the entire model could be estimated. Mother's education is much more important than father's education in influencing the educational attainment of the daughters. Family size has twice the negative impact on the educational attainment of the daughters that it does on the sons.

6. Purely "economic" programs which attempt to equalize educational opportunity by income supplementation and/or cost reduction will probably reduce the inequality to a certain extent. More important than these economic factors, though, is the socioeconomic status of the parents. A necessary condition for the success of a program is that it equalizes the effects of these socioeconomic status differences.

7. We have not discovered in this chapter the exact way in which socioeconomic factors affect education. We do find, however, that most of the effect does *not* operate through either cognitive skills or achievement motivation. Programs which attempt to equalize preschool cognitive skills may change the unequal distribution of these skills but they will not equalize educational opportunity.

References

Atkinson, John W., "Motivational Determinants of Risk-Taking Behavior," in Atkinson and Feather (eds.), A Theory of Achievement Motivation, New York: John Wiley, 1966, pp 11-29.

Bowles, Samuel, "Understanding Unequal Economic Opportunity," American Economic Review, Vol. LXIII, No. 2, May 1973, pp 346-356.

Duncan, Beverly, "Education and Social Background," American Journal of Sociology, Vol. 72, No. 4, January 1967, pp 363-372.

Duncan, Otis Dudley, David L. Featherman and Beverly Duncan, Socioeconomic Background and Achievement, New York: Seminar Press, 1972.

Jencks, Christopher, Inequality: A Reassessment of the Effect of Family and Schooling in America, New York: Basic Books, 1972.

Leibowitz, Arleen, "Discussion", American Economic Review, Vol. LXIII, No. 2, May 1973, pp 357-358.

_____, "Home Investment in Children," paper prepared for presentation at NBER Population Council Conference, "Marriage, Family Human Capital and Fertility," June 1973.

Masters, Stanley H., "The Effect of Family Income on Children's Education: Some Findings on the Inequality of Opportunity," Journal of Human Resources, Vol. 4, No. 2, Spring 1969, pp 158-175.

Sewell, William H., "Inequality of Opportunity for Higher Education," American Sociology Review, Vol. 36, No. 5, October 1971, pp 793-809.

Sewell, William H. and Vimal P. Shah, "Parents' Education and Children's Educational Aspirations and Achievement," American Journal of Sociology, Vol. 33, No. 2, April 1968, pp 191-209.

Veroff, Joseph, Lou McClelland and Kent Marquis, Measuring Intelligence and Achievement Motivation in Surveys, U. S. Department of Health, Education, and Welfare, Contract No. OEO-4180, October 1971.

TABLE A7.1

Zero Order Correlation Matrix for Educational
Attainment Variable – 18-to 30-Year Old Males

		(2)	(3)	(4)	(5)	(6)	(7)	(8)	(9)	(10)
(1)	Five year average total family income	-.15	.43	.39	.33	.19	.21	.22	.26	.37
(2)	Number of siblings of child		-.33	-.31	-.26	-.04	-.21	-.06	-.05	-.26
(3)	Father's education			.55	.53	.24	.32	.14	.30	.50
(4)	Mother's education				.42	.09	.32	.20	.22	.37
(5)	Parent test score					.29	.40	.10	.21	.30
(6)	Child's achievement motivation						.18	.03	.13	.29
(7)	Child's test score							.06	.19	.33
(8)	Wage rate for unskilled labor								.39	.00
(9)	Expenditure per pupil									.25
(10)	Child's educational attainment									

TABLE A7.2

Zero Order Correlation Matrix for Educational
Attainment Variables - 18-to 30-Year Old Females

		(2)	(3)	(4)	(5)	(6)	(7)	(8)
(1)	Five year average total family income	-.13	.43	.40	.34	.07	.21	.37
(2)	Number of siblings of child		-.20	-.18	-.23	-.02	-.14	-.27
(3)	Father's education			.48	.51	.02	.21	.31
(4)	Mother's education				.45	.13	.11	.38
(5)	Parent test score					.04	.19	.32
(6)	Wage rate for Unskilled labor						.31	.03
(7)	Expenditure per pupil							.12
(8)	Child's educational attainment							

MTR 7057

TABLE A7.3

Means, Standard Deviations and Ranges for
Educational Attainment Variables – 18-to 30-Year Old Males

		Mean	Standard Deviation	Minimum Value	Maximum Value
(1)	Five year average total family income	12,436	7037	1095	41,210
(2)	Number of siblings of child	3.57	2.40	0	8
(3)	Father's education	9.79	4.03	0	18
(4)	Mother's education	10.35	3.23	0	18
(5)	Parent test score	9.40	2.26	0	13
(6)	Child's achievement motivation	6.93	2.40	0	12
(7)	Child's test score	9.90	2.12	0	13
(8)	Wage rate for unskilled labor	2.37	0.92	1	5
(9)	Expenditure per pupil	5.54	2.26	1	9
(10)	Child's educational attainment	12.58	2.28	0	18

MTR 7055

TABLE A7.4

Means, Standard Deviations and Ranges for
Educational Attainment Variables — 18-to 30-Year Old Females

		Mean	Standard Deviation	Minimum Value	Maximum Value
(1)	Five year average total family income	12,120	8204	956	78,540
(2)	Number of siblings of child	3.36	2.34	0	8
(3)	Father's education	10.36	3.67	0	18
(4)	Mother's education	10.26	3.79	0	18
(5)	Parent test score	9.28	2.49	0	13
(6)	Wage rate for unskilled labor	2.38	1.20	1	5
(7)	Expenditure per pupil	6.03	2.51	1	9
(8)	Child's educational attainment	12.65	1.99	3	18

Chapter 8

SUMMARY OF FINDINGS

This volume is an investigation of the determinants of the level of family economic well-being and of its changes over time. Well-being is a composite concept, made up of components within and beyond the control of family members. Both overall well-being and some of its principal components -- family size and composition, earnings, labor force participation, transfer income, income instability, and educational attainment -- have been the subjects of separate chapters in this volume.

Traditional analyses have investigated the relation between the components of economic well-being and various background and demographic characteristics. It is not a recent finding that low income families tend to contain people who are old, disabled, or handicapped by inadequate education, who are discriminated against because of race or sex, or who grew up in areas with little economic opportunity. But for as long as we have known these facts, we have also observed that many people from deprived backgrounds attain high levels of economic well-being. The issue of what it is in the environment or in the individual and his or her behavior patterns that leads to improvement in economic status has not been resolved in traditional studies. That issue motivated the design of the study and the analysis of this volume.

Our data contain personality and attitudinal measures of 5000 families and patterns of their economic behavior over a five-year period. We have supplemented these measures and the usual demographic information with several environmental variables -- the condition of the local labor market, the level of public school expenditure and so on. The statistical techniques we employ to conduct the data analysis are extremely flexible. They seem more appropriate than even repeated application of ordinary methods for finding which of the attitudes, behavior patterns, background factors, and envronmental conditions are important in determining economic well-being in the entire population and in its major subgroups.

This chapter summarizes the effects of variables which may be subject to change through public policy. This task seems more important than detailing the

334

unchangeable results of predetermined background factors. We will report findings on both the presence and absence of effects for the policy relevant variables. In spite of our flexible search strategy, we can be less confident of
negative findings than positive ones because they may result from errors in
measurement or from the dominance of background factors. Yet the negative findings are often extremely important because they fail to confirm popular beliefs
on which policy is often based.

We consider the effects of each policy relevant variable across all of the
components of well-being. Readers interested in the way in which a particular
component relates to the determinants of family well-being are referred to the
summary at the end of each chapter and, of course, to the analysis of the chapter
itself. First discussed here are the set of environmental factors, many of which
are subject to change by public policy or through the migration decisions of families. Race and sex are the next variables considered. They, of course, are not
changeable but their *effects* in labor and commodity markets are subject to change
through public policy. Educational attainment levels can potentially be changed
either by the individual or by social encouragement and incentives. Public policy can also affect the composition of families. It can encourage children to
split off from parental homes, motivate individuals to move into and out of homes
of relatives, or change the incentives for parents to have children. All of
these composition changes affect the well-being of families. Finally we discuss
the effects of behavior patterns, attitudes, and personality.

ENVIRONMENTAL FACTORS

One of the most interesting environmental variables is the level of unemployment for the county in which the families reside.[1] It has no effect on wage
rates for either men or women and has no effect on a family's chances of remaining at the bottom end of the income distribution. Unemployment rates, however,
do affect labor force participation in two ways. First, they result in higher
unemployment experiences for the individuals in our sample, although the association is weaker than one might expect. Second, they decrease the number of hours
of work, even after taking into account unemployment experience. County unemployment levels also affect the instability of individual incomes and a family's
chances of getting off welfare.

Higher wage rates for unskilled labor in the county seem to lead the young

_____

[1]This and other information about local labor market conditions were obtained by
mail questionnaires from the county unemployment compensation officers each year.

to quit school, while higher than average expenditure per pupil in a school system encourages them to stay in school. Both of these effects are statistically significant but are much less important than family characteristics. Unskilled wage rates also are associated with high wage rates among all workers.

In counties where the relative job opportunities for unskilled nonwhites is worse than it is for whites, nonwhites report an increased incidence of unemployment and are much less likely to hold second jobs.

The amount of urbanization in the area reflects the variety of job opportunities and therefore affects people's economic fortunes. We find that among those in the target population, the likelihood of being *persistently* poor is less for those in urban areas. Living in a large city also tends to increase a worker's wage rate, and for women, it increases the economic benefits of education. The administration of welfare seems to differ in the large urban areas, covering the very poor better than elsewhere but excluding those who have higher incomes but are still in poverty.

We find that environment has an important impact on the level of a family's well-being and on the instability of income. Environment has an impressive *lack* of effect on *trends* in family well-being; this is especially true on the global level. It also has no influence on the changes in wage rates for men, and only a small effect for women. Environment is relatively unimportant in explaining which families got on welfare.

RACE

There are large racial differences in wage rate *levels* with blacks earning about 10% less than comparable whites. Unemployment is also more serious among blacks, even when differences in education are taken into account. Controlling for occupation reduces the differences, indicating that blacks have limited access to the more stable jobs. Whites are more likely than blacks to offset very low wage rates by working long hours. This may be due to more restricted opportunities for nonwhites in finding second jobs or jobs offering particularly long work hours.

Income instability is also greater among nonwhites, even when the effects of other factors are taken into account. Perhaps as a result of this instability blacks are more likely to go on welfare, although they are not more likely to stay on than whites.

We find an interesting difference in the benefit to education for blacks and for whites. On the global level, the chances of a white family being persistently poor are very small if the head has a high school education, but this is

336

not true for a black family. The reduced benefit of education to blacks does not operate through wage rates. Blacks have the same wage payoff to more education as whites. Rather, it seems to be a result of education failing to reduce the amount of unemployment blacks experience as effectively as it does for whites.

It may be possible to change the effects of race on economic well-being. Minority group members *are* exhibiting more rapid *rates* of economic improvement, particularly those in the middle years, ages 25 to 54. In considering wage rates, we find that blacks in the middle wage group are doing the best. Whether this improvement is because of changing public policy or changing attitudes is not known, but the gap is being narrowed.[1] The very small group of Spanish Americans in our sample have the largest rates of increase, but they also started out with the lowest level of economic status.

SEX

We estimate that women are paid $1.00 an hour less than similarly qualified men. The impact of sex discrimination on the poverty population is substantial since many poor families are headed by women and a family's chance of being persistently poor is about twice as great if the head is a women. During this five-year period there is evidence of greater increases in wage rates for women than for men, but the largest gains were made by women in white collar jobs or with more education rather than those with the lowest wage rates.

That women are more likely to be on welfare than men is not surprising and is the result of eligibility rules. However, families headed by a female and *not* on welfare at the beginning of the study are no more likely than other poor families to go on welfare. Families where the male head left, especially if there were three or more children, are most likely to turn to welfare for assistance and once a woman is on welfare, she has a high probability of staying on until her children grow up or until she marries.

The educational attainment of children leaving home does not depend on the sex of the child. The way in which the home environment relates to completed years of education, however, does differ by sex. The father's education affects how much school his son finishes while a mother's education influences the amount of education the daughter receives. While the effect of family income on educational attainment is the same for both sexes, a greater number of children in the family reduces the daughter's completed schooling much more than it does the son's.

---

[1] This same phenomenon appears in the Census data from the current Population Survey.

EDUCATION

The extent to which public policy measures can influence educational attainment is problematic. The amount of education received by men is influenced to some extent by local labor market conditions and school expenditure levels, but it is much more dependent upon family background factors independent of environmental conditions, family income levels, and need standards.

Education has a pervasive effect on the level of earnings of both men and women. This is especially true for individuals with high test scores, urban backgrounds, and military experience. Educational attainment levels also affect labor supply and unemployment experience. Highly educated people work more hours, suffer less unemployment (particularly whites), are more likely to have second jobs, and enjoy main jobs in which there are fewer constraints on work hours.

Although there is a strong static relationship between schooling and earnings and labor supply, there is almost no evidence that education explains *changes* in the components of family well-being. Trends in male wage rates are either unaffected or adversely affected by more eduation. Income instability has no relationship to education once occupational differences have been taken into account. We find no education effect on a family's chances of either getting on or off welfare except for children who moved out of parental homes during the period. Since education does not affect trend in the components of well-being, it is not surprising that it also fails to affect changes in any of the more global well-being measures.

CHANGE IN FAMILY COMPOSITION

Family composition change is the most important of all the variables we included in our analysis of changed well-being. Decisions about marriage, having children, and encouraging older children and other adults to stay in the household or to leave it seem to be the main individual decisions that affect one's status, and there is some evidence that these decisions can in turn be explained by economic status. When, for example, we look at the likelihood of children leaving home, we find that it is associated with the situation in the parental home and the individual's apparent situation if he or she moved out.

Public policies concerning income taxes, rights to transfer incomes (welfare), and rent subsidies could be expected to influence decisions about one's living arrangements. Since all of the economies of scale and most of the help that individuals give to each other are realized through living together rather than through cash transfers *between* households, changes in the level and distribu-

338

tion of well-being are mainly caused by changes in household composition. Perhaps this is the most important finding of all -- that the family and the responsibility that people have for one another are still more important than any
social policy or individual behavior in determining the changing distribution of
well-being.

BEHAVIOR PATTERNS

It was originally thought that observations on various types of "proper"
behavior would show which of them resulted in improved economic well-being. We
attempted to measure time horizon, planning ahead, risk avoidance, connectedness
to sources of information and help, economizing in the use of resources, and behavior such as home production which would increase real incomes. We find very
little evidence that any of these behavior patterns have consistent effects on
changes in well-being. The connectedness variable seems to affect the changes
over the five years in family money income adjusted for needs, particularly for
the low income population, while economizing is important for changes in a different global well-being measure -- taxable income of head and wife. Neither of
these behavior patterns seems to affect the other well-being measure so little
confidence can be put in them.

ATTITUDES AND PERSONALITY

Several self-rated attitudes were measured for each of the five years.
They included indexes of aspiration-ambition, trust-hostility, sense of personal
efficacy, and perceived propensity to plan ahead. These attitudes affect almost
none of the components of economic status and their changes over time. It is not
merely that these measures failed to show up for the entire sample of families
either by themselves or when other variables were taken into account; they also
failed to affect any of the important subgroups of the population. Insofar as
we have segregated important subgroups, some of whom may have some opportunities
to make adjustments in their situations, the negative evidence is impressive.

Achievement motivation was measured in the fifth year only because it took
several years of development to create a reliable measure that was brief and easy
to administer. We do *not* find systematic or powerful effects of achievement motivation on either level or trend in family well-being or its components.
Achievement motivation makes a difference only for young men who recently left
home. Those among them who are highly motivated complete more education and also
have higher wage rates.

CONCLUSION

What seem to matter are the backgrounds and unchanging characteristics of individuals: age, sex, education, race and family background. We have not been able to find much evidence that people's attitudes or behavior patterns affect the trends in their well-being. If these findings are confirmed by additional years of data collected on trends in the families' fortunes, they have dramatic implications for the way we view the poor. If the poor cannot control their own fates, it seems unfair to distinguish the old and disabled as deserving and the rest as undeserving and in need of persuasion to change.

Can one really assert that because we find little evidence that individual attitudes and behavior patterns affect individual economic progress, that massive changes in those attitudes and behaviors would have no effect? Of course we cannot. But it is difficult to believe that there would not be *some* examples of subgroups for whom doing the "right" things resulted in rapid improvement. Yet there were none.

Perhaps there has not been enough time for attitudes and behavior patterns to exert their effects over inertia, random fluctuations, and sluggish aggregate economic conditions. Perhaps we have not measured the right things or have not measured them well enough. Perhaps we have not adequately isolated the autonomous groups for whom individual factors can show their effects and not be dominated by other factors.

On the other hand, we may have been oversold on the Protestant Ethic and have refused to see the extent to which people are the victims of their past, their environment, luck, and chance.

It is after all difficult to believe that there are not some situations where individual effort matters -- in seizing opportunities for better jobs, moving to new areas or avoiding undue risks. But for public policy purposes and for arguments about the extent to which one could reduce dependency in our society by changing the behavior and attitudes of dependent members, the findings certainly do not encourage expectations that such changes would make much difference.

Appendix A

SAMPLE WEIGHTS AND INDEPENDENT SUBSAMPLES

An efficient sampling design for studying some particular part of the population, for example the poor, calls for oversampling the subgroup of interest, or rather for undersampling the rest of the population with whom they are to be compared. Since much of our analysis focuses on the poor, we sampled disproportionately to secure more interviews with this subgroup than would have resulted from selection with equal probabilities. To preserve the unbiased nature of our estimates, each interview must be weighted by the inverse of its probability of selection. The interview must also be weighted to take care of: differential non-response, the combination of two separate samples that could overlap (SRC and Census), and the fact that we could use only those in the census sample who had signed a release of their information (approximately three quarters signed). A single weight takes care of all of these things.

The Census sample had already been dramatically oversampled in low income and heavily non-white areas, and we selected only the families in the lower ranges of income/needs for our follow-up interviews. We also selected only a sample of the Census sampling areas, in order to save costs. Finally, when two samples are merged some households are eligible to be selected in either one, and some are not, so the weights must allow for this. The details of the weighting are to be found in the Documentation.[1]

The sample can be thought of as consisting of all individuals living in the families sampled for the first wave of interviews in the spring of 1968. For analysis based on *individuals*, a set of individual weights is used which is unaffected by anything which happened subsequently. Individuals who "married into" the sample appear in the families but have zero individual weights, but children born into them have the weights of the parents.

---

[1] See A Panel Study of Family Income Dynamics, Vol. I, Section II, Institute for Social Research, University of Michigan, Ann Arbor, 1972.

For *families* there is the additional complication that the original individuals can end up in diverse families, due to family changes such as divorce or children leaving home to form families of their own. It is, therefore, best to think of this as a sample of families as of early 1972, with records of the history of each. Because some members of original families have moved out since 1968, there are cases where two or more 1972 families have the same 1968 record.

All that the reader or user of the data needs to know about all this is that there are weights which should be used, whether the analysis is of individuals or of families, in order to minimize bias in estimates. The details of the basic samples are documented in an earlier volume.

The use of weights and the complexity of the sample design make tests of significance complex and require keeping track of the number of interviews on which each estimate is based as well as the fraction of the sample represented by them. In any case, sampling errors cannot be based on assumptions of simple random sampling but must take account of both the complexities of the original samples and the differential sampling rates as well. (See Appendix B). On the other hand, measures of association, such as Kendall's Tau and Cramor's V, and estimates of the proportion of variance explained, such as squared correlation coefficients and Eta squared, are little affected by these complications.

It is a mistake to focus on tests of significance and sampling errors in the traditional manner when elaborate analysis of a complex set of data is undertaken. The usual assumption of statistical inference, that a single set of hypotheses is tested against a set of data, is not met. Clearly if one selects the best five out of a hundred competing explanatory variables, he should be able to find some that appear "significant," because the predictors were selected by searching the data. In fact that situation is even more complex because we often search not only for individual predictors that matter, but for patterns, combinations and structural models using those predictors.

One answer to this problem is to use part of the data for searching and selecting the best explanatory model and to use an independent part to estimate how much the unexplained variance has been reduced and how sure of the estimated relationships one should be. The procedure used to divide our sample into independent parts for searching and testing is as follows: Area probability samples are clustered at several stages, which reduces costs per interview far more than it reduces the amount of information per interview. Primary sampling areas are selected, usually counties or clusters of counties involving large urgan areas. Then there are area segments selected within those primary areas, and so on until finally several dwellings near one another are selected. A random division

of the dwellings into two subsamples might easily put one of a pair of nearby
dwellings in each sample, making the two samples more alike than two simple random samples would be and thereby exaggerating the extent to which the second
would confirm findings from the first.

In order to have genuinely independent subsamples from a clustered probability sample, then, one must select and assign whole clusters to one subsample or another. Indeed, except for the largest, self-representing primary
sampling areas, it is whole primary sampling areas that must be allocated to one
subsample or another. This requires an intimate knowledge of the sample design.
Both for our analysis purposes and for other users of the data we have designated
four independent quarter samples which allow a search on one-quarter, one-half or
three-quarters of the data, and to assess the power and significance of the findings on a fresh independent remainder.

The ideal procedure is even more complex. Because of the small number of
primary areas the independent samples are not used to estimate sampling errors,
nor is the use of one or more of the independent subsamples an efficient way to
make the best final estimates of the parameters of the final model selected. The
independent subsample is best used to estimate the explanatory power of the selected model and to see whether the individual relationship parameters are consistent with those estimated with the other data.

In some cases we have tested the model on the independent data in exactly
this way. In other cases we have moved from a part sample to the full sample
in order to focus on the stability of the estimates, and to provide the best
final estimates of the relationships. A comparison of half-sample with full-sam-
ple estimates also provides some indication of the stability of the estimates.

Whether one looks at estimates from a fresh independent part sample or from
the whole sample, sampling error estimates must also take the sample design into
account. When part of the sample was searched to select the best model, a suggested procedure for using the sampling error estimates in Appendix B is to act
as though the number of cases on which the estimates were based is the number in
the independent part sample, even though the estimates were derived from the full
sample. For example, where the searching was done on a half sample and the final
estimate used the full sample, the reader should cut the number of cases in half
before entering the sampling error tables or before calculating an approximate
sampling error and allowing for the design effect.

The reader may wonder whether the costs of probability sampling are worth
it if statistical inference from the results is so difficult, complex, and impre-
cise. But in fact with any other kind of sampling, one has *no idea at all* what

the precision or stability of his estimates are or how likely another sample
would be to replicate them.

Appendix B

SAMPLING ERRORS

Any estimate based on a sample will have a variance resulting from the fact that only part rather than the whole population is measured; such estimates will vary from sample to sample from the same population. Measures of sampling variation of a proportion, mean, or other parameter are commonly called "sampling errors." For *simple random samples*, the standard error of a proportion is estimated from the expression $\sqrt{p(1-p)/n}$, where p is the sample proportion and n is the number of observations on which the proportion is based; for a sample mean the standard error is approximated by dividing the sample standard deviation by the square root of the number of sample cases. With complex probability samples, however, estimating sampling errors is more difficult. To prepare estimations of sampling variability for this report, we have relied on two estimation techniques:

1) for proportions and means we used formulas approximating sampling errors when only one primary unit is selected from a stratum;[1]

2) for MCA coefficients and adjusted means we used a repeated replication method.[2]

Since it is impossible to present an estimate of sampling error for each of the many estimates and differences between pairs of estimates cited in this report, we focus on measures of average variability for statistics of certain types -- proportions, means, and MCA adjusted means. In the case of means, for example, sampling errors have been computed and are presented only for certain variables and subgroups especially important in the analysis and thought to reflect the range and mix of variables and subgroups investigated.

It should be kept in mind that departures from simple random sampling can result in smaller or larger sampling errors per case according to the nature of the departure. Stratification and oversampling may reduce sampling variability while clustering and differential sampling rates not directly beneficial to a particular estimate may increase sampling variability. The combined effects of these

---

[1] See Leslie Kish, (1965), pp. 282-293.

[2] See Leslie Kish and Martin Frankel, (1970).

departures result in sampling errors that can vary from somewhat less than simple random sampling errors to a great deal more. Fortunately, it is possible to generalize about the kinds of items where the "design effect" (DEFF)[1] is large (sampling errors much larger than simple random sampling) and those where it is likely to be small. For example, anything involving race has substantially larger design effects because the races are clustered geographically. As mentioned in Appendix A, however, we oversampled the poor (and hence also blacks). The effect of this oversampling is to reduce the sampling error by increasing the number of cases, after it has already been made larger *per case* by the geographical concentrations of places where blacks live.

An intuitive way to understand the design effect of clustering in increasing the sampling error per interview is to think of some extreme cases. Suppose one took two interviews close together in each selected side-of-a-block, to save interviewers' travel costs. From this sample one may estimate the proportion of the population who are black. The second interview in each cluster provides almost no information, given present segregation patterns. As a result a sample of 1000 would have only about 500 effective degrees of freedom and a standard error about 40% larger than a simple random sample of 1000 cases.[2]

We present two sets of sampling errors: the first is for means and proportions and for the differences between pairs of means or pairs of proportions; the second is for the parameters of some sample multiple regressions using categorical predictors.

Sampling Errors for Percentages and Means

Sampling errors for percentages, means, differences of percentages, and differences of means were computed by a variation of the "collapsed stratum" method discussed in Kish (1965, pp. 283-286). This method involves pairing geographically and economically similar strata, aggregating the sample values for each primary selection member of a pair, and employing the differences between paired aggregates as measures of variability. To the extent that the paired primary selections differ, the method will slightly overestimate the actual variance. Details of the procedure used at the Survey Research Center are found in a paper by Kish and Hess (1965).[3]

---

[1] Design effect is defined to be the ratio of an estimated sample variance, as calculated from sample data, to the corresponding simple random sampling variance based on the same number of cases.

[2] That is, the standard error increases by a factor of $\sqrt{2}$ when the sample size is halved.

[3] Leslie Kish and Irene Hess, [The Survey Research Center's National Sample of Dwellings, 1965, p. 43 ff.]

A. PERCENTAGES AND DIFFERENCES OF PERCENTAGES

Table B.1 gives the approximate values of sampling errors associated with percentages in this report, according to the magnitudes of the percentages and the number of sample cases on which they are based. As demonstrated by the familiar formula for simple random sampling, standard error = $\sqrt{\dfrac{p(1-p)}{n}}$, sampling errors depend on both of those factors. "Sampling error" here refers to two standard errors, the range on either side of the estimated percentage which, for large samples, represents the 95% "level of confidence." If one requires a greater or lesser degree of confidence, a wider or narrower range than two standard errors can be chosen.

The numbers shown in Table B.1 result from the multiplication of the simple random sampling errors by a factor of 1.5, the square root of "design effect," representing the effect on sampling variability of departures -- specifically stratification, clustering, and disproportionate allocation selection -- from simple random sampling. In this case, the design effect employed is an estimated average design effect obtained for an assortment of percentages subjectively selected but thought to be representative of the variables and subgroups investigated in this study.

Although Table B.1 gives a satisfactory approximation of sampling variability for most percentages in this report, caution should be exercised in applying it to percentages based on samples of geographically clustered subpopulations. In particular, Table B.1 *does not apply* to percentages based on the black sample or subgroups of the black sample since the average square root of design effect for percentages based on blacks is about 2.25 rather than the 1.5 implicit in the Table. Thus, for inferences to the black population or subgroups thereof, the sampling errors in Table B.1 are to be multiplied by a factor of 1.5.

Approximate sampling errors for differences of percentages, computed in the same way [(average square root of design effect) x (srs standard error) = 1.5 ($\sqrt{p(1-p)} \ (1/n_1 + 1/n_2)$)] are shown in Table B.2. The sampling errors of differences provide a range on either side of the estimated difference which, in a long sequence of samples of this type, would include the true population difference about 95% of the time. The more complicated form of Table B.2 is due to the dependence of the sampling error on *two* base sizes as well as on the approximate magnitude of the percentages being compared.

As in the case of single proportions, inference to the black population requires that the numbers in Table B.2 be multiplied by a factor of 1.5.

TABLE B.1

Approximate Sampling Errors of Percentages*
(expressed in percentages)

Reported Percentages	Number of Interviews							
	5000	2500	1500	1000	700	500	300	100
50	2.1	3.0	3.9	4.7	5.7	6.7	8.7	15.0
30 or 70	1.9	2.7	3.5	4.3	5.2	6.1	7.9	13.7
20 or 80	1.7	2.4	3.1	3.8	4.5	5.4	6.9	12.0
10 or 90	1.3	1.8	2.3	2.8	3.4	4.0	5.2	9.0
5 or 95	.9	1.3	1.7	2.1	2.5	2.9	3.8	6.5

*The figures in this table represent two standard errors. Hence, for most items, we have "95% confidence" that the value being estimated lies within a range equal to the reported percentages, plus or minus the sampling error.

Note: The sampling errors in this table do not apply to percentages based on the black sample or subgroups of the black sample. To attain an approximate sampling error for a percentage of blacks (e.g. the percentage of blacks on welfare in 1970), multiply the appropriate tabular figure by 1.5.

TABLE B.2

Approximate Sampling Errors of Differences*
(expressed as percentages)

Size of Sample or Group	Size of Sample or Group						
	2500	1500	1000	700	500	300	100

For percentages from about 35% to 65%

Size of Sample or Group	2500	1500	1000	700	500	300	100
2500	4.1	4.7	5.5	6.4	7.3	9.1	15
1500		5.5	6.1	6.9	7.7	9.5	16
1000			6.7	7.4	8.2	9.9	16
700				8.0	8.8	10	16
500					9.5	11	16
300						12	17
100							21

For percentages around 20% and 80%

Size of Sample or Group	2500	1500	1000	700	500	300	100
2500	3.4	3.9	4.5	5.1	5.9	7.3	12
1500		4.4	4.9	5.5	6.2	7.6	12
1000			5.4	5.9	6.6	7.9	13
700				6.4	7.0	8.3	13
500					7.6	8.8	13
300						9.8	14
100							17

For percentages around 10% and 90%

Size of Sample or Group	2500	1500	1000	700	500	300	100
2500	2.6	2.9	3.4	3.9	4.4	5.5	9.2
1500		3.3	3.7	4.1	4.7	5.7	9.3
1000			4.0	4.4	4.9	5.9	9.4
700				4.8	5.3	6.2	9.6
500					5.7	6.6	9.9
300						7.3	10
100							13

For percentages around 5% and 95%

Size of Sample or Group	2500	1500	1000	700	500	300	100
2500	1.9	2.1	2.5	2.8	3.2	4.0	6.7
1500		2.4	2.7	3.0	3.4	4.1	6.8
1000			2.9	3.2	3.6	4.3	6.9
700				3.5	3.8	4.5	7.0
500					4.1	4.8	7.2
300						5.3	7.5
100							9.2

*See footnotes to Table B1.

B. MEANS AND DIFFERENCES OF MEANS

Summarization of sampling errors for means is difficult since standard errors for means, unlike those for percentages, depend on the *unit of measure* of the variable in question. The presentation adopted here is to provide sampling errors for a variety of means and differences of means, shown in Table B.3. For the total sample and for most of its subgroups, the square root of the design effect averages around 1.4. The square root of design effect for the black sample and relevant subgroups is about 2.1 or about 50% higher than for the total and white samples.

C. MCA ADJUSTED AND UNADJUSTED MEANS

To estimate the standard errors of the statistics produced by Multiple Classification Analysis (e.g., class means, coefficients, adjusted class means, etas and betas) we split the sample into balanced half samples using the "balanced repeated replication" (BRR) technique. [1] The MCA equation is then estimated twice: once using the whole sample and a second time using the half sample. The squared difference between the statistics of the half sample and the corresponding statistics of the whole sample provides an estimate of the variance of that statistic. Repeating this procedure 12 times and averaging the resulting variances provides a more stable estimate of the variance of the MCA results.

An estimate of the simple random samples (srs) standard errors is given by:

$$\sigma/\sqrt{n} \quad \text{for unadjusted class means and by}$$

$$\sqrt{1-R^2} \ \sigma/\sqrt{n} \quad \text{for adjusted class means,}$$

where σ = standard deviations of the dependent variable (from whole sample), n = number of cases used in estimating the mean, and R^2 = multiple correlation coefficient. The ratio of the standard errors computed from the 12 half samples to the estimated simple random sample standard errors yields an estimate of the square root of the design effect ($\sqrt{DEFF}$). In Tables B.4 and B.5 we present the average of these $\sqrt{DEFF}$ for each MCA predictor. Two different MCA regressions were estimated. In the first, the dependent variable was food consumption (Table B.4); in the second, the dependent variable was log of head's labor income (Table B.5). These dependent variables were selected to illustrate the types of variables analyzed in the text.

Several general conclusions may be drawn from the results presented. First, the average $\sqrt{DEFF}$ for the categories of a predictor range between 1.2 and 1.8 for the adjusted means. (For the unadjusted means the average $\sqrt{DEFF}$ is generally lower than for the adjusted means.) The reader may, therefore, use the following

---

[1] The technique described in this section has been described in more detail in Kish and Frankel (1970).

TABLE B.3

Estimated Sampling Errors for Selected Means
and Their Differences

A. 1971 WORK HOURS

Definition of Subgroups	Number of Sample Cases	Estimated Mean	Estimated Standard Error	Square Root of Design Effect ($\sqrt{DEFF}$)
All	5058	1639	22.9	1.55
Target Population	2608	1141	44.5	2.08
Difference		498	32.3	2.18
All	5058	1639	22.9	1.55
Splitoffs	1115	1738	36.5	1.35
Difference		99	34.8	1.39
All	5058	1639	22.9	1.55
Same Head, in labor force 5 years	2410	2227	18.0	1.34
Difference		587	22.0	1.45
All	5058	1639	22.9	1.55
Female Heads	1206	1277	39.3	1.51
Difference		363	37.1	1.54
Target Population, white	1080	1147	55.4	1.62
Target Population, black	1422	1069	50.6	1.90
Difference		78	71.8	1.66
Target Population, male	1563	1452	58.8	2.07
Target Population, female	1045	644	39.6	1.53
Difference		808	69.4	1.80
Splitoffs, white	651	1793	41.6	1.17
Splitoffs, black	431	1497	81.9	2.01
Difference		296	86.6	1.60
Splitoffs, male	838	1957	37.9	1.32
Splitoffs, female	277	1203	70.6	1.39
Difference		753	74.4	1.27
Same Head, in labor force 5 yrs., white	1571	2250	18.0	1.09
Same Head, in labor force 5 yrs., black	748	2037	48.9	1.93
Difference		213	49.7	1.64

TABLE B.3
(continued)

Definition of Subgroups	Number of Sample Cases	Estimated Mean	Estimated Standard Error	Square Root of Design Effect (√DEFF)
Female Head, <65, white	478	1378	43.9	1.08
Female Head, <65, black	698	974	66.7	1.98
Difference		403	74.9	1.42
Black	1753	1347	50.3	2.03
Spanish-American	124	1715	108.2	1.25
Difference		369	111.3	1.24
Splitoff, male employed, working 250 hrs. in 1971	723	2121	30.5	1.17
Splitoff, female employed, working 250 hrs. in 1971	142	1694	60.8	1.27
Difference		427	64.0	1.18

B. 1971 FAMILY INCOME

Definition of Subgroups	Number of Sample Cases	Estimated Mean	Estimated Standard Error	Square Root of Design Effect (√DEFF)
All	5058	$7090	$156	1.58
Target Population	2608	2815	112	1.67
Difference		4275	169	1.73
All	5058	7090	156	1.58
Splitoffs	1115	5596	152	1.18
Difference		1493	207	1.50
All	5058	7090	156	1.58
Same Head, in labor force 5 years	2410	10720	264	1.79
Difference		3631	171	1.65
All	5058	7090	156	1.58
Female Heads	1206	3782	159	1.55
Difference		3308	193	1.57
Target Population, white	1080	2835	137	1.28
Target Population, black	1422	2503	150	1.99
Difference		331	204	1.56
Target Population, male	1563	3823	154	1.61
Target Population, female	1045	1200	76	1.37
Difference		2622	177	1.59

TABLE B.3
(continued)

Definition of Subgroups	Number of Sample Cases	Estimated Mean	Estimated Standard Error	Square Root of Design Effect (√DEFF)
Splitoffs, white	651	$5901	$154	.90
Splitoffs, black	431	4188	429	2.63
Difference		1714	427	1.80
Splitoffs, male	838	6527	195	1.28
Splitoffs, female	277	3316	232	1.30
Difference		3211	312	1.33
Same Head, in labor force 5 yrs., white	1571	11113	279	1.57
Same Head, in labor force 5 yrs., black	748	6818	309	2.09
Difference		4295	449	1.94
Female Head, <65, white	478	4296	186	1.10
Female Head, <65, black	698	2142	176	1.90
Difference		2154	235	1.22
Black	1753	4096	218	2.20
Spanish-American	124	7588	135	1.26
Difference		3492	135	1.25
Splitoff, male employed, worked 250 hrs. in 1971	723	7166	215	1.33
Splitoff, female employed, worked 250 hrs. in 1971	142	4869	244	1.11
Difference		2297	358	1.31

C. FIVE-YEAR AVERAGE FAMILY MONEY INCOME

All	5058	$10031	151.2	1.59
Same Head Only	3568	10394	182.2	1.50
Difference		363	57.9	1.06
Same Head, black	1189	6495	318.2	2.45
Same Head, white	2259	10866	209.5	1.37
Difference		4370	390.4	1.95

TABLE B.4

Average Values of $\overline{\sqrt{DEFF}}$* For Unadjusted and Adjusted Class Means
from a Multiple Classification Analysis**

Dependent variable = Food consumption

$\overline{R^2} = .58$

N = 5060

Predictors	Number of Categories	Average $\sqrt{DEFF}$ for:	
		Unadjusted Class Mean	Adjusted Class Mean
Annual food standard	9	.97	1.4
Family money income	9	1.0	1.3
Head's race	2	1.3	1.4
Size of place	7	1.1	1.5

----

*Using 12 balanced half-samples.

**See Glossary. MCA is essentially regression using sets
of dichotomous predictors. We have averaged the design
effects over all the categories of each set of predictors.

TABLE B.5

Average Values of $\sqrt{\text{DEFF}}^*$ For Unadjusted and Adjusted Class Means
from a Multiple Classification Analysis

Dependent Variable = Log of Head's Labor Income

$$\overline{R}^2 = .26$$

$$N = 3593^{**}$$

Predictors	Number of Categories	Average $\sqrt{\text{DEFF}}$ For:	
		Unadjusted Class Mean	Adjusted Class Mean
Head's education	9	1.1	1.3
Head's race	4	1.3	1.2
Head's sex	2	1.5	1.8
Years of work experience	8	1.4	1.7

*Using 12 balanced half-samples.

**The MCA is based on those family heads who remained in the sample all 5 years and who were in the labor force each of those years.

356
rule of thumb to estimate sampling errors for MCA adjusted means presented in the text:

1) Estimate the srs standard error:

$$\sigma_{srs} = \sqrt{1-R^2} \; \sigma/\sqrt{n}$$

where, σ = standard deviation of the dependent variable.

n = number of cases in the category.

2) Multiply srs by an estimate of the DEFF.

While the design effect varies across predictors, 1.5 appears to be a reasonable estimate of $\sqrt{DEFF}$ for most predictors.

Reestimation of the $\sqrt{DEFF}$ based on the unweighted cross-section sample only, revealed generally lower design effects. This result indicates that a substantial portion of the design effect of the MCA adjusted means is due to weighting alone. The impact of weighting on the sampling errors, however, is ambiguous inasmuch as the precision *per case* is reduced by the weighting, but the sample size is increased for crucial estimates including poor people or blacks.

References

Kish, Leslie, Survey Sampling, John Wiley & Sons, Inc., New York, 1965.

Kish, Leslie and Frankel, Martin, "Balanced Repeated Replication for Standard Errors", Journal of the American Statistical Association, Vol. 65, Sept. 1970, pp. 1071-1094.

Appendix C

TECHNIQUES OF STATISTICAL DATA ANALYSIS

In addition to the usual tables and ordinary multiple regression, three other multivariate analysis procedures were used: regression using sets of dichotomous (dummy) variables (MCA), a sequential searching program for continuous dependent variables (AID), and a program for categorical dependent variables (THAID) which searches for subgroups with different *distributions* rather than different means.

MULTIPLE CLASSIFICATION ANALYSIS (MCA)[1]

Many of our explanatory factors have no scale but are classifications like region, occupation, or race. Others have a numerical scale but may have non-linear effects. To solve both these problems, it is possible to treat the membership in any one subclass of a classification as a dichotomous or dummy explanatory variable, and use ordinary multiple regression.

The extra degrees of freedom used in the estimation are no problem with samples in the thousands, and the loss of precision from converting a numerical variable into categories (bracket intervals) is minimal. If the relationship between a predictor and dependent variable is linear, as few as seven classes with their dummy variables as predictors can account for 98% of the variance that the full continuous variable could explain. If the relationship is not linear, the dummy variables can do better. Finally, a special group can be made of those who did not answer the question or for whom the question was inappropriate, rather than excluding them from the analysis and losing the other information they have provided.

It is only too common in presenting the results of dummy variable regression to express the effects of membership in some subclass as a deviation from another excluded subclass, which may even be small and extreme. A simple alge-

---

[1]The reader unfamiliar with regression in general or the MCA program should refer to Frank Andrews, James Morgan, John Sonquist, and Laura Klem, Multiple Classification Analysis (2nd Edition), Institute for Social Research, The University of Michigan, Ann Arbor, Michigan, 1973.

braic transformation allows one to express the effects as deviations from the grand mean and the weighted sum of the coefficients for any one classification that exhausts the sample will then add to zero. The MCA program makes this transformation.

It is easier for the reader, however, if the results are expressed as unadjusted and adjusted subgroup means, adding the grand mean to all the deviations. The difference between the unadjusted and adjusted means is the correction for intercorrelation among the predictors. Indeed, it is useful to think of the results of dummy variable regression as a set of subgroup means adjusted for the fact that that subgroup is not like the whole population in its distribution on several other characteristics. An adjusted wage rate for female family heads, for example, is an estimate of what their wage rate would be if they had the same distribution as the whole population on age, education, race, etc. The pattern of those adjusted means provides a direct sense of the stability and dependability of the results. A persistent monotonic rise or fall, without oscillations in the adjusted subgroup means, adds to one's confidence in the reliability of an estimated effect.

The program also produces estimates of the explanatory power not of individual subclasses, but of whole classifications such as race, or education. The gross power is estimated by the square of the correlation ratio (eta) or the fraction of the variance of the dependent variable accounted for by the subgroup means. The net power is estimated by an analogue to the normalized regression coefficient of numerical regression and is hence called beta squared. If the explanatory characteristics are not too highly intercorrelated, then beta squared is a good approximation to the square of the partial correlation coefficient, the best measure of the marginal explanatory power of a predictor.[1]

The MCA program can be used to analyze a dichotomous dependent variable provided the overall proportion classified 0 or 1 is not close to zero.[2] In that case the results are estimate probabilities, unadjusted and adjusted. The use of dummy variable predictors reduces the problem of explaining a dichotomous dependent variable since the possibility of predicting a probability less than zero or greater than 1 by using extreme values of the predictors is less because the extreme values are grouped in a class.

---

[1] A direct estimate of the partial correlation coefficient requires re-running the regression omitting a whole set of dummy variables for one classification. The decrease in the multiple correlation squared as a fraction of (1 - the multiple correlation without the marginal classification) is the partial correlation for that classification.

[2] See Appendix E for a detailed description of dichotomous dependent variables.

While MCA does not assume linearity in the relationships, it does assume additivity of effects (no interaction effects -- the effect of one predictor does not depend on the level of any other predictor). A limited number of interactions can be embodied in categorical variables which account for various combinations of characteristics. In several analyses incorporating very extensive interactions, however, they have been introduced as special predictors in linear regression models.[1]

AUTOMATIC INTERACTION DETECTOR (AID)

The Automatic Interaction Detector program is a computer program[2] for searching large data sets for a structure to explain some interval scale dependent variable. Unlike regression, it does not impose assumptions of linearity, additivity (i.e., the absence of interactions) or symmetry.

The way in which the program operates can best be explained with an example. In the initial chapter of the first volume, AID was used to help explain why some initially poor families "climbed out" of poverty over the five years of the study. The sample included those below a certain level of income relative to needs in the first two years of the study. Those families that managed to rise above that income/needs level by the final years of the study (i.e., climbed out) were scored "1" and those that failed were scored "0." Of all these initially poor families, 34% climbed out. AID was used to relate this dichotomous dependent variable to a set of independent variables measuring environmental conditions, background and demographic characteristics, attitudes and behavior patterns. Each of the independent variables is bracketed into a rather small number of categories (usually 5-10). As explained in the previous section of this Appendix which describes Multiple Classification Analysis, the collapsing of interval scaled variables into a small number of bracketed intervals loses surprisingly little precision. Variables both with and without a natural ordering can be used.

The program scans all possible dichotomous splits on a given independent variable and retains the one which explains the greatest fraction of the variance of the dependent variable. If, for example, the education variable consists of the classifications 0-8 years, 9-11 years, 12 years, and more than 12 years, then the program will first examine the population subgroups with fewer than 9 years of education and with 9 or more years and calculate the extent to which the

---

[1] See Appendix D on such interactions.

[2] See John A. Sonquist, Elizabeth Lauh Baker and James N. Morgan, Searching for Structure (2nd Edition), Institute for Social Research, The University of Michigan, Ann Arbor, Michigan, 1973.

unexplained variances of the dependent variable has been reduced by this division. It then compares the population subgroup consisting of those with 11 or fewer years of schooling to those with 12 or more and makes the identical calculation. This process continues until all such dichotomous splits of all independent variables have been examined.[1] The variable which proved to be most important in explaining which families climbed out of poverty was the education of the family head and the best division of the variable was at the level of high school graduation. The subgroups of those with and without high school diplomas differed more with respect to the chances of climbing out of poverty than any other two subgroups in the sample. The chances of the non-graduate group climbing out were 23%; the chances for the graduate groups were more than double that -- 52%.

The program then actually divides the sample by educational attainment and assesses all of the predictors for importance in explaining who among the families with heads who had not completed high school were able to climb out. It repeats the process on the population subgroups of families with heads who had a high school diploma. For both of these subgroups it turns out that the score on the sentence completion test was best able to explain movement out of poverty. Heads of families with higher test scores were more likely to climb out for both education subgroups. The four education-test score subgroups created by these two sets of splits have average proportions of families climbing out which range from 17% (for the low education-low test score group) to 65% (for those with high education-high test scores).

That the test score variable was important to both of the education subgroups *and* had similar effects on each of them indicates that the effects of test score on a family's chances of climbing out do not depend upon educational attainment; that is, there appears to be no interaction between test scores and education. If different variables had been important for the two education subgroups then the AID program would have shown it by splitting the two education subgroups on different predictors.[2] And if the same variable was most powerful for both groups, but had different effects, the subgroup data would show that.

After the four education-test score subgroups have been created, the program next assesses the host of independent variables for explanatory powers within each of these subgroups. New, smaller subgroups are created and, in turn,

---

[1] For independent variables with a natural order (such as education) the rank order of the predictor classes is maintained. For variables without order (such as region) the reordering of the classes is allowed and thus a much larger number of dichotomous splits are examined.

[2] The program output gives information on not only the division of the variable that proved most powerful, but on all splits of all independent variables.

searched. This process continues until splits either result in subgroups which are too small or the splits themselves do not explain some minimum amount of the total variance (usually half a percent) of the dependent variable.

The final results of the program are very transparent. One has a diagram (Figure 1.16 for the example of those climbing out of poverty) showing a successively finer set of population subgroups, defined by the sequence of divisions that created them. If the effects of the independent variables are additive then the same predictors should appear symmetrically in the brances of the diagram and with similar effects. If, however, different subgroups are further divided on quite different predictors, or their effects are different, this lack of symmetry implies interactive effects. Once discovered, they can be introduced into a linear model which can be estimated and tested by the usual procedures. This testing, however, can only be done on a fresh independent set of data and *not* with the data used to select the model. The separation of the searching and testing is crucial and it has been made possible in this study by the designation of four independent quarter samples (see Appendix A).

ANALYSIS OF CATEGORICAL DEPENDENT VARIABLES (THAID)

When the particular dependent variable of interest is measured on a continuous scale (such as wage scale or hours of labor force participation) or if it is dichotomous, taking values of zero or unity (such as whether climbed out of poverty) then AID is the appropriate search program. If, however, the dependent variable consists of a set of categories which have no **natural** ordering (such as mode of travel to work or kinds of change in family composition) the AID's criterion of reducing unexplained variance cannot be used. THAID was developed to apply the same flexible search process of AID to categorical dependent variables.[1]

While AID finds the division of the sample on an independent variable which maximally reduces the unexplained variance of the dependent variable, THAID finds the division which maximizes the differences in the *distributions* of the subgroups across the categories of the dependent variable.

An example will perhaps clarify this process. In Chapter 4 of Volume II, the dependent variable of interest is how people get to work. It was found that for those individuals living within two miles of work, the relevant mode of choices were driving, walking, and taking public transportation. These three

---

[1]For a full description of the program with examples, see James Morgan and Robert Messenger , THAID: A Sequential Analysis Program for the Analysis of Nominal Scale Dependent Variables, Institute for Social Research, The University of Michigan, Ann Arbor, Michigan, 1973.

choices are the categories of the dependent variable "travel mode" and it was found that the population was distributed across these categories as follows: 69% drove, 26% walked, and 5% took public transportation.

Several predictors could be expected to affect this distribution found that the variable which mattered most in terms of producing population sub-groups that had maximally different distributions was city size. Those living in cities larger than 500,000 were much more likely to use public transportation or walk and less likely to drive (39% drove, 44% walked, and 17% used public transportation). For those living in cities smaller than 500,000, the likelihood of using the various modes was, of course, reversed: 78% drove, 21% walked, and 1% took public transportation. The criterion measure that indicated that this division of the sample was more "powerful" than the division on any other cate-gory of this or other predictors is called *delta*. It is simply the weighted sum of deviations of subclass percentages from those of the parent class to which they belong.[1] Since the sum is weighted by the number of observations in each category of the dependent variable, a division of the sample on a predictor that is most powerful must result in two groups which are both of appreciable size and have widely different distributions across categories of the dependent variable.

As with the AID program, THAID finds the most powerful division of the en-tire sample and then searches through the subgroups formed from the division for the most powerful predictor for additional division.

In terms of the example of travel mode to work, the sample is divided by city size and then predictors are reassessed for their importance (delta) in explaining the distribution of those living in small cities and those living in large cities. As it turns out, different predictors are important for these two subgroups: the sex of head is most important for those living in large cities, and wage rate matters for those living in small cities. Thus, two interactions seem to have been uncovered[2] by THAID: the effects of both sex and wage rate on travel mode depend upon the city size.

KENDALL'S TAU-BETA AND CRAMER'S V

Two measures of association for cross-classifications were used in these analyses -- Kendall's Tau-b, a rank correlation coefficient, and Cramer's V.

---

[1] The Chi-square statistic is similar to delta although it is the sum of *squared* deviations. Thus, delta can be thought of as being equivalent to "Chi-unsquared."

[2] That these apparent interactions are, in fact, real can be investigated in sev-eral ways. First, it is necessary to check to see whether either sex or wage rate competed with one another for the two city size splits. A more formal test of significance can be made if the interactions are built into a linear model and tested on a fresh set of data.

Kendall's Tau-b assumes that the two classifications have natural ordering and that if an individual is higher than another individual on one rank, he should be higher on the other as well. It varies from -1.0 if all pairs show a reverse effect to +1.0 if all possible pairs show the expected effect.

Cramer's V makes no assumption about order of the classes but merely asks how well one could predict to which subclass of one characteristic a person belongs if it were known which class of another characteristic he was in. It assumes that whole distributions must be predicted rather than individuals; hence, it is similar to most Chi-squared measures. However, for large samples, it is also equivalent to the mean square canonical correlation between the two sets of dichotomies defined by the two classifications. It varies from 0, where there is no association, to 1, where one could predict perfectly from one classification to the other.

Appendix D

CATEGORICAL INTERACTIONS IN LINEAR REGRESSION MODELS

If a researcher suspects that all the parameters of a linear model are dissimilar in different subgroups of a population, he can run separate regressions on the different subgroups. He can then compare the residuals from the separate regressions with those from a single regression on the full population and use a Chow test for the significance of the interactions. If the number of parameters in the model is large, however, such tests for complete interactions become very expensive in degrees of freedom and their power in detecting limited interactions is very low.

Often, the researcher is concerned with interaction effects for only a small number of parameters. The remaining parameters are important for the model but are assumed to have consistent effects for the full population. For exposition we consider interactors on only one parameter, the coefficient of X. The model without interactions has the form:

$$1. \quad Y_i = a + \beta X_i + \sum_{k=1}^{K} \gamma_k Z_k + \varepsilon_i, \text{ for } i = 1 \ldots N$$

and the matrix of independent variables has the form:

$$
2. \quad
\begin{matrix}
1 & X_1 & Z_{11} & - - - & Z_{K1} \\
1 & \cdot & \cdot & \cdot\cdot\cdot & \cdot \\
1 & X_i & Z_{1i} & - - - & Z_{Ki} \\
1 & \cdot & \cdot & \cdot\cdot\cdot & \cdot \\
1 & X_N & Z_{1N} & - - - & Z_{KN}
\end{matrix}
$$

It is hypothesized that the coefficient of the variable X differs across subgroups. Using an indicator variable δ_{ij}, which takes value 1 if the ith observation is in the jth subgroup and zero otherwise, the interactive model may be specified as:

$$3. \quad Y_i = [\alpha_0 + \sum_{j=1}^{J} \alpha_j \delta_{ij}] + [\beta_0 + \sum_{j=1}^{J} \delta_{ij} \beta_j] X_i + \Sigma \gamma_k Z_{ki} + \sigma_i$$

and the matrix of independent variables has the form:

4. $1, X_1, \delta_1, \delta_1 X_1, \delta_2, \delta_2 X_1, \ldots\ldots \delta_J, \delta_J X_1, Z_{11} \ldots\ldots Z_{K1}$

    1

    $1, X_i, \delta_1, \delta_1 X_i, \delta_2, \delta_2 X_i, \ldots\ldots \delta_J, \delta_J X_i, Z_{1i} \ldots\ldots Z_{Ki}$

    1

    $1, X_N, \delta_1, \delta_1 X_n, \delta_2, \delta_2 X_N, \ldots\ldots \delta_J, \delta_J X_{11}, Z_{1N} \ldots\ldots Z_{KN}$

The coefficients for a particular subgroup are given by the complete expression within the brackets. The individual β_i's or α_i's represent deviations of the subgroup slope or intercept from that of the excluded group. If the subgroups for which interactions are allowed are mutually exclusive and exhaustive, it is possible to drop the overall intercept and X variable and enter X and the intercept separately for each subgroup. The estimated parameters may then be directly interpreted as the coefficients for their appropriate subgroups. As noted below, such a specification is not as flexible as that in equation 3 if the model is additive in first order interactions. The specification of equation 3 also has the advantage of yielding simple t tests for each interaction effect. It is, of course, always necessary to exercise care in specifications to avoid exact linear combinations and the resulting singular matrix.

As indicated in equation 3, it is generally necessary to allow a subgroup to differ in both slope and intercept. The specification of only a separate slope may result in anomalous estimates. In many cases a dummy variable for a subgroup will have been included in the simple additive model so that $\delta_i X_i$ is the only new variable entered in the model to allow for the interaction. The essential point is that the dummy or indicator variable is likely to be necessary for the proper specification of the interaction even if it does not appear to be significant in the simple additive specification. A graphical interpretation of the coefficients is given in Figure D.1, with the Z's held constant.

In Figure D.1a the estimated model includes a coefficient for X and a shift parameter or dummy variable for subgroup 1. In Figure D.1b the slope on X is allowed to differ for subgroup 1 but the indicator variable has been dropped so that a separate intercept is not allowed. In this admittedly extreme example the misspecifications in a and b show no effect at all for the variable X, the shift parameter, or the slope interaction. In the proper specification, shown in Figure 1c, all three are included and are highly significant.

The specification of equation 3 gains still further flexibility if additivity in first order interactions may be assumed. Under that assumption, the

FIGURE D.1

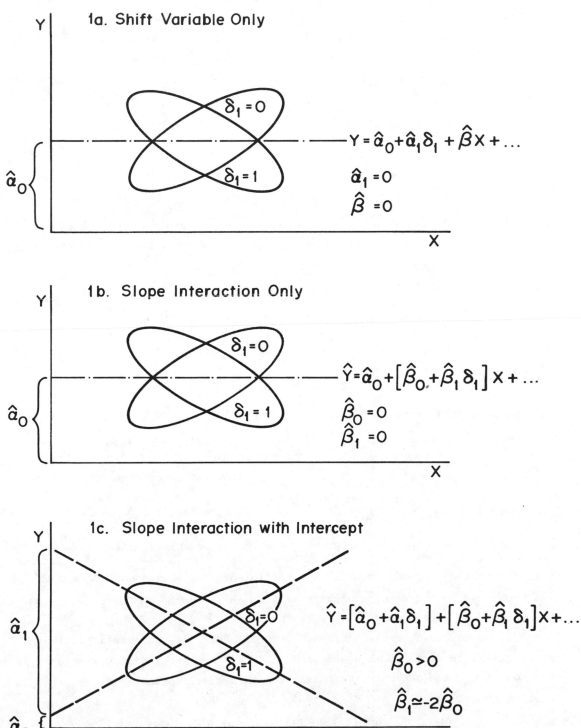

1a. Shift Variable Only

$Y = \hat{a}_0 + \hat{a}_1 \delta_1 + \hat{\beta} X + \dots$

$\delta_1 = 0$

$\delta_1 = 1$

$\hat{a}_1 = 0$

$\hat{\beta} = 0$

$\hat{a}_0$

1b. Slope Interaction Only

$\hat{Y} = \hat{a}_0 + [\hat{\beta}_0 + \hat{\beta}_1 \delta_1] X + \dots$

$\delta_1 = 0$

$\delta_1 = 1$

$\hat{\beta}_0 = 0$

$\hat{\beta}_1 = 0$

$\hat{a}_0$

1c. Slope Interaction with Intercept

$\hat{Y} = [\hat{a}_0 + \hat{a}_1 \delta_1] + [\hat{\beta}_0 + \hat{\beta}_1 \delta_1] X + \dots$

$\delta_1 = 0$

$\delta_1 = 1$

$\hat{\beta}_0 > 0$

$\hat{\beta}_1 \simeq -2 \hat{\beta}_0$

$\hat{a}_1$

$\hat{a}_0$

various subgroups for which interactions are specified need not be mutually exclusive.

The nature of assumption of additivity in first order interactions bears further clarification by a simple example. Suppose we wished to allow additive interactions between the slope of Y on X and race and union membership with all other factors held constant. We would define two indicator variables such as:

5. δ_1 = 0 for whites

         1 for nonwhites

     δ_2 = 0 for nonunion members

         1 for union members

Note that the choice of the base group (all δ_i=0) is arbitrary so long as a singular matrix is avoided, but interpretation is easier if it represents a plausible and relatively frequent combination of characteristics.

The model is then specified as:

6. $Y = \alpha_0 + \alpha_1\delta_1 + \alpha_2\delta_2 + \beta_0 X + \beta_1\delta_1 X + \beta_2\delta_2 X + \epsilon$

After estimation we would obtain the predictive equation:

7. $\hat{Y} = (\hat{\alpha}_0 + \hat{\alpha}_1\delta_1 + \hat{\alpha}_2\delta_2) + (\hat{\beta}_0 + \hat{\beta}_1\delta_1 + \hat{\beta}_2\delta_2)X$

and the estimated curves for different groups would be

8a. $Y = \hat{\alpha}_0 + \hat{\beta}_0 X$ for white, nonunion

 b. $Y = \hat{\alpha}_0 + \hat{\alpha}_1 + (\hat{\beta}_0 + \hat{\beta}_1)X$ for nonwhite, nonunion

 c. $Y = \hat{\alpha}_0 + \hat{\alpha}_2 + (\hat{\beta}_0 + \hat{\beta}_2)X$ for white, union

 d. $Y = \hat{\alpha}_0 + \hat{\alpha}_1 + \hat{\alpha}_2 + (\hat{\beta}_0 + \hat{\beta}_1 + \hat{\beta}_2)X$ for nonwhite, union

Note that the difference between the coefficients for white nonunion members and those for nonwhite union members is assumed to be the sum of the individual effects of race and union membership.

If we wished to relax the assumption of additivity in interactions and allow full interactions, we would need to define another indicator variable, δ_3, for nonwhite union members. Estimation of this model would then yield the predictive equation:

9. $Y = (\hat{\alpha}'_0 + \hat{\alpha}'_1\delta_1 + \hat{\alpha}'_2\delta_2 + \hat{\alpha}'_3\delta_3) + (\hat{\beta}'_0 + \hat{\beta}'_1\delta_1 + \hat{\beta}'_2\delta_2 + \hat{\beta}'_3\delta_3)X$

The primes affixed to the estimated coefficients indicate that the coefficients are expected to be different under the complete specification.

The coefficients, $\hat{\alpha}_3'$ and $\hat{\beta}_3'$, give the estimated difference between effect of the specific combination of race and union characteristic and the sum of their effects when they occur separately. If the assumption of additivity is correct, however, the coefficients $\hat{\alpha}_3'$ and $\hat{\beta}_3'$ will be insignificant and the changes in other coefficients will be minor.

The specification of higher order interactions may well be necessary for some models, but it rapidly becomes expensive in parameters as the number of interacted characteristics increases. Complete interactions with the five sets of characteristics, for instance, would involve $2^5=32$ combinations of characteristics and 64 estimated parameters as compared with the 10 necessary for the additive first order interactions.

It is possible, of course, to specify a selected subset of higher order interactions. If, for instance, we wished to allow interactions of a slope co-efficient with race, union membership, and sex we might specify the second order interaction for nonwhite females but allow other combinations of characteristics to be represented by the sums of first order terms.

This similarity of the specification in equation 3 to the common specification of multiplicative interactions for metric variables should be noted. The equation:

10. $Y = \alpha + \beta_1 X + \beta_2 W + \beta_3 X*W + \ldots$

can be arranged:

11. $Y = (\alpha + \beta_2 W) + (\beta_1 + \beta_3 W)X + \ldots$

In this specification both the intercept and the coefficient of X vary linearly with W. Clearly, the order could be reversed so that the coefficient of W varies with X.

The metric interaction is very tidy so long as these linearities hold. If there are non-linearities such as threshold effects, however, the specification of the interaction with a categorical step function may well provide a better approximation to reality. The categorical specification is also likely to be more robust in its sensitivity to "odd ball" extreme cases.

It has also been our experience that a larger number of interaction effects can be specified by the categorical method since multicollinearity problems rapidly become severe with metric interactions.

Presentation and Interpretation of Coefficients

Frequently a researcher may wish to compare regression results from a model with categorical interactions on some slope parameter with results from a model with a single slope parameter and only dummy variables for the corresponding categories. As mentioned earlier, the indicator variables are included in both regressions while the interactive model also includes their cross products with the slope variable. Though the included indicator variables are identical in both cases, one must be careful in comparing their estimated coefficients. In the simple model a single slope is estimated for all categories and the dummy variable coefficients are simple shift parameters which do not depend on the value of the slope variable at which they are evaluated. In the interactive model, however, the coefficients of the indicator variables represent the distances between the various regression lines evaluated at the zero point of the slope variable and since the slopes differ, the distances between the lines would change if evaluated at a different point. In many cases the mean of the slope variable is substantially removed from zero so that differences in intercepts evaluated at zero are quite unlike differences evaluated at the mean.

It is the latter set of values, the distances between the regression lines of various subgroups in the interactive model *evaluated at the point of means,* which is most nearly comparable to the set of dummy variable coefficients from the simple model.

The nature of this comparison is illustrated in Figure D.2. The distributions in Figure D.2a and D.2b are identical, but D.2a shows the estimated regression lines from a simple linear regression with two dummy variables while D.2b shows the regression lines from a properly specified model allowing additive slope interactions with the two dummy variable characteristics. It is clear from the figure that the differences between the regression lines of Figure D.2b at X=0 are not comparable to those in Figure D.2a. When the differences are translated to the mean of X as indicated by the $\hat{\alpha}'_i$ in Figure D.2b we can see direct comparability. In the figure the subgroups all have the same mean values of the X variable so that the translated intercepts in the interactive model are exactly equal to the dummy variable coefficients from the simple model. When the subgroups have different means on the interacted variable this exact comparability is lost, but evaluation at the mean of X generally provides values of the coefficients which are more easily interpretable. The translation of the coefficients is accomplished by use of the simple formula:

$$\hat{\alpha}'_i = \hat{\alpha}_i + \hat{\beta}_i \overline{X}$$

FIGURE D.2

2a

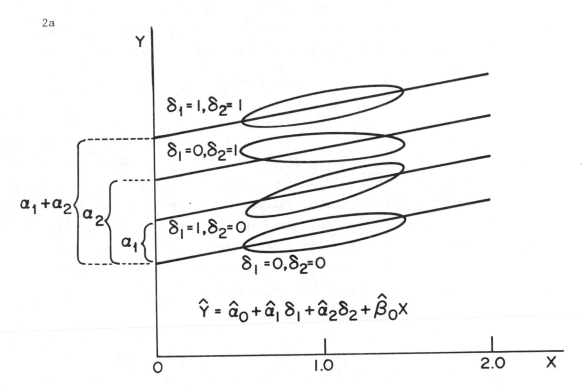

$$\hat{Y} = \hat{\alpha}_0 + \hat{\alpha}_1 \delta_1 + \hat{\alpha}_2 \delta_2 + \hat{\beta}_0 X$$

2b

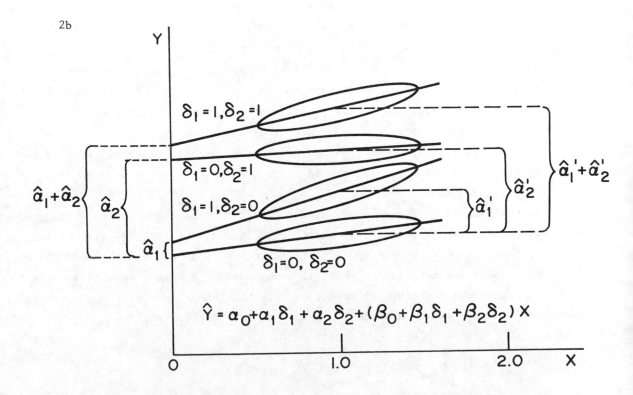

$$\hat{Y} = \alpha_0 + \alpha_1 \delta_1 + \alpha_2 \delta_2 + (\beta_0 + \beta_1 \delta_1 + \beta_2 \delta_2) X$$

Alternatively, the model can be specified so that the zero point of the interacted variables is at the sample mean or a selected value near the center of the distribution. The model of equation 6. would be specified as

$$12. \quad Y = \alpha_0 + \alpha_1 \delta_1 + \alpha_2 \delta_2 + \beta_0 X + \beta_1 \delta_1 (X - \bar{X}) + \beta_2 \delta_2 (X - \bar{X})$$

Under this specification the estimated coefficients $\hat{\alpha}_1$ and $\hat{\alpha}_2$ give the distances between the subgroup regression lines evaluated at $\bar{X}$. In our experience with models specified in this manner the estimated coefficients $\hat{\alpha}_i$ are the same as the translated coefficients from specification 6. and both are closely comparable to the dummy variable coefficients from the simple model. Further, the standard errors estimated under specification 12. are also very close to the standard errors of the dummy coefficients in the simple model. This indicates that those standard errors may be used as good approximations for coefficients estimated under specification 6. and translated to the mean value.

Other Useful Applications

A curvilinear relationship in a single variable may be treated as an interaction of that variable with itself. As illustrated in Figure D.3, indicator variables may be specified for intervals of the independent variable, so that the curve is approximated by a set of straight line segments. Again, one advantage of such a specification over a specific curved function, such as a polynomial or logarithm, is its robustness in the face of extreme cases.

Another related specification is useful in the case of an independent variable which takes value zero for some substantial subset of observations and has a continuous distribution on the positive or negative half-line for the remainder of the observations. In such cases there is often an effect associated with the simple presence of a non-zero value on the variable which may be different from the effect due to variations in the non-zero value. Two examples are illustrated in Figure D.4.

In the example of Figure D.4a, neither a slope nor a dummy variable for positive values of X_i would reveal any relationship if one were included without the other. In Figure D.4b, proper specification requires only a dummy variable, but if X_i alone were included in the model it would appear to have a significant effect. If the model is initially specified with both slope and intercept, unnecessary complications can be dropped if they prove insignificant.

FIGURE D.3

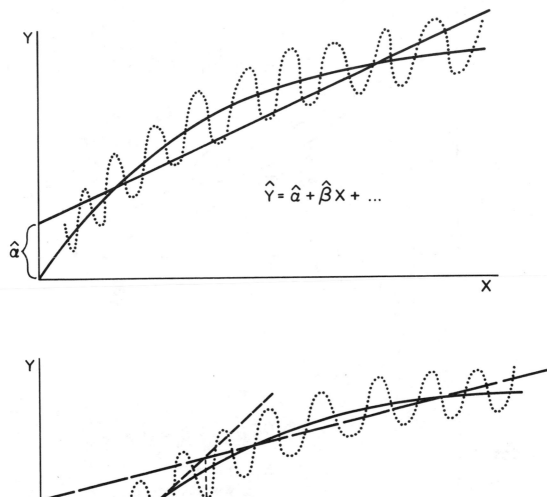

$$\hat{Y} = \hat{\alpha} + \hat{\beta}X + \ldots$$

$\hat{\alpha}$

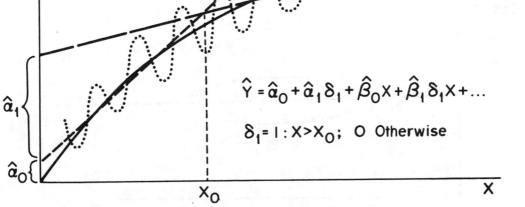

$$\hat{Y} = \hat{\alpha}_0 + \hat{\alpha}_1\delta_1 + \hat{\beta}_0 X + \hat{\beta}_1\delta_1 X + \ldots$$

$$\delta_1 = 1 : X > X_0; \quad 0 \text{ Otherwise}$$

$\hat{\alpha}_1$

$\hat{\alpha}_0$

X_0

FIGURE D.4

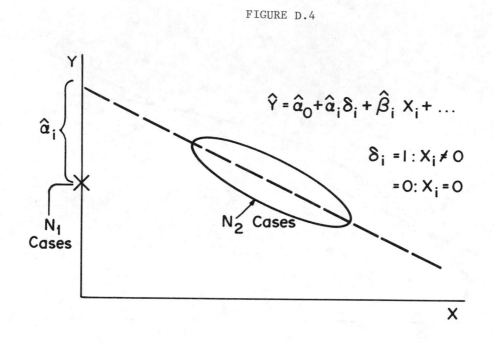

$$\hat{Y} = \hat{a}_0 + \hat{a}_i \delta_i + \hat{\beta}_i X_i + \ldots$$

$$\delta_i = 1 : X_i \neq 0$$
$$= 0 : X_i = 0$$

$\hat{a}_i$

N_1 Cases

N_2 Cases

X

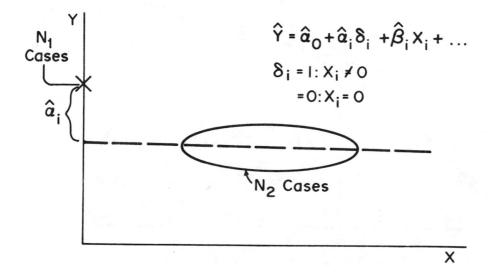

$$\hat{Y} = \hat{a}_0 + \hat{a}_i \delta_i + \hat{\beta}_i X_i + \ldots$$

$$\delta_i = 1 : X_i \neq 0$$
$$= 0 : X_i = 0$$

N_1 Cases

$\hat{a}_i$

N_2 Cases

X

Appendix E

DICHOTOMOUS DEPENDENT VARIABLES

Some of the analysis in this volume deals with dichotomous dependent variables. Geographic mobility is scored zero for stayers and one for movers. Labor force participation, movement from below to above the poverty line, and other occurences are scored similarly. This appendix discusses some statistical issues relating to dichotomous dependent variables analyzed by regression or Multiple Classification Analysis (MCA).

There are three specific problems associated with the application of least-squares regression to analysis of dichotomous dependent variables (referred to as estimation of a linear probability function). First, estimated probabilities, $\hat{y}$, are not constrained to the 0-1 range. For example, the regression of a dichotomous dependent variable y on a continuous x might produce a least squares regression line as drawn in Figure E.1. For the lowest values of x, $\hat{y}$ is less than zero, and for the largest x, $\hat{y}$ is greater than 1.[1] Dummy variable regression (e.g., MCA) can also produce estimated probabilities less than zero or greater than one. Estimated probabilities outside of the 0-1 range are obviously not easily interpreted.

A second problem is attributable to the linearity assumption of regression analysis. Consider the following bivariate distribution:[2]

x	y	probability
0	0	.1
1	0	.4
2	1	.4
3	1	.1

Here y can be predicted from x with certainty, but the squared simple correlation coefficient, ρ^2, is only .75. Linearity is not assumed in dummy variable regression, so this problem does not necessarily arise with MCA.

---

[1] Lansing, John B., and James N. Morgan, Economic Survey Methods (Ann Arbor: Institute for Social Research, The University of Michigan, 1971, pp. 296-297.

[2] Example taken from Neter, John and E. Scott Maynes, "On the Appropriateness of the Correlation Coefficient with a 0,1 Dependent Variable," Journal of the American Statistical Association, 65:330 (June 1970), pp. 501-509.

FIGURE E.1

Least Square Regression Line on Dichotomous Dependent Variable

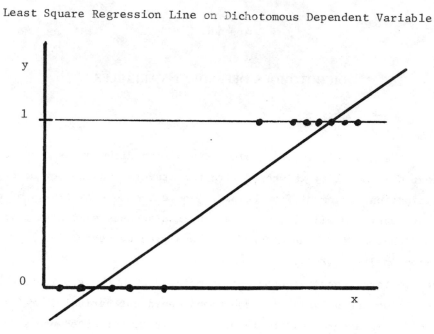

FIGURE E.2

Logit Transformation of Probability

$$\text{Logit} = \text{Log}\ \frac{p}{1-p}$$

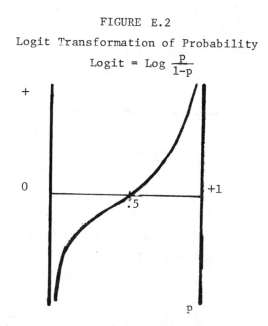

A third difficulty is that a dichotomous dependent variable results in a heteroscedastic error term.[1] In multiple regression, for a given vector of independent variables X, the error term for observation i is:

$$e_i = y_i - X_i'B.$$

B is the vector of estimated regression coefficients. Since y_i is either 0 or 1, e_i must be either $-X'B$ or $1-X'B$. If $E(e_i) = 0$, e_i must be distributed as follows in order to maintain the expected value of zero for the error term.

e_i	$f(e_i)$
$-X'B$	$1-X'B$
$1-X'B$	$X'B$

The variance of e_i is then:

$$E(e_i^2)=(-X'B)^2 (1-X'B) + (1-X'B)^2 (X'B) = (X'B) (1-X'B),$$

and since $X'B = y_i = Ey_i$,

$$E(e_i^2) = Ey_i(1-Ey_i).$$

The disturbance is therefore heteroscedastic, varying systematically with Ey_1. Ordinary least squares results in inefficient (non-minimum variance) estimates of the regression coefficients, if the error term is heteroscedastic, although the estimated coefficients remain unbiased. The degree of heteroscedasticity is determined by the specific distribution of the estimated probabilities. Models in which y does not vary substantially (i.e., a poor model in the sense that the independent variables do not markedly discriminate "1" responses from "0" responses on the dependent variable) are less heteroscedastic. And because of the distribution of $y(1-y)$ for $0 \leq y \leq 1$, for models with a given variance of the estimated probability $(Var \; \hat{y} = \sum(\hat{y}_i-\bar{y})/n)$, those with $\bar{y}$ near .5 will be less heteroscedastic than those with a large or small mean probability.

Solutions have been proposed for each of the above mentioned statistical problems associated with dichotomous dependent variables. To deal with the dilemma of estimated probabilities outside of the 0-1 range, a number of transformations of the estimated probability have been proposed. An early and prominent transformation is the probit,[2] the effect of which is to fit the probability to the independent variables with an S-shaped curve instead of with a straight line. The logit transformation is another method of fitting the data to an S-shaped curve. Theil[3] is one advocate of this transformation, which is considerably more

---

[1] Goldberger, Arthur, Econometric Theory(N.Y.: Wiley, 1964), pp. 248-250.

[2] Finney, D. J., Probit Analysis, 2nd ed., (Cambridge: Cambridge University Press, 1952).

[3] Theil, Henry, "On the Estimation of Relationships Involving Qualitative Variables," American Journal of Sociology, 76:1 (July 1970), pp. 103-154.

straightforward than the probit. The resulting model appears as

$$\log_e(p/(1-p)) = b_o + \sum_i b_i x_i.$$

The term on the left hand side, the log of the odds $(p/(1-p))$, is related to p as shown in Figure E.2.[1] When expressed in p, the model takes the logistic form, $p = 1/(1 + \exp(-b_o - \sum_i b_i x_i))$. The logit takes on the value $-\infty$ when p=0 and $+\infty$ when p=1. One characteristic of both the logit and probit transformation is that a given change in the value of an independent variable will have less effect on the estimated probability if the probability is near zero or one than if the probability is near one-half. The intuitive interpretation of this feature is that an individual's performance as indicated by the 0-1 dependent variable is more responsive to changes in the independent variables if that individual is "flexible" as indicated by a probability near .5. Note the contrast with the linear probability function, where a given change in an independent variable causes the same change in the estimated probability regardless of the value of the probability.[2] Berkson gives examples demonstrating that logistic and probit transformations result in similar conclusions as to the effects of the independent variables on the dependent variable.[3]

In response to the problem of the linearity assumption, Neter and Maynes[4] discuss several alternatives to the correlation coefficient in cases where the dependent variable is dichotomous. One proposed alternative is the familiar correlation ratio, eta^2, which in the case of a dichotomous y is defined by

$$eta^2_{yx} = \sum_h w_h (p_h - p)^2 / (p(1-p))$$

where y takes on the values 1 and 0 with probabilities p and 1-p, respectively, x takes on the values x_h (h=1,..,m) with probabilities w_h, and $p_h = E(y/x_h)$. The advantage of this procedure is that there is no assumption of linearity in the dependence of y on x. If x is a continuous variable, this approach requires that x be transformed into ordinal categories. This is precisely the procedure followed in MCA. The R^2 from an MCA analysis is actually a multiple eta^2, where the p_h values are derived from a multiple regression of the dependent variable on more than one x.

---

[1] Theil (1970), p. 107.

[2] A computer program for the non-linear estimates required to fit the multivariate logit has been developed and tested at the Institute for Social Research. Preliminary tests show that with samples of 1000 or more, even when the probability is around .05, the reduction in error variance is quite small.

[3] Berkson, Joseph, "Application of the Logistic Function to Bio-Assay," Journal of the American Statistical Association, 39: (Sept. 1944), pp. 357-365.

[4] Neter and Maynes (1970).

The standard procedure for adjusting for heteroscedastic residuals is to re-sort to generalized least squares. As Goldberger[1] demonstrates, in the case of a dichotomous dependent variable the appropriate procedure is to use the ordinary least squares regression to obtain the calculated values $\hat{y}_i = E y_i$ and then use $\hat{y}_i (1 - \hat{y}_i)$ as the diagonal elements of an estimated disturbance matrix Ω_*, and finally recompute $b_* = (x' \Omega_*^{-1} x)^{-1} (x' \Omega_*^{-1} y)$ to get best linear unbiased estimates of the b_* vector.

The purpose of this tedious procedure is to weigh more heavily in computing the regression coefficients those observations that give more precise estimates of the dependent variables. Adjustments for heteroscedasticity have not been made in the statistical analyses in this volume.

A current debate concerns R^2 statistics in the context of 0-1 dependent variables. Regression and MCA analyses in which the dependent variable is dichotomous typically result in low R^2s. R-squareds greater than .30 are practically unheard of. This can be understood if we recall that the regression or MCA equation generates a probability as the expected value of the dependent variable, whereas the observed values of y will all be either zero or one. Morrison[2] specifies a method for ascertaining upper bounds for R^2 corresponding to different distributions of the "true" probability of an event occuring. He uses the example of flipping a bent coin with (true) probability of .7 of falling heads. While the maximum likelihood prediction of the outcome would be 1, the prediction resulting in the minimum mean squared error would be .7. Morrison defines the true probability as that value resulting from a perfect model. His use of the adjectives "true" and "perfect" is questionable. A perfect model, as Morrison sees it, is apparently one that assigns probabilities correctly ($p_i = \hat{p}_i$ for all cases i) within the limits of the particular functional form and set of independent variables one selects. But as Goldberger notes,[3] the adjective "perfect" is best reserved for a model that predicts each outcome correctly. This would require that all the estimated probabilities, $\hat{p}$, be either 0 or 1 and coincide perfectly with the observed outcomes. This could be done in Morrison's bent coin example if measurements of wind velocity, thumb thrust, etc., were available. "However rarely it may occur in practice, in principle it is surely possible to have a model which is sufficiently sharp, i.e., contains enough explana-

[1] Goldberger (1964), pp. 249-250.

[2] Morrison, Donald G., "Upper Bounds for Correlations Between Binary Outcomes and Probabilistic Predictions," _Journal of the American Statistical Association_, 68:341 (March 1973), p. 84.

[3] Goldberger, Arthur, "Correlations Between Binary Outcomes and Probabilistic Predictions," _Journal of the American Statistical Association_, 68:341 (March 1973), p. 84.

tory variables, to correctly predict every outcome of a binary variable."
Goldberger concludes that "for a binary variable, as for a continuous variable,
the proper upper bound on R^2 is unity."

Most of the analyses of 0-1 dependent variables in this volume use the
structure of linear probability functions. But the linearity assumption is often
effectively discarded through use of MCA or traditional dummy variable methods.
Estimated probabilities outside the 0-1 range do occur but hopefully are few in
number. And the heteroscedasticity results in unbiased but inefficient coefficient estimates. It also may result in inconsistent standard errors and hence
wrong judgments on significance. Low R^2s are the rule rather than the exception
when the dependent variable is dichotomous and models should not be judged by
this criterion alone.

In conclusion, although there are statistical problems associated with
analysis of dichotomous dependent variables, they are unlikely to alter the general conclusions of the studies reported in this volume.

Appendix F

MEASURES OF ACHIEVEMENT MOTIVATION AND COGNITIVE ABILITY

The original model underlying this Panel Study called for a measure of mental ability. In the first wave of interviews a simplified version of the Ammon's Quick Test was administered experimentally to a small subsample of the panel. It was decided, however, that it was necessary to develop a measure more appropriate for use in voluntary interviews with an adult population. In the belief that psychological factors are essential variables in explaining economic behavior, we asked psychologists Joseph Veroff, Lou McClelland, and Kent Marquis of the Institute for Social Research to explore the feasibility of developing measure of motivation and cognitive ability which could be used in household interviews.

The measures would have to meet fairly stringent criteria:

1. Be feasible in a cross-section sample of the United State population.

2. Be reliable and valid for major groups within the population.

3. Not provoke hostility or anxiety, and have a reasonable and honest explanation to the respondents.

4. Be extremely brief -- no more than five minutes even for respondents who are difficult to interview.

Of these criteria, time was the most severe restriction. From past research it was clear that a single measure of achievement motivation by itself would not have much predictive value. Multiple measures would be essential. To avoid cultural bias in measuring intelligence, it was originally thought that here also at least two different assessment procedures would be necessary.

Pilot studies investigating the usefulness of existing intelligence and motivation measures were undertaken. After two preliminary surveys in Jackson, Michigan, seven measures of intelligence were selected for further testing in a final survey in Detroit. For testing verbal mediational facility the Lorge-

---

[1]See, Measuring Intelligence and Achievement Motivation in Surveys, by J. Veroff, L. McClelland, and K. Marquis, Survey Research Center, Institute for Social Research, Ann Arbor, Michigan, 1971.

Thorndike Sentence Completion Test, Ammon's Quick Test, and Weschler's Information Test were tried. To test perceptual performance Weschler's Digit Span,
Raven's Progressive Matrices, and Picture Order Central and Incidental Tests
were tried.

Although the study's directors had expected to recommend at least two types
of measures, each reflecting a different kind of intelligence, they found that
one test, the Sentence Completion Test, was significantly correlated with every
other measure, even when respondent's education, age, race, and sex were statistically controlled for. Thus it alone was included in the fifth wave.

The test asks the respondent to supply from a set of alternatives a missing
word in a sentence. Although it is a measure of verbal comprehension and learning, the Sentence Completion Test also requires hypothesis testing and skill in
patterning sentences similar to skills involved in the perceptual performance
measures which were used. It was, therefore, able to stand by itself as a valid
measure of intelligence.

The Detroit interview also included many varied achievement measures.
Among these were several new methods plus revisions of some traditional ones.
The measure finally selected was composed of a series of 14 questions. For most
groups, except for black females, this measure correlates moderately well with
both a projective measure of achievement and a behavioral assessment of moderate
risk taking.

We have found that both the "I.Q." test and achievement motivation scores
correlate well with other variables (see Table F.1), but not so well that they
have no potential explanatory power of their own.

Administering these tests to the respondents caused no particular problem.
Although some interviewers predicted trouble, there were, in fact, very few
refusals.

In the word test the interviewers read the sentences and choice of words to
the respondent and the respondent was given a booklet containing the same sentences and words to follow along. Most respondents accepted the test calmly --
even enthusiastically. The test did cause difficulties in telephone interviews
as the respondent had no booklet. It was almost impossible to administer to
people who could not read or had trouble with English and a very few respondents
were not able to cope with it at all.

Some of the respondents were confused and irritated by a few of the motivation questions of the "which would you rather" variety, complaining that no clear
alternatives were offered -- that sometimes both choices were desirable and could
probably be true at the same time. However, in 1972 our response rate was even

higher than in 1971, hence few respondents can have been seriously antagonized by these tests.

There is, of course, the problem that these two measures were taken on the fifth interview, and one can never be sure they do not in part reflect the results of the past five years, rather than permanent personality or ability characteristics which caused that experience. People in white collar jobs, for instance, might use words more often and learn how to handle them more effectively. And recent success might affect people's achievement imagery. So while both measures intend to measure a stable concept, the final proof of their explanatory power will only come if this panel is followed for enough future years so that the outcome can be measured *after* the measurement of these factors. And even then a complex dynamic model would have to be invoked.

Regardless of the causal mechanism, however, if people are given intelligence tests as part of the qualification requirements for jobs, then their ability to handle such tests is an important matter.

The Ammon's Quick Test was administered as an experiment to a small subsample of this panel in 1968, the first wave of interviews. It involved sets of four pictures and a list of words to be read off. Each word was related to one of the four pictures, and the respondent was asked to select which one. This involved not only vocabulary, but also some analogous reasoning. The original design of the test called for careful administration with more and more difficult words until the subject missed four in a row. We could not do this with interviewers and voluntary respondents, so we selected a relatively easy set, attempting to distinguish only the middle range, not the geniuses.

At any rate, for a few respondents, we have scores for this test in 1968 and for the sentence completion test in 1972.[1] The inter-person correlation between the two is relatively high, as can be seen in Table F.2.

---

[1] For details of the early test, see Volume II of the documentation, p. 46, and Martha J. Mednick, "The Relationships of the Ammon's Quick Test of Intelligence to Other Ability Measures," Psychological Reports, 72 (1965), pp 48-59.

TABLE F.2

Picture-Word Test in 1968

Sentence Completion Test in 1972	0-5	6-9	10-11	12	13	14 (All Right)
0	0	1	0	0	0	3
1-3	9	10	2	0	0	0
4-6	62	39	23	14	7	3
7	12	13	14	16	2	3
8	0	13	33	10	3	5
9	10	13	8	20	20	10
10	7	9	19	32	29	24
11	0	0	1	1	31	21
12	0	2	0	7	7	17
13	0	0	0	0	1	13
	100%	100%	100%	100%	100%	99%
Number of Cases	11	58	51	56	67	82

Rank Correlation (Kendall's TauB) = .47

NOTE: A very few cases where head was not the respondent in one year or the other may reduce the correlation, but most such cases were omitted.

TABLE F.1

Correlations of Test Score ("IQ") and Achievement Motivation (N/Ach) with Other Variables

Number	Variable	Test Score		Achievement Motivation	
		Tau-B[*]	Cramer's V	Tau-B	Cramer's V
2828	Race	-.23	.19	-.06	.07
2915	Geographic mobility	.01	.06	.04	.06
2907	Hourly earnings	.25	.13	.18	.10
2818	Number of states lived in	.06	.06	.10	.08
2543	Sex (femaleness)	-.10	.13	-.17	.21
2822	Father's education	.17	.11	.11	.08
2823	Head's education	.37	.19	.25	.13
2813	Religion	**	.08	**	.06
3825	Head a veteran	.12	.10	.11	.09
2911	Region	**	.07	**	.07
2975	Number of inter-county moves	.08	.08	.11	.09
2974	Number of changes of residence	.02	.06	.09	.08
2973	Changes in jobs	.14	.10	.10	.08
2972	Changes in family composition	-.01	.06	.04	.06
2934	Age	-.12	.09	-.14	.09
2950	Achievement motivation	.22	.12	--	--
2939	Efficacy-Planning index	.18	.12	.20	.13
2940	Trust-hostility index	.20	.19	.09	.08
2942	Aspiration-ambition index	-.02	.06	.12	.09
2943	Real earnings activity index	.03	.07	.07	.07
2944	Economizing index	-.11	.08	-.11	.08
2945	Risk avoidance index	.21	.12	.11	.07
2946	Planning acts index	.17	.11	.13	.09
2947	Connectedness index	.05	.08	.01	.05
2948	Money earning acts index	.14	.10	.14	.09
2804	Number of siblings of head	-.17	.09	-.08	.06

---

[*] For explanation of these two measures of association, see Appendix C.

** Inappropriate - no natural ranking.

Appendix G

THE COMPOSITION OF INCOME AND OTHER POLICY-RELEVANT CHARACTERISTICS OF FAMILIES AT DIFFERENT LEVELS OF WELL-BEING

In our attempts to measure income and well-being carefully, we have asked about components of money income, not merely its total, and have also asked about nonmoney components of income and about some of the costs involved in earning income. Hence, we can look at the composition of income, both as an explanation-description and as a base for assessing the impact of certain public policies. Since we are mostly interested in differences between persons at different levels of well-being, we concentrate on a single classification variable -- the ratio of total family money income to a needs standard. This makes use of the most common income measure, but also takes account of family size and structure to re-sort people by their level of well-being (or ability to pay). It is highly correlated with more sophisticated alternatives that take account of nonmoney income and/or leisure.

Total family money income can be thought of as having three main components: labor earnings, income from capital (interest, dividends, rent, royalties), and transfer income. Transfer is income that is not currently earned by the productivity of labor or capital. It includes payments from the social security system, retirement pensions, unemployment compensation, and workmen's compensation, all of which were in some part paid for earlier by contributions (explicitly or implicitly part of earnings). It also includes "non-contributory" transfers such as Aid to Dependent Children, Aid to Families with Dependent Children, and other welfare given purely on the basis of need.

Figure G.1 shows how two of these three components, and the major element of the third (head's labor income) vary as a fraction of total money income at different levels of well-being. Table G.1 gives more detail on the percentages, and Tables G.2 and G.3 give still more detail on the dollar amounts for those who may want to focus on individual items or combine them in different ways. Transfer incomes are a substantial fraction of income at the lower levels of well-being and capital income is important only at the very top. But when we include nonmoney capital income (imputed rent from owning a home) the picture changes.

388

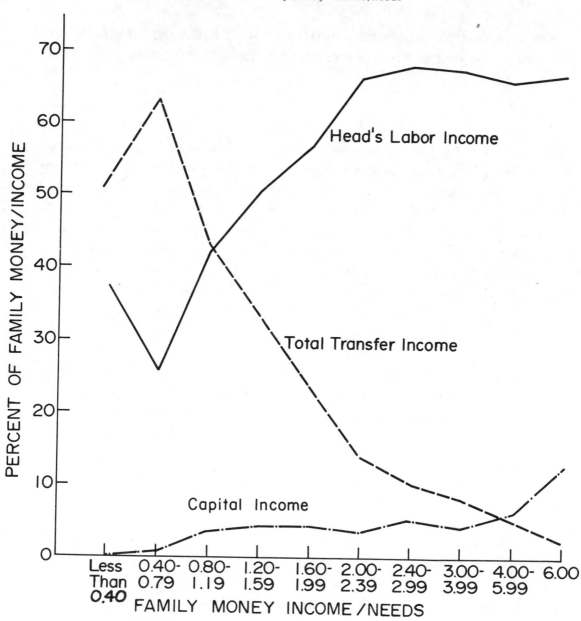

FIGURE G.1

Percentages of Total Family Money Income from Three Sources
by Level of Family Money Income/Needs

TABLE G.1

Some Major Components, as Percent of Total Family Money Income
by Family Income/Needs

Family Money Income/Needs	Head's Labor Income	Wife's Labor Income	Head & Wife Capital Income	Total Taxable Income	ADC, AFDC[*] Other Welfare (Non-Contributory Transfers)	Social Security, Other Ret. (Contributory Transfers)	Total Money Transfer Income[**]
Less than .40	.379	.047	.000	.490	.223	.182	.509
.40-.79	.258	.036	.007	.364	.224	.279	.635
.80-1.19	.421	.033	.035	.563	.139	.217	.436
1.20-1.59	.508	.051	.044	.661	.065	.199	.338
1.60-1.99	.571	.071	.044	.761	.022	.147	.238
2.00-2.39	.667	.080	.036	.859	.007	.097	.140
2.40-2.99	.681	.080	.055	.892	.002	.067	.107
3.00-3.99	.676	.115	.044	.914	.002	.053	.085
4.00-5.99	.665	.132	.065	.945	.003	.035	.054
6.00 or more	.672	.124	.130	.974	.000	.018	.025
All levels of income/needs	.650	.109	.071	.901	.010	.060	.098

*
 Includes taxable income of others in family.
**
 Includes transfer income of others in family, other transfer income of head and wife,
 e.g., unemployment compensation, workman's compensation, alimony, etc.

MTR 1061

TABLE G.2

Taxable Income*

Family money income/needs	Head's labor income	Wife's labor income	Head-Wife capital income	Total taxable income
Less than .40	$ 301	$ 38	$ 0	$ 389
.40 - .79	540	76	16	763
.80 - 1.19	1430	114	121	1913
1.20 - 1.59	2281	229	202	2968
1.60 - 1.99	3491	436	274	4648
2.00 - 2.39	5032	610	274	6482
2.40 - 2.99	6589	775	535	8630
3.00 - 3.99	7945	1354	527	10,750
4.00 - 5.99	10,255	2044	1012	14,569
6.00 or more	17,063	3164	3317	24,705
All	7089	1188	783	9818

*The sampling errors of these means depend on the number of cases (given in Table G.1), the standard deviation (which varies from half the mean to several times the mean, the latter for items which are zero for many people) and the sample design effect (which increases them by about 10-20%); see Appendix B.

MTR 1061

TABLE G.3

Transfer Income

Family money income/needs	Head and Wife							Others		Total Money Income
	ADC-AFDC	Other Welfare	Social Security	Other Retirement	Unempl. Comp; Workmen's Comp.	Alimony Child Support	Mis. cell.[*]	Other's Transfer Income	Total Money Transfer Income	
Less than .40	$116	$ 61	$ 108	$ 37	$ 1	$ 4	$ 65	$ 12	$ 404	$ 793
.40-.79	250	219	473	111	17	64	108	86	1328	2091
.80-1.19	301	174	581	158	41	60	95	70	1480	3394
1.20-1.59	128	166	710	185	86	22	133	90	1520	4489
1.60-1.99	94	45	649	249	79	69	82	191	1458	6107
2.00-2.39	40	14	515	222	71	40	79	81	1062	7544
2.40-2.99	12	17	375	282	64	57	96	133	1036	9667
3.00-3.99	21	7	345	284	75	49	130	90	1001	11,751
4.00-5.99	4	1	206	345	59	36	102	79	832	15,401
6.00 or more	0	0	110	366	10	31	25	117	659	25,363
All	$ 66	$ 49	$ 394	$266	$58	$46	$ 95	$102	$1076	$10,894

---

[*] Includes help from relatives, transfers explicitly to wife, and "other."

MTR 1061

The details on transfer income are illuminating, since only the non-contributory transfers are impressively redistributive. The contributory element of the others, even though they are also partially redistributive through insurance-like arrangements, means that those who earned more contributed more, and get more out later. But they are also more likely to have other income, so that these contributory transfers are less redistributive between people than across time for the same person, transferring income from when it was earned to when it is needed more.

Money income, however, does not include some important nonmoney income items that contribute to people's economic status. Some are earned by labor (home production), some earned by capital (imputed rent on equity in a home) and some are unearned transfers (free rent, free food, food stamp subsidies). There are also money deductions from income which leave somewhat less available for the family, deductions like federal income taxes, commuting costs, union dues, child care costs when parents are working, and support of relatives or ex-wives. Figure G.2 gives a broad picture of the relative importance of labor income, transfers, and income from capital when the nonmoney items are included too. The most obvious change is the increased importance of capital (imputed rent), which at the very bottom even rises in importance -- mostly because of retired people with low cash incomes but with a home paid for. Table G.4 shows somewhat more detail on the percentages of nonmoney incomes *as a percent of income*, and Table G.5 gives still more detail in dollar form. At the very lowest level of family income/needs, the nonmoney items are more than 100% of the money income more than doubling the family's real income.

What about the costs of earning income? The main cost is federal income taxes, which are estimated in the editing process, assuming average deductions but making use of direct information on blindness, age, and support of dependents outside the home (see Table G.6). *All* the costs go up with income, but it must be kept in mind that this is not an exhaustive coverage of costs. State and local income taxes are not included nor are property taxes, sales taxes, and charitable contributions. (Some of these would have to be estimated net of saving on federal income tax for those who itemize.)

Finally, we have not included in income the value of housework and child care, nor have we taken account of the labor time spent earning income which determines the amount of leisure time left to enjoy it. Table G.7 gives in hours, not dollars, the amount of housework "produced" by the members of the family or received free from outside. It also shows the leisure time per adult, which is lower at higher levels of family well-being, indicating that to some extent the

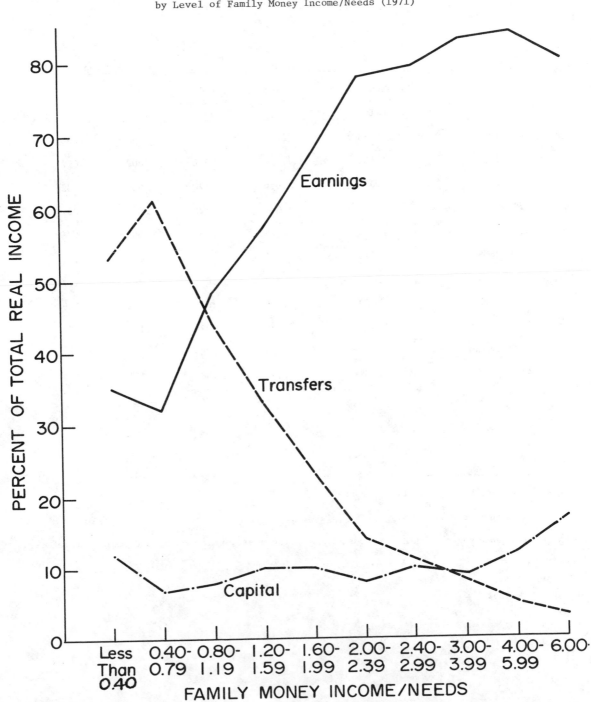

FIGURE G.2

Percentages of Total Real and Money Income from Three Sources
by Level of Family Money Income/Needs (1971)

TABLE G.4

Some Not-Included Elements as Percent of Total Family Money Income
by Family Money Income/Needs

| | Additions | | | Deductions | |
	Non-Money Labor or Capital Income*	Non-Money Transfer Income	Total Non-Money Income	Taxes	Total
Less than .40	.528	.621	.150	0	.004
.40-.79	.151	.164	.316	.002	.022
.80-1.19	.094	.076	.170	.008	.032
1.20-1.59	.030	.030	.128	.028	.057
1.60-1.99	.098	.024	.122	.045	.076
2.00-2.39	.079	.014	.093	.065	.100
2.40-2.99	.078	.010	.088	.083	.117
3.00-3.99	.073	.005	.079	.101	.139
4.00-5.99	.069	.005	.074	.124	.157
6.00 or more	.056	.003	.059	.180	.217
All	.072	.011	.084	.114	.149

---

*
 Includes home production, imputed rent.
**
 Includes free rent, free food, food stamp subsidy
***
 Includes taxes, child care costs, commuting costs, union dues, and help to relatives.

MTR 1061

TABLE G.5

Non-Money Components of Income

Family money income/needs	Labor			Capital	Transfers						Total Money Income
	Saved on A&R	Grow Own Food	Car Repair	Imputed Rent	Free Rent	Food Stamps	At Work School	Other Food Saved	Total Real Transfer		
Less than .40	$112	$36	$62	$209	$122	$245	$57	$69	$493		$912
.40-.79	78	27	21	190	67	210	34	33	344		660
.80-1.19	45	39	29	207	63	123	36	36	258		578
1.20-1.59	65	24	29	320	33	42	40	21	136		574
1.60-1.99	98	42	45	416	46	37	29	30	142		743
2.00-2.39	115	29	49	403	48	14	17	25	104		700
2.40-2.99	164	28	54	513	37	5	38	13	93		852
3.00-3.99	201	28	50	588	25	4	22	9	60		927
4.00-5.99	223	30	49	770	28	0	29	17	74		1146
6.00 or more	238	18	31	1152	24	0	36	5	65		1504
All	$157	$29	$43	$566	$38	$32	$31	$19	$120		$915

MTR 1061

TABLE G.6

Costs of Earning Income

Family money income/needs	Child care costs	Contri- butions	Union dues	Commuting costs head	wife	Taxes head & wife	others	Total
Less than .40	$ 0	$ 0	$ 4	$ 24	$ 0	$ 0	$ 0	$ 28
.40 - .79	0	8	1	27	5	3	2	46
.80 - 1.19	6	16	4	50	7	21	5	109
1.20 - 1.59	9	11	8	89	12	97	29	255
1.60 - 1.99	21	31	12	100	23	256	20	463
2.00 - 2.39	23	52	22	138	26	461	33	755
2.40 - 2.99	15	71	26	183	31	749	58	1133
3.00 - 3.99	38	151	33	189	44	1099	82	1636
4.00 - 5.99	31	158	28	226	65	1783	127	2418
6.00 or more	38	535	28	255	77	4427	141	5501
All	$24	$132	$27	$161	$38	$1174	$ 67	$1623

MTR 1061

TABLE G.7

Hours of Housework

Family money income/needs	Wife or Single head	Husband	Others	Free from Outside	Leisure* per Adult
Less than .40	1059	9	293	443	4135
.40 - .79	1125	67	361	263	4310
.80 - 1.19	1237	77	262	208	4142
1.20 - 1.59	1230	58	263	228	4000
1.60 - 1.99	1342	79	242	286	3810
2.00 - 2.39	1409	79	187	220	3575
2.40 - 2.99	1488	107	254	157	3572
3.00 - 3.99	1406	107	196	265	3485
4.00 - 5.99	1301	117	167	215	3404
6.00 or more	1131	91	116	128	3406
All	1315	93	213	225	3654

*Total time minus (work and commuting time, 8 hours of sleep per day, time unemployed or ill, home production hours, housework time). Leisure is averaged for head and wife.

MTR 1061

levels are illusory, having been paid for by a sacrifice of leisure time. The
inequality of a measure of well-being that takes account of leisure too would be
less than the inequality of income alone, since there is a preponderance of smaller families (mostly older or very young) at the lower income levels.

It should not be inferred that the choice between more income and more leisure to enjoy it is always voluntary since other analysis indicates there are
substantial constraints on people's choices. Some do not get paid for extra work
on their main job, and many find it difficult to get more work if they want it.

Table G.8 gives the percent of families that have various sources of income
(or costs) so that the reader will know how many zeroes were averaged into the
numbers in the preceeding tables. It is at the higher levels of well-being where
there are the most wives working, the most frequent cases of other earners, and,
of course, the highest probability that there is income from capital. And most
of the types of nonmoney income are more frequent at the upper income/needs
levels. Transfer incomes are more likely to be reported at lower levels, but
even at the highest economic levels some people receive transfer incomes.

The remaining tables give distributions rather than averages, since there
are some people for whom items such as commuting or consumption of alcohol are
irrelevant.[1] The tables focus on items relevant to the analysis of public policy
issues. The differential impact of various public policies requires knowing the
extent to which they may affect mostly people at higher or at lower levels of
well-being (or of ability to pay). We produced most of these tables a second
time using a more comprehensive measure of well-being that included nonmoney components of income and deducted the main costs of earning income, but the results
were so similar that we restrict the tables to a single classification of families -- by total family money income relative to needs.

Table G.9 shows that it is the better-off families who are doing the most
miles of commuting. It is they who would benefit most from speeding of commuting
traffic, or pay most if gas prices go up or pollution controls lower gas mileage.
(They are also more likely to drive than use public transportation.)

Table G.10 indicates the relation of housing cost, paid or imputed, to
economic level of the family and tells us who would benefit from the substitution of other taxes for the property tax. Table G.11 focuses on the equity in
owned homes which is given favorable tax treatment by the deductibility of property taxes and the non-taxability of the imputed rent earned. Clearly the benefits go to those who need them least. The third table on housing gives house-

---

[1]A measure of association -- Cramer's V -- is given at the bottom of each table.
It assumes no rank ordering for uniformity across tables, though a rank correlation coefficient would be more appropriate for some of them.

TABLE G.8

Percentages With Various Forms of Income,
by Ratio of Family Money Income/Needs

Income/Needs	Head Labor Income	Wife Labor Income	Others Income	Capital Income	Head & Wife Transfer Income	Others Transfer Income	Free Rent	Food Stamps	Subsidized Other Food at Work or School	Free Food
Less than .40	.46	.05	.09	24	62	1	21	33	20	18
.40-.79	.44	.08	.16	13	83	9	13	35	26	21
.80-1.19	.60	14	19	33	71	6	11	25	24	17
1.20-1.59	.66	19	17	31	70	6	5	12	22	18
1.60-1.99	.75	21	24	38	60	10	7	10	17	13
2.00-2.39	.89	28	24	37	47	6	5	4	13	16
2.40-2.99	.87	32	26	46	40	7	4	2	17	11
3.00-3.99	.71	41	25	51	34	7	2	1	13	13
4.00-5.99	.93	47	29	66	28	5	2	0	13	10
6.00 or more	.97	50	25	84	16	4	2	0	16	8

	Saved on A&R	Saved Growing Food	Saved Repairing Car	Imputed Rent	New Taxes	Others' Taxes	Free Help From Outside
Less than .40	21	30	18	31	0	0	10
.40-.79	21	26	13	43	1	2	14
.80-1.19	27	35	23	38	19	3	17
1.20-1.59	32	29	29	50	43	5	19
1.60-1.99	38	31	31	57	62	8	17
2.00-2.39	44	34	39	59	82	10	17
2.40-2.99	44	31	40	62	87	11	14
3.00-3.99	54	30	46	65	91	13	18
4.00-5.99	50	27	41	70	96	15	15
6.00 or more	47	21	30	77	99	14	9

MTR 1061

TABLE G.9

Miles to Work For Husband Plus Wife Family Money Income/Needs

Total Miles To Work (One Way) (For Husband Plus Wife)	Less than 0.40	.40-.79	.80-1.19	1.20-1.59	1.60-1.99	2.00-2.39	2.40-2.99	3.00-3.99	4.00-5.99	6.00+
0	71	73	61	51	42	24	25	18	17	15
1	5	8	6	10	11	15	12	12	10	10
2	0	3	3	3	4	6	4	6	4	5
3	1	3	5	5	7	8	6	7	9	7
4	2	0	3	3	2	5	3	3	3	2
5	3	1	3	5	4	7	7	7	8	7
6-7	4	3	3	5	5	5	8	8	8	6
8-9	0	1	1	2	3	3	5	8	5	7
10-14	3	3	6	6	8	9	12	12	15	17
15-19	2	2	2	2	5	6	6	5	5	10
20-29	4	1	2	3	4	4	6	7	7	7
30-39	1	0	1	1	1	2	2	3	4	2
40-	1	0	0	1	0	2	2	2	2	2
Not ascertained	1	2	3	2	3	2	2	1	1	3
TOTAL	98	100	99	99	99	100	100	99	98	100
Percent of sample	1.0	5.1	7.7	8.9	9.0	8.4	13.0	16.9	19.4	10.7
Number of cases	101	474	576	583	524	458	620	701	684	349

$V=.17$

MTR 1061

TABLE G.10

Cost of Housing By Total 1971 Family Money Income/Needs
(for all 5060 families in early 1972)

Annual Cost of Housing - Paid or Imputed*	Less than 0.40	.40-.79	.80-1.19	1.20-1.59	1.60-1.99	2.00-2.39	2.40-2.99	3.00-3.99	4.00-5.99	6.00+
Less than $250	7	4	3	1	1	1	0	1	0	0
250-499	17	24	11	8	4	3	3	2	1	0
500-999	43	40	38	30	25	20	15	11	5	3
1,000-1,499	17	18	30	35	33	31	26	19	13	8
1,500-1,999	10	10	11	17	18	21	23	25	21	14
2,000-2,499	4	3	4	5	10	14	13	18	25	19
2,500-2,999	2	0	1	3	5	6	9	9	12	18
3,000-3,499	0	0	1	2	1	2	6	8	9	9
3,500-3,999	0	0	0	0	1	1	2	4	6	6
4,000-	0	1	0	1	2	2	3	4	9	23
TOTAL	100	100	99	102	100	101	100	101	101	100
Percent of Sample	1.0	5.1	7.7	8.9	9.0	8.4	13.0	16.9	19.4	10.7
Number of cases	101	474	576	583	524	458	620	701	684	349

V=.21

MTR 1061

*Includes 6% of house value to represent actual or imputed interest costs, rent, rental value if free, utilities, property taxes, and expenditures on repairs and additions up to $1,000.

TABLE G.11

Imputed Rent by Total 1971 Family Money Income/Needs
(for all 5060 families in early 1972)

Imputed Rent (Non-Money Return on Equity in Home)*	Less than 0.40	.40-.79	.80-1.19	1.20-1.59	1.60-1.99	2.00-2.39	2.40-2.99	3.00-3.99	4.00-5.99	6.00+
0	69	57	62	50	43	41	38	35	30	23
1-299	8	18	11	12	10	13	11	10	5	5
300-599	7	12	11	14	18	18	15	16	10	9
500-899	6	7	10	11	12	12	12	12	12	11
900-1,199	3	3	2	7	8	7	11	11	15	9
1,200-1,499	6	2	2	3	5	5	4	7	12	12
1,500-1,799	1	1	2	1	2	2	4	4	6	8
1,800-2,399	0	0	1	1	3	2	3	4	7	11
2,400-2,999	0	0	0	1	1	1	1	2	2	5
3,000-	0	0	0	0	0	0	1	1	1	8
TOTAL	100	100	101	100	102	101	100	102	100	101
Percent of Sample	1.0	5.1	7.7	8.9	9.0	8.4	13.0	16.9	19.4	10.7
Number of cases	101	474	576	583	524	458	620	701	684	349

V=.14

MTR 1061

*6% of net equity in house (house value minus mortgage principal remaining)

TABLE G.12

House Value Per Room by Total 1971 Family Money Income/Needs
(for all 5060 families in early 1972)

Value Per Room*	Less than 0.40	.40-.79	.80-1.19	1.20-1.59	1.60-1.99	2.00-2.39	2.40-2.99	3.00-3.99	4.00-5.99	6.00+
Less than $500	14	8	4	2	1	0	1	1	1	0
500-999	6	19	16	9	6	5	4	4	1	1
1,000-1,499	7	17	20	13	16	10	8	5	3	2
1,500-1,999	20	13	13	17	9	11	10	8	5	4
2,000-2,999	20	20	25	26	28	26	24	20	16	6
3,000-3,999	14	11	10	15	17	25	20	25	21	22
4,000-4,999	9	6	6	8	11	11	16	16	19	18
5,000-7,499	4	4	5	7	9	9	11	17	25	28
8,000-9,999	3	0	0	1	1	0	2	2	4	10
10,000-	2	3	1	3	3	2	4	4	3	10
TOTAL	99	101	100	101	101	99	100	102	98	101
Percent of Sample	1.0	5.1	7.7	8.9	9.0	8.4	13.0	16.9	19.4	10.7
Number of cases	101	474	576	583	524	458	620	701	684	349

V=.17

MTR 1061

*House value or 10 x annual rent/number of rooms

value per room, an indicator of the quality of housing, which seems to increase rapidly at the higher levels of income needs, whereas rooms per person, an indicator of quantity, may well increase most at more moderate levels.

The next three tables, G.13-G.15, focus on expenditures often subject to special taxes. The first, money spent eating out, is heavily concentrated at the upper economic levels, whereas expenditures on cigarettes and alcohol, heavily taxed for other reasons, are substantial even at the lowest levels of family well-being. If only the rich had bad habits it would be easier to have taxes that were both redistributive and sumptuary.

Table G.16 shows the distribution of leisure time, one of the few things that is greater at lower levels of income/needs. A person working 50 40-hour weeks would have left, after deducting 8 hours a night for sleep and 2000 hours for work, some 3840 hours of leisure. Since many people have less leisure than this, a substantial fraction are working more than "full time" and have constraints on the time they have left to enjoy leisure. It seems to be the lower income people who have more leisure and, hence, might be more able to use recreational facilities that were conveniently located and inexpensive.

Table G.17 shows that it is the upper middle of the distribution that has the most children in school benefiting from the provision of free public education, or at least from the fact that everyone is taxed to provide education to the current crop of children. The longer range distributional implications are more complex and uncertain.

Tables G.18 and G.19 show the potential distribution of benefits from subsidized day care and other pre-school arrangments. The first table covers all families; the second covers only those where all the adults were working and where presumably the need for day care for younger children is more urgent.

The last two tables use the individual not the family as the unit of analysis. For all 16,138 sample individuals we look at the *individual's income* according to the *family* level of well-being. Clearly any income maintenance program providing each individual with a right to a basic minimum income would have to be concerned with the number of *individuals* who would qualify even though they were living in a family that was rather well off. Alternatives that focus on the family involve difficult admistration and enforcement problems.

Table G.21 looks only at individuals 18 or older who did not do any work for money in 1971 and who were probably not in school, since their age minus years of school was 8 or greater. We distribute them by a sequential sorting procedure which first isolates those 65 or older (presumably not able to work), then those disabled or requiring extra care, next those not old or disabled but

TABLE G.13

Amount Spent Eating Out by Total 1971 Family Money Income/Needs
(for all 5060 families in early 1972)

Annual Amount Spent Eating Out at Restaurants	Less than 0.40	.40-.79	.80-1.19	1.20-1.59	1.60-1.99	2.00-2.39	2.40-2.99	3.00-3.99	4.00-5.99	6.00+
0	74	74	61	54	47	42	32	25	15	10
1-99	5	9	9	10	11	16	10	8	7	3
100	12	7	14	14	16	12	17	18	16	10
200	6	5	10	11	14	17	20	19	20	15
300	1	1	1	3	2	4	6	7	9	7
400	0	0	1	1	1	2	2	2	3	3
500	3	3	4	4	7	4	8	14	18	25
750	0	1	1	1	1	2	3	3	6	10
1000	0	0	0	1	2	1	1	3	5	12
1500	0	0	0	0	0	0	1	1	1	6
TOTAL	101	100	101	99	101	100	100	100	100	101
Percent of Sample	1.0	5.1	7.7	8.9	9.0	8.4	13.0	16.9	19.4	10.7
Number of cases	101	474	576	583	524	458	620	701	684	349

$V = .17$

MTR 1061

TABLE G.14

Annual Amount Spent on Cigarettes by Total Family Money Income/Needs
(for all 5060 families in early 1972)

Amount Spent on Cigarettes	Less than 0.40	.40-.79	.80-1.19	1.20-1.59	1.60-1.99	2.00-2.39	2.40-2.99	3.00-3.99	4.00-5.99	6.00+
0	47	57	55	54	48	46	48	48	50	51
0-49	2	4	5	3	3	3	3	3	3	2
50-99	19	6	9	8	6	4	5	4	4	5
100-199	22	16	14	16	17	22	19	19	16	13
200-299	9	11	9	10	11	13	14	12	11	14
300-399	0	3	3	5	8	7	7	7	7	7
400-499	0	0	2	1	2	1	2	2	2	2
500-999	0	2	3	3	6	5	4	6	7	6
TOTAL	99	99	100	100	101	101	102	101	100	100
Percent of Sample	1.0	5.1	7.7	8.9	9.0	8.4	13.0	16.9	19.4	10.7
Number of cases	101	474	576	583	524	458	620	701	684	349

V=.06

MTR 1061

TABLE G.15

Annual Amount Spent on Alcohol by Total 1971 Family Money Income/Needs
(for all 5060 families in early 1972)

Annual Amount Spent On Alcohol	Less than 0.40	.40-.79	.80-1.19	1.20-1.59	1.60-1.99	2.00-2.39	2.40-2.99	3.00-3.99	4.00-5.99	6.00+
0	73	79	74	68	61	59	49	45	41	34
0-49	0	5	4	6	8	6	9	10	9	7
50-99	7	6	6	7	7	6	9	12	15	14
100-199	11	6	8	9	10	14	13	14	15	16
200-299	0	2	4	5	7	10	9	11	10	15
300-399	1	0	2	2	2	1	2	2	4	4
400-499	0	0	1	1	1	0	1	2	2	2
500 or more	7	1	2	3	5	5	7	7	5	7
TOTAL	99	99	101	101	101	101	99	103	101	99
Percent of Sample	1.0	5.1	7.7	8.9	9.0	8.4	13.0	16.9	19.4	10.7
Number of cases	101	474	576	583	524	458	620	701	684	349

V=.10

MTR 1061

TABLE G.16

Leisure Net of Commuting Time by Total 1971 Family Money Income/Needs
(for all 5060 families in early 1972)

Leisure Time Per Adult*	Less than 0.40	.40-.79	.80-1.19	1.20-1.59	1.60-1.99	2.00-2.39	2.40-2.99	3.00-3.99	4.00-5.99	6.00+
Less than 2,000	3	3	4	1	3	5	2	2	4	4
2,000-2,499	3	3	3	7	8	5	8	7	8	6
2,500-2,999	3	6	9	12	12	14	18	20	20	23
3,000-3,499	11	12	13	16	16	30	26	32	34	34
3,500-3,999	28	13	11	17	19	20	22	22	19	20
4,000-	51	62	60	48	40	26	24	18	15	14
TOTAL	99	99	100	101	98	100	100	101	100	101
Percent of sample	1.0	5.1	7.7	8.9	9.0	8.4	13.0	16.9	19.4	10.7
Number of cases	101	474	576	583	524	458	620	701	684	349

V=.13

*16 hour day (5840 hours per year) minus hours spent working, ill unemployed, or travelling to work and back, averaged for head and wife. Work includes unpaid home production and housework.

MTR 1061

TABLE G.17

Number of Children in School by Total 1971 Family Money Income/Needs
(for all 5060 families in early 1972)

Number of Children in School	Less than 0.40	.40-.79	.80-1.19	1.20-1.59	1.60-1.99	2.00-2.39	2.40-2.99	3.00-3.99	4.00-5.99	6.00+
None, Inap.	76	66	64	62	61	59	54	58	60	69
One	4	8	6	11	11	12	12	15	20	15
Two	3	8	10	10	10	15	15	14	12	10
Three	4	5	7	8	7	6	10	8	6	4
Four	6	5	6	4	6	4	4	3	2	1
Five	3	4	3	5	3	2	2	1	0	1
Six or more	3	2	4	0	2	0	2	1	0	0
N.A., DK	0	1	1	0	0	2	1	0	1	1
TOTAL	99	99	101	100	100	100	100	100	101	101
Percent of sample	1.0	5.1	7.7	8.9	9.0	8.4	13.0	16.9	19.4	10.7
Number of cases	101	474	576	583	524	458	620	701	684	349

$V = .09$

MTR 1061

TABLE G.18

Age of Youngest Child by Total 1971 Family Money Income/Needs
(for all 5060 families in early 1972)

Age of Young-est Child	Less than 0.40	.40-.79	.80-1.19	1.20-1.59	1.60-1.99	2.00-2.39	2.40-2.99	3.00-3.99	4.00-5.99	6.00+
Inap.	60	60	58	56	57	48	43	46	54	69
1 year	11	9	9	10	6	11	10	10	7	5
2	9	3	5	3	7	7	6	5	5	3
3	5	2	4	2	4	4	5	4	4	1
4	3	3	2	3	5	4	2	4	2	1
5	4	3	2	3	2	5	2	3	1	2
6	0	2	3	5	3	3	5	3	2	1
7-8	0	4	5	6	4	4	6	6	6	3
9-11	0	6	6	5	6	5	10	8	6	3
12-14	4	5	4	5	5	3	7	5	8	6
15-17	2	6	2	3	2	5	3	4	7	6
TOTAL	98	103	100	101	101	99	99	98	102	100
Percent of sample	1.0	5.1	7.7	8.9	9.0	8.4	13.0	16.9	19.4	10.7
Number of cases	101	474	576	583	524	458	620	701	684	349

V=.09

MTR 1061

TABLE G.19

Age of Youngest Child by Total 1971 Family Money Income/Needs
(for 2829 families in early 1972 where all adults were workers)

Age of Young-est Child	Less than 0.40	.40-.79	.80-1.19	1.20-1.59	1.60-1.99	2.00-2.39	2.40-2.99	3.00-3.99	4.00-5.99	6.00+
Inap.	72	58	53	46	49	48	38	43	53	70
1	5	11	10	10	8	8	8	9	7	3
2	11	1	5	2	9	8	5	4	4	2
3	3	1	3	2	3	3	5	4	3	1
4	5	3	3	5	5	3	3	4	2	1
5	2	4	3	3	2	4	2	5	1	3
6	0	4	2	5	4	5	6	4	3	1
7-8	0	2	8	11	5	6	7	7	6	3
9-11	0	8	9	8	7	5	13	10	6	2
12-14	0	3	5	6	5	5	10	6	9	6
15-17	2	3	0	4	3	6	5	6	7	8
TOTAL	100	98	101	102	100	101	102	102	101	100
Percent of sample	0.6	3.2	5.8	6.9	7.9	8.8	13.0	18.3	22.6	12.9
Number of cases	31	174	239	280	278	287	370	461	467	242

V=.12

MTR 1061

TABLE G.20

Income of Individuals by 1971 Family Money Income/Needs
(for all sample individuals)

Individual's Income	Less than 0.40	.40-.79	.80-1.19	1.20-1.59	1.60-1.99	2.00-2.39	2.40-2.99	3.00-3.99	4.00-5.99	6.00+	All Levels
0	76	72	67	63	58	53	53	46	39	32	51
1-499	9	12	9	7	8	6	6	6	6	7	7
500-	10	5	5	5	3	3	3	3	3	3	3
1,000-	4	8	5	5	6	7	4	4	3	3	4
2,000-	0	1	5	5	4	3	3	3	3	1	3
3,000-	0	2	6	9	10	11	8	7	7	5	7
5,000-	0	0	1	3	5	10	8	11	11	8	7
7,500-	0	0	0	1	3	4	6	9	10	7	6
10,000-	0	0	0	0	2	3	6	8	12	13	6
15,000-	0	0	1	1	1	1	2	3	7	22	4
TOTAL	99	100	99	99	100	101	99	100	101	101	98
Percent of sample	1	5	8	9	9	9	15	17	19	9	101
Number of individuals	398	1871	2171	1962	1693	1442	1943	1974	1834	850	16,138

MTR 1061

TABLE G.21

Characteristics of Individuals 18 or Older, Not Working for Money in 1971,
and Probably Out of School, by Family Money Income/Needs

	Less than 0.40	.40-.79	.80-1.19	1.20-1.59	1.60-1.99	2.00-2.39	2.40-2.99	3.00-3.99	4.00-5.99	6.00+	All Levels
65 or older	14	43	45	49	40	25	27	30	18	19	32
Not 1 but disabled or requires extra care	36	23	18	14	14	9	11	4	7	8	12
Not 1, 2 but was less than 6 grades of school	4	7	5	2	2	4	1	3	0	0	3
Not 1-3 but has a child under 6 at home	26	14	16	18	15	28	23	20	21	19	19
Not 1-3 but non-white female	11	2	3	2	3	1	3	1	1	3	2
Not 1-3 but white female	6	10	10	13	20	32	32	39	47	49	29
Not 1-3 but non-white male	3	1	1	0	2	0	2	0	0	0	1
Not 1-3 but white male	1	1	1	1	3	1	2	2	5	3	2
TOTAL	101	101	99	99	99	100	101	99	99	101	100
Percent of sample	1	8	11	11	11	8	14	15	14	7	100
Number of cases	82	336	371	295	239	156	263	241	221	103	2307

MTR 1061

with less than 6 grades of education, and finally those with a child under 6. The remainder are divided by race and sex. It is clear that most of the individuals not working or in school (and 18 or older) who are in difficult economic circumstances are old, disabled, or taking care of minor children, and only the last of these three groups would be potential workers (if child care were provided). Among individuals not working but in relatively good economic circumstances, most are mothers or housewives or aged and are presumably unwilling or unable to work.

Most of these results are what one would expect. But in examining the effects of public policy, it is often useful to be certain. For example, it does not appear to be true that commuting costs are a heavier burden on the poor, so that policies to reduce them (or to increase them in order to encourage better location or fuel economy) would not affect those at the bottom more than other families. If one counted the time cost of commuting, particularly at opportunity cost value, the total commuting cost would be even greater at upper levels of well-being.

The transfer system can be seen to have some effect on altering the distribution of income, but not much, largely because most transfers are contributory and have an insurance element in them. And nonmoney incomes except for food stamps are well spread over the income levels. In order to earn imputed income, one of the main nonmoney incomes, one must have equity in a house. Only among a few old people is this common at lower income levels.

The impact of taxes and subsidies, more carefully treated elsewhere in this analysis (see Chapter 8, Volume II), is seen to be perverse in many cases -- subsidies benefiting the affluent and taxes (on liquor and cigarettes, for instance) hitting many of the poor. The main exceptions would seem to be free education, whose benefits affect many families whose income/needs are on a lower rank than their incomes because their families are larger and their needs greater. Anything which makes leisure more pleasurable clearly benefits the lower economic level families as they have more free time than the more affluent.

It must be remembered that this is a small sample and subject to some biases because of its history as a panel. In addition, many of the items are measured casually with a single question. The data are presented to fill a gap and because we can relate them to a better measure of economic well-being.

GLOSSARY

The following is a description of some of the technical terms used in these volumes. For more details on the measures used in these analyses see the documentation, <u>A Panel Study of Income Dynamics</u>, 2 volumes, Survey Research Center, Institute for Social Research, University of Michigan, Ann Arbor, Michigan, 1972.

ACHIEVEMENT MOTIVATION - A personality measure from social psychology representing a propensity to derive satisfaction from overcoming obstacles by one's own efforts in situations where the outcome is ambiguous. It is believed to be developed by early independence training, to result in the taking of calculated but not extreme risks and in the raising of goals after success experiences (see Appendix F).

ASPIRATION-AMBITION - A seven-item index of attitudes and plans reflecting attempts to improve economic well-being; see Volume II of the documentation, p. 789. The items include the following:

> Might move on purpose
> Wanted more work, and/or worked more than 2500 hours last year
> Might quit a job if it was not challenging
> Prefers a job with chances for making more money to one
>   more pleasant
> Is dissatisfied with self
> Spends time figuring out how to get more money
> Plans to get a new job, knows what type of job and what
>   it might pay
> (Second and last items neutralized for those for whom
>   they are inappropriate.)

BETA - A measure of the explanatory power of an independent variable when considered in a multivariate context; see Appendix C on Multiple Classification Analysis.

BETA WEIGHTS - When the independent and dependent variables in the regression equation $Y = a + b_1X_1 + b_2X_2 + u$ are measured in their "natural" units (e.g., in dollars, years, hours) then the parameters b_1 and b_2 reflect the effect on Y of a one unit change in X_1 and X_2, respectively. If all variables are standardized so that each has a mean of zero and a standard deviation equal to one, then the equation becomes $Y = \beta_1 X_1 + \beta_2 X_2 + v$ and the β's can be interpreted as the fraction of a standard deviation that Y changes as a result of a change of one standard deviation in the X's. The b's are regression coefficients (sometimes called "partial regression coefficients"), the β's are *beta weights* or standardized regression coefficients. The unstandardized and standardized coefficients are related in the following way:

$$\beta_1 = \frac{b_1 \sigma_{X_1}}{\sigma_Y}$$

CANONICAL CORRELATION – Canonical correlation is the extension of ordinary least squares regression to the situation in which there is more than one dependent variable. In ordinary regression a single dependent variable is related to a linear combination of independent variables. The particular set of coefficients on the independent variables are those which maximize the correlation (R) between a linear combination of the independent variables and the dependent variable. Canonical correlation relates a linear combination of independent variables to a linear combination of dependent variables and finds the coefficients on both sets of variables that maximizes the correlation.

COGNITIVE ABILITY – See *TEST SCORE*

CONNECTEDNESS (to sources of information and help) – The following eight-item set of reported behaviors measuring the extent to which the respondent has friends or habits likely to keep him informed or provide help; see Volume II of the documentation, p. 793.

> Attended PTA meeting within the year
> Attends church once a month or more
> Watches television more than one hour a day
> Knows several neighbors by name (2 points if 6 or more)
> Has relatives within walking distance
> Goes to organizations once a month or more
> Goes to a bar once a month or more
> Belongs to a labor union and pays dues
> (First item is neutralized for families without children)

COUNTY WAGE RATE for unskilled casual labor – An estimate of the wage rate for unskilled labor in the county where the respondent lives, secured by mail questionnaires sent each year to the state official in charge of unemployment compensation.

COUNTY UNEMPLOYMENT – An estimate of the unemployment rate in the county where the respondent lives, secured by mail questionnaires sent each year to the state official in charge of unemployment compensation.

CRAMER'S V – A measure of association between two nominal scale variables when they have no natural rank order. It is similar to the Chi-square measure except it is adjusted for the number of observations and is constrained to take on values between 0 and 1. The higher Cramer's V, the greater the association between the classifications; see Appendix C.

DECILE - If all units are arranged in ascending order on some criterion such as income and each tenth marked off and identified, the ten groups formed are called deciles. The actual dividing points of incomes are given in Volume II of the documentation.

DESIGN EFFECT - The effect of departures from simple random sampling in probability samples, defined as the ratio of the actual sampling variance to the variance of a simple random sample of the same size; see Appendix B.

ECONOMIES OF SCALE - As the size of a family increases, if the costs do not increase proportionately, then we say there are economies of scale in large families.

ECONOMIZING INDEX - An index of six reported behaviors taken to indicate parsimonious use of money; see Volume II of documentation, p. 790.

> Spent less than $150 a year on alcohol
> Spent less than $150 a year on cigarettes
> Received more than $100 worth of free help
> Do not own late model car
> Eat together most of the time
> Spent less than $260 a year eating out
> (The fourth item is neutralized for those not owning cars).

EFFICACY INDEX - An index composed of six self-evaluations which reflect a sense of personal effectiveness, and a propensity to expect one's plans to work out; see Volume II of documentation, p. 787.

> Is sure life will work out
> Plans life ahead
> Gets to carry out plans
> Finishes things
> Would rather save for the future
> Thinks about things that might happen in future

ELASTICITY - Refers to the response of the quantity of a good consumed to a change in price or in income. If the percentage change in the quantity of food consumed, for example, is greater than the percentage change in the price, then the demand for food is said to be price-elastic; if it is less than the percentage change in price, it is price-inelastic.

ETA - A measure of the explanatory power of a set of subclass means based on a one-way analysis of variance. The square of eta for a single categorical variable is analogous to the unadjusted R^2 from regression with a single independent variable. Eta is sometimes called the correlation ratio.

EXOGENOUS VARIABLE - Variables whose levels and changes are determined by forces independent of those being studied, as contrasted with endogenous variables which are interdependent with variables in the system.

EXPECTED VALUE - When a dependent variable is determined by a combination of systematic and random effects, the expected value is that part which can be predicted from the systematic relationship. In the case of regression, it is the value predicted by the regression equation.

F-TEST - A test of the significance of the proportion of the variance explained by a set of several predictors or several classifications of a single predictor; see *STATISTICAL SIGNIFICANCE*.

FAMILY - All persons living in a household who are related by blood, marriage, or adoption. In occasional cases an unrelated person has been included in the family unit if he or she shares expenses and is apparently a permanent member of the unit. The definition of family used in this study includes single person families. This contrasts with the Census Bureau convention of classifying single persons separately as "unrelated individuals."

FAMILY COMPOSITION - Contains several dimensions, most of them related to the family's position in the standard life cycle: marriage, birth of first child, youngest child reaches age 6 and starts school, children leave home, one spouse dies. The sex and marital status of the head, the number of children, and age of the youngest are the main components.

FAMILY MONEY INCOME - Family income, unless otherwise designated, is the total regular money income of the whole family, including income from labor, capital, and transfers such as pensions, welfare, unemployment compensation, workmen's compensation, and alimony. It includes neither capital gains (realized or unrealized) nor irregular receipts from insurance settlements.

FAMILY TAPE - A data file containing all the data on that family from all five interviews. There is one record for each sample family. The final five-year data tape includes only families interviewed in 1972, so that there are no partial records. Where there are several families derived from an original sample family, the early family information will appear on each of their records.

GINI COEFFICIENT - A measure of inequality. If one orders all units (families) in ascending order on some measure (income) and plots the cumulative fraction of aggregate income against the cumulative proportion of families, the resulting curve sags below a straight diagonal line to indicate inequality. The ratio of the area between the curve and the diagonal line to the whole triangular area below the diagonal is the Gini coefficient. It varies from zero for total equality to 1 for total inequality. The curve is called the Lorenz curve.

HEAD OF FAMILY - In nuclear families the husband is defined as the head. In families with a single adult, he or she is defined as the head. In ambiguous cases of more than one adult, the head is the major earner or the one who owns the home or pays the rent. Note that the head of the family may change due to marriage, divorce, or death. For splitoff families, the head is similarly defined.

HORIZON INDEX - A six-item index of reported behavior indicating a propensity to plan ahead; see Volume II of documentation, p. 792.

> Is sure whether will or will not move
> Has explicit plans for children's education
> Has plans for an explicit kind of new job
> Knows what kind of training new job requires
> Has substantial savings relative to income
> Expects to have a child more than a year hence, or expects
>   no more children and is doing something to limit the
>   number.

HOUSEHOLD - Probability samples usually sample occupied dwellings, which may contain more than one household, which in turn may contain more than one family. However, the term household is often used loosely to mean family, since the number of individuals living with unrelated adults is very small. A family is a group of individuals related by blood, marriage, adoption.

HUMAN CAPITAL - The economically valued skills which result from the investment in one's self through education or other training.

IMPUTED RENT - A form of nonmoney income for home owners who can be thought of as in the business of renting a house to themselves. It is calculated by taking 6% of the owner's net equity in his house (house value minus mortgage).

INCOME - Unless otherwise specified, this means total family money income including regular money transfers. (See FAMILY MONEY INCOME.) When a year is given, it is the year of the income, not the (later) year when the interview was taken.

INCOME INSTABILITY - That portion of an individual's income variation not explained by either his cohort income movements or his consistent deviations from the cohort income pattern. A complete description may be found in the appendix to Chapter 6, Volume I.

INCOME/NEEDS RATIO - See NEEDS STANDARD

INDIVIDUAL TAPE - A data file with one record for each individual as of 1972, containing all the data for that individual over the whole period and all the data for the family that individual was in each of the five years. The file contains some individuals who are not in the sample and are thus excluded from the analysis but who are necessary to derive family information for those in the sample.

Individuals and families have separate weights; see WEIGHT and the documentation, Volume I.

INCOME TREND - Income trend is generally defined as the least squares regression slope of income on time. With five data points the trend is given by the following equation:

$$b = \frac{\sum\limits_{t=1}^{5} Y_t T_t}{\sum\limits_{t=1}^{5} T_t^2} = \frac{2Y_5 + Y_4 - Y_2 - 2Y_1}{10}$$

where T = -2, -1, 0, 1, 2. The trend is often divided by the five-year average.

INELASTICITY - See ELASTICITY

INTELLIGENCE - See TEST SCORE

KENDALL'S TAU - A measure of rank correlation between two classifications; see Appendix C.

LEAST SQUARES ESTIMATOR - That method of estimation which minimizes the squared deviations of the actual value from the predicted value of the dependent variable. Such estimators are sensitive to extreme cases and nonnormal distributions.

LINEAR REGRESSION - See REGRESSION

LORENZ CURVE - A curve plotting the cumulative proportion of some aggregate quantity against the cumulative fraction of families (arranged in ascending order). It is a measure of inequality--the more it sags, the greater the inequality. It depends heavily on the definition of the measure and the unit, particularly the latter.

MARGINAL PROPENSITY TO CONSUME - That fraction of an incremental increase in income which is spent on consumption.

MOTIVATION - See ACHIEVEMENT MOTIVATION

MULTICOLLINEARITY - A problem arising in estimation if two or more predictors are highly intercorrelated. It thus becomes difficult to estimate the separate effects of these variables.

MULTIPLE REGRESSION - See REGRESSION

MONEY EARNING ACTS INDEX - An index of behavioral reports that the family is doing things to increase its money income including working long hours, getting to work on time, changing jobs, looking for a better job; see documentation, Volume II, p. 794.

MTR - Tables and other computer output are indexed by a Machine Tabulation Request number for checking and filing purposes. The number appears at the bottom of each table.

NEEDS STANDARD - An estimate of the annual income necessary for a family. The standard is generated in the same way as the official Federal poverty line; food needs are determined according to age and sex, as estimated and priced by the USDA (in Family Economics Review), and food costs are adjusted for economies of scale; this figure is then multiplied by a factor to allow for other needs also differentially greater for smaller families.

The absolute level is to some extent arbitrary and is not adjusted for inflation in later years, but the standard adjusts for differences in family size and structure so the status of families that differ in composition can be compared.

The needs standard is corrected for changes in family composition during the prior year, so that it is legitimate to compare it with that year's income. See the documentation, Volume I, for further details.

NUMBER OF CASES - The actual number of families or individuals on which the estimate is based. The number does not reflect the proportion of the population represented by that group because of the differences in sampling and response rates. See *WEIGHTS*.

NULL HYPOTHESIS - See *STATISTICAL SIGNIFICANCE*

QUINTILE - If all cases are arranged in ascending order on some criterion such as income and each fifth is marked off and identified, these five groups are called quintiles.

PARTIAL CORRELATION COEFFICIENTS (partial R^2) - The partial correlation coefficient (squared) is a measure of the marginal or added explanatory power of one predictive variable or set of variables, over and above all the other predictors. It can be thought of as the correlation of two sets of residuals, after removing the effects of all other predictors from both the dependent variable and the predictor in question. It is also the fraction of the remaining distance to perfect explanation (1.00) the multiple correlation (squared) is moved by the added predictor. It is the best measure of the "importance" of a predictor or group of predictors.

PERCENT OF POPULATION - The fraction of the weight-sum represented by a subgroup is an estimate of the percent of the population (of families or of individuals) it represents. Aggregate estimates can be made by ratio-estimating procedures, i.e., multiplying the sample mean by the proportion of the population times an outside estimate of the aggregate number of families or individuals.

PLANNING INDEX - A subset of the efficacy index consisting of the following items:

> Plans ahead
> Prefers to save for future
> Thinks about the future

REAL EARNING ACTS INDEX - A five-item index, with neutralization of the inapplicable items, reflecting ways of earning nonmoney income or investing in self; see documentation, Volume II, p. 789-90.

> Saved more than $75 doing own additions or repairs
> Saved more than $75 growing own food
> Saved more than $75 repairing own car
> Head was taking courses or lessons with economic potential
> Head spent spare time productively

R^2 - The fraction of variance in the dependent variable which is explained by the set of explanatory variables.

REGRESSION - A statistical technique which estimates the separate, independent effect of each of several predictors on a dependent variable. It minimizes the sum of the squared deviations from predicted values (see LEAST SQUARE ESTIMATOR) and assumes that the dependent variable is a linear and additive function of the predictors and a random error term.

REGRESSION COEFFICIENT - The estimated effect of a predictor on the dependent variable obtained from a regression analysis. It shows the expected effect that a unit change in the predictor would have on the dependent variable if all other predictors were held constant.

RISK AVOIDANCE INDEX - An index of six reported behaviors indicating the avoidance of undue risks; see Volume II of the documentation, p. 791.

> Car (newest if several) in good condition
> All cars are insured
> Uses seat belts (2 points if all the time)
> Has medical insurance or a way to get free care
> Head smokes less than one pack of cigarettes a day
> Have liquid savings (2 points if more than two months
>   income in savings)

SIZE OF LARGEST CITY IN AREA - The primary sampling unit is a county or (rarely) cluster of counties and the size of the largest city in that area is intended to reflect the number and variety of jobs, as well as differences in costs and standards of living. When the city is 50,000 or more, the area is a Census Standard

Metropolitan Statistical Area.

SPLITOFF - A splitoff is someone who left a sample family and is living in a different household. Most splitoffs are children who left the parental home to set up their own households. When a couple is divorced, one of them is designated as the continuing family and the other is a splitoff.

SPLIT SAMPLE - In order to allow proper testing of the significance and explanatory power of the descriptive and explanatory models finally selected, we have divided the sample into independent subsamples. This requires attention to the original sample design and the allocation of whole primary sampling areas to one subsample or another, so that they are truly independent (households within a cluster in a clustered sample are more like each other than a purely random set). The sample is divided into four parts, so that some initial analysis can be done on half-sample and some on three-fourths depending on the amount of searching that may need to be done and the precision of the needed testing (see Appendix A).

STANDARD DEVIATION - A measure of the dispersion of a distribution of observations around their average (or predicted) value. If random effects are normally distributed, roughly two-thirds of the observations fall in a range of the mean plus or minus one standard deviation. It is equal to the square root of the variance and is denoted by the symbol σ. The standard deviations presented in the tables should be considered in context of the design effect; see Appendix B.

STATISTICAL SIGNIFICANCE - Traditional statistical inference tests the hypothesis that a finding (e.g., that some effect is greater than zero), is a chance result from the sample, not existing in the population. If the probability is sufficiently small, (e.g., less than 5%), this "null hypothesis" is rejected and it is believed that there is some effect which is "statistically significant." Tests of significance should consider the design effect; see Appendix B.

In most initial searching of data for what matters, and in what form, the assumptions of statistical testing are violated because many alternative models are tried. In addition, there are problems of estimating sampling variance with complex samples. Hence, we have used only part of the sample for searching and have reserved an independent part of the sample for assessing significance and explanatory power.

T-TEST - Under certain assumptions, estimated regression coefficients have a frequency distribution known as the t-distribution. This fact can be used to form a test of significance for the coefficients, called the t-test. See also *STATISTICAL SIGNIFICANCE*.

TARGET POPULATION - Those families who were in the lowest 20% of the income/needs distribution in any one of the five years, 1967-1971.

TEST SCORE - A 13-item sentence completion task developed as a culture-free, sex-free, and race-free measure of "intelligence." Of course, like all such measures, it may also test acquired skills or freedom from test anxiety. For further details, see Appendix F.

TREND - See INCOME TREND

TRUST IN OTHERS - An index composed of five self-evaluating items on trusting others, believing in the fairness of the system; see Volume II of the documentation, p. 788.

> Does not get angry easily
> It matters what others think
> Trusts most other people
> Believes the life of the average man is getting better
> Believes there are *not* a lot of people who have good
>   things they don't deserve.

WEIGHT - There are weights both for the file of individuals and families which make the weighted estimates representative of the national non-institutional population of the continental United States. They offset differences in sampling rates and response rates, and the extra probabilities of inclusion of those who married nonsample members. There will be more respondents in lower income and minority groups than the weighted proportions because of oversampling. The over-sampling simply made the estimates for those groups more reliable.

Weighted estimates essentially multiply each case by a number representing the number of households it represents. Each digit of the weight represents 500 households. See Appendix A for more details.

YEAR - Interviewing was done in the spring of 1968, 1969, 1970, 1971 and 1972, but the income questions refer to the year prior to each (1967-1971).

INDEX

Ability. See Cognitive ability

Accounting period, impact on instability measure, 279–281

Achievement motivation, effects, 338
    change in income/needs, 45, 77
    change in wage rates, 157
    educational attainment, 306, 307, 308, 310, 313, 322, 324, 325
    labor supply, female, 232, 236
    labor supply, male, 218
    persistently poor, 27
    target population, 23, 24
    wage rates, 126, 166
        male, 133
        splitoff, 152

Advisory committee, xi, 6

AFDC. See Noncontributory transfers, Welfare status

AFDC payment in county, effects, 235, 237, 239, 265, 268

AID, 45, 359–361

Age, effects
    amount of welfare, 260
    change in family composition, 102
    change in income/needs, 45, 47, 53, 59
    change in wage rates, 157, 163
    change in welfare status, 266
    income instability, 283, 286, 292
    labor supply, female, 225, 235
    labor supply, male, 218, 221
    persistently poor, 27, 30
    splitting off, 110
    target population, 21, 23, 24
    unemployment, 184
    wage rates, 167
        female, 143
        male, 131, 133, 136, 139
        splitoff, 150, 153

Andrews, Frank, 284, 357

Area where head grew up, effects
    change in welfare status, 265, 269
    wage rates, female, 143
    wage rates, male, 129, 136

Asset and savings levels, effects on educational attainment, 311

Atkinson, John W., xi, 308

426

Attitudes, effects, 338, 339
        change in family composition, 106
        change in income/needs, 45, 50, 78
        change in welfare status, 266, 268, 272, 273
        wage rates, 166
                splitoff, 152

Background, effects, 333
        change in welfare status, 265, 269
        target population, 77
        wage rates, 126
                female, 143
                male, 128-133

Baker, Elizabeth, 359

Baerwaldt, Nancy, xi, 251

Becker, Gary S., 294

Behavior patterns, effects, 338, 339
        change in family composition, 106
        change in income/needs, 45, 50, 78

Benus, Jacob, 277

Ben-Porath, Yoram, 294

Bergmann, Barbara, 145

Berkson, Joseph, 378

Betsey, Charles, 126

Block, M. K., 277

Boland, Barbara, 263

Bowles, Samuel, 125, 134, 324

Capital income, 13
        effects on labor supply, male, 217
        relation to family income instability, 290
        relative importance in change in total family income, 68
        relative importance in total family income, 68

Child, age of youngest, effects
        amount of welfare, 258
        change in income/needs, 47, 53, 59
        change in welfare status, 265, 268, 271
        labor supply, female, 236

Child, birth of, effects
        change in welfare status, 265, 268
        labor supply, female, 226

Children, number of, effects
        amount of welfare, 258, 262
        change in welfare status, 265, 268, 271
        labor supply, female, 231, 236
        labor supply, male, 218
        receiving welfare, splitoffs, 271
        unemployment, 187

Children, whether, effects
        amount of welfare, 258, 273
        change in family composition, 102
        change in welfare status, 263, 271, 273
        labor supply, female, 231
        persistently poor, 27, 30
        target population, 23, 24, 26

City size, effects, 335
        amount of welfare, 261
        change in wage rates, 160, 163
        change in welfare status, 265, 268
        persistently poor, 27, 33, 77
        target population, 23, 24
        wage rates, female, 145
        wage rates, male, 137, 139

Cognitive ability, effects
        change in income/needs, 50, 78
        change in wage rates, 157
        change in welfare status, 265, 266, 268, 273
        educational attainment, 306, 307, 308, 310, 311, 313, 322, 325
                female, 318
                male, 317, 322
        labor supply, female, 232, 236, 239
        persistently poor, 27, 33
        target population, 23, 24
        wage rates, 126, 166
                male, 133, 134
                splitoff, 152

Cognitive ability of parents, effects
        educational attainment, 310
                female, 322
                male, 316, 322

Cohen, Malcolm, S., 213

Connectedness index, effects on change in income/needs, 53

Constraints on work hours, 194–196, 199–204
        effects on labor supply, male, 222

Consumer Price Index, 5

DeJanosi, Peter, xi

Dickinson, Jonathan G., 177, 231

Dickinson, Katherine P., 7, 123, 231, 251

Disability, effects
        change in welfare status, 265, 266, 268, 272, 273
        labor supply, female, 232, 236
        unemployment, 187

Disadvantaged workers, moonlighting opportunities, 209

Distance to city, effects
        persistently poor, 27, 33, 77
        target population, 23, 24

428

Divorce, 104

Dreze, Jacques H., 277

Duncan, Beverly, 125, 306, 317

Duncan, Otis Dudley, 125, 306, 317

Earnings,
      expected cohort, 279, 296
      expected pattern, 279
      function, cross-section, 294
      residuals from expected, 296
      variation, anticipated, 294
      See also Labor income, Wage rates

Education, effects, 337
      change in income/needs, 45, 51, 78
      change in wage rates, 157, 163
      change in welfare status, 265, 268, 272, 273
      income instability, 283, 286, 294
      labor supply, female, 225, 232, 236, 239
      labor supply, male, 214, 218, 223
      moonlighting, 208
      persistently poor, 27, 30, 33
      receiving welfare, splitoffs, 271
      target population, 23, 24, 77
      unemployment, 182, 185, 237
      wage rates, 125, 167
          female, 143
          male, 128, 133-137
          splitoff, 152, 153

Education of father, effects
      educational attainment, 311, 325, 326
          female, 318
          male, 316, 318
      wage rates, 167
          female, 143
          male, 131

Education of mother, effects
      educational attainment, 311, 325, 326
          female, 318
          male, 316, 318

Education of parents, effects
      educational attainment, 310, 323, 324

Education, quality of, effects
      educational attainment, 309
          male, 317
      wage rates, splitoffs, 152, 153

Educational attainment, determinants of, 305-331
      female, 318-322
      male, 313-327

Efficacy index, effects
      change in welfare status, 266, 268

Employment mode, determinants of, 199-211, 237
     moonlighting, 207
     relationship to work hour preference, 202
     wage rate and work hours, 202-207

Environment, effects
     changes in family composition, 106
     income instability, 284
     See also Local conditions

Expenditure per pupil, effects
     educational attainment, 311
        female, 322
        male, 317

Family composition, determinants of, 99-121
     effects, 337

Family composition, effects
     change in income/needs, 45
     change in welfare status, 263, 266, 271
     receiving welfare, splitoffs, 271
     labor supply, female, 226, 231, 232, 235
     transfer income, 255

Family composition, change in, effects, 37-44
     changes in income/needs, 45, 47, 77, 78
     target population, 23

Family Economic Review, 5, 63

Family membership, changes in, effects on change in income/needs, 53, 59

Family size, effects on change in income/needs, 53. See also Number of siblings

Featherman, David L., 125, 306, 317

Ferber, Robert, xi

Finny, D. J., 377

Frankel, Martin, 380

Glennan, Tom, xi

Goldberger, Arthur S., xi, 288, 377, 379

Gramlich, Ned, xi

Griliches, Zvi, 133

Harrison, Bennett, 137

Hause, John C., 133

Heffernan, W. J., 256

Heineke, J. M., 277

Hess, Irene, 346

Hill, C. Russell, 221

Hours, importance in labor income, 71, 123

Hubbard, Robert, xi

430

Human capital investment, effects on income instability, 294

Illness, effects on labor supply, male, 213

Imputed rent from owner occupied home, effects on amount of welfare, 260, 261

Incentives to split off, 110, 113, 116

Income effect, 188
        income instability, 283, 292
        labor supply, female, 228
        labor supply, male, 214-218
        tests of differentials, 223

Income, relative importance in income/needs, 72

Income fluctuations, unexpected, 279

Income instability, determinants of, 277-302

Income/needs, effects
        amount of welfare, 255-257, 273
        unemployment, 181

Income/needs, changes in, 44-60

Income of family, relation to income instability, 287

Income of family, taxable, trend, 47

Income of head and wife, taxable, 13, 47

Income of others, relative to family income instability, 290

Income of others, taxable
        relative importance in change in total family income, 70
        relative importance in total family income, 68

Income uncertainty, 277, 278

Industry, effects
        labor supply, male, 221, 238
        payment mode, 192
        wage rates, female, 149
        wage rates, male, 139

Intelligence. See Cognitive ability

Institute for Research on Poverty, ix

IQ. See Cognitive ability

Jencks, Christopher, 125, 317

Kish, Leslie, 345, 346, 350

Klein, Lawrence, xi

Klein, Lester, xi, 20

Klem, Laura, 357

Kosters, Marvin, 190

Labor force participation, changes in, effects, 40-44, 78

Labor income of head, 13
 relation to family income instability, 287
 relative importance in total family income, 68
 relative importance in change in total family income, 70

Labor income of wife, 13
 effects on labor supply, male, 216
 relation to family income instability, 290
 relative importance in total family income, 68
 relative importance in change in total family income, 70

Labor supply, determinants of
 male heads of families, 211–224
 single women with children, 232–237
 wives, 224–232

Labor supply curves, 211

Lane, Jonathan P., xi, 20

Lansing, John B., xi, 129, 375

Leibowitz, Arleen, 324, 325

Leland, Hyane E., 277

Lerman, Robert I., 213

Levine, Robert, xi

Local demand conditions, effects on wage rates, 126
 female, 145
 male, 128, 139

Local employment conditions, effects
 educational attainment, 309, 326
  male, 317
 labor supply, female, 231, 232, 235, 237
 moonlighting, 209
 unemployment, 185

Lucas, Robert E. B., 125

Lyday, James, xi

Marginal pay, jobs without, 191–194
 relationship to employment mode, 202

Marginal wage rate,
 effects on labor supply, 189
 from moonlighting, 208
 from reducing work hours, 210
 from switching jobs, 204–207

Marital status, effects
 amount of welfare, 260
 change in family composition, 102
 change in welfare status, 263, 266, 273
 labor supply, female, 235, 236
 persistently poor, 27
 target population, 23–24, 26
 wage rates, female, 145

Marquis, Kent, xi, 310, 381

Mason, William, 133

Masters, Stanley H., 322, 323

Mathematica, ix

Maynes, F. Scott, xi, 375, 378

MCA. See Multiple classification analysis

McClelland, Lou, xi, 310, 381

Mednick, Martha, 383

Messenger, Robert, 102, 361

Mirer, Thad W., 281

Modigliani, Franco, 277

Moles, Oliver, 108

Moonlighting, effects on labor supply, male, 222
    relationship to constraints on work hours, 196

Morgan, James N., xii, 11, 99, 102, 129, 226, 251, 284, 357, 359, 361, 375

Morrison, Donald G., 379

Motivation. See Achievement motivation

Multiple classification analysis, 357–359

Needs standard, relative importance in income/needs, 72

Negative income tax, effects on labor supply, 189

Neter, John, 375, 378

Noncontributory transfers, adequacy and equity, 255–263

Nontransfer income, relationship to transfer income, 252–257, 272

Nonwage income, effects on labor supply, 189

Number of siblings, effects
    educational attainment, 310
        female, 317, 322, 323, 326

Occupation, effects
    change in wage rates, 160, 163
    income instability, 283, 286, 292
    labor supply, male, 221
    payment mode, 192
    unemployment, 182, 184, 237
    wage rates, 126
        female, 145
        male, 128, 137
    work hours constraints, 196

Occupation of father, effects
    educational attainment, 311
    wage rates, male, 131

Office of Economic Opportunity, ix, x, xi

Oi, Walter, 283

Okner, Benjamin, 252

Orcutt, Guy H., x, xi

Overcrowding, effects on change in family composition, 102

Parental income, effects
    change in family composition, 104
    educational attainment, 310, 323
        female, 322
        male, 313, 318
    receiving welfare, splitoffs, 269
    wage rates, splitoff, 152

Payment mode, effects on labor supply, male, 222

Payoff from splitting, 113, 114

Permanent income, as a measure of well-being, 277

Perrella, Vera, 207

Persistently poor, 12, 27-37

Planning index, effects
    change in income/needs, 50, 51
    change in family composition, 108
    change in welfare status, 266, 268, 272, 274

Race, effects, 335-336
    amount of welfare, 260
    change in income/needs, 47, 59
    change in wage rates, 157, 163
    change in welfare status, 265, 269, 272, 273
    educational attainment 311
    income instability, 283, 294
    labor supply, female, 225, 230, 231, 235, 237
    labor supply, male, 221, 238
    moonlighting, 209
    payment mode, 192
    persistently poor, 27, 30, 33, 37
    splitting off, 110, 113
    target population, 23, 24, 26, 77
    unemployment, 185, 237
    wage rates, 166
        female, 143
        male, 129, 137
        splitoff, 150, 152, 153

Rea, Samuel, A., 213, 226

Region, effects
    amount of welfare, 261, 262, 273
    change in welfare status, 265, 268, 272
    labor supply, female, 235, 237
    wage rate, female, 149
    wage rate, male, 139

Residential mobility, effects,
    amount of welfare, 260
    change in income/needs, 45, 50
    change in wage rates, 160, 166

434

Risk avoidance index, effects on change in income/needs, 51

Rural residence. See Distance to city

Sampling error, 3, 345–356

Sandmo, Agnar, 277

Self-employment, effects on unemployment, 184

Seniority on job, effects
    change in wage rates, male, 160
    labor supply, male, 218
    wage rates, 167
        male, 139
        splitoff, 150

Sentence completion test. See Cognitive ability

Sewell, William H., 306, 317, 324

Sex, effects, 336
    amount of welfare, 260
    change in family composition, 102
    change in income/needs, 47, 59
    change in welfare status, 263, 266, 271, 273
    educational attainment, 311
    income instability, 283, 284, 294
    persistently poor, 27, 30
    receiving welfare, splitoff, 271
    splitting off, 110, 113
    target population, 23, 24, 26, 77

Sex discrimination, effects on wage rates, 145, 149, 150, 163, 166

Shah, Vimal P., 306, 317

Smith, James D., xi

Sonquist, John, 284, 357, 359

Standard error of estimate, 297

Substitution effect, 189
    effect on labor supply, female, 228
    effect on labor supply, male, 217

Survey of Economic Opportunity, 1

Target population, 12, 20–37, 305

Taubman, Paul, 296

Test score. See Cognitive ability

THAID, 361–362

Theil, Henri, 296, 377, 378

Thurow, Lester C., 125

Tobin, James, xi

Tomlinson, Tom, xi

Transfer income, determinants of, 251–276

Transfer income, effects on labor supply, male, 216
        relation to family income instability, 290
        relative importance in total family income, 68

Transfer income, change in, relative importance in change in total family
   income, 70

Trust index, effects
        change in family composition, 108
        change in welfare status, 266, 268, 272, 274
        wage rates, splitoff, 152, 166

Unemployment, determinants of, 178-188
        effects on labor supply, male, 213, 216

Unemployment of husband, 231-232

Unemployment rate, effects, 334
        change in income/needs, 45, 59
        change in welfare status, 265, 268, 272
        income instability, 283, 284, 286, 292
        labor supply, female, 225, 230
        labor supply, male, 218
        persistently poor, 27, 77
        receiving welfare, splitoff, 271
        target population, 23, 24

Union membership, effects
        change in wage rate, 160
        labor supply, male, 221, 238
        payment mode, 192
        unemployment, 184
        wage rate, male, 137, 139

USDA weekly food cost, 5

Variability components, 66-75

Veroff, Joseph, xi, 310, 381

Veteran, effects on wage rates
        male, 131, 136
        splitoff, 152

Wachtel, Howard M., 126

Wage rate, determinants of. 123-175
        changes in, 155-166
        female, 141-150
        male, 128-141
        splitoff, 150-154

Wage rate. effects
        labor supply, female, 225, 226, 232, 236, 238, 239
        labor supply, male, 214, 219-224, 238
        payment mode, 194
        unemployment, 181
        work hours constraints, 196

Wage rate, measure of, 128

Wage rate, relative importance in labor income, 71, 123

Wage rate for unskilled labor, effects, 334, 335
    change in wage rate, 160, 166
    educational attainment, 311, 323
        female, 322
        male, 317, 323
    labor supply, female, 225, 230
    wage rates, female, 149
    wage rates, male, 139

Wage rate of husband, effect on labor supply, female, 225, 228, 239

Wage slopes, differences in, 218–222

Wales, Terrence, 296

Watts, Harold W., 160, 210

Welfare income. See Noncontributory transfers

Welfare status, change in, 263–272

Wilson, John, xi

Work experience, effects on instability, 294. See also Seniority on job

Weights, 1, 341–344

Zellner, Arnold, xi